Modern KOREAN Grammar

Routledge's *Modern Grammar* series is an innovative reference guide combining traditional and function-focused grammar in a single volume, with an accompanying workbook. The aim of *Modern Korean Grammar* is to provide an overview of the structures and functions of the Korean language. Designed for those who have already acquired the basics of the language, the book combines a comprehensive description of the grammatical structures of Korean with a functional/usage approach to the language. All target grammatical and functional points are illustrated with examples in Hangul with English translations for better understanding. In addition, the use of linguistic terminology is limited, to facilitate quick and easy comprehension.

Andrew Sangpil Byon is Department Chair and Associate Professor of Korean Studies at the University at Albany, USA. As a Korean applied linguist, his primary research areas are sociolinguistics, Korean-as-a-foreign/second language (KFL) pedagogy, and second language acquisition (for American KFL learners).

Routledge Modern Grammars

Other books in series
Modern Brazilian Portuguese Grammar, Second Edition
Modern Brazilian Portuguese Grammar Workbook, Second Edition

Modern French Grammar, Second Edition
Modern French Grammar Workbook, Second Edition

Modern German Grammar, Second Edition
Modern German Grammar Workbook, Second Edition

Modern Italian Grammar, Third Edition
Modern Italian Grammar Workbook, Second Edition

Modern Japanese Grammar
Modern Japanese Grammar Workbook

Modern Korean Grammar
Modern Korean Grammar Workbook

Modern Mandarin Chinese Grammar
Modern Mandarin Chinese Grammar Workbook

Modern Russian Grammar
Modern Russian Grammar Workbook

Modern Spanish Grammar, Third Edition
Modern Spanish Grammar Workbook, Third Edition

Modern KOREAN Grammar

A Practical Guide

Andrew Sangpil Byon

LONDON AND NEW YORK

First published 2017
by Routledge
2 Park Square, Milton Park, Abingdon, Oxon OX14 4RN

and by Routledge
711 Third Avenue, New York, NY 10017

Routledge is an imprint of the Taylor & Francis Group, an informa business

© 2017 Andrew Sangpil Byon

The right of Andrew Sangpil Byon to be identified as the author of this work has been asserted by him in accordance with sections 77 and 78 of the Copyright, Designs and Patents Act 1988.

All rights reserved. No part of this book may be reprinted or reproduced or utilised in any form or by any electronic, mechanical, or other means, now known or hereafter invented, including photocopying and recording, or in any information storage or retrieval system, without permission in writing from the publishers.

Trademark notice: Product or corporate names may be trademarks or registered trademarks, and are used only for identification and explanation without intent to infringe.

British Library Cataloguing-in-Publication Data
A catalogue record for this book is available from the British Library

Library of Congress Cataloging-in-Publication Data
A catalog record for this book has been requested

ISBN: 978-1-138-93130-5 (hbk)
ISBN: 978-1-138-93131-2 (pbk)
ISBN: 978-1-315-18783-9 (ebk)

Typeset in Times New Roman
by Apex CoVantage, LLC

Contents

Preface xxii
Acknowledgments xxiii

Part A Structures — 1

1 Nouns — 3
    Notes before reading *3*
    1.1   Three groups of Korean nouns *3*
    1.2   Noun formation *4*
    1.3   Prenouns and bound nouns *6*
    1.4   Some characteristics of Korean nouns *8*
        1.4.1   Positions *8*
        1.4.2   Gender *8*
        1.4.3   Plurality *8*
        1.4.4   Collocations *9*
        1.4.5   Honorific nouns *9*

2 Pronouns — 10
    2.1   The first person pronoun *10*
    2.2   The second person pronoun *11*
    2.3   The third person pronoun *12*
    2.4   Indefinite pronouns *12*

3 Numbers and counters — 14
    3.1   Numbers *14*
    3.2   Counters *15*
    3.3   Counting *17*
    3.4   Sino-Korean numbers vs. native Korean numbers *17*
    3.5   Ordinals *18*

4 Nominalizing endings — 19
    4.1   The nominalizing ending ~기 *19*
        4.1.1   ~기가 어렵다 "difficult to" *19*
        4.1.2   ~기가 무섭게/바쁘게 "just after" *20*
        4.1.3   ~기 나름이다 "depends on ~ing" *20*
        4.1.4   ~기는요? "What do you mean?" *20*
        4.1.5   ~기나 하다 "at least do" *21*
        4.1.6   ~기는 하다 "indeed" *21*
        4.1.7   ~기는 커녕 "far from ~ing" *21*

		4.1.8	~기도 하다 "indeed" *21*	
		4.1.9	~기 때문에 "because of ~ing" *21*	
		4.1.10	~기로 하다 "decide to" *22*	
		4.1.11	~기를 바라다/원하다 "hope" *22*	
		4.1.12	~기 마련이다 "bound to" *22*	
		4.1.13	~기 시작하다 "begin" *22*	
		4.1.14	~기 십상이다 "it is easy to" *22*	
		4.1.15	~기에는 "as for (doing something)" *23*	
		4.1.16	~기에 따라서 "according to" *23*	
		4.1.17	~기에 앞서서 "before ~ing" *23*	
		4.1.18	~기 위해서 "as for ~ing" *23*	
		4.1.19	~기 일쑤이다 "routinely" *23*	
		4.1.20	~기 전에 "before ~ing" *24*	
		4.1.21	~기 짝이 없다 "beyond measure" *24*	
	4.2	The nominalizing ending ~(으)ㅁ *24*	
	4.3	The nominalizing ending ~이 *25*	
	4.4	The use of ~는 것 to create a noun form *25*	

5 Case particles I 26
- 5.1 Case and special particles *26*
- 5.2 Characteristics of particles *26*
- 5.3 The subject particle 이/가 *27*
  - 5.3.1 The particle 이/가 in negation *27*
  - 5.3.2 Double subject constructions *27*
  - 5.3.3 Interplay between the subject and the topic particles *28*
- 5.4 The direct object particle 을/를 *28*
- 5.5 The possessive particle 의 *29*

6 Case particles II 30
- 6.1 Particles of location and movement *30*
  - 6.1.1 에 "to/in/at/per/in addition to" *30*
  - 6.1.2 에다(가) "in/on/addition to" *31*
  - 6.1.3 에서 "from/at/in" *31*
  - 6.1.4 (으)로부터 "from" *32*
  - 6.1.5 한테/에게/께 "to" *32*
  - 6.1.6 한테(서)/에게(서) "from" *32*
- 6.2 Instrumental particles *33*
  - 6.2.1 (으)로(서/써) "as/by/with" *33*
- 6.3 Comitative particles *34*
  - 6.3.1 와/과 "and/with" *34*
  - 6.3.2 (이)랑 "and/with" *35*
  - 6.3.3 하고 "and/with" *35*

7 Special particles I 36
- 7.1 The differences between case particles and special particles *36*
- 7.2 Particles of topic and focus *37*
  - 7.2.1 은/는 "as for" *37*
  - 7.2.2 (이)야 "if it be" *38*
  - 7.2.3 (이)야말로 "indeed" *38*
- 7.3 Particles of comparison and contrast *38*
  - 7.3.1 보다 "more than" *38*
  - 7.3.2 처럼/같이 "like" *39*
  - 7.3.3 만큼 "as . . . as" *39*

CONTENTS

		7.3.4 따라 "unusually" *39*	
		7.3.5 대로 "in accordance with" *39*	
	7.4	Particles of frequency *40*	
		7.4.1 마다 "every" *40*	
		7.4.2 씩 "each" *40*	

8 Special particles II — 41
- 8.1 Particles of extent *41*
  - 8.1.1 부터 "from" *41*
  - 8.1.2 까지 "to, until, including (even)" *41*
  - 8.1.3 도 "also, even" *42*
  - 8.1.4 마저/조차 "even" *42*
  - 8.1.5 만 "only" *42*
  - 8.1.6 밖에 "nothing but" *43*
  - 8.1.7 뿐 "only, just" *43*
  - 8.1.8 은/는커녕 "far from" *43*
- 8.2 Particles of approximation and optionality *44*
  - 8.2.1 쯤 "about" *44*
  - 8.2.2 (이)나 "about, or" *44*

9 Verbs, adjectives, and copula — 46
- 9.1 Verbs and adjectives *46*
  - 9.1.1 Stems *46*
  - 9.1.2 Vowel-based and consonant-based stems *47*
- 9.2 Endings *47*
  - 9.2.1 Pre-final endings *47*
  - 9.2.2 Non-sentence-final endings *47*
  - 9.2.3 Sentence-final endings *48*
- 9.3 The copula 이다 *48*

10 Irregular predicates — 50
- 10.1 ㄷ-irregular *50*
- 10.2 ㅂ-irregular *51*
- 10.3 ㅅ-irregular *51*
- 10.4 ㅎ-irregular *52*
- 10.5 으-irregular *52*
- 10.6 르-irregular *52*
- 10.7 ㄹ-irregular *53*

11 Past tenses — 54
- 11.1 Past tense marker ~었/았 *54*
- 11.2 Double past tense marker ~었었/았었 *55*
- 11.3 The retrospective suffix ~더 *56*

12 Future tenses and aspect — 57
- 12.1 Future tenses *57*
  - 12.1.1 ~(으)ㄹ 거 "will" *57*
  - 12.1.2 ~(으)ㄹ래 "will (intend)" *58*
  - 12.1.3 ~(으)ㄹ게 "will (promise)" *58*
  - 12.1.4 ~겠 "will (intend), conjecture" *59*
- 12.2 Continuous tense/aspect *60*
  - 12.2.1 ~고 있다 *60*
  - 12.2.2 ~어/아 있다 *60*

CONTENTS

13 Auxiliary verbs I   62
- 13.1 ~어/아 가다 /오다 "continue to"   62
- 13.2 ~어/아 내다 "do all the way (to the very end)"   63
- 13.3 ~어/아 놓다 (or 두다) "do for later"   63
- 13.4 ~어/아 대다 "do continuously"   64
- 13.5 ~어/아 버리다 "end up doing"   65
- 13.6 ~어/아 보다 "try (doing something)"   65

14 Auxiliary verbs II   67
- 14.1 ~어/아 보이다 "appear to be"   67
- 14.2 ~어/아 빠지다 "fall into a negative state"   67
- 14.3 ~어/아 주다 "do for"   67
- 14.4 ~어/아 치우다 "do hurriedly"   68
- 14.5 ~어/아하다 "be in the state of"   68
- 14.6 ~어/아지다 "become"   69

15 Auxiliary verbs III   71
- 15.1 ~고 말다 "end up ~ing"   71
- 15.2 ~고 보다 "try (something first) and then see what it is like"   71
- 15.3 ~고 싶다 "want to"   72
- 15.4 ~(으)ㄹ까 싶다 "afraid that it may"   72
- 15.5 ~(으)ㄹ까 보다 "am thinking of, worrying that"   73
- 15.6 ~(으)ㄹ까 하다/생각하다 "am thinking of (doing something)"   73
- 15.7 ~나/(으)ㄴ가 보다 "appears that"   73
- 15.8 ~게 되다 "turns out"   74
- 15.9 ~어/아야 되다 "must"   74

16 Clausal conjunctives I   76
- 16.1 Restrictions   76
- 16.2 Clausal conjunctives (reasons and cause)   78
  - 16.2.1 ~어/아서 "so, and then"   78
  - 16.2.2 ~(으)니까 "as, since, because"   79
  - 16.2.3 ~(으)ㄹ 테니까 "since"   80
  - 16.2.4 ~느라고 "as a result of, while doing"   80
  - 16.2.5 ~(으)므로 "because of"   80
  - 16.2.6 ~더니 "but, since"   81
  - 16.2.7 ~길래 "so, since"   81

17 Clausal conjunctives II   82
- 17.1 Clausal conjunctives (background)   82
  - 17.1.1 ~는/(으)ㄴ데 "and, but, while"   82
  - 17.1.2 ~(으)ㄹ 텐데 "I guess that . . ."   83
- 17.2 Clausal conjunctives (contrast)   83
  - 17.2.1 ~지만 "although"   83
  - 17.2.2 ~(으)나 "but, however"   84
  - 17.2.3 ~(으)나 마나 "whether . . . or not"   84
  - 17.2.4 ~어/아도 "even though"   84
  - 17.2.5 ~는/(으)ㄴ데도 "although, even after"   85
  - 17.2.6 ~더라도 "even though"   85
  - 17.2.7 ~어/아서라도 "even if it means"   85
  - 17.2.8 ~고도 "even after"   86
  - 17.2.9 ~(으)ㄴ들 "even if, granted that"   86
  - 17.2.10 ~(으)ㄹ지라도 "even if"   86

CONTENTS

        17.2.11 ~(으)ㄹ지언정 "even though" *87*
        17.2.12 ~(으)ㄹ망정 "even if" *87*
        17.2.13 ~느니 "rather, instead of doing X" *87*
        17.2.14 ~기로서니 "even though" *87*

18 Clausal conjunctives III   88

    18.1 Clausal conjunctives (intention) *88*
        18.1.1 ~(으)러 "to, in order to" *88*
        18.1.2 ~(으)려고 "to, intending to" *88*
        18.1.3 ~(으)려다가 "intending to" *89*
        18.1.4 ~고자 "intending to" *90*
        18.1.5 ~게 "so that" *90*
        18.1.6 ~도록 "so that, to the extent that" *90*
    18.2 Clausal conjunctives (conditions) *90*
        18.2.1 ~(으)면 "if, when" *90*
        18.2.2 ~(으)려면 "if, when (one intends to do)" *91*
        18.2.3 ~었/았더라면 "if, when (something had been the case)" *91*
        18.2.4 ~거든 "if, when" *92*
        18.2.5 ~어/아야 "only if" *92*
        18.2.6 ~(으)ㄹ수록 "the more . . . the more" *93*

19 Clausal conjunctives IV   94

    19.1 Clausal conjunctives (sequence) *94*
        19.1.1 ~고 "and, and also, as well" *94*
        19.1.2 ~고서 "and, and then" *95*
        19.1.3 ~거니와 "as well as" *95*
        19.1.4 ~(으)면서 "while" *95*
        19.1.5 ~(으)며 "and, while" *95*
        19.1.6 ~자마자 "as soon as" *96*
        19.1.7 ~다가 "while doing, do and then" *97*
    19.2 Clausal conjunctives (option) *97*
        19.2.1 ~거나 "or" *97*
        19.2.2 ~든지 "or, regardless" *98*
    19.3 Clausal conjunctives (comparison) *98*
        19.3.1 ~듯이 "like, as, as if" *98*
        19.3.2 ~다시피 "just as, as if" *99*

20 Negation   100

    20.1 The short-form negation [안/ 못 + predicate] *100*
    20.2 The long-form negation: ~지 않아요 and ~지 못해요 *101*
    20.3 The negative auxiliary verb ~지 말다 *103*
    20.4 Sino-Korean negative prefixes *104*

21 Modifiers   105

    21.1 The noun-modifying ending ~는 *105*
    21.2 The noun-modifying ending ~(으)ㄴ *105*
    21.3 The noun-modifying ending ~(으)ㄹ *106*
    21.4 The noun-modifying ending ~던 *107*
    21.5 Placing a noun-modifying unit in a sentence *107*

22 Expressions with modifier clauses I   109

    22.1 ~는/(으)ㄴ/(으)ㄹ/던 것 같다 "it seems" *109*
    22.2 ~는/(으)ㄴ 것이다 "the fact is" *110*

CONTENTS

22.3 ~(으)ㄹ 겸 "to do A and to do B" *110*
22.4 ~(으)ㄹ 계획이다 "plans to" *110*
22.5 ~는/(으)ㄴ 김에 "since/while you are at it/doing it" *111*
22.6 ~는/던 길에 "on the way to/from" *111*
22.7 ~(으)ㄴ 다음에 "after" *111*
22.8 ~(으)ㄴ 덕분에 "thanks to, by (someone's) favor" *112*
22.9 ~는/(으)ㄴ 대로 "as soon as" *112*
22.10 ~는 동안/사이에 "while" *112*
22.11 ~는/(으)ㄴ/(으)ㄹ 듯하다/듯싶다 "seems" *113*
22.12 ~(으)ㄹ 때 "when" *113*

23 Expressions with modifier clauses II   115
23.1 ~(으)ㄹ 리가 없다 "it is not possible that" *115*
23.2 ~(으)ㄹ 만하다 "worth" *115*
23.3 ~는/(으)ㄴ/(으)ㄹ 모양이다 "appears to" *116*
23.4 ~(으)ㄹ 바에 "rather . . . than" *116*
23.5 ~는/(으)ㄴ 바람에 "because of" *116*
23.6 ~는/(으)ㄴ 반면에 "on the other hand" *117*
23.7 ~는/(으)ㄴ 법이다 "it's certain that . . ." *117*
23.8 ~(으)ㄹ 법하다 "be likely" *117*
23.9 ~(으)ㄹ 뻔했다 "almost" *118*
23.10 ~(으)ㄹ 뿐 "only" *118*
23.11 ~(으)ㄹ 수 있다/없다 "can, cannot" *118*
23.12 ~는/(으)ㄴ 이상 "since, unless" *119*
23.13 ~(으)ㄴ 일/적/경험이 있다/없다 "ever, never" *119*

24 Expressions with modifier clauses III   121
24.1 ~(으)ㄹ 정도로 "to the extent that" *121*
24.2 ~는/(으)ㄴ/(으)ㄹ 줄 알다/모르다 "know, think" *121*
24.3 ~는 도중에 "in the middle of" *122*
24.4 ~는 중이다 "be in the middle of" *122*
24.5 ~(으)ㄴ 지 되다/지나다 "it's been . . . since" *123*
24.6 ~(으)ㄴ 채로 "just as it is, while" *123*
24.7 ~는/(으)ㄴ 척/체하다 "pretend" *124*
24.8 ~는/(으)ㄴ 탓/통에 "because of" *124*
24.9 ~는/(으)ㄴ 편이다 "tends to" *124*
24.10 ~는/(으)ㄴ 한 "as long as" *125*

25 Sentence endings I   126
25.1 ~거든(요) "you see" *126*
25.2 ~고말고(요) "of course" *127*
25.3 ~군(요) "oh, I see . . .!" *127*
25.4 ~네(요) "wow, I see that . . ." *128*
  25.4.1 ~겠네요 *128*
  25.4.2 ~었/았겠네요 *129*

26 Sentence endings II   130
26.1 ~(으)ㄹ걸(요) "regrets, guessing" *130*
26.2 ~(으)ㄹ까(요)? "wondering" *130*
26.3 ~(으)ㄹ 텐데(요) "I am afraid that, I suppose that" *131*
26.4 ~(으)렴 "may, go ahead (giving orders)" *132*
26.5 ~잖아(요) "you know" *132*
26.6 ~지(요) "right?" *132*

CONTENTS

27 Addressee honorifics: speech level endings — 135
- 27.1 Korean honorifics *135*
- 27.2 Addressee honorifics: speech level endings *136*
  - 27.2.1 The formal speech level *136*
  - 27.2.2 The polite speech level *137*
  - 27.2.3 The intimate speech level *138*
  - 27.2.4 The plain speech level *138*
  - 27.2.5 The familiar speech level and the blunt speech level *140*

28 Referent honorifics — 142
- 28.1 The subject honorific suffix ~(으)시 *142*
- 28.2 Honorific verbs/adjectives *142*
- 28.3 The honorific particles 께 and 께서 *143*
- 28.4 Object honorification by using "humble verbs" *143*
- 28.5 Honorific nouns *144*
- 28.6 Using the honorific elements together *144*

29 The passive construction — 146
- 29.1 The passive suffix ~이, ~히, ~리, ~기 *146*
- 29.2 Passives with ~어/아지다 *148*
- 29.3 Passives with "noun + 되다" *148*
- 29.4 Verbs with a passive-like meaning *149*

30 The causative construction — 150
- 30.1 Causative suffixes: ~이, ~히, ~리, ~기, ~우, ~구, ~추 *150*
- 30.2 The causative constructions ~게 하다 and ~도록 하다 *152*
- 30.3 Causatives with "noun + 시키다" *152*

31 Direct and indirect questions/quotations — 153
- 31.1 Indirect question form ~는/(으)ㄴ/(으)ㄹ지 *153*
- 31.2 Indicating a speculative mindset *154*
- 31.3 Direct quotations *155*
- 31.4 Indirect quotations *156*
- 31.5 Abbreviation of the indirect quotation endings in colloquial usages *158*
- 31.6 Reporting one's thoughts or feelings *158*

32 Prenouns — 159

33 Adverbs — 162
- 33.1 Adverbs *162*
  - 33.1.1 Semantic categorization of adverbs *162*
  - 33.1.2 Structural categorization of adverbs *164*
- 33.2 Mimetic/onomatopoetic words *165*

Part B Functions — 167

34 Ability — 169
- 34.1 Using words that indicate "ability" *169*
- 34.2 ~(으)ㄹ 줄 알다/모르다 "know how to" *169*
- 34.3 ~(으)ㄹ 수 있다/없다 "can/cannot" *170*
- 34.4 ~다 못해(서) "unable to" *170*

35 Addressing someone — 171
- 35.1 Address terms in Korean *171*
- 35.2 How to address a family member *172*
- 35.3 How to address a friend/familiar person *174*
- 35.4 How to address a colleague at your workplace *174*
- 35.5 How to address an unfamiliar person/stranger *175*

36 Advice — 176
- 36.1 Seeking advice *176*
  - 36.1.1 ~(으)ㄹ까요? "wondering" *176*
- 36.2 Giving advice *176*
  - 36.2.1 ~지 그래요? "why don't you . . . ?" *176*
  - 36.2.2 ~도록 하세요 "do" *177*
- 36.3 Seeking and giving advice *177*
  - 36.3.1 어때요/어떨까요? "How about?" *177*
  - 36.3.2 ~지 않을까요? "Don't you think . . . ?" *177*
  - 36.3.3 ~것이 어떨까 싶네요 "how about . . ." *178*
  - 36.3.4 ~(으)ㄹ 만하다 "worth . . ." *178*
- 36.4 Responding to advice *178*

37 Causes — 179
- 37.1 Asking about cause *179*
- 37.2 Expressing cause *179*
  - 37.2.1 N의 원인은 N이다 "N's cause is N." *179*
  - 37.2.2 N때문에 "because of N" *179*
  - 37.2.3 ~기 때문에 "because of ~ing" *180*
  - 37.2.4 N으로 말미암아(서) "owing to N" *180*
  - 37.2.5 N으로 인해서 "due to N" *180*

38 Changes — 181
- 38.1 Expressing a change in action/state *181*
  - 38.1.1 ~게 되다 "to turn out" *181*
  - 38.1.2 ~(으)ㄹ수록 "the more . . . the more" *181*
  - 38.1.3 ~어/아지다 "become" *182*
- 38.2 Verbs that express a change *182*

39 Choices — 184
- 39.1 A하고 B하고 어느 쪽으로 하시겠어요? "Which would you prefer, A or B?" *184*
- 39.2 ~거나 "or" *184*
- 39.3 ~건 ~건 "whether . . . or not" *185*
- 39.4 ~느니 "rather, instead of doing X" *185*
- 39.5 N 대신에 "instead of N" *185*
- 39.6 ~는/(으)ㄴ 대신에 "in place of ~ing" *186*
- 39.7 ~든지 ~든지 "or else" *186*
- 39.8 ~(으)ㄹ 바에(야) "rather . . . than" *186*
- 39.9 N(이)나 "or" *187*
- 39.10 N이라도 "even if it is" *187*

40 Comparing — 188
- 40.1 N보다 더/덜 "more/less than noun" *188*
- 40.2 ~는/ㄴ다기보다(는) "rather than" *188*

CONTENTS

	40.3	N와/과 비교해서 and N에 비해서 "when compared to" *189*	
	40.4	N 만큼 "as . . . as" *189*	
	40.5	~는 것보다 ~는 게 낫다 "Doing X is better than doing X." *190*	
	40.6	N중에서 N가 최고로/제일 *190*	

41 Complaining   **192**

    41.1   ~(으)면서 . . . 해요 "while" *192*
    41.2   아무리 ~기로서니 "no matter how . . . you may be . . ." *192*
    41.3   ~어/아 빠지다 "is extremely" *192*
    41.4   ~기 일쑤이다 "prone to" *193*
    41.5   ~어/아 대다 "do frequently" *193*
    41.6   ~(으)려고 들다 "rush to" *193*
    41.7   ~었/았어야지요 "should have" *193*
    41.8   Examples of complaining remarks *194*

42 Conditions   **196**

    42.1   Expressing conditions by conjunctives *196*
        42.1.1   ~거든 "when, if" *196*
        42.1.2   ~(으)면 "if, when" *196*
        42.1.3   ~(으)면 몰라도 "unless" *197*
        42.1.4   ~(으)려면 "if you intend to" *197*
        42.1.5   ~어/아야 "only if" *197*
    42.2   Other ways to express conditions *198*
        42.2.1   ~할 경우 "in the event that" *198*
        42.2.2   ~지 않는 한/이상 "unless" *198*
        42.2.3   ~(느)냐에 달려 있다 "it depends on" *198*
        42.2.4   ~기 나름이다 "it depends on" *199*

43 Congratulations, condolence, and gratitude expressions   **200**

    43.1   Congratulating someone *200*
    43.2   Expressing good wishes for special occasions *200*
    43.3   Expressing concerns and condolences *201*
        43.3.1   When you express concern *201*
        43.3.2   When you express condolences in person *201*
        43.3.3   When you express condolences in formal speech or writing *201*
    43.4   Gratitude *202*
        43.4.1   In casual conversations *202*
        43.4.2   In formal speech or writing *202*
        43.4.3   When you receive a gift *202*
        43.4.4   Before being treated to a meal/drink *202*
        43.4.5   After being treated to a meal/drink *203*
    43.5   Replying to expressions of gratitude *203*

44 Conjecture   **204**

    44.1   ~겠네요/겠어요 "you must be . . ." *204*
    44.2   ~나/(으)ㄴ가 보다 "it looks like" *204*
    44.3   ~나/(으)ㄴ가 했다 "I thought/guessed that" *205*
    44.4   ~는/(으)ㄴ/(으)ㄹ 것 같다 "I think/guess that" *205*
    44.5   ~는/(으)ㄴ/(으)ㄹ 듯하다 "it seems that . . ." *206*
    44.6   ~는/(으)ㄴ/(으)ㄹ 모양이다 "it appears that . . ." *206*
    44.7   ~는/(으)ㄴ/(으)ㄹ 줄 알았다/몰랐다 "knew/thought" *207*
    44.8   ~어/아 보이다 "appears to be" *207*

44.9 ~(으)ㄹ 거예요 "I think/guess" *207*
44.10 ~(으)ㄹ걸요 "I bet/think" *208*
44.11 ~(으)ㄹ까요 "Do you think . . .?" *208*
44.12 ~(으)ㄹ지도 모르다 "not sure if" *208*
44.13 ~(으)ㄹ 텐데 "I guess that" *209*
44.14 ~(으)ㄹ 테니까 "I suppose . . . so" *209*

45 Contrast 211
45.1 Expressing contrasts with clausal conjunctives *211*
    45.1.1 ~고도 "although, even after" *211*
    45.1.2 ~건만 "despite" *211*
    45.1.3 ~지만 "although" *211*
    45.1.4 ~기는 ~지만 "indeed . . . but" *212*
    45.1.5 ~어/아도 "although" *212*
    45.1.6 ~더라도 "even though" *212*
    45.1.7 ~으나 "but" *213*
    45.1.8 ~는/(으)ㄴ데(도) "even after" *213*
45.2 Expressing contrast with conjunctional adverbs *213*
45.3 Expressing contrast with the particle 은/는 *214*
45.4 Other expressions of contrast *214*
    45.4.1 ~는/(으)ㄴ가 하면 "on the other hand" *214*
    45.4.2 ~는/(으)ㄴ 반면에 "on the other hand" *215*
    45.4.3 ~(으)ㅁ에도 불구하고 "even after, in spite of" *215*
45.5 For writings and formal contexts *215*

46 Deciding 217
46.1 결정 + verb "decide" *217*
46.2 결심하다 "make a resolution" *217*
46.3 정하다 "decide on, choose, set" *218*
46.4 ~기로 하다 "decide to" *218*

47 Degree and extent 219
47.1 Expressing degree and extent *219*
    47.1.1 N만 "only" *219*
    47.1.2 N만하다 "be as . . . as" *219*
    47.1.3 N만 해도 "just talking about . . ." *219*
    47.1.4 N뿐 "only" *220*
    47.1.5 N밖에 "nothing but, only" *220*
    47.1.6 ~기 짝이 없다 "beyond measure" *220*
    47.1.7 ~도록 "to the extent that . . ." *220*
    47.1.8 ~(으)ㄹ 정도로 "to the extent that . . ." *220*
    47.1.9 ~(으)리만치 (similar to ~을 정도로) *221*
    47.1.10 ~는/(으)ㄴ/(으)ㄹ 만큼 "to the extent that . . ." *221*
47.2 Expressing the degree of satisfaction *222*

48 Describing people, places, weather, color, and taste 223
48.1 Describing people *223*
48.2 Describing places *223*
48.3 Describing the weather *224*
48.4 Describing color *224*
48.5 Describing the taste of food *225*

CONTENTS

49	**Discoveries**		**226**
	49.1	~군/네(요) "oh, I see . . ." *226*	
	49.2	~(으)니까 "when" *226*	
	49.3	~고 보니(까) "after having tried doing . . . and then realize" *227*	
	49.4	~다(가) 보니(까) "after tried doing X . . . and then realize" *227*	
	49.5	~다(가) 보면 "if/when continue to do something . . . then . . . will" *228*	
	49.6	~(었/았)더니 "since, seeing as" *228*	

50	**Emphasizing strategies**		**229**
	50.1	~거든요 "you see, you know" *229*	
	50.2	~잖아요 "you know" *229*	
	50.3	~기가 이를 데 없다 (~기가 그지없다/~기 짝이 없다) "extremely" *230*	
	50.4	~기는 커녕 "far from ~ing" *230*	
	50.5	여간 ~지 않다 "exceedingly" *230*	
	50.6	얼마나/어찌나 ~은/는지 (모르다) "don't know . . . how . . ." *231*	
	50.7	~(으)ㄹ 뿐이다 "only, just" *232*	
	50.8	~(으)ㄹ 수밖에 없다 "have no choice but" *232*	
	50.9	~(으)ㄹ래야 ~(으)ㄹ 수가 없다 "though I try . . . I can't" *232*	
	50.10	N(이)야말로 "indeed" *232*	
	50.11	~는/(으)ㄴ 데다가 "besides" *233*	
	50.12	Using exclamatory remarks *233*	

51	**Establishing a sequence**		**235**

52	**Experiences**		**239**
	52.1	Nouns and verbs that indicate one's experience *239*	
	52.2	~(으)ㄴ 적/일이 있다/없다 "have/don't have an experience of ~ing" *240*	
	52.3	~어/아 보다 "try (doing something)" *240*	
	52.4	~어/아 본 적/일이 있다/없다 "have/don't have an experience of trying" *240*	

53	**Greetings and leave taking**		**242**
	53.1	Greetings *242*	
		53.1.1 Greetings as phatic expressions *242*	
		53.1.2 When you meet someone for the first time *243*	
		53.1.3 When you greet someone who you have not seen for a long time *243*	
		53.1.4 When you enter unfamiliar places *243*	
		53.1.5 When you return from your work, school, or an outing *243*	
	53.2	Leave taking *243*	
		53.2.1 When you end a conversation *243*	
		53.2.2 When you leave for work/school *244*	
		53.2.3 When you leave the office/work *244*	
		53.2.4 When you say good-bye *244*	

54	**Hypothetical situations**		**246**
	54.1	~는/ㄴ다면 "if" *246*	
	54.2	~는/ㄴ다고 치다/가정하다/하다 "supposedly . . ." *246*	
	54.3	~는/ㄴ다고 해서 "saying we suppose" *247*	
	54.4	~더라도 "even if" *247*	
	54.5	~(으)ㄹ 뻔하다 "almost" *248*	
	54.6	~(으)ㄹ지라도 "even if . . . may" *248*	

CONTENTS

- 54.7 ~(으)ㄹ지언정 "even though . . . may" *248*
- 54.8 ~(으)ㄹ망정 "even if . . . may" *249*
- 54.9 ~기 망정이지 "it was good that . . . otherwise . . ." *249*
- 54.10 ~는/(으)ㄴ 셈치다 "suppose" *249*
- 54.11 ~었/았더라면 "if/when (something had been the case)" *250*
- 54.12 ~(으)나 . . . ~(으)나 "whether . . . or" *250*

55 Initiating and maintaining conversations — 251
- 55.1 Initiating a conversation *251*
- 55.2 Introducing topics *251*
  - 55.2.1 The particle 은/는 "as for" *251*
  - 55.2.2 N에 관해서는 "regarding" *252*
  - 55.2.3 N에 대해서 "about" *252*
- 55.3 Switching topics *252*
- 55.4 Listener responses *253*
  - 55.4.1 Paying attention *253*
  - 55.4.2 Asking for confirmation *253*
  - 55.4.3 Showing surprise *253*
  - 55.4.4 Requesting a repetition *253*
  - 55.4.5 Making corrections *254*
  - 55.4.6 Acknowledging what the other says *254*

56 Intentions and plans — 255
- 56.1 ~겠어요 "will" *255*
- 56.2 ~어야겠어요 "I think that I need to . . ." *255*
- 56.3 ~(으)ㄹ 거예요 "will" *256*
- 56.4 ~(으)ㄹ게요 "will (promise)" *256*
- 56.5 ~(으)ㄹ까 해요 "I am thinking of ~ing" *256*
- 56.6 ~(으)ㄹ래요 "will (intend)" *256*
- 56.7 ~어/아야지 "will, should" *257*
- 56.8 ~(으)ㄹ 겸 . . . ~(으)ㄹ 겸 "to do A and to do B" *257*
- 56.9 ~(으)려다가 "intending to" *257*
- 56.10 ~(으)리라 "will" *258*
- 56.11 Other ways to indicate intention or plans *258*

57 Likes and wishes — 259
- 57.1 좋아하다 "like" *259*
- 57.2 ~고 싶다 "want, wish, would like to" *260*
- 57.3 ~(으)면 좋겠다/하다 "It'd be great if . . ." *260*
- 57.4 ~기 바라다 "to hope" *261*
- 57.5 마음에 들다 "be to one's liking" *261*
- 57.6 희망 "hope" and 소원 "wish" *261*
- 57.7 원하다 "to want" *262*
- 57.8 Expressing good wishes in writing or in person *262*

58 Listing and including additional information — 263
- 58.1 Listing *263*
  - 58.1.1 ~고 "and" *263*
  - 58.1.2 ~는가 하면 "while" *263*
  - 58.1.3 ~(으)랴 ~(으)랴 "while doing X and doing X" *264*
  - 58.1.4 ~(으)며 "and" *264*
  - 58.1.5 N(이)며 N(이)며 "and" *264*

CONTENTS

    58.2   Expressing additional information *264*
           58.2.1   Particles and conjunctives *264*
           58.2.2   ~거니와 "as well as" *265*
           58.2.3   ~는/(으)ㄴ 데다가 "in addition to" *265*
           58.2.4   ~(으)ㄹ 뿐만 아니라 "not just . . . but also . . ." *266*
           58.2.5   ~(으)ㄹ뿐더러 "not only . . . but also" *266*
           58.2.6   N을/를 비롯해서 "including, starting with N" *266*

59 Location, direction, and distance   267

    59.1   Asking and describing the location of an object *267*
           59.1.1   N에 있다 "there is . . ." *267*
    59.2   Asking and indicating for directions/destination *268*
           59.2.1   N에 *268*
           59.2.2   N(으)로 *268*
    59.3   Asking and indicating distance *269*
           59.3.1   N에서 N까지 *269*

60 Means   270

    60.1   Expressing means *270*
           60.1.1   N(으)로 "as/by/with" *270*
           60.1.2   N(으)로써 "as/by/with" *271*
           60.1.3   N(을/를) 가지고 "by/with" *271*
    60.2   Describing means of transportation *271*

61 Obligation and necessity   273

    61.1   Obligation *273*
           61.1.1   ~지 않으면 안 되다 and 안 ~(으)면 안 되다 "must" *273*
           61.1.2   ~어/아야 되다/하다 "must/have to" *273*
           61.1.3   ~어/아야지요 "should" *274*
           61.1.4   ~(으)ㄹ 의무가 있다 "have an obligation to" *274*
           61.1.5   ~지 않아도 되다 "do not have to" *275*
    61.2   Necessity *275*
           61.2.1   ~이/가 필요하다 "be necessary" *275*
           61.2.2   필요 없다 "no need" *275*
           61.2.3   ~(으)ㄹ 필요가 있다 "it is necessary to" *275*
           61.2.4   ~(으)ㄹ 필요가 없다 "there is no need for" *276*

62 Permission and prohibition   277

    62.1   Seeking and giving permission *277*
           62.1.1   ~어/아도 되다 "you may" *277*
    62.2   Denying permission/expressing prohibition *278*
           62.2.1   ~(으)면 안 되다 "must not" *278*
           62.2.2   ~지 마세요 "do not" *279*
           62.2.3   Formal written words that specify prohibited activities *279*

63 Personal information   281

    63.1   Name *281*
    63.2   Age *281*
    63.3   Place of origin *282*
    63.4   Nationality *282*
    63.5   Occupation *283*

CONTENTS

      63.6   Marital status *283*
      63.7   Family *284*

64 Possibility   285
    64.1   가능하다 "be possible" *285*
    64.2   ~(으)ㄹ 수(도) 있다 "possible" *285*
    64.3   ~(으)ㄹ지도 모르다 "may" *286*
    64.4   ~(으)ㄹ 리가 없다 "it's hardly possible" *286*

65 Probability and inevitability   287
    65.1   Expressing probability *287*
        65.1.1 ~(으)ㄹ 거예요 "will probably" *287*
        65.1.2 ~(으)ㄹ 법하다 "be likely" *287*
    65.2   Expressing inevitability *288*
        65.2.1 ~(으)ㄹ 게 뻔하다 "bound to" *288*
        65.2.2 ~기 십상이다 "it is easy to" *288*
        65.2.3 ~기 마련이다 "bound to" *288*
        65.2.4 ~는 법이다 "it is certain that . . ." *288*
        65.2.5 ~(으)ㄹ 수 밖에 없다 "have no choice but" *289*
        65.2.6 안 ~(으)ㄹ 수 없다 "have no choice but" *289*
        65.2.7 ~는/(으)ㄴ 마당에 "in this situation" *289*

66 Purpose   290
    66.1   Asking about purpose *290*
    66.2   Expressing purpose *290*
        66.2.1 ~고자 "intending to" *290*
        66.2.2 ~으러 "in order to" *290*
        66.2.3 ~(으)려고 "to" *291*
        66.2.4 ~도록 "so that" *291*
        66.2.5 ~게 "so that" *291*
        66.2.6 N위해서 "for the sake of N" *292*

67 Reasons   293
    67.1   Asking about reasons *293*
    67.2   Expressing reasons *294*
        67.2.1 ~고 해서 "so" *294*
        67.2.2 ~기에 "since" *294*
        67.2.3 ~길래 "since" *294*
        67.2.4 ~느라고 "as a result of" *295*
        67.2.5 ~는/(으)ㄴ 바람에 "because of" *295*
        67.2.6 ~는/(으)ㄴ 이상 "since" *295*
        67.2.7 ~는/(으)ㄴ 탓/통에 "because" *296*
        67.2.8 ~어/아서 "so" *296*
        67.2.9 ~어/아서 그런지 "perhaps . . . so" *297*
        67.2.10 ~(으)니까 "since" *297*
        67.2.11 ~(으)므로 "because, since" *297*

68 Recollecting   298
    68.1   Some verbs, words, or phrases related to recollection *298*
    68.2   The use of past tense marker ~었/았 *298*
        68.2.1 ~었/았었어요 *298*
        68.2.2 ~었/았을 때 "when" *299*
        68.2.3 ~곤 했다 "used to" *299*

CONTENTS

- 68.3 The use of retrospective suffix ~더 *299*
  - 68.3.1 ~데요 "I notice/remember that..." *299*
  - 68.3.2 ~더라고(구)요 "I'm telling you, you know" *300*
  - 68.3.3 The use of the retrospective noun-modifying ending ~던 *300*
  - 68.3.4 ~었/았던 *300*
  - 68.3.5 ~던데요 "I perceived that..." *301*

69 Regret and futility — 302
- 69.1 후회스럽다/유감스럽다 "regretful" *302*
- 69.2 ~고 말다 "end up ~ing" *302*
- 69.3 왜...는지 모르겠다 "not sure why..." *303*
- 69.4 ~(으)ㄹ걸 그랬다 "should have" *303*
- 69.5 ~었/았더라면 ~(으)ㄹ 텐데 "if/when...I guess that..." *303*
- 69.6 ~었/았아야 했는데 "should have" *304*
- 69.7 ~(으)나 마나 "whether...or not" *304*
- 69.8 ~어/아 봤자 "though you try...no use" *304*
- 69.9 ~(으)ㄴ들 "no matter how" *304*
- 69.10 ~(으)ㄴ 나머지 "as a result of, driven by" *305*

70 Requests — 306
- 70.1 Direct request/command *307*
- 70.2 ~어/아 주세요 "(Please)...for me." *307*
- 70.3 ~(으)ㄹ 거지(요)? "You will..., right?" *307*
- 70.4 ~어/아 줄래(요)/주시겠어요? "Will/Would you...?" *308*
- 70.5 ~(으)ㄹ 수 있으세요? "Can/Could you...?" *308*
- 70.6 ~는지 아세요? "Do you know how to...?" *308*
- 70.7 ~어/아 주실 수 있을까(요)? "Would it be possible...?" *308*
- 70.8 ~어/아도 될까(요)/괜찮을까(요)? "Would it be fine even if...?" *308*
- 70.9 ~읍시다/어떨까 싶네요 "How about...Let's...I wonder..." *309*
- 70.10 ~(으)면 한다/고맙겠다/감사하겠습니다 "I would appreciate it if..." *309*
- 70.11 Indirect request (want/need) *309*
- 70.12 Indirect request (hint) *309*

71 Similarity — 311
- 71.1 Indicating resemblance *311*
  - 71.1.1 N처럼 "like" *311*
  - 71.1.2 N같이 "like" *311*
  - 71.1.3 닮다 "resemble, look alike, take after" *311*
  - 71.1.4 비슷하다 "similar" *312*
  - 71.1.5 흡사하다 "alike" *312*
- 71.2 Expressing sameness *312*
  - 71.2.1 같다 "the same" *312*
  - 71.2.2 마찬가지이다 "the same" *312*
  - 71.2.3 N(이)나 다름없다 "no different from" *313*
- 71.3 Expressing in the same manner or form *313*
  - 71.3.1 ~다시피 하다/되다 "as, in the same way, almost" *313*
  - 71.3.2 ~듯이 "as, as if" *313*
  - 71.3.3 ~는/(으)ㄴ 양 "as if" *314*
  - 71.3.4 ~는/(으)ㄴ 척/체하다 "pretend" *314*

CONTENTS

72 Simultaneous actions and states — 315
- 72.1 Indicating simultaneous actions by clausal conjunctives — 315
  - 72.1.1 ~다가 "while doing" — 315
  - 72.1.2 ~(으)면서 "while" — 315
- 72.2 Indicating simultaneous actions or states by modifier clauses — 316
  - 72.2.1 ~는/(으)ㄴ 가운데 "while doing" — 316
  - 72.2.2 ~는/(으)ㄴ 김에 "while you are at it" — 316
  - 72.2.3 ~는 길에 "on the way to/from" — 316
  - 72.2.4 ~는 동안(사이)에 "while" — 316
  - 72.2.5 ~는 (도)중에 "in the middle of" — 317
  - 72.2.6 ~(으)ㄴ 채로 "just as it is, while" — 317
  - 72.2.7 ~(으)ㄹ 때 "when" — 317
  - 72.2.8 ~(으)ㄹ 때마다 "every time" — 318

73 Softening strategies — 319
- 73.1 좀 "please" — 319
- 73.2 어떻게 "how" — 319
- 73.3 ~(으)ㄴ가(요)?/~나(요)? — 320
- 73.4 ~지(요) — 320
- 73.5 ~게 되다 "to become" and 그렇다 "to be so" — 321
- 73.6 ~는/(으)ㄴ 것 같다 "seems/appears to" and ~은/는 편이다 "tends to/kind of" — 321
- 73.7 ~어/아 주다 "do something" and ~어/아 보다 "to try something" — 321
- 73.8 ~는/(으)ㄴ 감이 있다 "feel like" — 321
- 73.9 The use of questions — 322
- 73.10 The use of clausal conjunctives as sentence endings — 322
- 73.11 The use of fillers — 322

74 Telling the time, date, etc. — 325
- 74.1 Telling the time — 325
- 74.2 Counting days — 325
- 74.3 Counting months and years — 326
- 74.4 Asking and telling the time — 327
- 74.5 Asking and telling dates — 327
- 74.6 Asking and telling when something will happen or happened — 328
- 74.7 Asking and telling how long something takes — 328
- 74.8 Asking and telling the time that has passed for a certain period — 329
  - 74.8.1 N동안 — 329
  - 74.8.2 ~(으)ㄴ 지 지나다/되다 — 329

75 Temporal relations — 331
- 75.1 Expressing "before" — 331
  - 75.1.1 N전(에) "before N" — 331
  - 75.1.2 ~기 전(에) "before ~ing" — 331
- 75.2 Expressing "after" — 331
  - 75.2.1 N다음/ 후(에) "after N" — 331
  - 75.2.2 ~(으)ㄴ 후/다음(에) "after" — 332
  - 75.2.3 ~(으)ㄴ 끝에 "after" — 332
  - 75.2.4 N만(에) "after" — 332
  - 75.2.5 ~고 나서 "after having (done something)" — 332
- 75.3 Expressing sequence "and then" — 333
  - 75.3.1 ~고 "and then" — 333
  - 75.3.2 ~어/아서 "and then" — 333

CONTENTS

		75.3.3	~고서 "after, and then" *334*
		75.3.4	~었/았다가 "did and then" *334*
	75.4	Expressing "as soon as" *334*	
		75.4.1	~기가 무섭게 "just after" *334*
		75.4.2	~는/(으)ㄴ 대로 "as soon as" *334*
		75.4.3	~자마자 "as soon as" *335*
	75.5	Expressing "about to" *335*	
		75.5.1	~(으)려는 참이다 "is about to" *335*
		75.5.2	~(으)려던 참이었다 "was about to" *336*

English Index   **337**
Korean Index   **339**

Preface

Modern Korean Grammar provides a concise overview of the structures and functions of contemporary Korean in a single volume. Designed for those who have already acquired the basics of the language, this book strives to combine an essential description of the grammatical structures of Korean with a "functional/usage" approach to the language. All target grammatical and functional points are illustrated with examples in Hangul (the Korean alphabet) with English translations to facilitate understanding. In addition, the use of technical linguistic terms and jargon is minimized throughout the book so that the readers without formal linguistic training can easily comprehend the material. Adhering to the format of the *Modern Grammar* series, this book is divided into two major parts: Part A, Structures, and Part B, Functions. In addition, it is accompanied by its sister volume, *Modern Korean Grammar Workbook*.

Built on and expanded from the core content and format of my previous grammar books, *Basic Korean: Grammar and Workbook* (Routledge, 2009) and *Intermediate Korean: Grammar and Workbook* (Routledge, 2010), Part A, Structures, consists of several chapters that provide an accessible and succinct description of major grammatical features of Korean in a familiar and conventional manner. The section does not take a functional/situational approach in grouping or sequencing target grammatical points. Rather it sequences and covers grammatical points according to their grammatical categories (e.g., nouns, pronouns, numbers, particles, verbs, sentence endings, conjunctives, and so on) so that readers can use the section as a quick reference. For instance, if you wish to review the topic particle/postposition, different speech levels, or the structure of auxiliary verbs, you should refer to Part A for information.

Part B, Functions, is the larger of the two parts. It is a guide to Korean language usage, and it is designed to provide linguistic resources for managing/conveying communicative acts or interpersonal meanings. It is organized in terms of how to do things with language. For instance, if you want to find out what kinds of linguistic resources you would need when addressing someone, asking/talking about your experiences, or making a request, you should consult this section. There is extensive cross-referencing between the structure and function sections of the book to minimize redundant and duplicate explanations but help readers see how target grammar can be utilized/understood in terms of function/usage.

There will be a wide range of readers for this volume. The first group of readers will be secondary and postsecondary Korean-as-a-foreign language (KFL) learners. They can use this book as a supplementary grammar reference to their textbooks or as self-study materials. Besides the classroom-based KFL learners, there are individuals and former classroom-based KFL learners who are interested in learning or maintaining the language. The second major group will be KFL educators. They may find the book helpful and useful to organize their knowledge of grammar and functional features of the language and later to present the relevant features in their classrooms. The other group of readers will be linguists and other academics who may be interested in the structures and functions of Korean.

Acknowledgments

I would like to express my sincere gratitude to anonymous reviewers for their constructive comments. In addition, I am grateful to the superb editorial and production team at Routledge, especially Andrea Hartill, Samantha Vale Noya, Camille Burns, and Kristina Ryan, for their support and patience throughout the process. My special thanks also goes to Sarah Matott for reading the entire manuscript and providing helpful comments and extensive suggestions on both content and editorial matters. Last but not least, I thank my wife, Isabel Keemin Byon, for her love and constant moral support. I dedicate this volume to my beloved sons, Daniel Youngin Byon and Evan Younghoon Byon.

Part A

Structures

1
Nouns

Notes before reading

Words are the primary elements that construct a sentence. Each word in a sentence has a different function. Based on its grammatical function, each word is sorted into separate classes, such as nouns, verbs, adjectives, and so forth. Korean has the following word classes.

1   Nouns
2   Prenouns (precede a noun, like English demonstratives such as "this," "that," "these," and "those")
3   Pronouns
4   Numbers and counters
5   Particles (adhere to a noun and indicate grammatical relationships or add special meanings)
6   Verbs (express action or progress)
7   Adjectives (describe state or quality)
8   Copula (like "be verbs" that denote an equational expression: 이다 "be" and 아니다 "be not")
9   Adverbs

Korean words are divided into two groups: inflected words and uninflected words. Inflection is the process of adding some kinds of affixes to the original word in order to signal grammatical features such as tense, number, aspect, and person. The addition of an affix alters the form of the original word in the process; however, it does not change its class. For instance, consider how the English word "take" becomes "takes" with the affix "~s" when it is used for a third person singular. Another example is when the verb "learn" modifies its form to "learned" with the affix "~ed." Notice that these inflected verbs end up carrying supplementary grammatical features (i.e., the third person verb usage and past tense) but their class does not change (i.e., they are still verbs).

In Korean, the group of words that goes through inflection includes verbs and adjectives. On the other hand, the group of words that does not undergo inflection includes nouns, pronouns, numbers, adverbs, and prenouns. All of these different classes of words are discussed in detail throughout this book. However, this chapter focuses on nouns. In general, nouns concern the part of speech that indicates the name of a thing, quality, place, person, or action. Nouns often serve as the subject or object of verbs and adjectives.

1.1 Three groups of Korean nouns

There are three components that make up Korean nouns: native Korean words (about 35 percent), Sino-Korean words (about 60 percent), and loan words (about 5 percent). In general, native Korean words designate ideas that are fundamental to basic human life and are associated with traditional Korean culture. For instance, native Korean words are associated with kinship relationships, body parts, natural objects, personal pronouns, seasons, terms for agriculture and fishery, and honorific expressions.

NOUNS

아버지	"father"	바다	"sea"
구름	"cloud"	우리	"we"
여름	"summer"	얼굴	"face"
손	"hand"	쌀	"rice"
물고기	"fish"	진지	"meal"

The second group consists of Sino-Korean words. Historically speaking, Korea had been a member of Sino-Centric world order until the late nineteenth century, and had borrowed advanced culture and knowledge, including its writing system, from Chinese civilizations. The extensive Chinese influence on the Korean language resulted in the sizable number of Sino-Korean words. Since these were borrowed a long time ago (i.e., before the nineteenth century), most of the Sino-Korean words are considered completely "Koreanized" for most Korean people. In general, Sino-Korean words express abstract, scholarly, and complex ideas.

학교(學校)	"school"	질문 (質問)	"question"
경제(經濟)	"economy"	변화 (變化)	"change"
부모(父母)	"parents"	의복 (衣服)	"clothes"
문법(文法)	"grammar"	관계 (關係)	"relationship"
한국(韓國)	"Korea"	일본 (日本)	"Japan"

The third group is loan words, mostly borrowed from English since the liberation from Japanese colonial rule in 1945.

골프	"golf"	아파트	"apartment"
택시	"taxi"	버스	"bus"
그룹	"group"	스타일	"style"
파티	"party"	댄스	"dance"
리포터	"reporter"	힌트	"hint"

You may encounter native Korean, Sino-Korean, and loan words with comparable meanings. In such situations, the meaning of the native Korean word tends to be informal, colloquial, and traditional; that of Sino-Korean words tends to be formal and academic, and that of the loan words tends to be stylish and modern.

	Native Korean	Sino-Korean	Loan Words
"dance"	춤	무용	댄스
"drinking bar"	술집	주점	클럽, 빠
"store"	가게	상점	마트
"bakery"	빵집	제과점	베이커리

1.2 Noun formation

Generally speaking, Korean nouns can be made of either a single morpheme (a meaningful unit), such as 비 "rain," 강 "river," 새 "bird," 불 "fire," or multiple morphemes (a combination of several single morphemes), such as 이슬비 "drizzle" (이슬 "dew" + 비 "rain") and 돼지고기 "pork" (돼지 "pig" + 고기 "meat").

Nouns that are built on more than two morphemes are commonly constructed through either a derivational or a compounding process. The derivational formation takes an affix (either a prefix or a suffix), which generally appears in a noun or a predicate. Prefixes refer to the affixes that come before the word, whereas suffixes refer to the affixes that come after the word.

Noun formation 1.2

Derivational prefixes:
- Native Korean prefix (e.g., 맨 "bare")
  - 맨손 "bare hand" = 맨 "bare" + 손 "hand"
  - 맨발 "bare foot" = 맨 "bare" + 발 "foot"
  - 맨땅 "bare ground" = 맨 "bare" + 땅 "ground"
- Sino-Korean prefix (e.g., 대 [大] "big")
  - 대도시 "big city" = 대 "big" + 도시 "city"
  - 대가족 "big family" = 대 "big" + 가족 "family"
  - 대기업 "conglomerate" = 대 "big" + 기업 "company"

Derivational suffixes:
- Native Korean suffix (e.g., 쟁이 "person")
  - 거짓말쟁이 "liar" = 거짓말 "lie" + 쟁이 "person"
  - 겁쟁이 "coward" = 겁 "fear" + 쟁이 "person"
  - 멋쟁이 "classy dresser" = 멋 "elegance" + 쟁이 "person"
- Sino-Korean suffix (e.g., 가 [街] "street")
  - 주택가 "residential area" = 주택 "housing" + 가 "street"
  - 식당가 "row of restaurants" = 식당 "restaurant" + 가 "street"
  - 상점가 "shopping street" = 상점 "shops" + "가 "street"
- Nouns, derived from verbs (e.g., 이/기/(으)ㅁ "act")
  - 놀이 "game" = 놀 "play" + 이 "act"
  - 달리기 "running" = 달리 "run" + 기 "act"
  - 웃음 "laughter" = 웃 "laugh" + 음 "act"
- Nouns, derived from adjectives (e.g., 이/기/(으)ㅁ "quality")
  - 크기 "size" = 크 "big" + 기 "quality"
  - 깊이 "depth" = 깊 "deep" + 이 "quality"
  - 기쁨 "happiness" = 기쁘 "happy" + ㅁ "quality"

On the other hand, compound nouns are constructed from two or more independent morphemes. They are grouped into native Korean and Sino-Korean compound nouns:

Native Korean compound words:
- noun + noun
  - 잠옷 "pajama" = 잠 "sleep" + 옷 "clothes"
  - 가을비 "autumn rain" = 가을 "autumn" + 비 "rain"
  - 나뭇잎 "foliage" = 나무 "tree" + 잎 "leaf"
- adverb + noun
  - 막말 "blunt remark" = 막 "just" + 말 "word"
  - 보통법 "common law" = 보통 "usually" + 법 "law"
  - 참말 "the truth" = 참 "really" + 말 "word"
- noun + predicate + nominalizer
  - 귀걸이 "earring" = 귀 "ear" + 걸 "hang" + 이 "act"
  - 돈벌이 "moneymaking" = 돈 "money" + 벌 "earn" + 이 "act"
  - 소매치기 "pickpocket" = 소매 "sleeve" + 치 "hit" + 기 "act"
- predicate + noun
  - 늦가을 "late autumn" = 늦 "late" + 가을 "autumn"
  - 고드름 "icicle" = 곧 "straight" + 얼음 "ice"
  - 늦잠 "oversleeping" = 늦 "late" + 잠 "sleeping"
- clause + noun
  - 못난이 "stupid person" = 못난 "foolish" + 이 "person"
  - 찬물 "cold water" = 찬 "cold" + 물 "water"
  - 지난밤 "last night" = 지난 "last" + 밤 "night"

NOUNS

Sino-Korean compound words

- Sino-Korean word + Sino-Korean word
  - 두통 "headache" = 두 [頭] "head" + 통 [痛] "pain"
  - 미국인 "American" = 미국 [美國] "America" + 인 [人] "person"
  - 교통사고 "traffic accident" = 교통 [交通] "traffic" + 사고 [事故] "accident"

1.3 Prenouns and bound nouns

Korean has a group of special nouns that always precede other nouns to change or describe the following nouns, such as 무슨 일 "what kind of work," 이 사진 "this photo," 그 사무실 "that office," and 어느 호텔 "which hotel." These nouns are called "prenouns" (like English words, such as "that," "this," and "which"). Prenouns are discussed in detail in Chapter 32.

Some nouns are used only after the aforementioned prenouns or a noun-modifying form, such as ~(으)ㄴ, ~ 는, and ~(으)ㄹ (as in 한국어 수업을 듣는 곳 "the place where I take a Korean language class"). These special nouns are called "bound nouns" (or "dependent nouns"). These bound nouns cannot be used by themselves but always with a prenoun (e.g., 이 곳 "this place," 그 분 "that person," or 저 것 "that thing") or a noun-modifying form (e.g., 가까운 데 "the place that is near," 우리가 자주 가는 곳 "the place where we go often," and 해가 질 무렵 "at around the time when the sun was setting"). What follows are some major bound nouns:

것 "thing, fact, affair"
  우리가 좋아하는 것은 없네요.
  "There's nothing that we like."
겸 "along with, combined with"
  아침도 먹고 구경도 할 겸 해서 왔어요.
  "(We) came here partly for eating breakfast and partly for sightseeing."
곳 "place"
  노인들이 살기 편한 곳이에요.
  "(It) is a convenient place for senior citizens to live."
김 "chance, occasion"
  여기까지 오신 김에 저녁이나 같이 하시지요?
  "Since (you) came all the way here, why not have dinner with us?"
나름 "style, dependence"
  생각하기 나름이에요.
  "(It) depends on how you think."
나위 "necessity"
  그 커피숍은 공부하기에 더할 나위 없이 좋은 장소예요.
  "That coffee shop is an ideal place for studying."
데 "place"
  가까운 데에 계세요.
  "Please stay nearby."
동안 "during"
  여름 방학 동안 유럽을 여행했어요.
  "(We) traveled Europe during summer vacation."
들 "etc."
  사과, 배, 바나나 들이 있었어요.
  "There are apples, pears, banana, etc."
듯 "likelihood"
  잘 모르겠다는 듯이 나를 쳐다봤다.
  "(He) stared at me as if (he) did not get (it)."
따름 "nothing but"
  그저 감사할 따름이에요.
  "(I) am nothing but thankful."

Prenouns and bound nouns

때 "when"
  그녀를 처음 만났을 때부터 좋아했어요.
  "(I) liked (her) from the first time (I) met her."
때문 "reason, because of"
  일이 많았기 때문에 고생 많이 했다.
  "(I) went through a lot of trouble because there was lots of work."
리 "reasons"
  틀릴 리가 없습니다.
  "There is no mistaking (it)."
만 "size, extent"
  한참 만에 휴가예요.
  "(It) is vacation after a good while."
만큼 "as much as"
  일한 만큼 대가를 받을 수 있습니다.
  "(You) can receive rewards for as much as (you) work."
말 "the end"
  학기 말이라 바빠요.
  "(I) am busy because (it) is the end of the semester."
무렵 "around the time when"
  해 질 무렵에 바닷가에 갑시다.
  "(Let's) go to the beach when the sun sets."
바 "way, thing"
  정말 어찌할 바를 몰랐어요.
  "(I) was really at a loss regarding what to do."
분 "person"
  찬성 하시는 분은 손드세요.
  "As for those who agree, please raise your hand."
뻔 "the verge, coming near"
  차 사고가 날 뻔했어요.
  "A car accident almost occurred."
뿐 "alone, only"
  그는 울기만 할 뿐 아무 말도 하지 않았어요.
  "He just cried without saying anything."
셈 "thinking, plan"
  어쩔 셈이에요?
  "What are (you) going to do (about it)?"
수 "way, case"
  어느 것이 어느 것인지 구별할 수가 없네요.
  "(I) can't tell which one is which."
적 "time, experience"
  전에 당신을 길에서 만난 적이 있습니다.
  "(I) have run into you on the street before."
줄 "method, probability"
  그이는 정말 아무것도 할 줄 몰라요.
  "He really doesn't know how to do anything."
중/도중 "middle"
  그는 병원으로 가는 도중에 사망했다.
  "(He) died on his way to the hospital."
즈음 "time"
  저희는 5월 즈음에 이사할 계획이에요.
  "We are planning to move sometime around May."
쪽 "direction, side"
  식당이 있는 쪽으로 오세요.
  "Please come in the direction where the restaurant is."

NOUNS

채 "intact, as it is"
>유니폼을 입은 채 물속으로 뛰어들었어요.
>"(They) plunged into the water with (their) uniforms on."

척 "pretense"
>자는 척하지 말아요.
>"Don't pretend to be asleep."

Korean has a number of idiomatic expressions that are made up of a noun-modifying form and a bound noun, and these are called "post modifiers." Post modifiers are discussed in detail in Chapters 21 through 24.

1.4 Some characteristics of Korean nouns

1.4.1 Positions

A Korean noun occurs in a sentence in one of the following ways: (i) by itself, (ii) before particles, (iii) before another noun, or (iv) before a copula. For instance, consider the following sentence:

>교수님, 요꼬가 일본인 유학생이에요.
>"Professor, Yoko is a Japanese international student."

Notice that 교수님 "professor" appears by itself. 요꼬 "Yoko" appears with the subjective particle 가. 일본인 "Japanese" appears before another noun, 유학생 "international student," and 유학생 appears before the copula 이에요.

The Korean copula is 이다 (or 이에요 with the polite speech level). Korean nouns can serve as the sentence predicate with the copula. A predicate describes the state of the subject. For instance, consider the following sentence: 제 남동생이 경찰이에요. "My younger brother is a police officer." Note that the copula 이에요 attaches to the noun 경찰 "police officer" as tightly as if it were a particle.

1.4.2 Gender

Unlike many European languages, such as French, Spanish, and Russian, Korean does not indicate gender with nouns. When you wish to highlight the gender difference of the people being referred to, you can add 남자/남 "man" or 여자/여 "woman" to the noun as follows:

>남학생 "male student"
>남자 판매원 "salesman"
>여자 직원 "female employee"
>여 선생님 "female teacher"

1.4.3 Plurality

English is so precise in reference to number that when there is more than one item, the item must be identified as plural with the addition of "s." In contrast, Korean is not specific about plurality. For instance, the Korean noun 숟가락 "spoon" can be translated into at least the following: spoon, a spoon, the spoon, some spoons, the spoons, and spoons. Moreover, "one kid" in Korean is 한 아이; "three kids" is 세 아이, and "ten kids" is 열 아이. Notice that the noun 아이 "kid" does not go through any change in form.

Korean uses the suffix 들 (that can be attached after a countable noun) to indicate the plurality of a noun. However, its usage is not obligatory for marking plurality; thus its purpose is rather for emphasizing the plurality of the noun. For instance, 학생이 태권도를 배워요 can be translated as "a student learns Taekwondo" or "some students learn Taekwondo." However, you can optionally attach 들 to 학생, as 학생들이 태권도를 배워요 "students learn Taekwondo,"

Some characteristics of Korean nouns

when/if you wish to highlight the plurality of 학생. You may use 들 for other cases too, such as adding the marker to pronouns. For instance, although it may sound redundant, you can attach 들 to 우리 "we," as in 우리들 "we." Notice that 우리 is already plural. Again, such usage is for placing emphasis.

1.4.4 Collocations

People tend to use nouns with certain verbs. For instance, in English, the word "crime" is collocated with the verb "commit," and "operation" is collocated with the verb "perform." The use of a noun with a verb that is not conventionally collocated (although the use of the verb may be grammatically correct) results in an awkward expression (e.g., "Stalin committed a crime" vs. "Stalin performed a crime"). Likewise, Korean nouns tend to collocate with certain verbs. Consider the following examples:

(X) 데니엘이 야구를 놀아요.
"Daniel plays baseball."
(O) 데니엘이 야구를 해요.
"Daniel plays (lit. does) baseball."

The verb 놀아요 literally means "play," and 해요 means "do." However, in Korean, the noun 야구 "baseball" does not collocate with 놀아요, but with 해요. When you talk about playing musical instruments, such as piano and guitar, you need to use a different verb 쳐요 "play" or "hit" instead of 해요 or 놀아요.

(X) 앤드류가 기타를 놀아요.
"Andrew plays guitar."
(X) 앤드류가 기타를 해요.
"Andrew plays (lit. does) guitar."
(O) 앤드류가 기타를 쳐요.
"Andrew plays (lit. hits/plays) guitar."

1.4.5 Honorific nouns

Korean is an honorific language in that it has grammatical elements that are used to indicate social meanings such as the speaker's attitudes (e.g., respect, formality, humility) toward whom he/she is talking to or talking about (see Chapters 27 and 28). Accordingly, some Korean nouns have corresponding honorific forms:

Plain	Honorific
나이 "age"	연세
말 "speech, word"	말씀
밥 "meal"	진지
생일 "birthday"	생신
이름 "name"	성함
집 "house"	댁

2

Pronouns

English has a lengthy list of pronouns: I (me, my, mine), you (your, yours), he (him, his), she (her, hers), it (its), we (us, our, ours), and they (them, their, theirs). Korean has its own list of pronouns as well, but its usage is much more restricted with different usage rules.

In general, pronouns are used much less frequently in Korean than in English for at least two reasons. First, in Korean, any contextually understood sentence components (including the subject and the object) are often left out. For instance, when two people are talking to one another, personal pronouns often get omitted in ordinary conversations because both speakers know who is talking and who is listening. This contrasts with English, where the use of the pronoun (or subject noun) is obligatory in all places. For instance, it would be grammatically incorrect or fragmentary to say "ate my lunch."

Second, in Korean, addressing someone by the pronoun sounds too direct and confrontational. Consequently, Koreans avoid using the second person pronoun unless the addressee is someone they know well (e.g., family members, friends) or is of equal or lower status (e.g., younger siblings, subordinates).

2.1 The first person pronoun

The Korean first person pronouns have plain and humble forms:

나 (plain singular) 　　　　　저 (humble singular)
내 (plain singular possessive)　제 (humble singular possessive)
우리 (plain plural possessive)　저희 (humble plural possessive)

There are two things to remember when using first person pronouns. First, the use of either plain or humble pronouns is contingent upon whom you are talking to. It is always safe to use the humble form when you talk to adult speakers whom you do not know well or when you speak in public or formal settings.

In addition, the use of the humble form is normally collocated with honorific elements (e.g., the formal speech level endings, the honorific suffix ~(으)시, euphemistic words, and so forth).

Second, 저희/우리, the first person plural pronoun, has a wider usage. Due to the collectivistic value system, profoundly reflected in the Korean language and culture, 저희/우리 is also used as the first person possessive pronoun when mentioning communal possessions (e.g., one's family or household, the school he/she attended, and so on). Consider the following two sentences:

저희(우리) 누나가 하와이 호놀루루에 있습니다.
"Our (my) older sister is in Honolulu, Hawaii."
제 (내) 누나가 하와이 호놀루루에 있습니다.
"My older sister is in Honolulu, Hawaii."

Both sentences are acceptable. However, the first sentence is favored over the second.

2.2 The second person pronoun

Korean second person pronouns include the following:

너 (plain singular) 너희들 (plain plural)
자네 (familiar singular) 자네들 (familiar plural)
자기 (intimate singular) 자기들 (intimate plural)
당신 (blunt singular) 당신들 (blunt plural)

The use of which second person pronoun depends on whom you are talking to. In addition, its use is much more restricted than that of English. For example, Koreans use 너 only when addressing a child, a childhood friend, one's younger sibling, one's son or daughter, and so forth.

오늘은 니(너)가 설거지 해라.
"As for today, you do the dishes."

A Korean (e.g., over 40 years old) may use 자네 when addressing an adult friend or a younger adult (e.g., son-in-law, graduate student, junior colleague, and so on).

자네가 이 일을 좀 맡게.
"You take charge of this task."

The use of 자기 can be found among young spouses or couples.

자기, 밥 먹었어?
"Did you eat breakfast?"

The use of 당신 is commonly observed between older spouses (e.g., over 40 years old).

당신만을 사랑해.
"(I) love only you."

However, its usage can be also found among Korean males who engage in arguments or confrontation.

당신 몇 살인데, 나한테 반말이야?
"How old do you think you are, speaking to me disrespectfully?"

Meanwhile, the following can be used as a second person pronoun or equivalent in more restricted contexts:

어르신 is used when addressing an elderly person respectfully.
어르신, 안녕하셨어요?
"How have you been?"
그쪽 can be used when addressing a stranger.
그쪽이 먼저 들어가시지요?
"Why don't you enter first?"
그대 is used in song lyrics or poems.
그대여, 울지 마세요.
"You, please do not cry."
본인 is used when one intends to obviously avoid the use of any other address term.
본인이 직접 전화 하셔야 해요.
"You need to call (them) by yourself."
여러분 is used when addressing a group of people.
여러분, 안녕하십니까?
"How is everyone?"
귀하 is used in automated calling instructions.
귀하의 4 자리 비밀번호를 입력하여 주십시오.
"Please enter your four-digit security code."

PRONOUNS

2.3 The third person pronoun

Strictly speaking, Korean has no true third person pronoun. Koreans use a demonstrative (e.g., this, these, that, and those) and a noun (e.g., child, man, woman, thing, people, and so on) when referring to the third person.

He

그 "that," 그 애 "that child," 그 사람 "that person," 그 분 "that esteemed person," 그 남자 "that man" . . .
저 사람이 범인이에요.
"That person (over there) is the suspect."

She

그 "that," 그 애 "that child," 그 사람 "that person," 그 분 "that esteemed person," 그 여자 "that lady" . . .
그 분이 어제 사무실에 오셨어요.
"(She) came to (my) office yesterday."

They

그들 "those," 그 애들 "those children," 그 사람들 "those people," 그 분들 "those esteemed people" . . .
그들은 졸업식에 참석하고 그 다음 날 한국으로 돌아갔다.
"As for them, (they) participated at the graduation ceremony and then returned to Korea on the next day."

Beside these terms, Koreans use various family or kinship terms in place of the third person pronoun (see Chapter 35).

2.4 Indefinite pronouns

People use indefinite pronouns when they designate something that does not have a specific referent. The examples of indefinite pronouns in English are "anything," "anyone," "something," "someone," "sometimes," "somewhere," and so on. Korean question words such as 누구 "who," 무엇 "what," 어디 "where," 언제 "when," 어떻게 "how," 어떤 "which/what type of," 몇 "what/how many," and 어느 "which" serve as question words as well as indefinite pronouns. What decides the use of these words as question words or indefinite pronouns is intonation. When the word functions as a question, the sentence that contains the question word has a rising intonation at the end. However, with a falling intonation, the question word takes the role of an indefinite pronoun.

As a question word:

누가 와요? (with a rising intonation)
"Who is coming?"

As an indefinite pronoun:

누가 와요. (with a falling intonation)
"Someone is coming."

Indefinite pronouns

As a question word:

뭐 먹었어요? (with a rising intonation)
"What did (you) eat?"

As an indefinite pronoun:

뭐 먹었어요. (with a falling intonation)
"(I) ate something."

As a question word:

어디 가요? (with a rising intonation)
"Where is (he) going?"

As an indefinite pronoun:

어디 가요. (with a falling intonation)
"(He) is going somewhere."

As a question word:

어떻게 고쳤어요? (with a rising intonation)
"How did (you) fix (it)?"

As an indefinite pronoun:

어떻게 고쳤어요. (with a falling intonation)
"(I) fixed (it) somehow."

3
Numbers and counters

3.1 Numbers

Korean makes use of two sets of numbers. The first set is called native Korean numbers, and they stop at 99. The second set was borrowed from Chinese a long time ago and is now part of the Korean number system. The numbers belonging to this set are called Sino-Korean numbers, and they can be as long as 14 digits.

Arabic	Native Korean	Sino-Korean
0	–	영/공
1	하나 (한)*	일
2	둘 (두)*	이
3	셋 (세)*	삼
4	넷 (네)*	사
5	다섯	오
6	여섯	육
7	일곱	칠
8	여덟	팔
9	아홉	구
10	열	십
11	열하나	십일
12	열둘	십이
13	열셋	십삼
14	열넷	십사
15	열다섯	십오
16	열여섯	십육
17	열일곱	십칠
18	열여덟	십팔
19	열아홉	십구
20	스물 (스무)*	이십
30	서른	삼십
40	마흔	사십
50	쉰	오십
60	예순	육십
70	일흔	칠십
80	여든	팔십
90	아흔	구십
100	–	백
1,000	–	천
10,000	–	만
100,000	–	십만
1,000,000	–	백만
10,000,000	–	천만
100,000,000	–	억
1,000,000,000	–	십억

Counters

Arabic	Native Korean	Sino-Korean
10,000,000,000	–	백억
100,000,000,000	–	천억
1,000,000,000,000	–	조
10,000,000,000,000	–	십조

As seen in the table, when it concerns the formation of higher numbers, the Korean number system is more orderly than the English number system. For instance, whereas English uses special words for 11 through 19 (e.g., eleven, twelve, thirteen, and so on), Korean numbers are formed as "ten + one" (십일) or (열하나), "ten + two" (십이) or (열둘), "ten + three" (십삼) or (열셋), and so forth.

In addition, it is optional to add 일 to the number that starts with 1, such as 100, 1,000, 10,000, and so forth. However, it is more commonly said without it. Therefore, for 100, saying "백 (hundred)" is more common than saying "일백 (one hundred)," for 1,000, it would be "천 (thousand)" rather than "일천 (one thousand)," and so forth.

For multiples of ten, Sino-Korean numbers are simple combinations: 20 is "two + ten" (이십), 30 is "three + ten" (삼십), 40 is "four + ten" (사십), and so on. However, native Korean numbers have special words, as 20 is 스물, 30 is 서른, 40 is 마흔, and so forth. In addition, the native Korean number set does not have the number "zero."

Meanwhile, note that, as indicated by the asterisk in the table, native Korean numbers "one," "two," "three," "four," and "twenty" have somewhat changed forms: 하나/한, 둘/두, 셋/세, 넷/네, and 스물/스무. Koreans use these modified forms when they count one of these native numbers with a counter. For instance, the counter for animal is 마리. Consequently, counting one dog would be 개 한 마리, not 개 하나 마리; two dogs would be 개 두 마리, not 개 둘 마리; three dogs would be 개 세 마리, not 개 셋 마리, and so on.

3.2 Counters

The function of a counter (also called a classifier) is to categorize nouns according to common attributes for numbering purposes. Consequently, by using a counter, you can indicate more information about the object you count. In English, counters are usually used for uncountable nouns, as in "three loaves of bread," "two sheets of paper," and "five grains of rice." However, in Korean, counters are used for both countable and uncountable nouns, and there is an extensive list of counters.

There are a few things to remember when using counters in Korean. First, some counters are used only with native Korean numbers, whereas some counters are used only with Sino-Korean numbers. Table 3.1 shows the counters that are commonly used with native Korean numbers. However, when the number is above 20, these counters can also be used with Sino-Korean numbers. For instance, when counting 35 people using the counter 명, you can say either 서른 다섯 명 or 삼십 오명.

Table 3.2 shows some counters that are used only with Sino-Korean numbers.

In addition, although very limited in number, there are counters, such as 주간/주일 "weeks" that can be used with both Sino-Korean numbers as well as native Korean numbers. For instance, one week can be either 한 주간 or 일 주간, eight weeks can be either 팔 주간 or 여덟 주간, and so on.

Also, when asking a question using a counter, you need to use the question word 몇 "how many." This question word cannot be used on its own but must precede a counter. For example, a specific question such as "how many items" would be 몇 개, "how old" would be 몇 살, "what month" would be 몇 월, and so on.

Table 3.1 Some major Korean counters used with native Korean numbers

Counter	Typical kinds of things counted	Examples
가지	kinds	반찬 네 가지 "four kinds of side dishes"
개	items, units	오렌지 한 개 "one orange"
건	items	교통사고 두 건 "two car accidents"
곡	pieces of music/songs	노래 다섯 곡 "five songs"
군데	places	식당 한 군데 "one restaurant"
권	books	책 세 권 "three books"
그루	trees	소나무 열 그루 "ten pine trees"
그릇	bowls of rice/soup	국 한 그릇 "one bowl of soup"
다발	bunches (of flowers)	장미 세 다발 "three bouquets of roses"
달	months (duration)	한 달 "for one month"
대	machines, cars	차 세 대 "three cars"
마리	animals	고양이 두 마리 "two cats"
명	persons	학생 다섯 명 "five students"
모금	a sip, a puff	물 한 모금 "a sip of water"
번	times	여섯 번 "six times"
벌	clothes	정장 한 벌 "one formal suit"
병	bottles	맥주 여덟 병 "eight bottles of beer"
봉지	paper bags	두 봉지 "two paper bags"
사람	persons	세 사람 "three people"
살	years of age	서른두 살 "33 years old"
상자	boxes	일곱 상자 "seven boxes"
송이	flowers	장미 열 송이 "ten stems of roses"
숟갈	spoonfuls	밥 한 숟갈 "one spoonful of rice"
시	time	세 시 "three o'clock"
시간	hours (duration)	한 시간 "for one hour"
쌍	couples (people & animals)	부부 세 쌍 "three married couples"
알	eggs, grapes, pills	계란 세 알 "three eggs"
자루	pencils, pens	연필 세 자루 "three pencils"
잔	cupfuls	커피 한 잔 "one cup of coffee"
장	pieces of paper	복사지 다섯 장 "five sheets of copying paper"
접시	main dishes	요리 네 접시 "four dishes of gourmet food"
조각	slices	피자 세 조각 "three slices of pizza"
쪽	small slices	사과 네 쪽 "four slices of apple"
채	houses, buildings	집 여덟 채 "eight houses"
척	ships	배 한 척 "one boat"
컵	cups	우유 두 컵 "two cups of milk"
켤레	pairs of shoes, socks	양말 세 켤레 "three pairs of socks"
통	letters (in an envelope)	추천서 세 통 "three recommendation letters"
편	movie, poems	영화 다섯 편 "five movies"
포기	cabbage	배추 세 포기 "three heads of cabbage"
해	years	한 해 "one year"

Table 3.2 Some major Korean counters used with Sino-Korean numbers

Counter	Kinds of things counted	Examples
개월	months (duration)	일 개월 "for one month"
년	years	이 년 "two years"
월	month names	팔 월 "August"
일	days	삼 일 "three days"
마일	miles	칠십 마일 "70 miles"
분	minutes	십 분 "ten minutes"
초	seconds	이 초 "two seconds"
층	floors (of a building)	삼십사 층 "34 floors"
파운드	pounds (sterling)	일 파운드 "one pound"

3.3 Counting

You count countable objects in three ways. First, you can just use a number by itself without using a counter. For instance, you simply use native Korean numbers. Therefore, for "three friends," you can say 친구 셋 (noun + number).

의자 하나	one chair
화장실 둘	two bathrooms
햄버거 셋	three hamburgers
학생 다섯	five students

Second, you can use a number with a counter. In this case, the function of a counter is to indicate the type of noun being counted. Counting items with a counter can take the following structure: "noun (being counted) + number + counter." Consequently, for "200 customers" you would say "손님 + 이백 + 명."

빵 한 개	one piece of bread
국 세 그릇	three bowls of soup
계란 세 알	three eggs
양말 두 켤레	two pairs of socks

Third, in formal settings (both in speech and writing), you can use the possessive particle 의, as in 세 대의 자동차 "number + counter + 의 noun (being counted)."

네 권의 책	four books
십 년의 세월	ten years of time
열 명의 한국인	ten Koreans
한 컵의 물	one glass of water

3.4 Sino-Korean numbers vs. native Korean numbers

The use of native Korean numbers and Sino-Korean numbers is different in a number of ways. First, Koreans use native Korean numbers when counting a small number of objects. For instance, two bottles of red wine would be 포도주 두 병 (red wine + two + bottles). However, when counting a large number of objects, they prefer using Sino-Korean numbers, so "35 bottles of red wine" would be 포도주 삼십오 병. Second, as for numbers beyond 100, Koreans use only Sino-Korean numbers.

134	백삼십사
259	이백오십구
487	사백팔십칠
615	육백십오
3,726	삼천칠백이십육
94,821	구만사천팔백이십

It is unusual, but you can read a number that is larger than 100 by combining a Sino-Korean number and a native Korean number. However, the use of Sino-Korean numbers alone is more common than a mixed use of both sets of numbers. That is, it is more common to read 429 as 사백이십구 rather than 사백스물아홉.

NUMBERS AND COUNTERS | **3.5**

Lastly, Koreans, in general, use Sino-Korean numbers for mathematical calculations:

5 × 4 = 20	오	곱하기 사는	이십
13 + 6 = 19	십삼	더하기 육은	십구
7 − 3 = 4	칠	빼기	삼은 사
30 ÷ 5 = 6	삼십	나누기 오는	육

3.5 Ordinals

Sino-Korean and native Korean numbers differ in the formation of ordinals (i.e., concerning order, rank, or position in a series). As for Sino-Korean numbers, you need to add the prefix 제 to a number. For instance, "the first" is 제 일, "the second" is 제 이, "the third" is 제 삼, "the seventh" is 제 칠, "the fourteenth" is 제 십사, and so forth. In addition, when used with a counter, you need to add the counter after the number, as in 제 7일 "the seventh day," 제 14주 "the fourteenth week," and so on. However, 제 can be omitted in informal/spoken communication.

오늘은 (제) 팔과를 공부할 거예요.
"Today, (we) will study the eighth chapter."
제 사무실은 이 빌딩 (제) 10층에 있어요.
"My office is on the tenth floor of this building."

As for native Korean numbers, you need to attach 째 to a number. Consequently, "the first" is 첫째, "the second" is 둘째, "the third" is 세째, "the fourth" is 네째, "the sixteenth" is 열여섯째, and so on. The only exception is that 하나/한, the native number for one, is not used for the ordinal, so you need to use the special word, 첫, as 첫째, not 한째.

Ordinal	Native Korean	Sino-Korean
The first	첫째	제 일
The second	둘째	제 이
The third	세째	제 삼
The fourth	네째	제 사
The fifth	다섯째	제 오
The sixth	여섯째	제 육
The seventh	일곱째	제 칠
The eighth	여덟째	제 팔
The ninth	아홉째	제 구
The tenth	열째	제 십
The fifteenth	열다섯째	제 십오
The twentieth	스무째	제 이십
The twenty-fourth	스물 네째	제 이십사
The thirty-eighth	서른 여덟째	제 삼십팔
The ninety-ninth	아흔 아홉째	제 구십구

When counting something with a counter, you need to attach 째 after the counter, as in 첫 병째 "the first bottle," 두 달째 "the second month," 다섯 번째 "the fifth time," and so forth.

세 달째 방세를 못 냈어요.
"(I) have not been able to pay the rent for the third month in a row."
벌써 맥주 네 병째예요.
"It's the fourth bottle of beer already."
제 방은 엘리베이터에서 두 번째 방이에요.
"My room is the second room from the elevator."

4

Nominalizing endings

Nominalizing endings transform a verb or an adjective into a noun form. Examples of English nominalzing endings include "~tion" (e.g., inform = information) "~ing" (e.g., serve = serving), "~ment" (e.g., agree = agreement), "~ance (e.g., accept = acceptance) and "~sion" (e.g., collide = collision). This chapter discusses three Korean nominalizing endings ~기, ~(으)ㅁ, and ~이, as well as the form ~는 것, which can also change a verb or adjective into a noun form.

4.1 The nominalizing ending ~기

When the nominalizing ending ~기 is added to a verb stem, it changes the meaning of the verb to "the act of ~ing" (e.g., 말하다 "speak" => 말하기 "speaking"). When it attaches to an adjective stem, it changes the meaning of the adjective to "a state of being ~" (e.g., 슬프다 "sad" => 슬프기 "state of being sad").

주말마다 쇼핑하기를 정말 좋아해요.
"(She) really likes going shopping every weekend."
수업 시간에 주로 한자 읽기를 배웠어요.
"(We) mainly learned reading Chinese characters in class."
오늘은 춥기 때문에 집에 있을 것 같은데요.
"It seems that (they) will stay home because (it) is cold today."
이 곳은 파스타가 맛있기로 유명합니다.
"This place is famous for delicious pasta."

Korean has a number of expressions that incorporate the nominizaling ending ~기, and what follows are some major examples.

4.1.1 ~기가 어렵다 "difficult to"

~기가 어렵다 means "(it) is difficult to." This form is built on the ending ~기, the subject particle 가, and the adjective 어렵다 "difficult."

구멍이 너무 작아서 맞추기가 어려워요.
"Since the hole is too small, (it) is difficult to put (them) together."
믿기 어렵겠지만 사실로 받아들어야 돼요.
"Although (it) may be difficult to believe, (you) must accept (it) as a fact."
모두 다 예뻐서 하나만 고르기가 어려웠어요.
"Since (they) were all pretty, (it) was difficult to choose only one."

Besides 어렵다, other adjectives, as follows, can be used to convey different meanings:

~기가 쉽다 *"(it) is easy to"*
빙판 길에서는 미끄러지기 쉬우니까 조심하세요.
"(It) is easy to slip on ice, so be careful."
~기가 힘들다 *"(it) is laborious to"*

NOMINALIZING ENDINGS   4.1

주말마다 가게에서 일하면서 <u>공부하기가 힘들었어요</u>.
"(It) was toilsome to study while working at the shop every weekend."
~기가 좋다 *"(it) is good to"*
오늘 날씨는 <u>스키타러 가기 좋아요</u>.
"As for today's weather, (it) is good to go skiing."
~기가 편하다 *"(it) is convenient to"*
지하철역이 가까워서 아침에 <u>출근하기가 편해요</u>.
"Since the subway station is near, it is convenient to go to work in the morning."
~기가 싫다 *"(it) is unwilling/unpleasant to"*
매일 같은 음식을 <u>먹기가 싫었어요</u>.
"(It) was unpleasant to eat the same food every day."
~기가 재미있다 *"(it) is fun to"*
한국 친구들이 많아서 한국어 <u>배우기가 재미있었어요</u>.
"(It) was fun to learn Korean, since (I) had many Korean friends."
~기가 귀찮다 *"(it) is bothersome to"*
피곤해서 설거지 <u>하기 귀찮았어요</u>.
"Since (I) was exhausted, (it) was bothersome to do dishes."

4.1.2 ~기가 무섭게/바쁘게 "just after"

~기가 무섭게/바쁘게 takes on the meaning of "just after." This form is constructed from the ending ~기, the subject particle 가, and the adverb 무섭게 "horribly" or 바쁘게 "busily."

집에 <u>들어오기가 무섭게</u> 화장실로 들어가 버렸어요.
"(He) went into the restroom as soon as (he) entered the house."
날이 <u>어두워지기가 무섭게</u> 추워졌어요.
"As soon as the day became dark, (it) became cold."
수업이 <u>끝나기가 바쁘게</u> 모두 학교 식당으로 달려갔어요.
"(They) ran into the school cafeteria as soon as the class ended."

4.1.3 ~기 나름이다 "depends on ~ing"

~기 나름이다 means "depends on ~ing." It combines the ending ~기, the bound noun 나름 "dependence," and the copula 이다.

성공은 <u>노력하기 나름이다</u>.
"The success depends on (your) effort."
이 일은 네가 <u>생각하기 나름이야</u>.
"As for this task, it depends on the way you think about it."

4.1.4 ~기는요? "What do you mean?"

~기는요? is used to mildly contend another speaker's comment, corresponding to "No way" or "What do you mean?" It is made of the ending ~기, the topic particle 는, and the politeness marker 요.

A: 뉴욕 날씨가 따뜻했지요?
   "The weather in New York was warm, right?"
B: <u>따뜻하기는요</u>? 생각했던 것보다 추웠어요.
   "Warm? No way, (it) was much colder than (I) thought."

A: 골프를 잘 치시네요.
   "(You) play golf well."
B: <u>잘 치기는요</u>? 오늘 좀 운이 좋은 것 같습니다.
   "No way, (I) think that (I) am lucky today."

The nominalizing ending ~기 | 4.1

4.1.5 ~기나 하다 "at least do"

~기나 하다 is used to express your smallest or lowest wish for someone to do something, meaning "at least do." It consists of the ending ~기, the particle 나, and the verb 하다 "do."

> 한번 입어 보기나 하고 결정하세요.
> "Decide at least after you try it on."
> 조용히 먹기나 해라.
> "At least eat quietly."

4.1.6 ~기는 하다 "indeed"

~기는 하다 is usually translated as "indeed." It is the combination of the ending ~기, the topic particle 는, and the verb 하다 "do."

> 수인이가 예쁘기는 하지요.
> "Sooin is indeed pretty."
> 배가 고프면 뭐든지 맛있기는 해요.
> "When (you) are hungry, anything is indeed tasty."

4.1.7 ~기는 커녕 "far from ~ing"

~기는 커녕 is used to negate the content of the ~기 ending predicate emphatically, translated as "far from ~ing." This form is built on the ending ~기, the topic particle 는, and the particle 커녕 "not at all."

> 싸기는 커녕 아주 비쌌어요.
> "It is far from being cheap; (it) was really expensive."
> 점심을 먹기는 커녕 아침도 아직 못 먹었네요.
> "Far from eating lunch, (I) could not even eat breakfast yet."

4.1.8 ~기도 하다 "indeed"

~기도 하다 takes on the meaning of "also does," and it is constructed from the ending ~기, the particle 도 "also," and the verb 하다 "do."

> 점심은 주로 학교 식당에서 먹는 편이지만 가끔 한국 식당에 가서 먹기도 해요.
> "Although (I) normally tend to eat lunch at the school cafeteria, (I) also eat at Korean restaurants from time to time."
> 주말에는 여자 친구하고 자전거를 타기도 해요.
> "(I) also ride a bike with (my) girlfriend on the weekend."
> 주로 버스를 이용하지만 비가 올 때는 가끔 지하철을 타기도 해요.
> "Normally, (we) use the bus, but when (it) rains, (we) sometimes take the subway."

4.1.9 ~기 때문에 "because of ~ing"

~기 때문에 simply means "because of ~ing." This form combines the ending ~기, the bound noun 때문 "cause," and the particle 에.

> 배가 아프기 때문에 오늘은 아무것도 먹고 싶지 않네요.
> "Because (my) stomach aches, (I) don't want to eat anything today."
> 매일 운동하기 때문에 건강해요.
> "(I) am healthy since (I) exercise every day."
> 그 때 지갑이 없었기 때문에 집까지 걸어서 갔었어요.
> "(I) went all the way home on foot because (I) did not have (my) wallet at that time."
> 갖고 싶었지만 너무 비쌌기 때문에 못 샀어요.
> "(I) really wanted to have (it), but (I) could not buy (it) because (it) was too expensive."

NOMINALIZING ENDINGS   4.1

4.1.10 ~기로 하다 "decide to"

~기로 하다 is used to indicate the meaning of "plans/decides to." It consists of the ending ~기, the particle ~로, and the verb 하다 "do."

신혼여행은 어디로 <u>가기로 했나요</u>?
"As for (your) honeymoon, where have (you) decided to go?"
내일 오후 2시에 호텔 로비에서 <u>만나기로 했습니다</u>.
"(We) decided to meet at the hotel lobby at 2 p.m. tomorrow."

Instead of 하다, you can use other verbs such as 결정하다 "make a decision," 결심하다 "make up one's mind," and 정하다 "decide."

오늘부터 담배를 <u>끊기로 결심했어요</u>.
"(I) decided to quit smoking starting today."
비가 오니까 가게 안에서 <u>만나기로 정합시다</u>.
"Since it is raining, (let's) decide on meeting inside the store."

4.1.11 ~기를 바라다/원하다 "hope"

~기를 바라다/원하다 is used to convey the meaning of "hope" or "wish." It is the combination of the ending ~기, the objective particle 를, and the verb 바라다 "wish" or 원하다 "want."

하루속히 <u>완쾌되시기를 바랍니다</u>.
"(I) hope that you get better soon."
제 부모님께서는 제가 금년안에 <u>결혼하기를 원하십니다</u>.
"My parents wish for me to get married within this year."

4.1.12 ~기 마련이다 "bound to"

~기 마련이다 takes on the meaning of "bound to." It is built on the ending ~기, the noun 마련 "preparation," and the copula 이다.

성격차이는 어느 부부에게나 <u>있기 마련이에요</u>.
"Personality differences are bound to exist for all married couples."
인간은 누구나 언젠가 죽음을 <u>맞이하기 마련이다</u>.
"All humans are bound to face death someday."

4.1.13 ~기 시작하다 "begin"

~기 시작하다 is used to indicate the beginning of an action or state. It is constructed from the ending ~기 and the verb 시작하다 "begin/start."

어젯밤부터 눈이 <u>오기 시작했어요</u>.
"(It) started snowing since last night."
지금부터 <u>쓰기 시작하십시오</u>!
"Start using (it) now!"

4.1.14 ~기 십상이다 "it is easy to"

~기 십상이다 is used similarly to the English expression "it is easy to." It combines the ending ~기, the noun 십상 "the right thing (for)," and the copula 이다.

여기 있으면 시간 가는 걸 <u>잊기 십상인걸요</u>.
"It is easy to lose track of time in here."
이렇게 더운 날씨에는 음식이 <u>상하기 십상이지요</u>.
"In this hot weather, food can spoil easily."

The nominalizing ending ~기　　　　　　　　　　　　**4.1**

4.1.15 ~기에는 "as for (doing something)"

~기에는 usually translated as "as for (doing something)." It is made up of the ending ~기, the particle 에, and the topic particle 는.

이 집은 <u>학생이 살기에는</u> 시끄러운 편이지요.
"As for this house, (it) is kind of noisy for students to live in."
오늘은 <u>조깅하기에는</u> 좀 싸늘하네.
"As for jogging today, (it) is a bit chilly."
미국 사람이 <u>먹기에는</u> 너무 매웠어요.
"As for an American to eat, (it) was too spicy."

4.1.16 ~기에 따라서 "according to"

~기에 따라서 simply means "depending on." It consists of the ending ~기, the particle 에, and 따라서 (따르다 "follow" + 어서 "because/and").

얼마나 열심히 <u>운동하기에 따라서</u> 체중이 어느 정도 내려갈 수 있습니다.
"(Your) weight can go down to a certain degree, depending on how diligently (you) exercise."
<u>생각하기에 따라서</u> 돈은 축복일 수도 있고 저주일 수도 있습니다.
"Depending on how (you) think, money can be a blessing or a curse."

4.1.17 ~기에 앞서서 "before ~ing"

~기에 앞서서 takes on the meaning of "before ~ing." It is the combination of the ending ~기, the particle 에, and 앞서서 (앞서다 "to get ahead" + 어서 "because/and").

저희 가족을 <u>소개해 올리기 앞서서</u> 먼저 감사의 말씀을 드리고 싶습니다.
"(I) want to thank (you) before introducing my family members (to you)."
제 발표를 <u>시작하기에 앞서서</u> 여러분 모두에게 감사의 말씀을 드리고 싶습니다.
"Before starting (my) presentation, (I) would like to offer a word of gratitude to you all."

4.1.18 ~기 위해서 "as for ~ing"

~기 위해서 has the meaning of "as for the sake of ~ing." It is built on the ending ~기, and 위해서 "for the sake of."

그 꿈을 <u>이루기 위해서</u> 뭘 먼저 해야 할 까요?
"(I) wonder what (I) should do first for the sake of achieving that dream?"
공항으로 <u>떠나기 위해서</u> 택시를 불렀어요.
"(I) called a taxi in order to leave for the airport."
변호사가 <u>되기 위해서</u> 정말 열심히 공부했어요.
"(I) studied really hard in order to become a lawyer."

4.1.19 ~기 일쑤이다 "routinely"

~기 일쑤이다 is used to express an unpleasant or negative action/state that takes place frequently (often unintentional). It is constructed from the ending ~기, the bound noun 일쑤 "routine," and the copula 이다.

기선이는 늦게 자는 편이라서 <u>지각하기 일쑤예요</u>.
"Keesun tends to sleep late, so (she) is often tardy."
우진이는 건망증이 심해서 열쇠를 <u>잃어버리기 일쑤였어요</u>.
"Woojin has a bad memory, so (he) frequently lost (his) keys."
먼저 인터넷에서 알아보고 사지 않으면 <u>비싸게 사기 일쑤예요</u>.
"Unless (you) buy (it) after researching (it) online, (it) is easy to buy (it) at an expensive price."

NOMINALIZING ENDINGS

4.1.20 ~기 전에 "before ~ing"

~기 전에 takes on the meaning of "before ~ing." It combines the ending ~기, the noun 전 "before," and the particle 에.

자기 전에 꼭 샤워하세요.
"Make sure to take a shower before going to bed."
나가기 전에 방 청소를 했어요.
"(I) cleaned the room before going out."
친구가 런던으로 떠나기 전에 호텔에 전화 할 거예요.
"(My) friend will make a phone call to the hotel before (he) leaves for London."

4.1.21 ~기 짝이 없다 "beyond measure"

~기 짝이 없다 "beyond measure" is made of the ending ~기, the noun 짝 "pair," the subject particle 이, and the verb 없다 "not exist." This form is used with an adjective to stress the extreme degree denoted by the adjective.

정말 한심하기 짝이 없네요.
"(She) is deplorable beyond measure."
영화 줄거리가 유치하기 짝이 없었어요.
"The story of the movie was childish beyond measure."

4.2 The nominalizing ending ~(으)ㅁ

The use of the nominalizing ending ~(으)ㅁ is more restricted and less frequent than that of ~기. For instance, the ending ~(으)ㅁ is used only when the activity or state of the predicate has already occurred and has been actualized or completed. Consider the following examples:

우리는 세일 기간이 어제로 끝났음을 몰랐다.
"We did not know that the sale period ended yesterday."
하와이의 공기는 깨끗함과 맑음으로 유명하지요.
"As for Hawaii's air, (it) is well known for its purity and clarity."

Notice that the ~(으)ㅁ ending phrases imply that the activity or state has already been ensured or determined. Here are more examples:

저는 그들이 사기꾼임을 정말 몰랐었습니다.
"As for me, (I) really did not know that they were the con men."
이별의 아픔을 경험해 본 적이 있나요?
"Have (you) ever experienced the pain of separation?"

Meanwhile, a number of Korean nouns are made of the ~(으)ㅁ ending. The ~(으)ㅁ ending nouns include:

살다 "to live"   삶 "life"
죽다 "to die"   죽음 "death"
웃다 "to smile"   웃음 "smile/laughter"
자다 "to sleep"   잠 "sleep"

아프다 "to be sore"   아픔 "pain"
기쁘다 "to be joyous"   기쁨 "joy"
즐겁다 "to be glad"   즐거움 "gladness"
어렵다 "to be hard"   어려움 "hardship/distress"

The use of ~는 것 to create a noun form   4.4

In restricted contexts, such as when one wishes to state, inform, or record a certain fact in a concise manner, the nominalizing ending ~(으)ㅁ can be used as a sentence ending. Consider the following examples:

아침 아직 <u>안 먹었음</u>.
"Did not eat breakfast yet."
오늘 강의 <u>없음</u>.
"No class today."
회사에 도착하는대로 <u>연락 주기 바람</u>.
"Contact (us) as soon as (you) arrive at work."
열쇠 <u>찾았음</u>.
"Found the key."
변상필 <u>드림</u>/<u>올림</u>.
"Respectably, Sangpil Byon" (in closing letter or e-mail message)

4.3 The nominalizing ending ~이

The use of the nominalizing ending ~이 is even more confined than that of ~기 and ~으(ㅁ). For instance, the following is a list of the small number of nouns that are constructed from the predicate stem and the nominalizing ending ~이:

벌다 "to earn"   벌이 "income"
먹다 "to eat"   먹이 "prey, food"
놀다 "to play"   놀이 "game"

길다 "to be long"   길이 "length"
높다 "to be high"   높이 "height"
넓다 "to be wide"   넓이 "width"

4.4 The use of ~는 것 to create a noun form

Besides the use of the aforementioned nominalizing endings, Koreans can change a verb into a noun form by attaching ~는 것 to the stem of the verb. ~는 것 is the combination of the noun-modifying ending ~는 and the bound noun 것 "the fact/the one/the being" (or 거 for colloquial settings).

조깅하다 "to jog"   조깅하는 것 "jogging"
놀다 "to play"   노는 것 "playing"
일하다 "to work"   일하는 것 "working"
쉬다 "to rest"   쉬는 것 "resting"

그냥 <u>걸어가는 게</u> 낫겠어요.
"(I) think that just walking will be better."
밖에서 <u>먹는 것</u>보다 집에서 <u>먹는 것</u>이 건강에 더 좋아요.
"Eating at home is better than eating out for health reasons."
<u>공부하는 것</u>보다 컴퓨터 게임을 <u>하는 것</u>을 더 좋아해요.
"(He) likes playing computer games more than studying."
<u>요리하는 것</u>이 <u>먹는 것</u>보다 더 즐거워요.
"Cooking is more fun than eating."

5

Case particles I

5.1 Case and special particles

One special word class in Korean that has no corresponding equivalent in English is "particles" (also called postpositions or suffixes). Particles typically attach to the end of a noun to indicate grammatical roles or add special meanings. There are two kinds of particles in Korean: case particles and special particles.

In English, the grammatical role of nouns in a sentence is typically determined by the word order. For instance, in the sentence "Andrew practices Taekwondo," the subject is "Andrew" because it appears in the beginning of the sentence, while "Taekwondo" is the object because it appears after the verb "practices."

In Korean, however, this is primarily determined by case particles, whose primary function is to signal the grammatical role of the noun (or noun phrase) to which they are attached. Case particles include 이/가 "subject case particle," 을/를 "object case particle," 의 "possessive particle," and so on. Consider the following sentence:

영호가 저녁을 먹어요.
"Youngho eats dinner."

영호 is the subject, as it is marked by the subject particle 가, and 저녁 is the object, because it is marked by the object particle 을.

"Special particles" function not to designate grammatical roles of the noun but rather to express special meanings, such as indicating the noun as a topic of the sentence, highlighting the singularity or plurality of the noun, and so on. Special particles include the topic particle 은/는 "as for" and delimiters such as 만 "only," 도 "also," and so forth. Consider the following example:

한국 음식은 비빔밥이 맛있어요.
"As for Korean food, bibimbap is tasty."

In the example, 한국 음식 is not the subject but the topic of the sentence in that it is marked by the topic particle 은. Instead, 비빔밥 is the subject of the sentence, as it is marked by the subject particle 이.

5.2 Characteristics of particles

Particles are tightly bound to the noun. For instance, notice in the previous example sentences that there is no space between the noun and the particle (e.g., 영호가 not 영호 가, 음식은 not 음식 은). The particle is an integral part of the noun to which it is attached.

In addition, particles can often be dropped during casual spoken communication. This omission in colloquial usages is possible because the contextual understanding of the conversation is often sufficient to indicate the syntactic roles of the nouns being used (e.g., knowing who is a subject or an object, and so forth). However, the deletion of the particles is not permitted in formal written communication. For example, the sentence "Lisa drank coffee" in Korean should be 리사가 커피를 마셨다 in writing, but it can be 리사(가) 커피(를) 마셨어요 in colloquial speech.

Moreover, due to the case particle's role of signaling the grammatical role of the nouns, the word order can be scrambled. For instance, notice that the following two sentences have the same meaning, even though their word orders (e.g., the subject 정우 and the object 아침) are different.

정우가 아침을 먹어요.
"Jungwoo eats breakfast."
아침을 정우가 먹어요.
"Jungwoo eats breakfast."

What follows next in the remaining chapter are case particles. As for special particles, they will be discussed in detail in Chapter 7.

5.3 The subject particle 이/가

The subject case particle 이/가 is a two-form particle, with 이 being used after a noun that ends in a consonant (e.g., 집이 "house-particle") and 가 after a noun that ends in a vowel (e.g., 아파트가 "apartment-particle"). The primary function of 이/가 is to indicate that the noun to which it is attached is the subject of the sentence.

조슈아가 오늘 수업에 안 왔어요.
"Joshua did not come to class today."
저 집이 우리 집이에요.
"That house (over there) is our home."

5.3.1 The particle 이/가 in negation

Although the main function of 이/가 is to indicate the subject case, its usage extends beyond case marking. For example, in negation, the noun it marks is not the subject of the sentence. Consider the following example:

나오미는 일본인이 아니에요.
"As for Naomi, (she) is not a Japanese person."

나오미 is not the subject but the topic of the sentence, as it is marked by the topic particle 는. Notice that the subject of the sentence is omitted, and 일본인, marked by the particle 이, is not the subject of the sentence.

5.3.2 Double subject constructions

Some Korean sentences may have two nouns marked by the subject particle, as shown here:

학생이 다섯 명이 장학금을 신청했어요.
"Five students applied for a scholarship."

Notice that there are two nouns, marked by the subject particle: 학생 and 다섯 명. Korean grammarians call such a sentence "double-subject construction." Double-subject sentences are common in Korean. However, its interpretation is not that the sentence has two subjects. In this sentence, the focus is on the number five rather than students.

Here is another example:

수지가 얼굴이 작아요.
"Suzie's face is small."

CASE PARTICLES I

In this sentence, the relationship between the two nouns, 수지 and 얼굴, is that of the possessor-possessed. It may be confusing which noun marked by the particle should be considered as the highlighted subject. Koreans, however, use contextual understanding as well as other linguistic/prosodic cues (e.g., intonation) to figure out where the emphasis lies.

5.3.3 Interplay between the subject and the topic particles

When asking a question in Korean, the question word (e.g., 무엇 "what," 누구 "who") is usually marked by the subject particle 이/가. However, when answering the question, the question word is often marked by the topic particle 은/는. Consider the following examples:

    Peter: 전공이 뭐예요?
               "What is (your) major?"
    Susan: 전공은 한국어예요.
               "As for (my) major, (it) is Korean."

In Peter's question, the particle 이/가 is used since 전공 "major" is the subject of the question. However, when responding to this question, Susan answers 전공은 한국어예요 "As for (my) major, (it) is Korean," instead of 전공이 한국어예요 "The major is Korean." Notice that 전공 is marked by the topic particle 은/는, not the subject particle 이/가.

When Peter asks the question, 전공 is the subject of the sentence, and it is not the topic of the conversation yet. In other words, the word 전공 is new information which was just brought up in the conversation. However, after Peter's question, 전공 becomes the topic. As a result, Susan replies with 전공은 rather than 전공이.

This may sound confusing, but it should become clear with more examples. Consider the following:

    A: 이름이 뭐예요?
         "What is (your) name?"
    B: 제 이름은 앤드류예요.
         "As for my name, (it) is Andrew."

    A: 고향이 어디예요?
         "Where is (your) hometown?"
    B: 제 고향은 서울이에요.
         "As for my hometown, (it) is Seoul."

5.4 The direct object particle 을/를

The direct object is a noun (or pronoun) that receives or experiences the action indicated by the verb. In Korean, the direct object is marked by the particle 을/를. Just like the subject particle, the direct object particle 을/를 is a two-form case particle. 을 is used after a noun that ends in a consonant, and 를 is used after a noun that ends in a vowel.

    화장실을 청소해요.
    "(They) clean the bathroom."
    한국 드라마를 봐요.
    "(They) watch a Korean drama."

Although the particle 을/를 typically marks the direct object of transitive verbs in Korean, there are few exceptions where the noun marked by 을/를 does not appear to be the direct object. For instance, consider the following sentences:

    기민이가 오전 9시에 회사에 가요.
    "Keemin goes to work at 9 a.m."

기민이가 오전 9시에 회사를 가요.
"Keemin goes to work at 9 a.m."

Notice that 회사 "company/work" can be marked by the locative particle 에 as well as the direct object particle 를. Here are other examples:

아침에 공원에서 산책했어요.
"(We) took a walk in the park in the morning."
아침에 공원을 산책했어요.
"(We) took a walk in the park in the morning."

Note that 공원 "park" can be marked by dynamic locative particle 에서 as well as 을/를.

Meanwhile, just like subject particle 이/가 can appear twice in one sentence, 을/를 can appear twice in casual speech as well. Consider the following examples:

스펜서가 한국인 학생들한테 영어를 가르쳤어요.
"Spencer taught Korean students English."
스펜서가 한국인 학생들을 영어를 가르쳤어요.
"Spencer taught Korean students English."

Notice in the previous example that sometimes 을/를 can replace the particle 한테 "to."

5.5 The possessive particle 의

In English, the possessor–possession relationship between two nouns is often indicated by the apostrophe -'s or "of." In Korean, it is expressed by the possessive particle 의, as in 교수님의 책 "professor's book." The first noun is typically the possessor (since the particle 의 is attached to it), and the second noun is the possession. The case particle 의 is a one-form particle. It is the same regardless of whether it attaches to a noun that ends in a vowel or a consonant, as in 김은미 씨의 책상 "Ms. Kim Eunmee's desk" and 데니엘의 컴퓨터 "Daniel's computer."

Although the function of the particle 의 resembles that of the English suffix -'s, there is one difference in their usages. English allows the possessor + 's construction, as in "It is Peter's" or "It is Susanna's." However, Korean does not allow the possessor noun ending with the particle. As a result, a sentence like 그 시계가 사이몬의예요 "That watch is Simon's" is not acceptable. For this purpose, the bound noun 것 "thing" typically appears after the particle, as in 그 시계가 사이몬의 것이에요 "That watch is Simon's thing."

In colloquial conversations, the particle 의 can be often omitted. For instance, 사유리 가방 can be used instead of 사유리의 가방 "Sayuri's bag" and 사유리 것 (or 사유리 거 for a more informal usage) can be used instead of 사유리의 것 "Sayuri's thing." In summary, there are three ways to express a possessor–possession relationship in Korean:

NOUN 의 NOUN, as in 경호의 자전거 "Kyoungho's bicycle."
NOUN NOUN, as in 경호 자전거 "Kyoungho bicycle."
NOUN 것 (or 거), as in 경호 거 "Kyoungho thing."

6

Case particles II

6.1 Particles of location and movement

6.1.1 에 "to/in/at/per/in addition to"

The case particle 에 is a one-form particle that expresses the following six things: (i) the static location, (ii) the goal of the action (e.g., destination), (iii) times, (iv) quantity, (v) the cause of a certain condition, and (vi) addition.

First, the particle 에 marks the static location, corresponding to "in," "at" or "on" in English. The static location points to the place where something is (being) at or in.

혜지가 지금 집에 있어요.
"Haeji is at home now."
에펠 탑이 파리에 있어요.
"The Eiffel Tower is in Paris."
프린터는 책상 위에 올려놓아 주세요.
"As for the printer, please put it on the desk."

Second, the particle 에 expresses the goal of the action (e.g., inanimate objects or destinations), corresponding to "to" or "at' in English.

내일 도서관에 갈 거예요.
"(I) will go to the library tomorrow."
경찰서에 연락했어요.
"(I) contacted the police station."
은행에 돈을 입금했어요.
"(I) deposited money to a bank."

If the goal of the action is animate (e.g., persons or animals), the particles 한테 and 에게 should be used instead.

"(I) make a phone call to mom."
(O) 엄마한테 전화해요.
(X) 엄마에 전화해요.
"(I) gave water to the puppy."
(O) 강아지한테 물을 줬어요.
(X) 강아지에 물을 줬어요.

Third, the particle 에 marks references to time, corresponding to "at," "in," or "on" in English.

우리 이번 주 수요일에 만나요.
"Let's meet on this Wednesday."
이번 주말에 바빠요.
"(I am) busy this weekend."
토요일 오후 3시에 만날 거예요.
"(I) will meet (her) at 3 p.m. on Saturday."

Particles of location and movement | 6.1

Fourth, the particle 에 is used to mean "for" or "per," as in "per day."

하루에 몇 시간 TV를 보세요?
"How many hours do (you) watch TV per day?"
그 와인은 한 병에 얼마예요?
"As for that wine, how much is (it) per bottle?"

Fifth, the particle is used after a noun that causes a certain state or condition.

좋은 시험 결과에 정말 기뻐요.
"(I) am really glad because of the good test result."
비바람에 나무가 쓰러졌어요.
"The tree fell over due to the rainstorm."

Lastly, the particle 에 is used to express "in addition to."

큰 집에 좋은 차도 있어요.
"(He) has an expensive car in addition to a huge house."
햄버거하고 콜라에 피자도 시켰어요.
"In addition to hamburgers and cola, (we) also ordered pizzas."

6.1.2 에다(가) "in/on/addition to"

In colloquial conversation, the one-form case particle 에다(가) can be used instead of 에 when expressing two things: (i) static location and (ii) addition, as shown in the following examples:

식탁 위에 올려놓았습니다.
"(I) put (it) on the top of the table."
식탁 위에다가 올려놓았어요.
"(I) put (it) on the top of the table."
피자 큰 거 두 판에 맥주 두 병 주문했어요.
"(I) ordered two bottles of beer in addition to two large pizzas."
피자 큰 거 두 판에다가 맥주 두 병 주문했는데요.
"(I) ordered two bottles of beer in addition to two large pizzas."

6.1.3 에서 "from/at/in"

The one-form particle 에서 expresses two things: (i) the dynamic location or (ii) the source of action. A dynamic location refers to the place where an action takes place. Consider the following sentence:

승훈이가 학교 식당에서 점심을 먹어요.
"Sunghoon eats lunch at the school cafeteria."

Notice that 학교 식당 "the school cafeteria" is a dynamic location where the action (i.e., eating lunch) takes place. In fact, the use of the particle 에서 is determined by the type of verb the sentence has. Whenever the verb denotes an activity such as playing, doing, meeting, working, studying, and so forth, 에서 must be used.

공원에서 운동했어요.
"(We) exercised at the park."
로비에서 잠시만 기다려 주세요.
"Please wait a moment in the lobby."

Further, the particle 에서 marks a source of action (e.g., starting location/point), corresponding to "from" in English. Consider the following examples:

보스톤에서 뉴욕시까지 가요.
"(I) go to New York City from Boston."
부엌에서 여기까지 청소해 주세요.
"Please clean from kitchen to here."

CASE PARTICLES II

6.1

Notice that the sources of action in the previous examples are all inanimate entities (e.g., places such as Boston and kitchen). If the sources of the actions are animate, such as persons and animals, different particles such as 한테서 or 에게서 should be used.

6.1.4 (으)로부터 "from"

The particle (으)로부터 is a two-form particle. 으로부터 is used after a noun that ends in a consonant (as in 병원으로부터 "from the hospital"), and 로부터 is used after a noun that ends in a vowel (as in 학교로부터 "from school") or the consonant ㄹ (as in 절로부터 "from the Buddhist temple").

The particle (으)로부터 is also used to mark a source, meaning "from" in English. However, differing from 에서 (which marks an inanimate source) or 한테서/에게서 (which marks an animate source), 으로부터 can be used to mark both an animate and an inanimate source. In addition, 으로부터 sounds more formal than 에서 and 한테서/에게서.

> 회사로부터 반가운 소식을 받았습니다.
> "(I) received good news from the company."
> 이 시계가 학생들로부터 받은 생일 선물입니다.
> "This watch is the birthday present that (I) received from (my) students."

6.1.5 한테/에게/께 "to"

The one-form particles 한테, 에게, and 께 mark the animate indirect object of the sentence (e.g., persons, animals), which corresponds to "to" in English. The only difference among these particles is that 한테 is most widely used in informal/colloquial conversations, 에게 tends to be used in a more formal context, and 께 is used when the direct object is an esteemed person or senior (e.g., one's boss, teachers, and so forth).

> 우리 엄마한테 전부 이야기할 거예요.
> "(I) will tell my mom all of it."
> 말한테 먹이를 줬어요.
> "(I) gave horse feed to the horses."
> 이 소포를 서울에 있는 제 친구에게 보낼 겁니다.
> "(I) will send this package to my friend in Seoul."
> 변 교수님께 편지를 드렸어요.
> "(I) gave the letter to Professor Byon."

One thing to remember when using 께 is that it is an honorific element; therefore its usage should be collocated with other honorific elements such as the honorific suffix, euphemistic words, proper address or reference terms, and so on. For example, in the previous examples, 드리다 "give (honorific)" is used instead of 주다 "give (plain form)."

> 사장님께 서류를 드렸어요.
> "(I) gave the document to the boss." (O)
> 사장님께 서류를 줬어요.
> "(I) gave the document to the boss." (X)

6.1.6 한테(서)/에게(서) "from"

The one-form particles 한테(서) and 에게(서) mark an animate source (e.g., persons and animals), taking on the meaning of "from" in English. The only difference between 한테(서) and 에게(서) is that the former is used in a colloquial context whereas the latter is used for a more formal setting.

> 어제 아빠한테서 백불을 받았어요.
> "(I) received 100 dollars from Dad yesterday."

Instrumental particles

현재 아직 회사 동료들<u>에게서</u> 답변을 기다리고 있는 중입니다.
"Currently, (we) are still waiting for the response from (our) company colleagues."

Note that in conversation, 서 can be often omitted, as in these examples:

친구<u>한테(서)</u> 컴퓨터를 빌렸어요.
"(I) borrowed a computer from (my) friend."
마이클<u>한테(서)</u> 전화 왔어요.
"A phone call came from Michael."

6.2 Instrumental particles

6.2.1 (으)로(서/써) "as/by/with"

The case particle (으)로 is a two-form particle: 으로 appears after a noun that ends in a consonant (as in 책<u>으로</u> "by books"); 로 appears after a noun that ends in a vowel (as in 버스<u>로</u> "by bus") or the consonant ㄹ (as in 신발<u>로</u> "by shoes"). The particle (으)로 can express the following six things: (i) instrument, (ii) direction, (iii) selection, (iv) the change of state, (v) in the role/status of, and (vi) cause.

First, the particle (으)로 (or 으로써 for more formal situations) indicates that the noun it attaches to is a tool or an instrument. It is translated in English as "by means of" or "with."

펜<u>으로</u> 싸인하세요.
"Please sign with a pen."
와인은 포도<u>로</u> 만들어요.
"As for wine, (one) makes it with grapes."
꿀<u>로써</u> 단 맛을 내십시오.
"Please add a sweet taste to (it) with honey."
이 집은 나무<u>로써</u> 지었다.
"This house was built with wood."
이 도시의 아름다움은 말<u>로써</u> 다 표현할 수 없었습니다.
"(I) could not fully express the beauty of this city with words."

Second, the particle (으)로 indicates the direction "to" or "toward." Note that the direction (e.g., destination) can be marked by the case particle 에 as well. The difference between 에 and (으)로 is that while 에 indicates a specific location or destination, (으)로 indicates a more general direction of the target location, as in the following examples:

어디<u>에</u> 가세요?
"Where are (you) going?"
어디<u>로</u> 가세요?
"In what direction, are (you) going?"

Here are some more examples:

오른쪽<u>으로</u> 가세요.
"Go toward the right side."
식탁은 TV쪽<u>으로</u> 움직여 주세요.
"As for the table, please move (it) toward the side with the TV."

Third, the particle (으)로 indicates that the preceding noun is a selection from several options. For instance, consider the following conversation:

Salesman: 무슨 색<u>으로</u> 드릴까요?
"In what color shall (I) give (it to you)?"
Customer: 하얀 거<u>로</u> 주세요.
"Give (me) the white one."

CASE PARTICLES II

Notice that by using (으)로, the salesman implies that there are items in different colors. Here are more examples.

> 금요일 오후로 정합시다.
> "Let's decide it on Friday afternoon."
> 피자 큰 것으로 두 판 주세요.
> "Please give (us) two large pizzas."

Fourth, the particle (으)로 marks "the result of the change" or "change of the state."

> 좀 더 큰 것으로 바꿔 주세요.
> "Please change (this) into a bigger one."
> 전화를 새거로 바꿨어요.
> "(I) replaced (my) phone with a new one."
> 비가 눈으로 변했어요.
> "The rain changed into snow."

Fifth, the particle (으)로 (or 으로서) expresses "in the role or function of."

> 영어교사로 한국에서 2년 있었어요.
> "(I) was in Korea as an English teacher for two years."
> 평일에는 회사 사장으로 주말에는 요리사로 일해요.
> "(He) works as a company CEO on weekdays and as a chef on the weekend."

Meanwhile, as for more formal situations, one can use (으)로서 "as" instead of (으)로, as shown here:

> 저는 교수로서 학자로서 지난 20년간 최선을 다해 왔습니다.
> "As an educator and a scholar, I have done my best in the past 20 years."
> 의사로서 충고 한마디 해도 되겠습니까?
> "As a medical doctor, may I give you a word of advice?"

Lastly, the particle (으)로 indicates "the cause," as shown in these examples:

> 지난 달에 감기로 엄청 고생했어요.
> "(I) suffered greatly because of a cold last month."
> 샌프란시스코가 금문교로 유명합니다.
> "San Francisco is well known because of the Golden Gate Bridge."

6.3 Comitative particles

The particles 와/과, (이)랑, and 하고 serve to link nouns together and take on the meaning of "and" or "with."

6.3.1 와/과 "and/with"

The particle 와/과 is a two-form particle. 와 is used with a noun that ends in a vowel (e.g., 사과와 오렌지 "apple and orange"), and 과 is used with a noun that ends in a consonant (e.g., 연필과 지우개 "pencils and erasers"). The particle 와/과 tends to be used in formal or written communication.

> 겐타 씨와 하사꼬 씨가 일본 사람입니다.
> "Kenta and Hisako are Japanese."
> 제 형과 누나는 지금 시카고에서 대학을 다니고 있습니다.
> "My older brother and older sister are attending colleges in Chicago."

Comitative particles

6.3.2 (이)랑 "and/with"

The particle (이)랑 is also a two-form particle, with 이랑 being used with a noun that ends in a consonant and 랑 being used with a noun that ends in a vowel. The particle (이)랑 is used for colloquial settings.

영호랑 재은이가 미국 교포예요.
"Youngho and Jaeun are Korean Americans."
형이랑 누나는 한국에 있어요.
"(My) older brother and older sister are in Korea."

6.3.3 하고 "and/with"

The particle 하고 is a one-form particle that comes after a noun regardless of whether it ends in a vowel or a consonant. There is no apparent difference in meaning between 하고 and the other two particles 와/과 and (이)랑. However, 하고 seems to be less informal than 와/과 but more formal than (이)랑.

집 주소하고 집 전화 번호를 쓰시면 돼요.
"(All you need to do is to) write (your) home address and (your) home phone number."
김치찌개하고 소주 한 병 주문했어요.
"(We) ordered kimchi stew and a bottle of Soju."

When the subject is understood from the context, it can be omitted. In such cases, the noun with 와/과, (이)랑, or 하고 can stand alone, as in (제가) 영주하고 갈 거예요 "(I) will go with Youngjoo." Then, the translation of the particle will be "with" rather than "and."

7

Special particles I

Whereas the preceding chapter discussed case particles, this chapter discusses another set of particles: the special particles.

7.1 The differences between case particles and special particles

What distinguishes case particles from special particles lies in their functions. Whereas the primary function of the case particle is to indicate the syntactic role of the noun it attaches to (e.g., whether the noun is the subject, object, indirect object, and so on), that of the special particle is to add a special meaning (e.g., whether the word it attaches to is the topic of the sentence, or indicate special meanings such as "also," "even," "only," and so forth).

Case particles also differ from special particles in the places they appear in a sentence. A case particle can appear only after a noun (i.e., subject, object, indirect objects, etc.). However, a special particle can appear in one of three places.

First, it can appear in the place of a case particle. For instance, the special topic particle 은/는 can appear where you expect to see the subject case particle 이/가.

지하철 역이 저희 집에서 가까워요.
"The subway station is close to our home."
지하철 역은 저희 집에서 가까워요.
"As for the subway station, (it) is close to our home."

They can also appear in the place where you expect the object case particle 을/를.

성희가 과일을 좋아해요.
"Sunghee likes fruits."
성희가 과일은 좋아해요.
"As for fruits, Sunghee likes (them)."

Second, a special particle can appear after an existing case particle (e.g., 에, 에서, and 으로) in order to add that particle's particular meaning.

언니가 거실에서 안 자요.
"(My) older sister does not sleep in the living room."
언니가 거실에서는 안 자요.
"As for the living room, (my) older sister does not sleep (there)."

Third, a special particle can appear not only after a noun but also after an adverb, such as 잘 "well," 맛있게 "deliciously," 싸게 "at a low price," 자주 "frequently," and 빨리 "fast."

그 학생이 한글로 이메일을 빨리 써요.
"That student writes e-mails in Korean fast."

Particles of topic and focus

그 학생이 한글로 이멜일을 빨리는 써요.
"(I don't know about other things but) that students writes e-mails in Korean fast."
이 슈퍼마켓이 야채를 싸게 팔아요.
"This supermarket sells vegetables at cheap prices."
이 슈퍼마켓이 야채를 싸게는 팔아요.
"(I don't know about other things but) this supermarket sells vegetables at a low price."

Consequently, you cannot simply assume and memorize where a certain particle (including both case and special particles) always appears in a certain context. This is because, as just seen, a special particle can appear in the place where you expect another particle to be.

7.2 Particles of topic and focus

7.2.1 은/는 "as for"

The particle 은/는 is a two-form particle. 은 is used after a noun that ends in a consonant (e.g., 아이스크림은 "ice cream-particle"), and 는 is used after a noun that ends in a vowel (e.g., 커피는 "coffee-particle"). The main function of 은/는 is to indicate that the noun to which it is attached is the sentence topic (e.g., what the sentence is about). Consider the following two sentences:

캐서린은 호주 사람이에요.
"As for Katherine, (she) is an Australian."
데니는 영국 사람이에요.
"As for Danny, (he) is an Englishman."

Notice that the previous two sentences are "topic-comment" structures. Both sentences begin with the topic of the sentence (marked by the topic particle 은/는), followed by the predicate (e.g., an equational expression). In the first sentence, 캐서린 is the topic and 호주 사람이에요 is the comment. In the second sentence, 데니 is the topic, whereas 영국 사람이에요 is the comment. Such a topic-comment structure is the most basic sentence type in Korean.

To understand its usage in more detail, let us consider the following examples:

나오미는 캐나다 사람이에요.
"As for Naomi, (she) is a Canadian."
간호사예요.
"(She) is a nurse."
25살이에요.
"(She) is 25 years old."
겐타는 일본 사람이에요.
"As for Kenta, (he) is Japanese."

Notice that the first three sentences are about Naomi. Because of the fact that Naomi was noted as the topic in the first sentence, it would be redundant to raise Naomi as the topic again. Consequently, the second and the third sentence omit the topic 나오미. (In addition, 나오미 as the subject is omitted here as well, since we know that the subject is 나오미 anyway from the context.) However, as the fourth sentence is about a different person 겐타, the sentence begins with the new topic, 겐타.

Meanwhile, notice that the introduction of the new topic, 겐타 (after talking about 나오미) may signal a contrast with the preceding information of 나오미. That is, while the primary function of 은/는 is to mark a topic, it can also indicate contrast. Here are more examples:

형은 미국에서 공부하고 있어요.
"As for (my) older brother, (he) is studying in the U.S."
누나는 서울에서 대학교에 다녀요.
"As for (my) older sister, (she) attends a college in Seoul."

Notice that the particle 은/는 marks 형 and 누나 as the topic of each sentence. In addition, the particle marks 형 in order to be contrasted with 누나.

The noun marked by 은/는 appears to be the subject of the sentence. However, 은/는 is not a subject particle, and it does not mark the noun as the subject. For instance, consider the following sentence:

커피는 하와이 코나 커피가 맛있어요.
"As for coffee, Hawaii Kona Coffee is tasty."

Notice that "coffee" is the topic of the sentence (what the sentence is talking about), while "Hawaii Kona Coffee" is the subject of the predicate "tasty."

7.2.2 (이)야 "if it be"

The particle (이)야 is a two-form particle: 이야 (after a consonant) and 야 (after a vowel), and its major function is to put an emphasis on the noun it attaches to. It is translated as "if it is" in English, as shown in the following examples:

비싸지만 맛이야 정말 최고예요.
"Although (it) is expensive, if it is taste, (it) is indeed the best."
골프야, 우리 아버지가 진짜로 잘 치세요.
"If it is golf, my father is really good at (it)."
돈이야, 물론 많이 벌지만, 주말에도 나가서 일해요.
"If it is money, (he) certainly earns a lot, but (he) goes to work even on the weekend."

7.2.3 (이)야말로 "indeed"

The two-form particle (이)야말로, with 이야말로 being used after a consonant and 야말로 after a vowel, adds the meaning of "indeed" or "exactly" to the noun it attaches to.

뉴욕시야말로 대도시예요.
"New York City is indeed a mega city."
제 어머님이야말로 이 세상에서 저를 제일 사랑해 주시는 분이세요.
"My mother is indeed the person who loves me the most in this world."

7.3 Particles of comparison and contrast

7.3.1 보다 "more than"

The particle 보다 is used to make a comparative sentence. This particle is attached to a noun that is being compared, and it is translated as "more than" or "rather than." You can use adverbs like 더 "more," 훨씬 "by far" or 엄청 "exceedingly" to intensify the meaning.

이 방이 저 방보다 더 커요.
"This room is bigger than the room over there."
지하철이 택시보다 편해요.
"The subway is more convenient than a taxi."

Meanwhile, with the adverb 덜 "less," the particle 보다 indicates "less than."

오늘 야채가 어제 거보다 덜 싱싱해요.
"The greens today are less fresh than those yesterday."
제가 동생보다 훨씬 덜 많이 먹어요.
"I eat much less than (my) younger brother."

Particles of comparison and contrast

7.3.2 처럼/같이 "like"

The particles 처럼 and 같이 are used to compare two nouns. They are translated as "as if" and "like."

정말 개미처럼 열심히 일했어요.
"(We) really worked hard like ants."
수잔이 한국 사람처럼 한국말을 잘하네요.
"Susan speaks Korean well, as if (she) were a Korean."
제 목소리가 원래 남자같이 허스키했었어요.
"My voice used to be husky like a man's."
어제는 여름같이 더웠어요.
"As for yesterday, (it) was hot like summer."

7.3.3 만큼 "as . . . as"

The particle 만큼 is used when the two things that are being compared are equal in some way, corresponding to "as much as" or "to the extent that" in English. Consider the following examples:

아이구, 벌써 아버지만큼 키가 컸네요.
"Wow, (you) became as tall as (your) father."
오늘은 어제만큼 덥지 않아요.
"As for today, (it) is not as hot as yesterday."
이 차가 저 차만큼 비싸요.
"This car is as expensive as that car (over there)."
규리도 언니만큼 예뻐요.
"As for Kyuri, (she) is as pretty as (her) older sister."
기대만큼 점수가 나왔어요.
"The score came out to the extent of (my) expectations."

7.3.4 따라 "unusually"

The particle 따라 commonly attaches to a time noun, such as 오늘 "today," 어제 "yesterday," or 그날 "that day," and adds the meaning of "unusually" or "of all times."

어제따라 매일 늦게 들어오시던 아버지께서 일찍 퇴근하셨다.
"Yesterday, (my) father, who used to come home late every day, got off work unusually early."
오늘따라 수업이 평소보다 일찍 끝났네요.
"The class ended early today unusually."
이상하게도 그 날따라 손님이 많았어요.
"Strangely, there were many customers on that day, which was unusual."

7.3.5 대로 "in accordance with"

The particle 대로 adds the meaning of "according to."

더 이상 망설이지말고 법대로 합시다!
"Let us not hesitate anymore, but proceed in accordance with the law!"
너도 이제 성인이니 네 마음대로 해라.
"You are an adult now, so do as you wish."

SPECIAL PARTICLES I

7.4 Particles of frequency

7.4.1 마다 "every"

The particle 마다 means "every" or "each," as shown in the following examples:

아버지가 달마다 돈을 부쳐 주세요.
"(My) father sends (me) money every month."
4시간마다 약을 꼭 드셔야 돼요.
"(You) must take the medicine every four hours."
방마다 책상하고 침대가 있나요?
"Does each room have a desk and a bed?"
교수님마다 연구실이 있어요.
"Each professor has an office."

7.4.2 씩 "each"

The particle 씩 is used to indicate regularity or equal distribution, adding the meaning of "apiece," "each," and "respectively" to the noun it attaches to.

천천히 순서대로 한명씩 들어오세요.
"Slowly, please come in one at a time in the order named."
잊지말고 약은 하루에 세번씩 꼭 드셔야 돼요.
"As for the medicine, don't forget that (you) must take it three times a day."
매일 세 네시간씩만 자면서 열심히 공부했어요.
"(I) studied for the exam while sleeping only three to four hours every day."

8

Special particles II

8.1 Particles of extent

8.1.1 부터 "from"

The particle 부터 indicates a beginning point, corresponding to "from" in English.

가을학기가 내일부터 시작해요.
"Fall semester begins from tomorrow."
뭐부터 먹을까요?
"What shall (we) eat first?"
어제 밤 9시부터 잤어요.
"(I) slept from 9 o'clock last night."
다음 회의가 오후 2시 반부터 있어요.
"The next meeting is from 2:30 p.m."
4 페이지부터 읽으세요.
"Please read (the book) from page 4."
노트북 컴퓨터 가격은 700달러부터예요.
"As for the price of notebook computers, (it) is from 700 dollars."

8.1.2 까지 "to, until, including (even)"

The particle 까지 marks an ending point, and it corresponds to "to," "until," or "as far as" in English. When the particle is used with a temporal noun, it indicates an ending temporal point, as in:

3 시까지 기다려 주시겠어요?
"Could you please wait until 3 o'clock?"
밤 11시까지 도서관에서 공부했어요.
"(I) studied at the library until 11:00 p.m."

The particles 부터 and 까지 are often used together to express "from [time expression] to [time expression]."

오전 8시부터 오후5시까지.
"From 8:00 a.m. to 5:00 p.m."
밤부터 새벽까지.
"From night to dawn."

When the particle is used with a place noun, it indicates an ending location (e.g., destination), as in:

서울까지 비행기로 두 시간 걸려요.
"(It) takes two hours to Seoul by plane."
공항까지 멀어요.
"(It) is far to the airport."

SPECIAL PARTICLES II 8.1

The particle 까지 can be used with a nontime or a nonplace noun, such as persons, clothes, and so forth. When it is used with a nonplace or a nontime noun, the particle 까지 means "including (even)," or "even (as far as)."

남동생<u>까지</u> 집으로 돌아갔어요.
"Even (my) younger brother went back home."
사장님<u>까지</u> 유니폼을 입고 오셨습니다.
"Even the president came wearing the uniform."

8.1.3 도 "also, even"

The particle 도 serves to express emphasis, adding the meaning of "also," "too," or "even" to the noun it attaches to.

내일<u>도</u> 또 들르세요.
"Please stop by again tomorrow as well."
돼지고기<u>도</u> 사요.
"(Let's) buy some pork too."
점심 먹을 시간<u>도</u> 없어요.
"(I) do not even have time to have a lunch."
아직 샤워<u>도</u> 안 했어요.
"(I) haven't even taken a shower yet."
당신<u>도</u> 이제 많이 늙었네요.
"You also got much older now."

8.1.4 마저/조차 "even"

The particles 마저 and 조차 are used to express "even," and their meaning is similar to that of 까지 "including (even)" or 도 "also/even." However, differing from 까지 or 도, the particles 마저 and 조차 are in general used for unfavorable or undesirable situations. Compare the following examples:

제 예전 여자 친구<u>까지</u> 만났어요.
"(She) even met my ex-girlfriend."
제 예전 여자 친구<u>마저</u> 만났어요.
"(She) even met my ex-girlfriend."

Although the translation of both examples is the same, the second example with 마저 implies that meeting the ex-girlfriend was not a favorable event, whereas the first example with 까지 simply indicates "including (even)." Here are more examples:

빚 때문에 집을 팔고 차<u>마저</u> 팔았어요.
"Because of the debt, (he) sold the house and even the car."
아침도 굶고 점심<u>조차</u> 못 먹었어요.
"(I) skipped breakfast and could not eat even lunch."
그의 부인<u>조차</u> 그의 말을 안 믿었어요.
"Even his wife did not believe his word."
토마스<u>마저</u> 파티에 안 왔어요.
"Even Thomas did not come to the party."
그 학생은 자기 이름<u>조차</u> 못 써요.
"As for that student, (he) cannot write even his name."

8.1.5 만 "only"

The particle 만 is a one-form particle, and it means "only" or "just."

슈퍼에서 우유하고 치즈<u>만</u> 샀어요.
"(I) bought only milk and cheese."

Particles of extent　　　　　　　　　　　　　　　　　　　　　　　　**8.1**

세현이는 하루 종일 컴퓨터 게임만 해서 걱정이에요.
"As for Sayhyun, (we) worry about (him) since (he) plays only computer games all day long."
언니는 수요일에만 회사에 가요.
"As for (my) older sister, (she) goes to work only on Wednesday."
필요한 것 없으니까 빨리만 오세요.
"There is nothing we need, so just come in a hurry."

8.1.6 밖에 "nothing but"

The particle 밖에 is used to indicate "only," and its meaning is similar to that of 만 "only." However, differing from 만, the particle 밖에 always co-occurs with a negative predicate. For instance, compare the following sentences:

20달라만 있어요.
"(I) have only 20 dollars."
20 달라밖에 없어요.
"(I) have only 20 dollars (lit. I have nothing but 20 dollars)."

Notice that, although the meanings of both sentences are similar, the second sentence ends in 없어요 "do not have." Here are more examples:

10분밖에 안 기다렸어요.
"(I) waited nothing but 10 minutes."
커피는 두 잔밖에 안 마셨어요.
"As for coffee, (I) drank nothing but two cups."
한국어를 조금밖에 못 해요.
"(I) can speak nothing but a little Korean."

8.1.7 뿐 "only, just"

The particle 뿐 adds the meaning of "only" to the noun it attaches to.

모두에게 인생은 한 번뿐이다.
"Everyone lives only once."
내가 믿고 의지할 수 있는 사람은 오직 당신뿐이에요.
"You are the only one that I can trust and rely on."

Meanwhile, 뿐 is commonly used with the particle 만 "only" and the negative copula 아니라 to convey more emphatic effects, as in 뿐만 아니라 "it is not only/just."

진훈이는 영어뿐만 아니라 불어도 유창해요.
"Jinhoon is not just fluent in English but French as well."
어머니뿐만 아니라 아버지도 화가 엄청 나셨었어요.
"It was not only Mother, but Father was also very angry."

8.1.8 은/는커녕 "far from"

The particle 커녕 is commonly used with 은/는, as in 은/는커녕, and it adds the meaning of "far from," "on the contrary," or "anything but." 은/는커녕 is a two-form particle, with 은커녕 being used after a consonant and 는커녕 being used after a vowel.

아버지한테 칭찬은커녕 꾸지람만 들었어요.
"Far from receiving praise, (I) was scolded by (my) father."
이메일은커녕 전화 한 통도 없었어요.
"There was not even a phone call from (her), let alone an e-mail."
제 동생은 영어는커녕 한국어도 아직 잘 모르는데요.
"My younger sibling does not even know Korean yet, let alone English."

SPECIAL PARTICLES II

8.2 Particles of approximation and optionality

8.2.1 쯤 "about"

The particle 쯤 is used to indicate approximation, meaning "about" or "around."

> 보험 회사에서 1,000불쯤 받았어요.
> "(We) received about 1,000 dollars from the insurance company."
> 이따가 한 6시쯤에 오세요, 알았지요?
> "Come around 6 o'clock later, okay?"
> 어젯밤 파티에 한국 사람은 10명쯤 온 것 같아요.
> "It seems that about 10 Koreans showed up at the party last night."

8.2.2 (이)나 "about, or"

The particle (이)나 is a two-form particle, with 이나 being used after a noun that ends in a consonant, and 나 after a noun that ends in a vowel. The particle indicates four different meanings depending on the context in which it is being used: (i) "or something (like that)," (ii) "or," (iii) "as many/much as," and (iv) "about."

First, the particle (이)나 means "or something (like that)" when it is used after a single noun. Consider the following examples:

> 집에 가서 낮잠이나 잘 거예요.
> "(I) will go home and take a nap or something."
> 피자나 시켜서 먹읍시다.
> "(Let's) order and eat pizza or something."

As seen in the previous examples, the particle (이)나 marks the object of the sentence and reduces the importance of the object noun. For instance, the object being chosen may not be the best possible action or item for the given situation, or there may be more choices.

In addition, when the particle is used with certain question words such as 어디 "where," 무엇 "what," and 누구 "who," the particle (이)나 reduces the interrogative meaning of these question words and generalizes their meanings, as in:

어디 "where"	=	어디나 "anywhere"
누구 "who"	=	누구나 "whoever," "anyone," or "everyone"
무엇 "what"	=	무엇이나 "anything" or "whatever"

Second, the particle (이)나 simply means "or" when it is used between two nouns. Consider the following examples:

> 보스턴이나 뉴욕으로 갈 거예요.
> "(We) will head toward Boston or New York."
> 맥주나 와인 주세요.
> "Please give (us) beers or wine."

Third, the particle (이)나 means "as many as," "as much as," or "up to" when it is attached to an expression of quantity. The particle expresses the speaker's surprise that the quantity of the item is more than the speaker's expectation.

> 열 시간이나 운전해서 왔어요.
> "(We) came driving as many as ten hours."
> 여기서는 오렌지 주스가 10불이나 해요.
> "Orange juice here costs as much as ten dollars."

Particles of approximation and optionality

Fourth, the particle (이)나 means "about" or "approximately" when it is used with certain question words, such as 몇 "how many" and 얼마 "how much."

이 티셔츠는 얼마<u>나</u> 줬어요?
"As for this T-shirt, about how much did (you) pay?"
뉴욕에서 런던까지 비행기로 몇 시간<u>이나</u> 걸려요?
"About how many hours does (it) take from New York to London by plane?"

9

Verbs, adjectives, and copula

This chapter discusses the category of words in Korean that undergo inflection: verbs (that denote actions or processes), adjectives (that denote states or quality), and the copula (that denote an equational expression).

9.1 Verbs and adjectives

Verbs normally indicate actions and processes. Adjectives typically indicate states or qualities (e.g., size, weight, quality, quantity, shape, appearance, perception, and emotion). In English, one can distinguish a verb from an adjective either by comparing their meanings or by looking at their structure.

For example, we know "learn" is a verb since its meaning signals an action/process, while "smart" is an adjective since its meaning refers to a state/quality. Moreover, structurally speaking, we know that a verb does not require a copula when it is used as a predicate as in "John learns Korean," but the adjective needs to use the "be" verb, as in "John is smart."

In Korean, however, verbs and adjectives resemble one another in how they inflect and how they function in a sentence. That is, there is no obvious structural difference between verbs and adjectives. In fact adjectives behave like verbs so much that Korean grammarians categorize adjectives as "descriptive verbs." Hence, the only way to distinguish a verb from an adjective is from their meanings.

9.1.1 Stems

Korean verbs and adjectives consist of stems and endings. The stems of verbs and adjectives do not stand by themselves, and they are always conjugated by inflectional endings. These endings indicate various grammatical information and roles (e.g., tense, aspect, speech levels, and so on).

When you search for the meaning of certain verbs or adjectives in your dictionary or textbook word lists, you are most likely to encounter verbs and adjectives with 다 as their endings (e.g., 보다 "see," 믿다 "believe," and 작다 "small"). Remember that stems do not stand alone. Consequently, for a dictionary-entry purpose, Korean verbs and adjectives take a special dictionary form ending ~다. Therefore, finding the stem of a verb or an adjective is simple. The stem is what remains after you remove 다 from the dictionary form.

Dictionary form	Meaning	Stem
주다	"give"	주
배우다	"learn"	배우
가르치다	"teach"	가르치
좋다	"good"	좋
나쁘다	"bad"	나쁘
아름답다	"beautiful"	아름답

9.1.2 Vowel-based and consonant-based stems

Stems of Korean verbs and adjectives are sorted into two types: consonant based and vowel based. An example of the vowel-based stem is 사 of 사다 "buy," and an example of the consonant-based stem is 팔 of 팔다 "sell."

Vowel-based verbs

만지다	"touch"
타다	"ride"

Consonant-based verbs

살다	"live"
앉다	"sit"

Vowel-based adjectives

쓰다	"bitter"
흐리다	"cloudy"

Consonant-based adjectives

가깝다	"near"
많다	"many"

9.2 Endings

The stems of verbs and adjectives are always used with endings, since they cannot stand alone. Korean has many different endings that convey grammatical functions such as tense, aspects, sentence types, conjunctions, speech levels, and so on. The endings can be categorized into two types: pre-final endings and final endings, depending on where they are placed in the verb or adjective.

9.2.1 Pre-final endings

Pre-final endings are inflectional elements that come between the stem and the final ending. They include the honorific suffix ~(으)시, the past tense marker ~었/았, and so on.

Consider the following example:

어제 도서관에서 책을 빌리셨어요?
"Did (you) borrow a book at the library yesterday?"

Notice that the pre-final endings (e.g., 셨 = 시 + 었) appear between 빌리, the stem "borrow," and 어요, "a sentence final ending."

9.2.2 Non-sentence-final endings

There are two types of final endings: one that ends a verb or an adjective but does not end the sentence (non-sentence-final endings), and one that ends both the verb and the sentence (sentence-final endings). Non-sentence-final endings include various clausal conjunctives such as ~고 "and then," ~어/아서 "because," ~으면서 "while," ~지만 "although," ~도록 "in order to," and so on. Consider the following sentence.

숙제를 하고 저녁을 먹어요.
"(I) do homework and then eat dinner."

On one hand, the conjunctive ~고 "and then" does not end the sentence but does end the verb stem 하 "do." On the other hand, the ending ~어요 ends the verb stem 먹 "eat" as well as the sentence.

9.2.3 Sentence-final endings

The typical examples of sentence-final endings are various speech level endings. Korean has six speech levels as shown in the following table. These speech level endings indicate the speaker's interpersonal relationship with the addressees or attitude toward them (e.g., social meanings such as intimacy and formality of the situation).

The formal speech level is the highest among the six, followed by the polite speech level and so on. In addition, each speech level has four endings that indicate the type of sentences: declarative (statement), interrogative (question), imperative (command/request) and propositive (suggestion):

Speech level	Declarative	Interrogative	Imperative	Propositive
(1) Formal	~습니다/ㅂ니다	~습니까/ㅂ니까	~(으)십시오	~(으)십시다
(2) Polite	~어요/아요	~어요/아요	~어요/아요	~어요/아요
(3) Blunt	~(으)오	~(으)오	–	–
(4) Familiar	~네	~나/는가	~게	~세
(5) Intimate	~어/아	~어/아	~어/아	~어/아
(6) Plain	~ㄴ(는)다	~(으)니/냐	~어라/아라	~자

Among these six speech levels, the use of (3) blunt and (4) familiar speech levels have been declining, especially among young generations. Korean Foreign Language (KFL) learners however must be familiar with the formal, polite, intimate, and plain levels, which are still widely used for all Koreans regardless of age.

Let's apply four of the endings to the verb stem 믿 "believe." When saying "Do (you) believe (it)?" one needs to use one of the four interrogative endings (~습니까, ~어요, ~어, or ~냐).

Level	Conjugation	Possible social settings
Formal	믿습니까?	(e.g., in a formal situation)
Polite	믿어요?	(e.g., to an adult colleague)
Intimate	믿어 ?	(e.g., to an adolescent friend)
Plain	믿냐?	(e.g., to a child)

Notice that the verb stem in each speech level and the referential meaning are the same. In addition, different endings render different social meanings, such as the speaker's attitude toward the listener and the formality of the situation. Consequently, choosing the right speech level is critical, and it all depends on whom you talk to. The speech level endings are discussed in detail in Chapter 27.

9.3 The copula 이다

In English, copulas "am," "are," and "is" are used to indicate equational expressions (i.e., something equals something), as in "Daniel is a student" or "Kia is an automobile company." For equational expressions in Korean, the copula 이다 (or 아니다 for negation) is used.

The dictionary form for the Korean copula is 이다. The stem of the copula is 이 (as you take 다 "the dictionary ending" out). With the polite speech level ending, the copula 이다 becomes 이에요 if the preceding noun ends in a consonant, as in 이사벨이에요 "(I) am Isabel." If the preceding noun ends in a vowel, the copula 이다 becomes 예요, as in 앤드류예요 "(I) am Andrew." With

The copula 이다   9.3

another speech level, such as the formal speech level ending, the copula becomes 입니다 (이 + ㅂ니다).

이에요/예요 always follows the noun it expresses. In other words, it cannot be used separately from the noun. For instance, consider the following sentences:

> 바비는 경찰관<u>이에요</u>.
> "As for Bobby, (he) is a police officer."
> 토마스는 과학자<u>예요</u>.
> "As for Thomas, (he) is a scientist."

In the first sentence, notice that 이에요 attaches to 경찰관 (since the last syllable 관 ends in the consonant ㄴ), whereas in the second sentence, 예요 comes after 과학자 (as the last syllable ends in the vowel ㅏ).

The Korean copula for negation is 아니다. The stem of the negative copula 아니 becomes 아니에요 with the polite speech level ending. For negating an equational expression, the subject particle 이/가 is used with 아니에요, as in:

> 유리는 중국 사람<u>이 아니에요</u>.
> "As for Yuri, (she) is not Chinese."
> 지은이는 간호사<u>가 아니에요</u>.
> "As for Jieun, (she) is not a nurse."

Notice that the noun that is being negated has the subject particle 이 (after the noun ending in a consonant) or 가 (after the noun ending in a vowel) (see 5.3.1).

10

Irregular predicates

Korean predicates (for example, verbs and adjectives) are either regular or irregular. The regularity of a predicate depends on whether the stem of the predicate is subject to variation. The predicates whose stems do not change, regardless of the sound of the following suffix, are called regular predicates. On the other hand, those predicates whose stems are subject to variation depending on the sound of the following suffix are called irregular predicates. This chapter introduces seven irregular predicates: ㄷ-irregular, ㅂ-irregular, ㅅ-irregular, ㅎ-irregular, ㅇ-irregular, 르-irregular, and ㄹ-irregular.

10.1 ㄷ-irregular

Some verbs whose stems end with ㄷ are irregular. For instance, consider the verb 묻다. ㄷ of the stem 묻 changes to ㄹ when followed by a suffix that begins with a vowel, for example:

	~습니다	~어/아요
묻다 "ask"	묻습니다	물어요

Here are more examples of ㄷ-irregulars:

걷다 "walk"	걷습니다	걸어요
깨닫다 "realize"	깨닫습니다	깨달아요
듣다 "listen"	듣습니다	들어요
싣다 "load"	싣습니다	실어요

However, not all verbs that end with ㄷ are irregular. The following are examples of regular predicates:

	~습니다	~어/아요
닫다 "close"	닫습니다	닫아요
받다 "receive"	받습니다	받아요
믿다 "believe"	믿습니다	믿어요
얻다 "gain"	얻습니다	얻어요

Notice that these ㄷ-ending verbs conjugate regularly. The stems of these regular predicates do not undergo any change whether the ensuing suffix begins with a vowel or a consonant.

10.2 ㅂ-irregular

The ㅂ-irregular predicates are subject to the following variation: ㅂ changes to either 우 (or 오 for a few predicates) when the ensuing suffix begins with a vowel. For instance, consider how 춥다 "cold" is conjugated: 춥 + 어요 => 추우 + 어요 => 추워요. Here are more examples:

	~습니다	~어/아요
가볍다 "light"	가볍습니다	가벼워요 (가벼우 + 어요)
고맙다 "thankful"	고맙습니다	고마워요 (고마우 + 어요)
그립다 "longed for"	그립습니다	그리워요 (그리우 + 어요)
무섭다 "fearful"	무섭습니다	무서워요 (무서우 + 어요)
밉다 "hateful"	밉습니다	미워요 (미우 + 어요)

Not all predicates that end with ㅂ are irregular. For example, the following are regular ㅂ-ending predicates:

	~습니다	~어/아요
입다 "wear"	입습니다	입어요
잡다 "catch"	잡습니다	잡아요
접다 "fold"	접습니다	접어요
좁다 "narrow"	좁습니다	좁아요
집다 "pick up"	집습니다	집어요

10.3 ㅅ-irregular

Some verbs that end with ㅅ are subject to the following irregular conjugation: ㅅ of the stem gets deleted when followed by a suffix that begins with a vowel. Examples of ㅅ-irregular verbs are as follows:

	~습니다	~어/아요
긋다 "draw"	긋습니다	그어요
낫다 "get better"	낫습니다	나아요
붓다 "swell"	붓습니다	부어요
잇다 "connect"	잇습니다	이어요
짓다 "build"	짓습니다	지어요

Not all predicates that end with ㅅ are irregular. The following are regular ㅅ-ending predicates:

	~습니다	~어/아요
벗다 "take off"	벗습니다	벗어요
빗다 "comb"	빗습니다	빗어요
빼앗다 "take (by force)"	빼앗습니다	빼앗아요
씻다 "wash"	씻습니다	씻어요
웃다 "laugh"	웃습니다	웃어요

IRREGULAR PREDICATES

10.4 ㅎ-irregular

Some predicates that end with ㅎ are subject to the following irregular conjugation: ㅎ of the stem drops out when followed by a suffix that begins with a vowel. A number of color-related adjectives as well as demonstratives fall into this group of irregular predicates:

	~습니다	~어/아요
노랗다 "yellow"	노랗습니다	노래요
파랗다 "blue"	파랗습니다	파래요
하얗다 "white"	하얗습니다	하얘요
그렇다 "be that way"	그렇습니다	그래요
어떻다 "be how"	어떻습니다	어때요

Regular ㅎ-ending predicates include the following:

넣다 "insert"	넣습니다	넣어요
놓다 "place"	놓습니다	놓아요
좋다 "good"	좋습니다	좋아요

10.5 으-irregular

All Korean predicates that end with the vowel 으 are subject to the following irregular conjugation: The vowel 으 of the stem drops out when the following suffix begins with a vowel. For example:

	ㅂ니다	~어/아요
따르다 "follow"	따릅니다	따라요 (따 르 + 아요)
쓰다 "write, use"	씁니다	써요 (쓰 + 어요)
기쁘다 "happy"	기쁩니다	기뻐요 (기 쁘 + 어요)
바쁘다 "busy"	바쁩니다	바빠요 (바 쁘 + 아요)
크다 "big"	큽니다	커요 (크 + 어요)

10.6 르-irregular

Most Korean predicates that end with 르 conjugate irregularly: 르 of the stem drops out and the consonant ㄹ is added, when followed by a suffix that begins either 어 or 아.

For instance, consider the verb 가르다 "divide." Notice that 르 of the stem is deleted but the consonant ㄹ is inserted when followed by polite speech level ending -아요:

	~ㅂ니다	~어/아요
가르다 "divide"	가릅니다	갈라요 (가르 + 아요 => 갈 ㄹ + 아요 => 갈라요)

Here are more examples:

	~ㅂ니다	~어/아요
누르다 "press"	누릅니다	눌러요
오르다 "go up"	오릅니다	올라요
자르다 "cut (off)"	자릅니다	잘라요
다르다 "different"	다릅니다	달라요
빠르다 "fast"	빠릅니다	빨라요

10.7 ㄹ-irregular

All Korean predicates that end in ㄹ are subject to the following irregular conjugation: ㄹ drops out when the following suffix begins with ㄴ, ㅂ, or ㅅ.

	~ㅂ니다	~어/아요	~는	~세요
열다 "open"	엽니다	열어요	여는	여세요
풀다 "untie"	품니다	풀어요	푸는	푸세요
길다 "long"	깁니다	길어요	긴	기세요
달다 "sweet"	답니다	달아요	단	–
멀다 "far"	멉니다	멀어요	먼	–

11
Past tenses

11.1 Past tense marker ~었/았

The stems of verbs and adjectives cannot be used by themselves. Consequently, they are always conjugated with endings. Korean has many different endings that indicate grammatical functions such as tense, aspect, sentence type, conjunction, honorific, and so forth. The endings can be sorted into two types: final endings and pre-final endings, depending on where they are placed in the verb or adjective.

Final endings are various speech level endings, such as the polite level ~어/아요 and the formal level ~습니다. Pre-final endings include inflectional elements that appear between the stem and the final ending. Pre-final endings are the past tense marker ~었/았, the retrospective suffix ~더, the intentional suffix ~겠, the honorific suffix ~(으)시, and so forth. For example, consider the following sentence:

변 교수님이 새 컴퓨터를 사셨어요.
"Professor Byon bought a new computer."

Notice the honorific suffix ~시 and the past tense marker ~었 appear between the stem 사 "buy" and the speech level ending ~어요, as in 사셨어요 (contracted from 사 + 시었 + 어요) "bought."

The past tense marker ~었/았 is a two-form pre-final ending, with ~았 being used after a stem that ends in a bright vowel (e.g., 아 or 오), and ~었 being used after a stem that ends in all other vowels. The following list shows how the marker is placed between the stem and the polite speech level ending ~어/아요.

Verb stem	Past	Polite speech level ending	
먹 "eat"	었	어요	= 먹었어요 "ate"
보 "see"	았	어요	= 봤어요 "saw" (from 보았어요)
이 "copula"	었	어요	= 이었어요 (or 였어요) "was/were"
있 "exist/have"	었	어요	= 있었어요 "existed/had"
작 "small"	았	어요	= 작았어요 "was small"
크 "big"	었	어요	= 컸어요 "was big" (contracted from 크었어요)
하 "do"	았	어요	= 했어요 "did" (irregular)

Note that ~어요 is used after the past tense marker ~았/었. In addition, the conjugation of verb 하다 "do" is irregular in that the stem 하 is changed to 해 when it is combined with the past tense marker, as in 했어요 "did."

In general, the Korean past tense is similar to the English past tense in that they both indicate a past action or situation. However, there is one subtle difference between them. Whereas the English past tense primarily signals something that happened in the past, the Korean past tense indicates not only something that happened in the past but also can signal whether the action or event is complete or not. For example, consider the following sentences:

운동화를 신었어요.
"(I) wore sneakers" or

Double past tense marker ~었었/았었

"(I) am wearing sneakers" (as a result of the complete action of wearing sneakers).
우리 결혼했어요.
"We are married" or "We got married."
티셔츠를 입었어요.
"(I) wore a T-shirt" or "(I) am wearing a T-shirt."
우리 어머니는 늙으셨어요.
"As for my mother, (she) is old" or "As for my mother, (she) became older."

Notice that the examples all have two interpretations. The first interpretation simply expresses something that occurred in the past. The second interpretation indicates the completion of an action or event. For example, one may be wearing a coat, since the action of putting on the coat is complete.

As for some verbs, such as 살찌다 "gain weight," 화나다 "get angry," 닮다 "resemble," and 생기다 "be formed," ~었/았 primarily indicates the present state (as a result of the complete action or event). For example:

요새 운동도 안 하고 많이 먹어서 살쪘어요.
"(He) is fat/gained weight, since (he) does not exercise but eats a lot recently."
왜 화났어요?
"Why are (you) angry?"
동생이 형을 많이 닮았어요.
"The younger brother resembles (his) older brother."
정말 잘생겼어요.
"(He) is really good looking."

11.2 Double past tense marker ~었었/았었

In Korean, one can change a past tense sentence into a double-past tense sentence by adding 었 to the existing past tense marker ~았/었.

Verb stem	Past + past		Polite speech level ending	
먹 "eat"	었	었	어요	= 먹었었어요 "ate (long before)"
보 "see"	았	었	어요	= 봤었어요 "saw (long before)"
이 "copula"	었	었	어요	= 이었었어요 (or 였었어요) "was/were"
있 "exist/have"	었	었	어요	= 있었었어요 "existed/had (long before)"
작 "small"	았	었	어요	= 작았었어요 "was small (long before)"
크 "big"	었	었	어요	= 컸었어요 "was big (long before)"
하 "do"	았	었	어요	= 했었어요 "did (long before)"

The double past tense marker ~았었/었었 makes the past action or situation more remote than the regular past tense marker ~았/었 does. The double past tense marker signals that the past event is no longer relevant to the present activity or situation. In addition, it denotes that the past action or situation is totally complete. For instance, consider the following sentences:

결혼 반지를 꼈어요.
"(I) wore a wedding ring" or "(I) am wearing a wedding ring."
결혼 반지를 꼈었어요.
"(I) wore a wedding ring (no longer wear it)" or "(I) used to wear a wedding ring."
구두를 신었어요.
"(I) wore shoes" or "(I) am wearing shoes."
구두를 신었었어요.
"(I) wore shoes" or "(I) used to wear shoes."
보름달이 떴어요.
"The full moon came up" or "The full moon is up."

PAST TENSES

보름달이 떴었어요.
"The full moon was up (back then)."
집에 왔어요.
"(I) came home" or "(I) am home."
집에 왔었어요.
"(I) came home" or "(I) was home (at that time and no longer here)."
한국어를 전공했어요.
"(I) majored in Korean studies."
한국학을 전공했었어요.
"(I) used to major in Korean studies."

11.3 The retrospective suffix ~더

Besides the past tense marker ~었/았, Korean has another pre-final ending that is used to signal the past: the retrospective suffix ~더. The suffix ~더 is used in place of or in addition to the past tense ~었/았 to indicate a speaker's past observation or experience.

Korean has several grammatical forms that incorporate the suffix ~더. For instance, consider the sentence ending ~더라구(요) and clausal conjunctive ~더니/었더니.

The sentence ending ~더라구(요) is constructed from the suffix 더, the statement suffix 라, the quotation particle 구 (the informal counterpart of 고), and the politeness marker 요. The ending is mainly used in informal conversation, and it is used to report what a speaker has observed or experienced. The ending also highlights the authenticity of the speaker's observation or experience and conveys meanings such as "I am telling you" or "you know."

그 영화가 참 재미있더라구요.
"That movie was pretty interesting (you know)."
그 카페 커피가 정말 맛있더라구요.
"The coffee of that café was really tasty (you know)."
요리를 꽤 잘 하시더라구요.
"(She) was quite good at cooking (you know)."
맥주를 정말 많이 잘 마시더라구요.
"(He) really drank beer a lot."

Meanwhile, the clausal conjunctive ~더니 is made of the suffix 더 and the suffix 니. It is used when the speaker recollects what he/she has directly observed or experienced, as shown here:

유명해지더니 우리를 모른 체했어요.
"Since (he) became famous, (he) pretended that (he) does not know us."
매일 꾸준히 운동을 하더니 많이 날씬해졌네요.
"Since (you) have exercised every day steadily, (now I see that you) became much slimmer."
지난 주는 날씨가 엄청 춥더니, 이번 주는 많이 따뜻해졌네요.
"As for last week, the weather was terribly cold, but as for this week, (it) has become much warmer."
학교 도서관에 갔더니 모두 열심히 공부하고 있었어요.
"(I) went to the school library, and everyone was studying hard."
공부를 열심히 했더니 성적이 많이 올랐어요.
"Since (I) studied hard, (my) grades went up significantly."

12

Future tenses and aspect

12.1 Future tenses

12.1.1 ~(으)ㄹ 거 "will"

In English, the future tense is marked by "will" or the "be going to" pattern, as in "I will go to Seoul," or "He is going to study Korean." In Korean, many forms involving ~(으)ㄹ "future/prospective modifier" and 겠 "will/conjecture" are used to talk about the future. Among these forms, the most common way to express a future event is to use the probable future marker ~(으)ㄹ 거.

The ~(으)ㄹ 거 form is built on the prospective modifier ~(으)ㄹ and the bound noun 거, which is a colloquial form of 것 "thing" or "fact." The following shows how the marker is placed between the stem and different speech level endings.

볼 겁니다	(보 + ㄹ 거 + ㅂ니다)	"will see" (formal speech level)
볼 거예요	(보 + ㄹ 거 + 예요)	"will see" (polite speech level)
볼 거야	(보 + ㄹ 거 + 야)	"will see" (intimate speech level)
볼 거다	(보 + ㄹ 거 + 다)	"will see" (plain speech level)
먹을 겁니다	(먹 + 을 거 + ㅂ니다)	"will eat" (formal speech level)
먹을 거예요	(먹 + 을 거 + 예요)	"will eat" (polite speech level)
먹을 거야	(먹 + 을 거 + 야)	"will eat" (intimate speech level)
먹을 거다	(먹 + 을 거 + 다)	"will eat" (plain speech level)

One must remember however that this ending does not express "future" but "probable future." In Korean, an event that will surely happen in the future is expressed by the present tense with a time adverb. Consider the following three sentences:

서울에 가요.
"(I) go to Seoul."
내일 서울에 가요.
"(I will) go to Seoul tomorrow."
내일 서울에 <u>갈 거예요</u>.
"(I) will (probably) go to Seoul tomorrow."

Notice that the first and the second sentences have the present tense. However, the second sentence differs from the first sentence in that it indicates the future event with the time adverb 내일 "tomorrow." The third sentence uses the probable future ending ~(으) ㄹ 거예요. Notice that the possibility that the future event (i.e., going to Seoul) will occur in the future is less certain in the third sentence when compared to the second sentence. In other words, ~(으)ㄹ 거예요 indicates "a probable future event" rather than "a definite future event."

The English "will" can sometimes express a speaker's intention in addition to the future event, as in "I will practice singing." In a similar manner, ~(으)ㄹ 거 can also signal the intention of the

FUTURE TENSES AND ASPECT   12.1

speaker in addition to the future probability depending on the context. This is particularly true when the subject of the sentence is the first person. Consider the following examples:

서울에서 공부할 때 한국인 친구를 많이 <u>사귈 거예요</u>.
"(I) will make many Korean friends while studying in Seoul."
취직하면 오토바이를 꼭 <u>살 거예요</u>.
"Surely, (I) will buy a motorcycle, if (I) get a job."

When the subject is not the first or second person, the ~(으)ㄹ 거예요 ending can indicate the speaker's conjecture. Consider the following examples:

소포가 이번 주 금요일쯤 <u>도착할 거예요</u>.
"(I guess that) the package may arrive (here) this week on Friday."
동경 물가가 꽤 <u>비쌀 거예요</u>.
"(I guess) the cost of living in Tokyo may be fairly high."
부인이 아마 중국 사<u>람일 거예요</u>.
"(I guess that his) wife is probably Chinese."
도착지가 로<u>마일 거예요</u>.
"(I guess that) the destination is Rome."

12.1.2 ~(으)ㄹ래 "will (intend)"

The ~(으)ㄹ래 ending denotes the speaker's intention or immediate desire, and its equivalents in English are "intend to" or "will." The politeness marker 요 can be added to make this ending polite, as in ~(으)ㄹ래요. The ~(으)ㄹ래요 ending is a three-form ending, with ~을래요 (after a stem that ends in a consonant, as in 먹을래요), ~ㄹ래요 (after a stem that ends in a vowel, as in 갈래요), and ~래요 (for a ㄹ-irregular stem, as in 만들래요).

There are a few things to remember when using ~(으)ㄹ래요. First, the ending is commonly used in colloquial settings. Second, since this ending conveys one's intention, the ending is used only with verbs. Third, the ~(으)ㄹ래요 ending is only used for first person and second person subjects. Consider the following conversation:

A: 뭐 <u>마실래요</u>?
 "What will (you) drink?"
B: 아메리카노 한 잔 <u>시킬래요</u>.
 "(I) will order a cup of Americano." (intention)

In this example, the ~(으)ㄹ래요 ending is used in the second person question (for the first sentence) and the first person statement (in the second sentence). The ~(으)ㄹ래요 ending cannot be used for the third person subject, since one cannot speak for the third person's intentions. Consequently, a sentence like 제 남동생은 오렌지 주스 마실래요 "My younger brother will (intend to) drink orange juice" is ungrammatical in Korean.

The meaning of the ~(으)ㄹ래요 ending is similar to that of the ~(으)ㄹ 거예요 ending in that both signal the intention of the first person speaker, as shown in the following examples:

스타벅스에서 <u>기다릴래요</u>.
"(I) will wait for (her) at Starbucks."
스타벅스에서 <u>기다릴 거예요</u>.
"(I) will (probably) wait for (her) at Starbucks."

However, note that the usage of ~(으)ㄹ 거예요 is much wider than that of ~(으)ㄹ래요 in that ~(으)ㄹ 거예요 can be used for the third person subject as well. When the subject is not the first or second person, ~(으)ㄹ 거예요 indicates the speaker's supposition.

12.1.3 ~(으)ㄹ게 "will (promise)"

The ~(으)ㄹ게 ending indicates the speaker's promise or willingness to do something for the listener's interest. It is a three-form ending, with ~을게 (after a stem that ends in a consonant, as

Future tenses

in 먹을게), ~ㄹ게 (after a stem that ends in a vowel, as in 갈게), and ~게 (for ㄹ-irregular verbs, as in 살게 or 만들게). Meanwhile, to present this ending in the polite speech level, you can add the politeness marker 요, as in ~(으)ㄹ게요.

The ~(으)ㄹ게요 ending is used only for the first person subject and only with verbs. Consider the following sentences:

    A: 몇 시에 로비에 내려올 거예요?
         "What time will (you) come down to the lobby?"
    B: 오전 8시까지 <u>갈게요</u>.
         "(I) will go (there) by 8 a.m." (promise)

Notice that the speaker A asks what time B will come to the lobby. Speaker B's reply with (으)ㄹ게요 conveys a sense of promise or reassurance of "arriving at the library by 8 a.m." for speaker A's sake.

The ~(으)ㄹ게요 ending and the ~(으)ㄹ래요 ending seem to resemble each other since they both can be translated as "will" in English. However, there are two clear differences. First, whereas ~(으)ㄹ래요 can be used to ask a question in the second person, ~(으)ㄹ게요 cannot. This is because the ~(으)ㄹ게요 ending is used only for the first person subject.

    몇 시에 공항에 <u>갈래요</u>?
    "What time will (you) go to the airport?" (intention)
    (X) 몇 시에 공항에 <u>갈게요</u>?
    "What time will (you) go to the airport?" (promise)

The second difference is that whereas ~(으)ㄹ래요 indicates the speaker's intention, ~(으)ㄹ게요 carries the speaker's sense of promise. Here are some examples for comparison:

    음료수는 제가 <u>가져갈래요</u>.
    "As for the drink, (I) will bring (it)." (intention)
    음료수는 제가 <u>가져갈게요</u>.
    "As for the drink, (I) will bring (it)." (promise)

As ~(으)ㄹ게요 indicates a sense of promise, it is often used when the speaker volunteers to do something.

    디저트는 제가 <u>살래요</u>.
    "As for the dessert, I will buy (it)." (intention)
    디저트는 제가 <u>살게요</u>.
    "As for the dessert, I will buy (it)." (volunteer/promise)

12.1.4 ~겠 "will (intend), conjecture"

The suffix ~겠 is a pre-final ending, and it is used to indicate two things. First, when the subject of the predicate is the first or second person, the suffix ~겠 expresses the speaker's intention or asks for the listener's intention, and it corresponds to "will" in English. It is used for first person statements and second person questions.

    열심히 일하<u>겠</u>습니다.
    "(I) will work hard."
    내일 오후에 다시 오<u>겠</u>습니다.
    "(I) will come again tomorrow afternoon."
    신용 카드로 지불하시<u>겠</u>습니까?
    "Will (you) pay by a credit card?"
    어디로 가시<u>겠</u>습니까?
    "Where will (you) go?"

Notice that the meaning of the suffix ~겠 is similar to ~(으)ㄹ래요 "will." However, whereas ~(으)ㄹ래요 is normally used in colloquial situations, the suffix ~겠 is used for more formal situations.

FUTURE TENSES AND ASPECT   12.2

Second, when the subject of the predicate is not either the first or second person (i.e., the third person or entity), the suffix ~겠 indicates the speaker's conjecture or asks the listener's idea regarding the topic in question. It is corresponding to "I guess/think" (for the first person statement) or "do you think that . . ." (for the second person question) in English.

내일 시합이 힘들겠어요.
"(I guess that) tomorrow's game will be tough."
다리가 아팠겠어요.
"(I guess that) your legs were sore."
기름 값이 쌌겠어요?
"Do (you) think that the price of oil was cheap?"

The suffix ~겠 is used in formal or broadcasting contexts such as weather forecasts and news reports. Consider the following examples:

오늘 밤부터 눈이 오겠습니다.
"(I guess that) snow will fall (starting) from tonight."
주말은 날씨가 흐리겠습니다.
"(I guess that) as for the weekend, the weather will be cloudy."

12.2 Continuous tense/aspect

12.2.1 ~고 있다

The progressive form is used to express an action in progress. The English progressive form takes a copula ("am," "is," and "are") and a verb that ends with "~ing," as in "John is sleeping." The Korean progressive form takes ~고 있다. For instance, consider the following sentences:

피자를 먹고 있어요.
"(They) are eating pizza."
영화를 보고 있어요.
"(We) are watching a movie."

To express a past action that was in progress, the past tense marker ~었/았 is added to the stem of 있다 as in 책을 읽고 있었어요 "(I) was reading a book." Here are more examples:

노래를 부르고 있었어요.
"(We) were singing a song."
라디오를 듣고 있었어요.
"(I) was listening to the radio."

To express respect to the subject, the verb 계시다 (~고 계세요) is used instead of 있다 (~고 있어요). Here are some examples:

사장님이 손님을 만나고 계세요.
"The president is meeting the guest."
어머니가 케이크를 만들고 계세요.
"Mother is making a cake."
아직도 기다리고 있습니다.
"(We) are still waiting."
이번 학기에 한국어 수업을 듣고 있어요.
"(I) am taking a Korean language course this semester."

12.2.2 ~어/아 있다

Whereas ~고 있다 is used to talk about an action in progress, ~어/아 있다 is mainly used with intransitive verbs (that do not take an object, such as 가다 "go" and 넘어지다 "fall") to indicate

Continuous tense/aspect 12.2

a continuous state that results from a completed action. For instance, compare the following three examples:

> 소파에 앉아요.
> "(He) sits on the couch."
> 소파에 앉고 있어요.
> "(He) is sitting on the couch."
> 소파에 앉아 있어요.
> "(He) is seated on the couch."

The first sentence simply states what the subject does. The second sentence indicates the progressive action of the main verb. However, ~어/아 있다 in the third sentence expresses that the state (seated) resulting from the main verb (sit) continues to exist. Here are more examples:

> 창문이 열려요.
> "The window opens."
> 창문이 열리고 있어요.
> "The window is being opened."
> 창문이 열려 있어요.
> "The window is open."

The first sentence simply indicates that the door opens. The second sentence indicates the progressive action. The third sentence, however, indicates the continuing state of "being open," brought about after the completion of or by the main verb 열리다 "to be opened."

> A: 문이 열려 있네요. 안 닫고 나갔어요?
> "The door is open. Did (you) go out without closing (it)?"
> B: 미안해요. 아침에 급히 나오느라 그냥 나갔나 봐요.
> "Sorry. (I) guess that (I) went out without closing (it) because (I) was rushing."

> 지금 호텔 로비에 와 있어요.
> "(They) are in the hotel lobby (as a result of coming here)."
> 지난 달부터 하와이 이모 집에 가 있어요.
> "(She) has been in (her) aunt's house in Hawaii since last month (as a result of going there)."
> 피곤해서 소파에 누워 있어요.
> "(I) am still lying down on the couch since (I) am tired."
> 문 옆에 아직도 서 있어요.
> "(They) are still standing next to the door."
> 봄방학이라 학교 정문이 닫혀 있어요.
> "Since it is spring break, the school's main gate is closed."
> 여행 가방 안에 여권하고 서류가 들어 있어요.
> "(My) passport and documents are inside of the suitcase."

Meanwhile, a limited number of verbs involved with "wearing" do not take the ~어/아 있다 pattern but take the ~고 있다 pattern to indicate the resultant state. For instance, "(I) am wearing socks" is 양말을 신고 있어요 not 양말을 신어 있어요.

> 장갑을 끼고 있어요.
> "(I) am wearing gloves."
> 목걸이를 매고 있어요.
> "(I) am wearing a necklace."
> 스웨터를 입고 있어요.
> "(I) am wearing a sweater."
> 선글라스를 쓰고 있어요.
> "(I) am wearing sunglasses."

13

Auxiliary verbs I

An auxiliary verb (also called a "helping verb") combines with a main verb to indicate distinctions of tense, aspect, mood, or voice. For instance, English auxiliary verbs include "can," "have," "may," "must," "shall," and "will," since they combine with a main verb, as in "You must get there on time."

Korean has a number of auxiliary verbs as well, but there are a few things to note about Korean auxiliary verbs. First, unlike English auxiliary verbs that always precede a main verb, Korean auxiliary verbs always appear after the main verb (or adjective for limited auxiliary verbs). Second, the main verb is always used with the infinitive form ~어/아 (or with endings like ~고, ~을까, ~는/은가, ~게, and ~어/아야). Third, Korean auxiliary verbs are in fact all regular verbs. However, when these verbs are used as auxiliary verbs, they express different meanings, as shown in the following examples:

Regular verbs	Auxiliary verbs
가다 "go"	~어/아 가다 "continue to"
오다 "come"	~어/아 오다 "continue to"
내다 "produce"	~어/아 내다 "do all the way/completely"
놓다 "put down"	~어/아 놓다 "do for later"
대다 "put [X] over on [Y]"	~어/아 대다 "do continuously"
버리다 "throw away"	~어/아 버리다 "end up doing/do completely"
보다 "see"	~어/아 보다 "try (doing something)"
보이다 "be seen"	~어/아 보이다 "appear to be"
빠지다 "fall"	~어/아 빠지다 "fall into a negative state"
주다 "give"	~어/아 주다 "do for"
치우다 "tidy up"	~어/아 치우다 "do hurriedly"
하다 "do"	~어/아 하다 "be in the state of"
지다 "bear/owe"	~어/아 지다 "become"

This chapter introduces the auxiliary verbs that occur after ~어/아. The auxiliary verbs that occur after other endings, such as ~고, ~을까, ~는/은가, and so forth, are discussed in the next chapter.

13.1 ~어/아 가다 /오다 "continue to"

Korean has two motion verbs: 가다 "go" and 오다 "come." When these motion verbs are used as auxiliary verbs, both indicate that an action of the main verb is carried out continually. Since 가다 denotes the motion away from the speaker, ~어/아 가다 is used to express a continuous action that goes into the future.

밤이 깊어 가요.
"The night advances."
영화 시간이 다 끝나 가요.
"(The) movie time runs out."

~어/아 놓다 (or 두다) "do for later"   **13.3**

졸업 파티의 분위기가 무르익어 가고 있었어요.
"The festive mood of the graduation party was heightening."

On the other hand, 오다 signifies the motion toward the speaker. Therefore ~어/아 오다 is used to express a continuous action that comes toward the present.

지금까지 주로 한국 역사만 연구해 왔어요.
"Until now, (I) have mainly researched on Korean history."
지난 15년 동안 한국어만을 가르쳐 왔어요.
"(I) have taught the Korean language only for the last 15 years."
김 박사님이 병원을 잘 운영해 오셨어요.
"Dr. Kim has managed the hospital well."
지난 학기부터 한국어를 공부해 왔어요.
"(I) have been studying Korean since last semester."
7살 때부터 피아노를 배워 왔어요.
"(I) have learned piano since the age of 7."
어렸을 때부터 교회를 쭉 다녀 왔어요.
"Since (I) was young, (I) have attended church."

13.2 ~어/아 내다 "do all the way (to the very end)"

The verb 내다 means "produce/put forth" as in 힘을 내세요 "put forth strength" or 모두 의견을 냈어요 "Everyone put forth (his/her) opinion." However, the auxiliary verb ~어/아 내다 denotes "do all the way (to the very end)." It is used to indicate that although a certain task or action is burdensome or difficult, he/she completes the action to the very end (or does it all the way). Compare the following two examples:

2년 만에 책을 썼어요.
"(I) wrote the book within two years."
2년 만에 책을 써 냈어요.
"(I) wrote the book (to the very end) within two years."

Notice that the first sentence simply indicates that the speaker finished writing the book in two years. On the other hand, the second sentence with ~어/아 내다 denotes that although writing the book within two years was a difficult task, the speaker did it anyway. Here are more examples:

결국 비밀번호를 알아 냈어요.
"Finally, (I) found out the secret code."
한 달안에 운전면허를 따 냈어요.
"(He) got a driver's license within a month."
환불을 받아 냅시다!
"(Let's) get a refund!"
고생하더니 결국 만들어 냈네요.
"(You) really worked hard for it, and you finally invented it!"
3년간의 연구를 통하여 치료제를 개발해 냈습니다.
"After three years of research, (we) developed the drug."
꼭 진실을 밝혀 내겠습니다.
"By all means, (we) will reveal the truth."

13.3 ~어/아 놓다 (or 두다) "do for later"

The verb 놓다 means "release/place/put down," as in 손잡이를 놓으세요 "Let the handle go/loose," or 열쇠를 어디에 놓으셨어요? "Where have (you) left the key?"

AUXILIARY VERBS I　　　　　　　　　　　　　　　　　　　　　　　　　　**13.4**

However, the auxiliary verb ~어/아 놓다 expresses two things. First, ~어/아 놓다 is used to indicate the continuation of a certain action or state after the completion of the action or state. For instance, compare the following sentences:

창문을 <u>열었어요</u>.
"(I) opened the window."
창문을 <u>열어 놓았어요</u>.
"(I) opened the window (and it is still open)."

Notice that the action of the main verb 열다 "open" is completed in both sentences, since they are marked by the past tense. However, while the first sentence simply indicates the past action (opened the window), the second sentence with the auxiliary verb ~어/아 놓다 signals the continuation of the completed action (i.e., the door continues to be opened). Here are more examples:

부엌에 불을 <u>켜 놓았어요</u>.
"(I) left a light on in the kitchen (and it is still on)."
전화기를 <u>꺼 놓았어요</u>.
"(I) turned off the cell phone (and it is off)."
문을 <u>잠가 놓았어요</u>.
"(I) locked the door (and it is still locked)."

Second, ~어/아 놓다 takes on the meaning of "doing something for later (future use)." Compare the following two sentences:

세일이 끝나기 전에 많이 <u>샀어요</u>.
"(I) bought a lot of (them) before the sale ends."
세일이 끝나기 전에 많이 <u>사 놓았어요</u>.
"(I) bought a lot of (them for later), before the sale ends."

Notice that the first sentence simply indicates the past action, 샀어요 "bought." However, the auxiliary verb ~어/아 놓다 in the second sentence expresses that the past action (e.g., buying) was done for later. Here are more examples:

물을 많이 <u>마셔 놓으세요</u>.
"Drink a lot of water (for later)."
양념을 <u>만들어 놓을 거예요</u>.
"(I) will make seasoning (for later)."
과일을 좀 <u>사 놓을게요</u>.
"(I) will buy some fruits (for later)."

Alternatively, the verb 두다 "place/keep" can be used instead of 놓다, as shown in the following examples:

필요한 서류를 <u>준비해 두었어요/놓았어요</u>.
"(We) prepared the necessary documents (and they are still there, for later)."
부엌을 <u>청소해 두었어요/놓았어요</u>.
"(I) cleaned the kitchen (for later, and it is clean)."
여름 방학 동안 아르바이트를 해서 돈을 좀 <u>모아 둘 거예요/ 놓을 거예요</u>.
"(I) will work part time and save some money during summer break (for later)."

13.4　~어/아 대다 "do continuously"

The verb 대다 means "put" or "touch" as in 오른손을 가슴에 대세요 "Put (your) right hand to your chest." However, the auxiliary verb ~어/아 대다 is used to express repeated or continued action that is considered tiresome or negative. For instance, compare the following sentences:

레고를 사달라고 계속 <u>졸랐어요</u>.
"(He) nagged (me) to buy (him) LEGOS."

레고를 사달라고 계속 <u>졸라 댔어요</u>.
"(He) kept nagging (me) to buy (him) LEGOS."

Whereas the first sentence simply indicates the past action, the second sentence with the auxiliary verb ~어/아 대다 indicates a repeated action that is considered negative. Here are more examples:

아기가 하루 종일 <u>울어 대요</u>.
"The baby cries all day long."
밤새 코를 <u>골아 대서</u> 도저히 잠을 잘 수 없었어요.
"(I) could not sleep at all because (he) snored all night long."

13.5 ~어/아 버리다 "end up doing"

The verb 버리다 means "throw away," as in 쓰레기를 이 곳에 버리세요 "Please throw away the garbage here." However, the auxiliary verb ~어/아 버리다 is used to indicate the terminality or completion of an action denoted by the main verb. It can be translated as "finish up/end up doing" or "do completely." For instance, compare the following sentences:

밥 한 그릇을 금방 다 <u>먹었어요</u>.
"(He) ate the whole bowl quickly."
밥 한 그릇을 금방 다 <u>먹어 버렸어요</u>.
"(He) ended up eating the whole bowl quickly."

Note that the first sentence simply expresses the past action (i.e., eating). However, the second sentence with the auxiliary verb ~어/아 버리다 signals the terminality of the action. Here are more examples:

케이블 요금이 너무 비싸서 <u>끊어 버렸어요</u>.
"(We) cancelled the cable service because the bill was too high."
콘서트가 한 시간만에 <u>끝나 버려서</u> 아쉬웠어요.
"(I) was sorry because the concert ended up finishing within an hour."
제가 피자를 다 <u>먹어 버렸어요</u>.
"I finished eating the entire pizza."
화가 나서 그냥 인사도 받지 않고 <u>나와 버렸어요</u>.
"Because (I) was mad, (I) just came out without receiving a greeting."
얼마 남지 않았는데 오늘 다 <u>끝내 버립시다</u>.
"There is not a lot left, so (let's) finish doing (them) all today."
날씨도 덥고 해서 머리를 짧게 <u>잘라 버렸어요</u>.
"The weather is also hot, so (I) cut my hair short."
좋아한다고 <u>고백해 버렸어요</u>.
"(I) ended up confessing that (I) like her."

13.6 ~어/아 보다 "try (doing something)"

When the verb 보다 "see" is used as an auxiliary verb, it is used to denote "try (doing something)/experience." It is used when a speaker tries doing some action at least once so that he/she can explore the results.

그리스에 <u>가 봤어요</u>.
"(I) have been to Greece. (lit. I have an experience of going to Greece)"
이거 한 번 <u>먹어 보세요</u>.
"Try this (food)."
좀 더 큰 사이즈로 <u>입어 보실래요</u>?
"Would (you) like to try a bigger size?"

AUXILIARY VERBS I

같이 <u>배워 봅시다</u>.
"(Let's) try learning (it) together."
의사하고 <u>상의해 봤어요</u>?
"Have (you) tried to discuss (this) with a doctor?"
서울에 가면 전통차를 <u>마셔 볼 거예요</u>.
"When (I) get to Seoul, (I) will try drinking traditional Korean tea."

14

Auxiliary verbs II

14.1 ~어/아 보이다 "appear to be"

The verb 보이다 means "come in sight," as in 나무 사이로 바다가 <u>보여요</u> "The sea was seen through the trees." As an auxiliary verb, ~어/아 보이다 is used when the speaker expresses his/her opinion regarding the appearance of something. It is only used with adjectives and corresponds to "(it) appears to be" in English.

> 시계가 <u>비싸 보여요</u>.
> "(Your) watch appears to be expensive."
> 커피가 <u>맛있어 보이네요</u>.
> "The coffee appears to be delicious."
> 기분이 <u>좋아 보였어요</u>.
> "(Her) mood appeared to be good."
> 어제 많이 <u>피곤해 보였어요</u>.
> "(He) appeared to be exhausted yesterday."

14.2 ~어/아 빠지다 "fall into a negative state"

The verb 빠지다 means "fall," as in 물에 빠졌어요 "(He) fell into the water." The auxiliary verb, ~어/아 빠지다 is often used with an adjective to indicate a worsening state of affairs denoted by the adjective. It usually carries a negative connotation, as shown in the following examples:

> 집이 <u>낡아 빠져서</u> 수리할 데가 많아요.
> "The house is extremely old, and there are many places to repair."
> 걔네들 정말 <u>게을러 빠졌어요</u>.
> "Those kids are really lazy."
> 요새 한국에 수입 외제차가 <u>흔해 빠졌어요</u>.
> "There are so many imported foreign cars in Korea recently."

14.3 ~어/아 주다 "do for"

The verb 주다 means "give," as in 매달 여동생한테 용돈을 <u>줘요</u> "(I) give pocket money to (my) younger sister every month." However, as an auxiliary verb, ~어/아 주다 means "do something as a favor (for someone)." Compare the following two sentences:

> 소피아가 제 생일 파티에 <u>왔어요</u>.
> "Sofia came to my birthday party."
> 소피아가 제 생일 파티에 <u>와 줬어요</u>.
> "Sofia came to my birthday party (for me)."

AUXILIARY VERBS II   14.5

Notice that the first sentence simply expresses that Sofia came to the party. On the other hand, the second sentence means that Sofia came to the party for the benefit of the speaker (or somebody). Here are more examples:

제가 문 <u>열어 줄게요</u>.
"I will open the door (for you)."
아빠가 명품 가방을 <u>사 주실 거예요</u>.
"(My) dad will buy (me) a luxury bag."
엄마가 맛있는 한국 음식을 <u>만들어 주셨어요</u>.
"(My) mom made delicious Korean food (for me)."

14.4 ~어/아 치우다 "do hurriedly"

The verb 치우다 means "clean (up/out)," as in 어제 방을 깨끗히 치웠어요 "(I) cleaned up (my) room yesterday." The auxiliary verb ~어/아 치우다 is used to express doing something completely and hurriedly. Its meaning is similar to ~어/아 버리다 "end up doing" but ~어/아 치우다 has an additional meaning of doing hurriedly. In addition, its usage is less common than that of ~어/아 버리다.

언제 다 벌써 <u>먹어 치웠냐</u>?
"When did (you) end up eating them all already?"
지난 주에 차하고 집에 있는 가구까지 다 <u>팔아 치웠어요</u>.
"(We) sold (our) car and even all the furniture at home last week."
한국어 숙제는 오늘 아침에 다 <u>해 치웠다</u>.
"As for the Korean homework, (I) did (it) all this morning."
빨리 담당자를 <u>갈아 치우도록</u> 하세요.
"Do replace the person in charge in haste."
너무 배가 고파서 피자 한 판을 10분 안에 <u>먹어 치웠다</u>.
"(I) was so hungry that (I) finished eating the entire pizza within 10 minutes."
남은 일을 되도록 빨리 <u>해 치웁시다</u>.
"(Let's) finish doing the work that remains."

14.5 ~어/아하다 "be in the state of"

The aforementioned auxiliary verbs are all mainly used with verbs. However, Korean has a limited number of auxiliary verbs, such as ~어/아하다 and ~어/아지다, that are used primarily with adjectives. In English, one can state how another person feels using emotion- or sense-related adjectives, such as "sad," "happy," and "cold." For instance, it is grammatically correct to say a sentence like "Susan is sad" or "Chris is cold." However, in Korean, one cannot use adjectives to express how a third person or people feel or think. Since Korean emotive or sensory adjectives denote unobservable internal feelings, a speaker cannot speak for how other people feel or think. Consequently, the sentence like 수잔이 추워요 "Susan is cold" is grammatically wrong.

In order to speak for a third person's or other people's feelings or emotions, one has to modify an emotive or sensory adjective into a verb form, using the auxiliary verb construction ~어/아하다, as shown in the following examples:

Adjectives	Adjective stem + 어/아하다
가엽다 "pitiful"	가여워하다 (가여우 + 어하다) "pity"
괴롭다 "painful"	괴로워하다 "suffer (from)"
귀엽다 "cute"	귀여워하다 "hold (a person) dear"
기쁘다 "glad"	기뻐하다 "rejoice"
덥다 "hot"	더워하다 "feel hot"
무섭다 "scary"	무서워하다 "fear"

~어/아지다 "become"

Adjectives	Adjective stem + 어/아하다
밉다 "detestable"	미워하다 "hate"
부럽다 "enviable"	부러워하다 "envy"
슬프다 "sad"	슬퍼하다 "grieve"
싫다 "unpleasant"	싫어하다 "dislike"
싶다 "desirous"	싶어하다 "want"
좋다 "good"	좋아하다 "like"
피곤하다 "tired"	피곤해하다 "feel tired"
춥다 "cold"	추워하다 "feel cold"

Notice that 하다 as a regular verb means "do." However, as an auxiliary verb ~어/아하다 denotes "be in the state." For instance, compare the following three sentences:

> 제가 <u>무서워요</u>.
> "I am scared."
> 예원 씨, <u>무서워요</u>?
> "Yewon, are (you) scared?"
> 경찬 씨가 <u>무서워해요</u>.
> "Kyongchan fears (it)."

Notice that when the subject of the sentence is the third person, the verb 무서워하다 "fear" is used instead of the adjective 무섭다 "be scared."

When speaking of another person's emotion or feeling in the past tense, one can use an adjective (without using the 어/아하다 construction). This is because the speaker could have information about the third person's internal feeling. Consider the following examples:

> (X) 종규는 기뻐요.
> "As for Jongkyu, (he) is glad."
> (O) 종규는 <u>기뻐해요</u>.
> "As for Jongkyu, (he) rejoices."
> (O) 종규는 <u>기뻤어요</u>.
> "As for Jongkyu, (he) was glad."
> (O) 종규는 <u>기뻐했어요</u>.
> "As for Jongkyu, (he) rejoiced."

Notice that 기뻤어요 as well as 기뻐했어요 are both acceptable, since both express the third person's feeling in the past tense.

Meanwhile, note that unlike other auxiliary verb compounding structures that normally leave a space between the main verb and the auxiliary verb, as in 열어 놓다 "open (for later)," there is no space between the main adjective and 하다 (e.g., 기뻐해요 not 기뻐 해요). This is simply a Korean spelling convention.

14.6 ~어/아지다 "become"

The verb 지다 means "bear/owe," as shown in the following examples:

> 김 부장님이 책임을 <u>지시고</u> 물러나셨습니다.
> "Manager Kim took all the responsibility and left office."
> 그 사람한테 얼마나 빚을 <u>졌어요</u>?
> "How much money do (you) owe (him)?"
> 이 일에 대해서 모든 책임을 <u>지세요</u>.
> "Take all the responsibility for this matter."

However, as an auxiliary verb, ~어/아지다 is typically used with an adjective, and it is used to express a gradually intensified change that occurs in the meaning of the adjective. It can be

AUXILIARY VERBS II

translated as "become/begin to be/get to be" in English. For instance, compare the following two sentences:

> 하늘이 흐려요.
> "The sky is cloudy."
> 하늘이 흐려져요.
> "The sky becomes cloudy."

Notice in the second sentence that the auxiliary verb ~어/아지다 adds the meaning of progressive change in the meaning of the adjective (e.g., "is cloudy" = "becomes cloudy"). In addition, ~어/아지다 changes the adjective 흐리다 "cloudy" into an intransitive verb, 흐려지다 "becomes cloudy." Moreover, just like ~어/아하다, ~어/아지다 does not leave a space between the main adjective and 지다. Again, this is simply a Korean spelling convention.

> 겨울에는 밤이 길어져요.
> "In winter, the nights become longer."
> 낙서 때문에 벽이 많이 더러워졌어요.
> "The walls got messy with all the graffiti."
> 날씨가 많이 싸늘해졌지요?
> "The weather has become very chilly, hasn't it?"

15
Auxiliary verbs III

15.1 ~고 말다 "end up ~ing"

The verb 말다 means "stop," as in 비가오다가 <u>말았어요</u> "(It) started to rain and then (it) stopped." However, as an auxiliary verb, ~고 말다, consisting of the connective 고 and the verb 말다, expresses that the speaker does something completely, regrettably, or inadvertently. It is used when the action is carried out despite the subject's previous effort or wishes against the completed action. Compare the following two sentences:

돌부리에 걸려 넘어졌어요.
"(I) fell over a stone."
돌부리에 걸려 <u>넘어지고 말았어요</u>.
"(He) ended up falling over a stone."

When compared to the completed action denoted in the first sentence, notice that the completed action of the second sentence (falling) is against the subject's will. Here are more examples:

겁이 나서 거짓말을 <u>하고 말았어요</u>.
"(I) ended up lying because (I) was scared."
침대에 쥬스를 <u>쏟고 말았어요</u>.
"(I) ended up spilling juice on the bed."
시험에 결국 <u>떨어지고 말았어요</u>.
"(I) ended up failing the exam in the end."
그들은 사귄 지 2주만에 <u>헤어지고 말았어요</u>.
"As for them, (they) ended up breaking up within two weeks of dating."

15.2 ~고 보다 "try (something first) and then see what it is like"

The auxiliary verb ~고 보다 means "try (doing something first) and then see what it is like." It is made of the connective ~고 and the verb 보다 "see." Note that the meaning of ~고 보다 is similar to ~어/아 보다 "try (doing something)" in that both mean "try doing something." However, ~고 보다 indicates an additional meaning of "then seeing how things progresses from there," as shown in the following examples:

한국어를 <u>배워 보자</u>.
"(Let's) try learning Korean."
한국어를 <u>배우고 보자</u>.
"(Let's) try learning Korean (first and then see what it is like).

Here are more examples:

먼저 이야기를 다 <u>듣고 봅시다</u>.
"(Let's) try hearing the story first (then see what really happens)."

AUXILIARY VERBS III | **15.4**

일단 배가 고프니까 뭐든지 먹고 봐요.
"For now, since (we) are hungry, (let's) try eating something (first and then see what to do)."
하여튼 가능한한 빨리 병원에 가고 봅시다.
"Anyway, (let's) try going to the hospital as soon as possible (and then see how it progresses thereafter)."

15.3 ~고 싶다 "want to"

In English, verbs such as "want" and "wish" are used to express one's desire, as in "I want to sleep" or "I wish to buy it." In Korean, ~고 싶다, consisting of the connective ~고 and the auxiliary adjective 싶다 "wish/appear," is used to indicate the first person's desire or wish.

한국 음식을 먹고 싶어요.
"(I) want to eat Korean food."
변 교수님을 만나고 싶어요.
"(I) wish to meet Professor Byon."

Since one cannot speak for the second person's desire, ~고 싶다 cannot be used for a second person statement. However, it can be used for second person questions.

무슨 영화를 보고 싶어요?
"What kind of movie do (you) want to see?"
이번 주말에 뭐 하고 싶어요?
"What do (you) want to do this weekend?"

To indicate the third person's wish in both statements and questions, ~고 싶어하다 is used.

모두 다 중국 음식을 먹고 싶어해요.
"All of them want to eat Chinese food."
집에서 쉬고 싶어해요?
"Does (she) want to rest at home?"

One thing to remember is that ~고 싶다 and ~고 싶어하다 do not take the copula 이다 "be." For saying "(I) want to be a teacher," the verb 되다 "become" is used instead, as in 선생님이 되고 싶어요. Consequently, a sentence like 선생님이 이고 싶어요 is ungrammatical. This contrasts with English in that sentences like "I want to be a teacher" and "I want to become a teacher" are both acceptable.

저는 변호사가 되고 싶어요.
"As for me, (I) want to become a lawyer."
현우는 의사가 되고 싶어했어요.
"As for Hyunwoo, (he) wanted to become a doctor."

15.4 ~(으)ㄹ까 싶다 "afraid that it may"

The auxiliary verb ~(으)ㄹ까 싶다 combines ~(으)ㄹ까, which is used to indicate a speaker's wondering mindset or to seek the listener's opinion, with the auxiliary adjective 싶다 "wish/seem." ~(으)ㄹ까 싶다 is used to express one's conjecture, and it can be translated as "afraid that it may/might" in English, as shown in the following examples:

사이즈가 좀 클까 싶어요.
"(I) am afraid that the size may be a bit big."
모두 다 집에 갔을까 싶다.
"(I) am afraid that everyone might return home already."
바빠서 이번에도 오지 못할까 싶어요.
"(I) am afraid that (he) may not be able to come this time again because (he) is busy."

15.5 ~(으)ㄹ까 보다 "am thinking of, worrying that"

The auxiliary verb ~(으)ㄹ까 보다 is made of ~(으)ㄹ까 and the verb 보다 "look." The meaning and usage of ~(으)ㄹ까 보다 is twofold. First, it is used to express what the speaker is thinking of doing.

점심에 햄버거나 <u>먹을까 봐요</u>.
"(I) am thinking of having a hamburger for lunch."
여름 방학 동안 골프를 <u>배워 볼까 봐요</u>.
"(I) am thinking of trying to learn golf."

Second, it is used to indicate a worry about a possible negative future event.

<u>실수할까 봐</u> 긴장되네요.
"(I) am nervous, worrying that (I) will make mistakes."
길이 막히면 약속 <u>시간에 늦을까 봐</u> 일찍 나가려고요.
"(I) will go out early, worrying that (I) may be late to (my) appointment because of the congested road."
<u>감기에 걸릴까 봐</u> 조심하고 있어요.
"(I) am trying to be careful not to catch a cold."
부모님께서 <u>걱정하실까 봐</u> 아직 말씀 드리지 않았어요.
"(I) have not told (my) parents yet, worrying that they might worry."
식당에 자리가 <u>없을까 봐</u> 미리 예약해 놓았어요.
"(I) made a reservation already, thinking that there may not be an available table."
아버지가 <u>싫어하실까 봐</u> 안 갔어요.
"Thinking that (my) father would disapprove of it, (I) did not go."
담배 때문에 폐암에 걸려 일찍 <u>죽을까 봐</u> 끊었어요.
"(I) quit smoking, worrying that (I) may die early because of lung cancer."
<u>고장 났을까 봐</u> 걱정돼서 서비스센터에 곧바로 연락했어요.
"(I) immediately contacted the service center, worrying that (it) is out of order."

15.6 ~(으)ㄹ까 하다/생각하다 "am thinking of (doing something)"

When the verbs 하다 "do" and 생각하다 "think" are used with ~(으)ㄹ까, they express the speaker's provisional idea regarding what he/she may do. Consequently, the auxiliary verb ~(으)ㄹ까 보다/하다/생각하다 means "I am thinking of doing something" in English.

저도 한국에 <u>갈까 해요</u>.
"I am also thinking of going to Korea."
저녁을 6시에 <u>먹을까 해요</u>.
"(We) are thinking of having dinner at 6 o'clock."
다음 학기부터 도서관에서 <u>일할까 생각해요</u>.
"(I) am thinking of working at the library from next semester on."

15.7 ~나/(으)ㄴ가 보다 "appears that"

The auxiliary ~나/(으)ㄴ가 보다 is built on the ending ~나/(으)ㄴ가 and the verb 보다 "see," and it expresses the speaker's inferential judgment. It corresponds to the English expressions, "it appears that," "I guess that," "it seems that," and "it looks like."

For verb stems, ~나 보다 is used, as shown in the following examples:

경제학을 <u>전공하나 봐요</u>.
"(I) guess that (he) majors in economics."
일요일마다 교회에 <u>가나 봐요</u>.
"(I) guess that (they) go to church every Sunday."

AUXILIARY VERBS III

For adjectives and copulas, ~(으)ㄴ가 보다 is used: ~은가 보다 is used after a stem that ends in a consonant, and ~ㄴ가 보다 is used after a stem that ends in a vowel.

기분이 좋은가 봐요.
"(It) looks like (she) is in a good mood."
가방이 아주 비싼가 봐요.
"(It) looks like the bag is very expensive."
중국 사람인가 봐요.
"(I) guess that (he) is Chinese."

For verbs, adjectives, and copulas in the past tense, ~나 보다 is used after the past tense marker 었/았.

아침을 아직 안 먹었나 봐요.
"(It) looks like (they) did not eat breakfast yet."
음식이 좀 매웠나 봐요.
"(It) looks like the food was a bit spicy."
어제 많이 피곤했나 봐요.
"(It) looks like (he) was very tired yesterday."
누나의 생일이 금요일이였나 봐요.
"(It) looks like (his) older sister's birthday was Friday."

Note in the previous examples that the main verb 보다 does not take the tense marker. It is not grammatically incorrect to add the past tense marker to 보다. However, adding the past tense to the main verb generates a different meaning, as shown in the following examples:

진규가 학교에 가나 봐요.
"(I) guess that Jinkyu goes to school."
진규가 학교에 갔나 봐요.
"(I) guess that Jinkyu went to school."
진규가 학교에 가나 봤어요.
"(I) checked whether Jinkyu goes to school."
진규가 학교에 갔나 봤어요.
"(I) checked whether Jinkyu went to school."

15.8 ~게 되다 "turns out"

The auxiliary verb ~게 되다 consists of the adverbial form ~게 and the verb 되다 "become/be." It is used to express how things happened/resulted (often by chance or outside of the speaker's control). Its English equivalent would be "turns out" or "comes out to be."

그의 모든 과거를 용서하게 됐어요.
"(I) reached the point where (I) forgave all of his past."
다음 달부터 회사에 출근하게 됐어요.
"It turned out that (I) am to begin working at the company."
생일 파티는 일식당에서 하게 됐어요.
"It turned out that (we) will have the birthday party at a Japanese restaurant."
못 가게 돼서 정말 미안해요.
"(I) am really sorry that it turned out that (I) can't go."

15.9 ~어/아야 되다 "must"

The auxiliary verb ~어/아야 되다 (or ~어/아야 하다 for more formal usages) expresses the idea of obligation or necessity. It is constructed from the clausal connective ~어/아야 "only if"

~어/아야 되다 "must" 15.9

and the verb 되다 "become/be" (or 하다 "do"), and it can be translated as "must" or 'should" in English.

매일 밤 약을 <u>먹어야 돼요</u>.
"(You) must take medicine every night."
크리스마스 전까지 카드를 <u>보내야 해요</u>.
"(I) must send the card before Christmas."
꼭 <u>행복해야 돼요</u>.
"(You) must be happy by all means."
집이 일단 <u>커야 합니다</u>.
"The house has to be big first."
한국 사람<u>이라야 돼요</u>.
"(He) has to be Korean."
아버지의 <u>사인이라야 합니다</u>.
"(It) has to be (your) father's signature."

16

Clausal conjunctives I

Clausal conjunctives are used to combine clauses into longer sentences and to express special meanings, such as simultaneous actions, contrastive actions or states, paralleling actions, and so on. Examples of English clausal conjunctives include "so," "but," "and," "whereas," "while," and "though."

Korean has an extensive list of clausal conjunctives that indicate various meanings, such as "and" (i.e., ~고), "because/and then" (i.e., ~어/아서), "while" (i.e., ~으면서), "although" (i.e., ~지만), "in order to" (i.e., ~도록), and so forth. Korean clausal conjunctives are non-sentence-final endings, since they attach to the predicate stem of the preceding clause. For instance, consider how the conjunctive ~(으)면서 "while" serves to connect two different clauses.

[커피를 마셔요 "(I) drink coffee."] + [신문을 읽어요 "(I) read a newspaper."] =
커피를 마시면서 신문을 읽어요.
"(I) read a newspaper while drinking coffee."

In this example, the conjunctive ~(으)면서 attaches to the verb stem of the first clause 마시 "drink" and indicates the new meaning "while" to the first clause: 커피를 마셔요 "(I) drink coffee" changes to 커피를 마시면서 "while drinking coffee." Notice that the conjunctive ~(으)면서 is not a sentence-final ending since it does not end the sentence. Instead, ~어/아요 in the main clause is the sentence-final ending since it attaches to the verb stem of the main clause 읽 "read" and ends the whole sentence. Consider another example:

평일에 일하고 주말에 쉬어요.
"(I) work on weekdays and rest on the weekend."

The clausal conjunctive ~고 "and" links two clauses: 평일에 일하다 "work on weekdays" and 주말에 쉬다 "rest on the weekend." Again, the conjunctive ~고 ends the verb stem of the first clause 일하다 "work," while the polite speech level ending ~어/아요 ends the verb stem of the main clause 쉬다 "rest" as well as the whole sentence.

16.1 Restrictions

Some Korean conjunctives may be subject to various restrictions regarding how they are used in sentences. The first restriction concerns the "tense agreement." Since a clausal conjunctive connects two different clauses, there are at least two predicates within a clausal conjunctive sentence. In English, the tense of each clause embedded within the sentence must be the same. Consider the following example:

"I drink a cup of coffee and cleaned up the room."

The above sentence is grammatically incorrect because the tense of the two predicates is not the same. In contrast to English, the tense of each clause can be different in Korean. This is

Restrictions 16.1

possible because some Korean conjunctives do not take tense markers. Consider the following examples:

열심히 <u>준비했지만</u> 재판에서 졌어요.
"Although (he) prepared hard, (he) lost the lawsuit."
열심히 <u>준비해서</u> 재판에서 이겼어요.
"Because (he) prepared hard, (he) won the lawsuit."

Notice that both sentences are about past actions. In the first example, both the conjunctive ~지만 "although" in the first clause as well as the predicate of the main clause 지다 take the past tense marker. However, in the second example, the conjunctive ~어/아서 "because" of the first clause does not take the past tense marker, but the predicate of the main clause 이기다 takes the past tense marker.

The second restriction concerns the subject agreement. Some conjunctives can have different subjects, whereas some cannot. In other words, for some conjunctives, the subject of the clauses within a sentence must be the same. Consider the following examples:

친구가 커피를 <u>시켰지만</u> 저는 우유를 시켰어요.
"Although (my) friend ordered coffee, as for me, (I) ordered milk."
의대에 <u>들어가려고</u> 지난 2년 동안 열심히 준비하고 공부했어요.
"(I) prepared and studied hard for the last two years in order to enter medical school."

In the first example, each clause has its own subject. However, in the second example, both clauses have the same subject.

The third restriction is about whether the conjunctive may be used with adjectives, copulas, and verbs. Some conjunctives must be used only with verbs, whereas some conjunctives may be used with verbs, adjectives, and copulas. For instance, the conjunctive ~지만 "although" can be attached to verb, adjective, and copula stems, as shown in the following examples:

매일 <u>연습하지만</u> 실력이 늘지 않아요.
"Although (I) practice (it) every day, (my) ability has not improved."
<u>피곤하지만</u> 오늘도 출근합니다.
"Although (I) am tired, (I) go to work even today."
<u>중국 사람이지만</u> 중국 음식을 좋아하지 않아요.
"Although (he) is Chinese, (he) does not like Chinese food."

On the other hand, a certain conjunctive such as ~(으)려고 "in order to" must be used only with verb stems.

근처에 맛있는 한국 식당이 있는지 <u>물어보려고</u> 로비에 갔어요.
"(He) went to the lobby to ask whether there are any delicious Korean restaurants around here."

The fourth restriction is that there are conjunctives that can be used for all sentence types, such as declarative, interrogative, imperative, and propositive, whereas some conjunctives must be used only for certain sentence types (see 9.2.3). For instance, consider the conjunctives ~(으)니까 and ~어/아서, which both mean "because/since."

너무 <u>더우니까</u> 일찍 퇴근합니다.
"(I) get off work early because (it) is so hot."
너무 <u>더우니까</u> 일찍 퇴근합니까?
"Do (you) get off work early because (it) is so hot?"
너무 <u>더우니까</u> 일찍 퇴근하십시오.
"Get off work early because (it) is so hot."
너무 <u>더우니까</u> 일찍 퇴근합시다.
"(Let's) get off work early because (it) is so hot."

CLAUSAL CONJUNCTIVES I

16.2

너무 더워서 일찍 퇴근합니다.
"(I) get off work early because (it) is so hot."
너무 더워서 일찍 퇴근합니까?
"Do (you) get off work early because (it) is so hot?"
(X) 너무 더워서 일찍 퇴근하십시오.
"Get off work early because (it) is so hot."
(X) 너무 더워서 일찍 퇴근합시다.
"(Let's) get off work early because (it) is so hot."

Notice that ~(으)니까 can be used for all sentence types, whereas ~어/아서 must be used only for declarative and interrogative sentences.

16.2 Clausal conjunctives (reasons and cause)

16.2.1 ~어/아서 "so, and then"

The conjunctive ~어/아서 means "since," "so," "because" or "and then." It is a two-form ending: ~아서 is used after a predicate stem that ends in 아 or 오 (e.g., 찾다 "find" = 찾아서), whereas ~어서 is used after a predicate stem that ends in all other vowels (e.g., 가르치다 "teach" = 가르쳐서). Meanwhile, as for the copula 이다, it has two forms: 이어서 and (이)라서. The negative copula 아니다 also has two forms: 아니어서 and 아니라서. The use of 이라서/아니라서 is more common than that of 이어서/아니어서:

미국 사람이라서/이어서   "since (I) am an American"
돼지고기가 아니라서/아니어서   "because (it) is not pork"

~어/아서 expresses two things. First, it indicates a cause-and-effect relation between two actions or states, equivalent to "so" or "because/since" in English. In other words, it is used when the action or state of the first clause provides a cause or reason for the action or state of the main clause.

디자인이 너무 예쁘고 독특해서 얼마냐고 물어봤어요.
"The design was really pretty and unique, so (I) asked how much (it) is."
내일부터 여름 방학이라서 모두 곧 집으로 돌아갈 거예요.
"(It) is summer vacation from tomorrow, so everyone will return home soon."
기름 값이 너무 올라서 요즈음은 대중교통을 이용하고 있습니다.
"The gas price went up too much, so (we) are using public transportation nowadays."
다음 주 토요일에 아들 생일 파티가 있어서 시간이 없겠는데요.
"(My) son's birthday party is on Saturday next week, so (I guess that I) will not have any time."

Second, ~어/아서 links two chronologically ordered actions or events without implying any cause-and-effect relation between them. Its English translation is equivalent to "and then."

사과는 깎아서 먹읍시다.
"As for apples, (let's) peel and then eat (them)."
약국에 들러서 감기약을 샀어요.
"(I) stopped by the pharmacy and then bought cold medicine."
학교에 가서 선생님을 만났어요.
"(I) went to school and then met (my) teacher."
오늘은 은미 씨 집에 가서 저녁을 먹을 거예요.
"As for today, (we) will go to Eunmi's house and then eat dinner (there)."

Meanwhile, ~어/아서 is subject to two restrictions. First, it is not conjugated for the tense. Consider the following example:

아침을 안 먹어서 배고팠어요.
"(I) did not eat breakfast, so (I) was hungry."

Clausal conjunctives (reasons and cause)

Notice that the past tense is only marked in the main clause (e.g., 배고팠어요) but not in the first clause (e.g., 먹어서).

Second, ~어/아서 must be used only for declarative or interrogative sentence types, as shown in the following examples:

한국 음악을 <u>좋아해서</u> 한국어를 공부합니다.
"(I) like Korean music, so (I) study Korean."
한국 음악을 <u>좋아해서</u> 한국어를 공부합니까?
"Do (you) study Korean because (you) like Korean music?"
(X) 한국 음악을 <u>좋아해서</u> 한국어를 공부하십시오.
"Study Korean because (you) like Korean music."
(X) 한국 음악을 <u>좋아해서</u> 한국어를 공부합시다.
"(Let's) study Korean because (we) like Korean music."

16.2.2 ~(으)니까 "as, since, because"

The conjunctive ~(으)니까, equivalent to "since," "so," and "because," is used to specify a reason for the main clause. ~(으)니까 is a two-form ending, with ~으니까 used after a predicate stem that ends in a consonant (e.g., 좋다 "good" = 좋으니까) and ~니까 after a predicate stem that ends in a vowel (e.g., 기다리다 "wait" = 기다리니까).

The function of ~(으)니까 is similar to that of ~어/아서 since both provide a cause or reason for the action or state of the main clause. However, there are three differences between these two conjunctives.

First, the reason or cause provided by ~(으)니까 sounds more specific than those given by ~어/아서. Second, whereas ~어/아서 must be used only for declarative and interrogative sentences, ~(으)니까 may be used for any sentence type.

(O) 국이 <u>뜨거워서</u> 천천히 먹습니다.
"Since the soup is hot, (I) eat (it) slowly."
(O) 국이 <u>뜨거워서</u> 천천히 먹습니까?
"Do (you) eat (it) slowly because the soup is hot?"
(X) 국이 <u>뜨거워서</u> 천천히 먹으십시오.
"Since the soup is hot, eat (it) slowly."
(X) 국이 <u>뜨거워서</u> 천천히 먹읍시다.
"Since the soup is hot, (let's) eat (it) slowly."
(O) 국이 <u>뜨거우니까</u> 천천히 먹습니다.
"Since the soup is hot, (I) eat (it) slowly."
(O) 국이 <u>뜨거우니까</u> 천천히 먹습니까?
"Do (you) eat (it) slowly because the soup is hot?"
(O) 국이 <u>뜨거우니까</u> 천천히 먹으십시오.
"Since the soup is hot, eat (it) slowly."
(O) 국이 <u>뜨거우니까</u> 천천히 먹읍시다.
"Since the soup is hot, (let's) eat (it) slowly."

Third, ~(으)니까 is conjugated for the tense, while ~어/아서 is not, as shown in the following examples:

(X) 지난 번에 내가 빨래 <u>했어서</u> 오늘 네가 해.
"Since I did the laundry last time, you do (it) today."
(O) 지난 번에 내가 빨래 <u>했으니까</u> 오늘 네가 해.
"Since I did the laundry last time, you do (it) today."
(X) 아침 일찍 공항으로 <u>떠날 거여서</u> 일찍 잡시다.
"(Let's) sleep early, since (we) will leave for the airport early in the morning."
(O) 아침 일찍 공항으로 <u>떠날 거니까</u> 일찍 잡시다.
"(Let's) sleep early, since (we) will leave for the airport early in the morning."

CLAUSAL CONJUNCTIVES I

16.2.3 ~(으)ㄹ 테니까 "since"

The conjunctive ~(으)ㄹ 테니까 is used to express "since" or "as." It is a two-form ending, with ~을 테니까 being used with a predicate stem that ends in a consonant (e.g., 맞다 "correct" = 맞을 테니까) and ~ㄹ 테니까 in a vowel (e.g., 비슷하다 "resemble" = 비슷할 테니까). The difference between ~(으)ㄹ 테니까 and ~(으)니까 is that the former indicates a sense of conjecture or an event/action that would take place in the future, as shown in the following examples:

저녁은 재호가 <u>살 테니까</u> 커피는 내가 살게요.
"Since Jaeho is going to pay for dinner, coffee will be on me."
내일 <u>추울 테니까</u> 옷 두껍게 입고 나가세요.
"Since it is going to be cold tomorrow, please go out wearing warm."
좋은 <u>사람일 테니까</u> 걱정하지 맙시다.
"(Let's) not worry, since (he) will be a nice person."
이번 주 많이 바쁘고 <u>피곤했을 테니까</u> 다음 주에 만나요.
"Since you must have been busy and tired this week, (let's) meet next week."

16.2.4 ~느라고 "as a result of, while doing"

The conjunctive ~느라고 is a one-form ending, and it means "as a result of/because of." Similar to ~어/아서 and ~(으)니까, ~느라고 is also used to express that the action of the first clause is the reason or cause for the main clause. However, there is a subtle meaning difference between ~느라고 and ~어/아서 (or ~(으)니까). The clause with ~느라고 generates a negative implication that the action of the main clause is performed at the expense of the action of the first clause. In other words, it indicates that the action of the first clause leads to the undesirable action of the main clause. Consider the following example:

<u>야근하느라고</u> 집에 못 갔어요.
"(I) could not go home because (I) worked all night."

Notice that the action of the first clause with ~느라고 contributes to the undesirable action of the main clause (e.g., could not go home). Here are more examples:

늦게 <u>일어나느라고</u> 세수도 못 하고 출근했어요.
"As a result of getting up late, (I) went to work without even washing (my) face."
밤새 여자 친구하고 <u>통화하느라고</u> 학교에 지각했어요.
"(He) was late for school because (he) talked to (his) girlfriend over the phone all night."
집에서 급히 <u>나오느라고</u> 사무실 열쇠를 안 가지고 왔어요.
"(I) did not bring (my) office key because (I) rushed coming out from home."

Meanwhile, ~느라고 is subject to more restrictions than ~어/아서 and ~(으)니까. First ~느라고 cannot be used for imperative or propositive sentences. Second, it must be used only with verbs. Third, it is not conjugated for the tense. Fourth, the subject of the ~느라고 clause must be the same as that of the main clause.

16.2.5 ~(으)므로 "because of"

The conjunctive ~(으)므로 is a two-form ending: ~으므로 is used after a predicate stem that ends in a consonant (e.g., 안다 "hug" = 안으므로), and ~므로 is used after a predicate stem that ends in a vowel (e.g., 떨어지다 "fall" = 떨어지므로). The meaning of ~(으)므로 is "as a result of/because of." However, it conveys a formal nuance; hence it is usually used in formal written language.

그분이 이 세상에 <u>오시므로</u> 기쁨이 충만하였습니다.
"As a result of his coming to this world, (it) was full of joy."
다음 주는 추석<u>이므로</u> 길이 많이 막히겠습니다.
"Since Chuseok is next week, the road will be congested."

Clausal conjunctives (reasons and cause) | **16.2**

김성지의 생일은 이정훈의 생일보다 세 달쯤 <u>늦으므로</u> 5월입니다.
"Since Kim Sungji's birthday is three months later than Lee Junghoon's birthday, it's in May."

16.2.6 ~더니 "but, since"

The one-form conjunctive ~더니, consisting of the retrospective suffix 더 and the suffix 니, means "but (now)/as/since/and as a result." The conjunctive ~더니 is used when the speaker recollects what he/she has directly observed. Consider the following examples:

밤 12시까지 텔레비전을 <u>보더니</u> 아직도 자고 있어요.
"(He) watched TV until midnight last night, and (he) is still sleeping."
열심히 <u>공부하더니</u> 결국 시험에 합격했어요.
"(He) studied hard, and (he) finally passed the exam."
밤새도록 <u>일하더니</u> 결국 몸살로 누웠어요.
"(He) worked the whole night through, and as a result, (he) was laid up with fatigue."

Notice in the examples that the ~더니 ending clause (i.e., watching TV, studying hard, and working the whole night through) is based on the speaker's direct observation.

Meanwhile, the use of past tense marker ~었/았 with ~더니, as in ~었/았더니, is used when the speaker recollects what he/she has directly experienced. Consider the following examples:

교실에 <u>갔더니</u> 아무도 없었어요.
"(I) went to the classroom, but nobody was there."
어제 두 시간 넘게 운동을 <u>했더니</u> 몸이 쑤셔요.
"Since (I) exercised more than 2 hours yesterday, (my) body aches."
어젯밤에 맥주를 너무 많이 <u>마셨더니</u> 머리가 아파요.
"Since (I) drank too much beer last night, (my) head aches"

Notice in the examples that the ~었/았더니 ending clause (i.e., going to the classroom, exercising, drinking too much) is based on what the speaker has directly experienced.

16.2.7 ~길래 "so, since"

The conjunctive ~길래 is a one-form ending, and it also expresses cause or reason; it is translated as "since," "because," or "so." However, in contrast to ~(으)므로, which is mainly used for formal and written communication, ~길래 is mostly used for informal and spoken communication.

너무 맛있게 <u>보이길래</u> 두 개나 먹었어요.
"(It) looked so delicious, so (I) ate two of them."
얼마나 <u>바쁘길래</u> 전화도 안 하니?
"Just how busy are (you) that (you) do not even call?"
뭘 <u>먹었길래</u> 배탈이 났어요?
"Just what did (you) eat that (you) have a stomachache?"
생각보다 훨씬 더 <u>비싸길래</u> 안 샀어요.
"(I) did not buy (them) since (they) were far more expensive than (my) expectation."

17

Clausal conjunctives II

17.1 Clausal conjunctives (background)

17.1.1 ~는/(으)ㄴ데 "and, but, while"

The conjunctive ~는/(으)ㄴ데 is used to attract the listener's attention by providing background information for the main clause (or second clause). It can be translated as "and," "so," and "but" depending on context. Consider the following example:

> 지금 드라마 1회를 보고 있는데 이미 재미있어요.
> "Right now, (I) am watching the first episode, and (it) is already interesting."

In this example, the first clause 드라마 1회를 보고 있다 "(I) am watching the first episode of the drama" is the background information for the main clause 재미있다 "(it) is interesting."

The conjunctive ~는/(으)ㄴ데 is a three-form ending. ~는데 is used after a verb stem or after adjective stems that are made of 있다/없다, such as 재미있다 "interesting" and 맛없다 "tasteless."

가다 "go"	가는데
먹다 "eat"	먹는데
있다 "have"	있는데
재미없다 "uninteresting"	재미없는데
맛있다 "delicious"	맛있는데

As for adjectives and copulas, ~은데 is used after a stem that ends in a consonant, and ~ㄴ데 is used after a stem that ends in a vowel.

맑다 "clear"	맑은데
싸다 "cheap"	싼데
행복하다 "happy"	행복한데
이다 "be"	인데
아니다 "be not"	아닌데

As for the past tense, ~는데 is used after the past tense marker ~었/았. In addition, as for the future, it is used after the future marker ~겠. This applies to any predicate type, as shown in the following examples:

> 어제 한국 식당에 갔는데 손님이 많았어요.
> "(I) went to a Korean restaurant yesterday, and there were many customers."
> 어제까지는 세일이라 쌌었는데 오늘은 가격이 올랐네요.
> "Until yesterday, (it) was on sale, so (it) was cheap, but today, the price went up."
> 작년까지는 고등 학생이었는데 이제는 대학생이에요.
> "Until last year, (she) was a high school student, but now, (she) is a college student."
> 내일부터는 날씨가 더 추워지겠는데 가실 거예요?
> "The weather will be colder from tomorrow, but (you) will still go?"

Clausal conjunctives (contrast)

~는/(으)ㄴ데 is not subject to any restrictions. That is, it is conjugated for the tense, it does not have a subject agreement restriction, it can be used for all sentence types, and it may be used with any predicate type. Consider the following examples:

어제 스티브를 길에서 <u>마주쳤는데</u> 하나도 안 변했던데요.
"Yesterday, (I) ran into Steve on the street, but (he) has not changed a bit."
생일 선물을 <u>사야 하는데</u> 뭘 좋아할까요?
"(I) need to buy a birthday gift, and (I) wonder what (she) will like."
눈이 많이 <u>오는데</u> 오늘은 집에 계세요.
"(It) is snowing a lot, so please stay home today."
이번 주 금요일은 시간이 <u>없는데</u> 대신 토요일에 만납시다.
"As for this week Friday, (I) do not have time, so (let's) meet on Saturday instead."
오늘은 좀 <u>피곤한데</u> 내일 이야기합시다.
"(I) am a bit tired today, so (let's) talk tomorrow."
누나는 의사<u>인데</u> 형은 변호사예요.
"(My) older sister is a doctor, and (my) older brother is a lawyer."

17.1.2 ~(으)ㄹ 텐데 "I guess that . . ."

Similar to ~는/(으)ㄴ데, the conjunctive ~(으)ㄹ 텐데 is also used to indicate background information for the main clause. However, it indicates an additional meaning that the background information of the first clause is an inference rather than a fact. For instance, compare the following sentences:

<u>더운데</u> 에어컨 틀어요.
"(It) is hot, so turn on the air conditioner."
<u>더울 텐데</u> 에어컨 틀어요.
"(My guess is that it) must be hot, so turn on the air conditioner."

Notice that in both sentences, the first clause 덥다 "hot" is the background information for the main clause 틀다 "turn on." However, in the second sentence, the background information, marked by ~ㄹ 텐데, is a conjecture of the speaker.

~(으)ㄹ 텐데 is a two-form ending, with ~ㄹ 텐데 being used after a predicate that ends in a vowel (e.g., 가다 "go" = 갈 텐데) and ~을 텐데 after a predicate that ends in a consonant (e.g., 먹다 "eat" = 먹을 텐데).

많이 <u>아플 텐데</u> 잘 참네요.
"(I guess it) must hurt a lot, but (you) hold (it) in well."
한국은 몹시 <u>추울 텐데</u> 감기 조심하시구요.
"(I guess that) it must be very cold in Korea, so please don't catch a cold."
지금쯤 사무실에 <u>도착했을 텐데</u> 좀 더 기다려 봅시다.
"(I guess that they) arrived at the office by now, so (let's) wait a little more."
그 영화 꽤 <u>재미있을 텐데</u>, 꼭 보세요.
"(I guess) that movie must be quite interesting, so please see (it)."
<u>바쁠 텐데</u> 와 줘서 고마워요.
"(I guess that you) must be busy, so thanks for coming."

17.2 Clausal conjunctives (contrast)

17.2.1 ~지만 "although"

The one-form conjunctive ~지만 is used to acknowledge the action or state of the first clause but to indicate something contrary or opposite to that of the main clause. It is equivalent to "but" or "although" in English.

몸은 <u>쑤시지만</u> 마음은 행복합니다.
"Although (my) body aches, (my) mind is happy."

CLAUSAL CONJUNCTIVES II   17.2

월급은 <u>많지만</u> 업무가 엄청나게 많지요?
"Although the salary is high, the workload is enormously heavy, isn't it?"
4년 동안 피아노를 <u>배웠지만</u> 잘 못 쳐요.
"(He) learned piano for four years, but (he) cannot play (it) well."
밖이 좀 <u>춥지만</u> 운동하러 나갑시다!
"(It) is a bit cold outside, but (let's) go out to exercise!"
좀 <u>비싸겠지만</u> 마음에 드시면 사십시오.
"(It) will be a bit costly, but please buy (it) if (you) like it."

17.2.2 ~(으)나 "but, however"

The conjunctive ~(으)나 is used to indicate that the content of the first clause does not comply with that of the main clause. It is also equivalent to "but/although" in English. ~(으)나 is a two-form conjunctive: ~으나 is used after a stem that ends in a consonant (e.g., 읽다 "read" = 읽으나) and ~나 is used after a stem that ends in a vowel (e.g., 시작하다 "begin" = 시작하나). Consider the following examples:

이 식당은 분위기는 <u>좋으나</u> 서비스가 나쁜 편이에요.
"As for the restaurant, (its) atmosphere is good, but (its) service is kind of bad."
건강을 위해서 매일 운동을 <u>하고 싶으나</u> 헬스클럽에 갈 시간이 없어요.
"Although (I) want to exercise for (my) health, (I) do not have time to go to the fitness center."
계속 많이 <u>먹고 있으나</u> 체중이 늘지 않네요.
"Although (I) continue to eat a lot, (my) weight does not increase."

17.2.3 ~(으)나 마나 "whether . . . or not"

The conjunctive ~(으)나 마나 is the combination of ~(으)나 and the verb 마나 (e.g., 마나 = 말다 "stop" + [으]나). It is used to signal that either the action or the state denoted by the predicate of the first clause does not influence the final content of the main clause. It can be translated as "whether . . . or not" in English, as shown in the following examples:

우리가 <u>가나 마나</u> 해결이 안될 것 같아요.
"Whether we go (there) or not, (the situation) will not be settled."
약을 <u>먹으나 마나</u> 별 차이가 없었어요.
"Whether (I) took the medicine or not, there was no difference."
네가 <u>오나 마나</u> 기다릴게.
"Whether (you) come or not, (I) will wait."
<u>재미있으나 마나</u> 볼 시간이 없어요.
"Whether (it) is interesting or not, (I) have no time to watch (it)."

17.2.4 ~어/아도 "even though"

The conjunctive ~어/아도 is also used to express "but" or "even though." It is a two-form ending, with ~아도 being used after a stem that ends in a bright vowel (e.g., 아 or 오) and ~어도 after a stem that ends in all other vowels.

에어콘을 <u>틀어도</u> 방이 금방 시원해지지 않을 거예요.
"Even though (you) turn on the air conditioner, the room will not cool soon."
두 시간을 <u>기다렸어도</u> 결국 안 왔어요.
"Even though (I) waited for (her) for 2 hours, (she) did not come after all."
도서관이 집에서 <u>가까워도</u> 절대로 공부하러 가지 않아요.
"Even though the library is close to (his) home, (he) never goes (there) to study."
돈이 많이 <u>있어도</u> 한 푼도 안 줄 거예요.
"Even though (he) has lots of money, (he) will not give (me) even a penny."

Clausal conjunctives (contrast)

Meanwhile, as for the copula, it can take two forms: 이어도/아니어도 for more formal style of speech or 이라도/아니라도 for conversational style.

> 하루에 십 분씩<u>이라도</u> 일찍 일어나 보세요.
> "Try getting up early even if it's only 10 minutes a day."
> 한국 사람이 <u>아니라도</u> 괜찮아요.
> "It is fine (with me) even if (he) is not Korean."

17.2.5 ~는/(으)ㄴ데도 "although, even after"

The combination of the conjunctive ~는/(은)ㄴ데 and the particle 도 "even/also" is the conjunctive ~는/(으)ㄴ데도, meaning "although/despite (the fact that)/even if." Similar to ~는/(으)ㄴ데, the conjunctive ~는/(은)데도 is also a three-form ending: ~는데 is used after a verb stem or after adjective stems that are made with 있다/없다 (e.g., 믿다 "believe" = 믿는데도, 맛있다 "delicious" = 맛있는데도); as for adjectives and copulas, ~은데 is used after a stem that ends in a consonant (e.g., 작다 "small" = 작은데도) and ~ㄴ데 is used after a stem that ends in a vowel (e.g., 크다 "big" = 큰데도).

> 공부를 열심히 <u>했는데도</u> 시험이 어려웠어요.
> "Even after (I) studied hard, the exam was difficult."
> 어제 푹 <u>쉬었는데도</u> 감기가 안 낫네요.
> "Even after (I) got a good rest last night, (my) cold is not better."
> 오늘이 크리스마스 이<u>브인데도</u> 손님이 별로 없네요.
> "Although today is Christmas Eve, there are not many customers."
> 방이 매우 <u>시끄러운데도</u> 잘 자네요.
> "Despite the fact that the room is very noisy, (he) sleeps well."

17.2.6 ~더라도 "even though"

The one-form conjunctive ~더라도 is used when the speaker acknowledges the content of the ~더라도 ending clause but stresses that the following clause must be the case. It is corresponding to "even though (it may be the case)." Consider the following example:

> 취직 시험에 <u>떨어지더라도</u> 너무 낙심하지 마세요.
> "Even though (it may be the case that you) fail the employment exam, do not be too disappointed."

Notice that the content of the first clause is acknowledged, but the content of the main clause is highlighted (i.e., don't get too disappointed). ~더라도 is not subject to any restrictions. Here are more examples:

> 연락이 <u>없더라도</u> 우리가 먼저 찾지 맙시다.
> "Even if (it may be the case that) there is contact (from her), let's not look for (her) first."
> 내가 안 <u>보이더라도</u> 걱정하지 마세요.
> "Even if (it may be the case that) I am not around, do not worry about me."
> 늦게 <u>도착하더라도</u> 기다릴게요.
> "Even if (it may be the case that he) arrives (here) late, (I) will wait."
> 다시 <u>실패하더라도</u> 용기를 잃지 말고 다시 일어나셔야 해요.
> "Even if (it may be the case that you) fail again, (you) should not lose (your) courage, but rise up again."

17.2.7 ~어/아서라도 "even if it means"

The conjunctive ~어/아서라도 "even if it means" is a two-form ending, with ~아서라도 being used after a predicate stem that ends in 아 or 오 (e.g., 찾다 "find" = 찾아서라도) and ~어서라도

CLAUSAL CONJUNCTIVES II

being used after a predicate stem that ends in all other vowels (e.g., 가르치다 "teach" = 가르쳐서라도).

  차를 <u>팔아서라도</u> 유학을 가고 싶었습니다.
  "(I) wanted to study abroad even if it meant selling (my) car."
  밤을 <u>새서라도</u> 꼭 일을 마치세요.
  "Please finish the work even if it means staying up all night."
  하루 종일 <u>기다려서라도</u> 만날 거지요?
  "(You) will meet (her) even if it means waiting the whole day, right?"

17.2.8 ~고도 "even after"

The one-form conjunctive ~고도 is used to express "even after." It is the combination of the conjunctive ~고 "and/and then" and the particle 도 "also." ~고도 is subject to one restriction: it cannot be conjugated for tense.

  <u>혼나고도</u> 거기에 또 갔니?
  "Even after being reprimanded, (did) you go there again?"
  디저트까지 <u>먹고도</u> 배가 고팠어요.
  "Even after (I) ate desserts, (I) was still hungry."
  대학원을 <u>졸업하고도</u> 아직 취업을 못 하고 있습니다.
  "Even after (he) graduated from graduate school, (he) has not found a job yet."
  실수를 <u>하고도</u> 절대로 사과하지 않을 사람이에요.
  "(He) is the (type of) person who will never apologize, even after (he) makes a mistake."

17.2.9 ~(으)ㄴ들 "even if, granted that"

The clausal conjunctive ~(으)ㄴ들 is a two-form ending. ~은들 is used after a stem that ends in a consonant (e.g., 받다 "receive" = 받은들), and ~ㄴ들 is used after a stem that ends in a vowel (e.g., 배우다 "learn" = 배운들). The conjunctive ~(으)ㄴ들 is used when one acknowledges the content of the first clause but expresses the result of the main clause that is negative. It can be translated as "even if" in English. Consider the following example.

  지금 네가 <u>사과한들</u> 무슨 소용있겠니?
  "Even if you apologize now, what's the use?"

Notice that the speaker acknowledges the content of the first clause 사과하다 "apologize," but the main clause confirms the futility of the first clause (i.e., 무슨 소용있겠니?). Here are more examples.

  유명한 <u>의사인들</u> 이런 상태에서 뭘 할 수 있었겠어요?
  "Granted that (he) is a well-known doctor, what could (he) do in such conditions?"
  비싸다고 <u>한들</u> 우리 집만큼 하겠어요?
  "(His house) may be expensive, but (I) am sure (it) is not as expensive as our house."
  아무리 <u>똑똑한들</u> 너만큼 똑똑하겠니?
  "Even though (he) may be smart, how can (he) be as smart as you?"

17.2.10 ~(으)ㄹ지라도 "even if"

The conjunctive ~(으)ㄹ지라도 also means "even if," and it is a two-form ending, with ~을지라도 after consonants (e.g., 괜찮다 "fine" = 괜찮을지라도) and ~ㄹ지라도 after vowels (e.g., 들어오다 "come in" = 들어올지라도).

  한국 <u>사람일지라도</u> 영어로 말할 거예요.
  "Even if (he) is Korean, (I) will talk to (him) in English."
  가격이 좀 <u>비쌀지라도</u> 사 가지고 갑시다.
  "(Let's) go and buy (it) even if the price may be a bit expensive."

Clausal conjunctives (contrast) | **17.2**

시험에 <u>떨어질지라도</u> 낙심하지 마세요.
"Even if (you) fail the test, do not be frustrated."

17.2.11 ~(으)ㄹ지언정 "even though"

The conjunctive ~(으)ㄹ지언정 means "even though," and it is a two-form ending, with ~ㄹ지언정 after vowels (e.g., 고치다 "repair" = 고칠지언정) and ~을지언정 after consonants (e.g., 씻다 "wash" = 씻을지언정).

시합에 <u>패했을지언정</u> 그들은 당당했다.
"Even though (they) lost the game, they stood tall."
<u>굶어죽을지언정</u> 도둑이 되고 싶지 않았어요.
"Even if (I) had to starve, (I) didn't want to be a thief."
아무리 <u>바쁠지언정</u> 부모님 생신을 잊어서는 안 돼요.
"No matter how busy you may be, (you) must not forget (your) parents' birthdays."

17.2.12 ~(으)ㄹ망정 "even if"

The conjunctive ~(으)ㄹ망정 is another two-form conjunctive that means "even if." ~ㄹ망정 is used after vowels (e.g., 아프다 "sick" = 아플망정), and ~을망정 is used after consonants (e.g., 죽다 "die" = 죽을망정).

이 동네에서 <u>살망정</u> 절대로 가난하지 않았어요.
"Even if (we) lived in this neighborhood, (we) were never poor."
저희 회사는 작은 <u>회사일망정</u> 일하기 좋은 곳이에요.
"Even if (our) company is small, (it) is a good place to work."
미안하다고는 <u>못 할망정</u> 오히려 왜 화를 내요?
"Even though (you) can't say sorry, why are (you) mad (at me) instead?"

17.2.13 ~느니 "rather, instead of doing X"

The one-form conjunctive ~느니 is used only with verb stems, and it indicates that the content of the main clause is preferable to that of the first clause. It can be translated as "it would be better" or "would rather" in English.

이렇게 노예같이 <u>일하느니</u> 차라리 그만두고 싶어요.
"(I) would rather quit than work like a slave like this."
결혼해서 가난하게 <u>사느니</u> 싱글로 남겠어요.
"(It) would be better to remain single than to get married and live in poverty."
이 식당에 가서 밥을 <u>먹느니</u> 커피나 마실래요.
"(I) would rather drink coffee (or something) than go to this restaurant for a meal."

17.2.14 ~기로서니 "even though"

The one-form conjunctive ~기로서니 is used similarly to an English expression "even though, admitting that." It is made of the ending ~기 and 로서니 "though." ~기로서니 is usually used in a negative context, as shown in the following examples:

아무리 <u>배가 고프기로서니</u> 어떻게 먼저 먹을 수 있나?
"No matter how hungry (you) are, how dare (you) eat first?"
내가 아무리 <u>밉기로서니</u> 어떻게 그럴 수 있어요?
"No matter how much (you) hate me, how on earth can (you) do that?"
아무리 <u>화가 나기로서니</u> 어떻게 그냥 그렇게 나가 버릴 수 있어요?
"No matter how angry (he) is, how can (he) go out like that?"

18

Clausal conjunctives III

18.1 Clausal conjunctives (intention)

18.1.1 ~(으)러 "to, in order to"

The conjunctive ~(으)러 is used to express the purpose of the speaker's action. It is translated as "for the purpose of" or "to" in English. ~(으)러 is a two-form ending: ~으러 is used after a verb stem that ends in a consonant (e.g., 입다 "wear" = 입으러), whereas ~러 is used after a verb stem that ends in a vowel (e.g., 쉬다 "rest" = 쉬러).

~(으)러 is usually used with a motion verb, such as 가다 "to go" and 오다 "to come," to indicate the purpose of going or coming, as shown in the following examples:

점심 먹<u>으러</u> 식당가는데 같이 갈래요?
"(We) are going to the cafeteria to eat lunch, and would (you) like to go together?"
뭘 <u>사러</u> 오셨어요?
"What did (you) come to buy?"

~(으)러 is subject to the following three restrictions. First, it is not conjugated for the tense. Second, the subjects of both clauses must be the same. Third, it is used only with verbs.

머리 <u>깎으러</u> 미장원에 갔어요.
"(I) went to the beauty parlor to get a hair cut."
(X) 머리 <u>깎았으러</u> 미장원에 갔어요.
"(I) went to the beauty parlor to get a hair cut."
<u>운동하러</u> 왔습니다.
"(I) came (here) to exercise."
(X) <u>행복하러</u> 결혼하고 싶어요.
"(I) want to marry (her) to be happy."

However, there is no restriction regarding sentence type. For instance, it can be used with any of the four sentence types as shown here:

학회에 <u>참석하러</u> 내일 서울로 떠나요.
"(I) will leave for Seoul tomorrow to participate at a conference."
언제 선물 <u>사러</u> 갈 거예요?
"When will (you) go to buy a gift?"
커피 한 잔 <u>마시러</u> 저희 집에 언제 한 번 들르세요.
"Stop by our house sometime to have a cup of coffee."
언제 같이 골프 <u>치러</u> 갑시다.
"(Let's) go sometime to play golf together."

18.1.2 ~(으)려고 "to, intending to"

The conjunctive ~(으)려고 is used to express the speaker's intention or plan. It is a two-form ending: ~으려고 is used after a verb stem that ends in a consonant (e.g., 벗다 "take

Clausal conjunctives (intention) **18.1**

off" = 벗으려고) and ~려고 is used after a verb stem that ends in a vowel (e.g., 보내다 "send" = 보내려고).

The meaning of ~(으)려고 is similar to that of ~(으)러. However, in contrast to ~(으)러, which is normally collocated with motion verbs such as 가다 or 오다, ~(으)려고 can be used with any verb.

제가 가고 싶은 대학에 <u>들어가려고</u> 열심히 공부했어요.
"(I) studied hard (intending) to enter the college that I wanted to go to."
내년에는 새집을 <u>사려고</u> 해요.
"(We) intend to buy a new house next year."
미국에서도 <u>운전하려고</u> 국제면허를 땄어요.
"(I) earned an international license (intending) to drive even in the states."
이번 여름에 중국을 <u>여행하려고</u> 돈을 모으고 있어요.
"(I) am saving money (intending) to travel in China this summer."
오늘은 집에서 대신 푹 <u>쉬려고</u> 헬스클럽에 안 갔어요.
"(I) did not go to the fitness center today, intending to get a good rest at home instead."

~(으)려고 is subject to the following restrictions: (i) it is not conjugated for the tense, (ii) the subject of the clauses must be the same, (iii) it is used only with verbs, and (iv) it is used only for declarative and interrogative sentences.

바이어를 <u>만나려고</u> 호텔 로비에서 기다리고 있었어요.
"(I) was waiting at the hotel lobby to meet a buyer."
용돈 <u>받으려고</u> 왔니?
"Did (you) come to get spending money?"
(X) 티켓을 <u>받으려고</u> 가십시오.
"Go (intending to) receive a ticket."
(X) 영화 <u>보려고</u> 갑시다.
"(Let's) go (to the theatre) to see a movie."

18.1.3 ~(으)려다가 "intending to"

The combination of ~(으)려고 "intending to" and ~다가 creates a new conjunctive ~(으)려다가. The conjunctive ~(으)려다가 is used when one tries to do something but comes across another situation. It indicates that the intentional action of the first clause was never actualized, but the action of the main clause was realized instead. Consider the following example:

도서관에 <u>가려다가</u> 서점에 갔어요.
"As (we) intended to go the library, (we) went to the bookstore."

Notice that the action of the first clause (e.g., going to the library) was never actualized. Instead, the action of the main clause was realized.

~(으)려다가 is subject to the following restrictions: (i) it is not conjugated for the tense, (ii) the subject of the clauses must be the same, (iii) it is used only with verbs, and (iv) it is used only for declarative and interrogative sentences. In addition, it has a two-form ending: ~으려다가 is used after a verb stem that ends in a consonant (e.g., 막다 "block" = 막으려다가), and ~려다가 is used after a verb stem that ends in a vowel (e.g., 던지다 "throw" = 던지려다가).

개를 <u>잡으려다가</u> 넘어졌어요.
"As (I) intended to catch the dog, (I) fell (on the ground)."
프린터를 <u>사려다가</u> 대신 컴퓨터를 샀어요.
"As (we) intended to buy a printer, (we) bought a computer instead."
무엇을 <u>사려다가</u> 못 샀어요?
"What did (you) intend to buy but could not buy?"
학위를 마치고 한국에 <u>돌아가려다가</u> 미국에서 직장을 알아보기로 했어요.
"As (I) intended to go back to Korea after getting (my) degree, (I) decided to look for a job in the states."

CLAUSAL CONJUNCTIVES III

18.1.4 ~고자 "intending to"

The conjunctive ~고자 is a one-form ending, and it is also used to indicate the intention of the speaker's action. However, when compared to ~(으)려고, ~고자 tends to occur more often in formal contexts.

당신을 <u>경배하고자</u> 모인 저희들을 축복하여 주옵소서.
"Do bless us who gathered here to worship you."
먼저 이 제품에 대해서 간단히 설명드리고 발표를 <u>시작하고자</u> 합니다.
"(I) intend to briefly explain about this product first and then begin my presentation."
김 교수님을 <u>뵙고자</u> 왔습니다.
"(We) came to pay respect to Professor Kim."

18.1.5 ~게 "so that"

The one-form conjunctive ~게 has two functions depending on whether it attaches to a verb stem or an adjective stem. When it is used with a verb, it means "so that," as shown here:

모두가 <u>읽게</u> 책상 위에 놨어요.
"(I) put it on the table so that everyone can read (it)."
잠 좀 <u>자게</u> 조용히 해 주세요.
"Please be quite so that (I) can fall asleep."

When it is used with an adjective, it changes the adjective into an adverb (e.g., 쉽다 "easy" = 쉽게 "easily"). Consider the following examples:

좀 더 <u>크게</u> 말씀 해 주시겠어요?
"Could you speak a bit louder?"
<u>예쁘게</u> 찍어 주세요.
"Please take (a picture of us) nicely."

18.1.6 ~도록 "so that, to the extent that"

The conjunctive ~도록 is used to express "so that" or "to the extent that." ~도록 is subject to only one restriction: it is not conjugated for the tense.

푹 <u>쉬시도록</u> 조용한 방을 예약해 드렸어요.
"(I) made a reservation for a quiet room so that (they) can get a good rest."
구급차가 <u>지나갈 수 있도록</u> 길을 비켜 주세요.
"Please step aside so that the ambulance can pass."
회의에 <u>늦지 않도록</u> 10분 일찍 만납시다.
"(Let's) meet 10 minutes early so that (we) will not be late for the meeting."
목이 <u>터지도록</u> 우리 팀을 응원했습니다.
"(We) cheered for our team to the point of breaking our throats."
그들은 서로 <u>죽도록</u> 사랑했다.
"As for them, (they) loved each other to death."
독감에 <u>안 걸리도록</u> 독감 주사를 맞았어요.
"(I) got a flu shot so that (I) would not catch the flu."
전쟁이 하루속히 빨리 <u>끝나도록</u> 기도할 거예요.
"(We) will pray so that the war will end as soon as possible."

18.2 Clausal conjunctives (conditions)

18.2.1 ~(으)면 "if, when"

The conjunctive ~(으)면 is used to express that the first clause is the condition of the main clause. It is equivalent to "if" or "when" in English. It is a two-form ending: ~으면 is used after a stem

Clausal conjunctives (conditions) 18.2

that ends in a consonant (e.g., 신다 "wear" = 신으면), and ~면 is used after a stem that ends in a vowel (e.g., 일어나다 "get up" = 일어나면).

오늘 오후에도 계속 <u>눈이 오면</u> 안 갈 거예요.
"If snow continues to fall even in the afternoon today, (we) will not go (there)."
질문 <u>있으시면</u> 언제든지 연락주세요.
"Contact (me) anytime if (you) have any questions."
모두 <u>모였으면</u> 이제 회의를 시작할까요?
"If everyone is gathered, shall (we) begin the meeting?"
오늘 오후에 시간 <u>있으면</u> 좀 들르실래요?
"If (you) have some time in the afternoon today, will (you) stop by?"
공항에 <u>도착했으면</u> 저희한테 연락했을 거예요.
"If (he) arrived at the airport, (he) would have contacted us."

The conjugation of ~(으)면 with the copula 이다 has two forms: ~(이)면 and ~(이)라면. ~면/라면 is used after a noun that ends in a vowel (e.g., 스파게티면 "if it is spaghetti"), whereas ~이면/이라면 is used after a noun that ends in a consonant (e.g., 호텔이면 "if (it) a hotel").

한국 사람<u>이면/이라면</u> 저한테 보내세요.
"If (he) is Korean, send (him) to me."
카페인이 없는 커피<u>면/라면</u> 마실래요.
"If (it) is decaffeinated coffee, (I) will drink (it)."

When ~(이)면/(이)라면 occurs after a time word, it means "in" or "at the end of."

11시<u>면</u> 대통령 취임 연설이 시작할 거예요.
"By 11 o'clock, the president's inaugural address will begin."
한 달<u>이면</u> 18살이 돼요.
"In one month, (he will) be 18 years old."

18.2.2 ~(으)려면 "if, when (one intends to do)"

The conjunctive ~(으)려면 "if one intends to do" is the combination of ~(으)려고 "intending to" with the conjunctive ~(으)면 "if." It is a two-form ending: ~려면 is used after a stem that ends in a vowel (e.g., 쓰다 "write/use" = 쓰려면) and ~으려면 is used after a stem that ends in a consonant (e.g., 얻다 "gain" = 얻으려면).

이 근처에 차를 <u>고치려면</u> 어디로 가야 합니까?
"If (I) intend to repair a car in this area, where should (I) go?"
이 드레스를 <u>입으려면</u> 먼저 다이어트를 하세요.
"If (you) intend to wear this dress, please go on a diet first."
한국 식당을 <u>찾으시려면</u> 여기서 30분을 더 가셔야 해요.
"If (you) intend to find a Korean restaurant, (you) need to drive 30 more minutes from here."
이 대학에 <u>입학하려면</u> 뭐가 필요하지요?
"If (I) intend to get admitted into this university, what would (I) need?"
김 박사님을 <u>만나시려면</u> 미리 예약하셔야 합니다.
"If (you) intend to meet Dr. Kim, (you) must make an appointment in advance."
이 회사에 <u>취직하려면</u> 2개의 외국어에 능통해야 한다고 합니다.
"(I heard that) if one intends to find employment in this company, one needs to be fluent in two foreign languages."
질문을 <u>하려면</u> 수업 끝나고 해라.
"If (you) intend to ask (me) a question, do so after class."

18.2.3 ~었/았더라면 "if, when (something had been the case)"

The conjunctive ~었/았더라면 means "if (something had/had not been the case)." The conjunctive is constructed from the past tense marker ~었/았, the retrospective suffix ~더, the statement

CLAUSAL CONJUNCTIVES III

suffix 라, and the conjunctive ~(으)면 "if." The conjunctive ~었/았더라면 is used when the speaker wishes to express a sense of regret or supposition. Consider the following examples:

술을 더 일찍 <u>끊었더라면</u> 더 건강했을 거예요.
"If (it was the case that he) quit drinking earlier, (he) would have been healthier."
의대를 <u>졸업했더라면</u> 좋은 의사가 되어 있었을 거예요.
"If (it was the case that he) graduated from medical school, (he) would have become a good doctor."

Notice that the main clauses of both examples indicate a sense of disappointment or assumption. Here are more examples:

눈이 많이 오던 그 날 그냥 집에 <u>있었더라면</u> 사고가 안 났을 거예요.
"If (it was the case that I) stayed home on that snowy day, the accident would not have occurred."
가족하고의 대화의 시간을 많이 <u>가졌더라면</u> 이혼을 안 했을 거예요.
"If (it was the case that they) had more time for conversation with (their) family, (they) would not have divorced."
친구들의 도움이 <u>없었더라면</u> 취직할 수 없었을 거예요.
"If (it was the case that I) didn't have (my) friends' help, (I) would not be able to get a job."

18.2.4 ~거든 "if, when"

The conjunctive ~거든 is used to indicate that the clause ending with ~거든 is the condition for the main clause. The meaning of ~거든 is similar to ~(으)면 in that they are both equivalent to "if" in English. However, ~거든 is usually used for commands, requests, or promises, as shown in the following examples:

서울에 <u>도착하거든</u> 작은아버지한테 꼭 연락해라.
"If (you) arrive in Seoul, make sure (you) contact (your) uncle."
혜연이를 이따가 학교에서 <u>만나거든</u> 꼭 메세지를 전해 줘요.
"If (you) meet Hyeyeon at school later, please pass (my) message (to her)."
방이 <u>덥거든</u> 에어컨을 켜세요.
"If the room is hot, please turn on the AC."
할 말이 <u>있거든</u> 하세요.
"If (you) have something to say, say (it)."
다시 <u>고장나거든</u> 이곳으로 연락해 보세요.
"If (it) breaks again, try contacting this place."

18.2.5 ~어/아야 "only if"

The conjunctive ~어/아야 indicates that the clause ending in ~어/아야 is a prerequisite or necessary condition of the main clause. It is corresponding to "only if" in English. Consider the following example:

학교에 <u>가야</u> 교수님을 만날 수 있어요.
"Only if (you) go to school, (you) can meet (your) professor."

Notice that the action of the first clause "going to school" is the necessity for the action of the main clause "meeting the professor."

~어/아야 is a two-form ending: ~아야 is used after a stem that ends in either 아 or 오, whereas ~어야 is used after a stem that ends in all other vowels.

잡다 "catch"	잡아야
믿다 "believe"	믿어야
작다 "small"	작아야
어렵다 "difficult"	어려워야 (어려우 + 어야)

Clausal conjunctives (conditions)

이다 "to be"	이어야/이라야
아니다 "not be"	아니어야/아니라야

To add an emphatic meaning, one can use the particle 만 "only" along with ~어/아야, as shown in the following examples:

앤드류를 <u>만나야만</u> 데니엘에 대해 들을 수 있어요.
"Only if (you) meet Andrew, (you) can hear about Daniel."
의과 대학을 <u>졸업해야만</u> 의사가 될 수 있어요.
"Only if (you) graduate from medical school, (you) can become a doctor."
열쇠를 <u>찾아야만</u> 집에 갈 수 있어요.
"Only if (we) find the key, (we) can go home."

18.2.6 ~(으)ㄹ수록 "the more . . . the more"

The conjunctive ~(으)ㄹ수록 expresses a continuous increase in the nature of an action or state. It can be translated as "the more . . . the more" in English. ~(으)ㄹ수록 is a two-form ending: ~을 수록 is used after a stem that ends in a consonant (e.g., 적다 "few" = 적을수록), whereas ~ㄹ수록 is used after a stem that ends in a vowel (e.g., 모으다 "accumulate" = 모을수록).

돈이 <u>많을수록</u> 욕심도 많아요.
"The more money (you) have, the more greed (you) have."
한자는 <u>배울수록</u> 어려워요.
"As for Chinese characters, the more (I) learn (it), the more difficult (it) is."

In addition, the conjunctive ~(으)면 "if" can be optionally used along with ~(으)ㄹ수록, as shown here:

나이가 <u>어리면 어릴수록</u> 외국어를 쉽게 배울 수 있대요.
"(I heard that) the younger (one) is, the easier (one) can learn a foreign language."
<u>친한 사람이면 친할수록</u> 예의를 꼭 지켜야 합니다.
"One must pay more attention to the courtesy, the closer the person is."
이 책은 <u>읽으면 읽을수록</u> 더 모르겠네요.
"As for this book, the more (I) read, the more (I) do not understand."
부부 관계는 시간이 <u>지나면 지날수록</u> 더 소중해져요.
"As for the relationship of married couples, the more time passes, the more precious (it) becomes."
술은 <u>마시면 마실수록</u> 더 마실 수 있게 된대요.
"(They say that) as for alcohol, the more (you) drink, the more (you) will be able to drink."
노트북은 <u>작으면 작을수록</u> 더 비싸요.
"As for laptops, the smaller (it) is, the more expensive (it) is."

19

Clausal conjunctives IV

19.1 Clausal conjunctives (sequence)

19.1.1 ~고 "and, and also, as well"

The one-form conjunctive ~고 has two functions. First, it simply connects two different clauses, regardless of their sequence. Consider the following examples:

> 제가 <u>청소하고</u> 제 아내가 요리해요.
> "I clean up, and my wife cooks."
> 제 아내가 <u>요리하고</u> 제가 청소해요.
> "My wife cooks, and I clean up."

Notice that the meanings of the previous sentences are the same even if the sequences of the clauses are different. Here are more examples:

> 히사꼬는 일본으로 <u>가고</u> 상필이는 한국으로 가요.
> "As for Hisako, (she) goes to Japan, and as for Sangpil, (he) goes to Korea."
> 희연이는 미술사를 <u>전공하고</u> 주영이는 회계학을 공부해요.
> "As for Heeyeon, (she) majors in art history, and as for Jooyoung, (she) studies accounting."

Second, the conjunctive ~고 links two sequential actions or events; equivalent to "and then" in English. Consider the following examples:

> 먼저 집 청소를 <u>하고</u> 요리를 시작할 거예요.
> "(I) will clean up the house first and then start cooking."
> 일단 뭐 좀 <u>주문하고</u> 전화해 봅시다.
> "(Let us) order something for now and then try calling (her)."

Notice that the conjunctive ~고 indicates the order of the action in these situations. In other words, changing the sequence of the clauses generates a different meaning. Here are more examples:

> 잠옷을 <u>입고</u> 주무세요.
> "Wear (your) pajamas and then go to sleep."
> 친구를 <u>만나고</u> 집에 갈 거예요.
> "(I) will meet (my) friends and then go home."
> 샤워 <u>하고</u> 잘 거지요?
> "(You) will take a shower and then go to bed, right?"
> 저녁을 <u>먹고</u> 공원에 산책하러 나갑시다.
> "(Let's) eat dinner and then go out to the park for a walk."

The conjunctive ~고 is subject to one restriction: it is not conjugated for the tense. Consider the following examples:

> 지난 금요일은 눈이 많이 <u>오고</u> 아주 추웠어요.
> "As for last Friday, it snowed a lot and was very cold."
> 점심 <u>먹고</u> 떠났어요.
> "(They) ate lunch and then left."

Clausal conjunctives (sequence)

Notice that both sentences are about the past action and state. However, the past tense is not marked by the ~고 ending clauses but by the main clauses.

19.1.2 ~고서 "and, and then"

The one-form conjunctive ~고서 is used to express sequential events or actions.

매일 한 시간쯤 <u>운동하고서</u> 출근해요.
"(I) exercise about an hour every day and then go to work."
<u>숙제하고서</u> 나갔어요?
"Did (he) go out after doing (his) homework?"
저녁은 각자 모두 집에서 <u>먹고서</u> 오세요.
"As for dinner, please come after eating it at (your) home."
일단 손을 <u>씻고서</u> 시작합시다.
"First, (let's) wash (our hands) and then begin."

19.1.3 ~거니와 "as well as"

The one-form conjunctive ~거니와 also connects two statements, meaning "and," "as well as," and "besides." The meaning of ~거니와 is similar to ~고, but its usage is much less frequent than that of ~고.

정훈이는 피아노도 잘 <u>치거니와</u> 노래도 잘 해요.
"As for Junghoon, (he) plays piano well and sings well too."
술도 잘 안 <u>마시거니와</u> 담배도 피우지 않으세요.
"(He) does not drink alcohol and does not smoke either."
기민이는 얼굴도 <u>예쁘거니와</u> 마음씨도 곱다.
"Keemin has not only a pretty face but also a lovely disposition."

19.1.4 ~(으)면서 "while"

The conjunctive ~(으)면서 is used when two actions (or states) are carried out simultaneously by the same subject. It corresponds to "while" in English. The conjunctive ~(으)면서 is a two-form ending, with ~으면서 being used after a predicate stem that ends in a consonant (e.g., 닫다 "close" = 닫으면서) and ~면서 after a predicate stem that ends in a vowel (e.g., 걸어가다 "go on foot" = 걸어가면서). The conjunctive ~(으)면서 is subject to one restriction; that is, the subject of the clauses within a sentence must be the same.

우리는 캠퍼스를 같이 <u>걸으면서</u> 많은 이야기를 했다.
"We talked a lot while taking a walk round the campus together."
이 식당은 음식값이 <u>비싸지 않으면서</u> 맛도 제법 괜찮아요.
"As for this café, while (its) food price is not expensive, the taste (of its food) is quite nice."
컴퓨터을 <u>쓰면서</u> 먹지 말아요.
"Do not eat while working on a computer."
뭐 좀 <u>마시면서</u> 이야기합시다.
"(Let's) talk while drinking something."
혹시 이 한심한 드라마 <u>보면서</u> 울고 있었어요?
"By any chance, were (you) crying while watching this pathetic drama?"
여기는 <u>일식당이면서</u> 중국 음식도 주문 받아요.
"As for this place, while (it) is a Japanese restaurant, (they) also take orders for Chinese food."

19.1.5 ~(으)며 "and, while"

The conjunctive ~(으)며 means "and" or "while." The conjunctive ~(으)며 is a two-form ending: ~으며 is used after consonants (e.g., 찾다 "find" = 찾으며), and ~며 is used after vowels

CLAUSAL CONJUNCTIVES IV

(e.g., 만나다 "meet" = 만나며). The meaning of ~(으)며 is similar to that of ~고 since both connect two actions or states. However, whereas the conjunctive ~고 can indicate both nonsequential as well as sequential actions/states (e.g., "and," "and," and "and then"), ~(으)며 indicates only nonsequential actions/states. In addition, whereas ~고 is widely used both in spoken and written communication, ~(으)며 tends to be used only in writing.

> 누나는 병원에서 <u>일하며</u> 형은 군에 있습니다.
> "As for (my) older sister, (she) works in the hospital, and as for (my) older brother, (he) is in the military."
> 내일은 매우 <u>덥겠으며</u> 오후에는 비도 오겠습니다.
> "As for tomorrow, (it) will be very hot, and (it) will rain in the afternoon too."
> 은행은 오른쪽에 <u>있으며</u> 지하철역은 왼쪽에 있습니다.
> "As for the bank, (it) is on the right side, while as for the subway station, (it) is on the left side."

Notice in the previous examples that the conjunctive ~(으)며 simply links two separate or nonsequential actions or states.

When the subjects of both clauses are the same, the conjunctive ~(으)며 indicates that two or more actions or events occur simultaneously. Consider the following examples:

> 보통 카페인이 많은 커피와 녹차를 <u>마시며</u> 공부해요.
> "Usually, (we) study while drinking coffee and green tea that have amounts of high caffeine."
> 재즈 음악을 <u>들으며</u> 춤 연습을 같이 할 거예요.
> "(We) will practice dancing together while listening to jazz music."

Note in the previous examples that ~(으)며 is translated as "while" rather than "and" in English.

The conjunctive ~(으)며 is subject to one restriction: it is not conjugated for the tense.

> 교수님의 강의를 <u>들으며</u> 많이 느끼고 배웠습니다.
> "While listening to the professor's lecture, (I) felt and learned a lot."
> 같이 재미있는 영화도 <u>보며</u> 좋은 시간을 보냈어요.
> "(We) had a good time watching interesting movies together."

Notice in the examples that only the predicates of the main clauses take the past tense marker.

19.1.6 ~자마자 "as soon as"

The one-form conjunctive ~자마자 is a one-form ending, and it means "as soon as" or "immediately after." The conjunctive ~자마자 is subject to two restrictions: it must be used only with verbs, and it is not conjugated for the tense.

> <u>일어나자마자</u> 샤워할 거예요?
> "Will (you) take a shower as soon as (you) get up?"
> 호텔에 <u>도착하자마자</u> 전화해 주셔야 해요.
> "Please (you) must call (me) as soon as (you) arrive at the hotel."
> 우리는 방에 <u>들어가자마자</u> 전등을 켰다.
> "We turned the electric lamp on as soon as (we) entered the room."
> 편지를 <u>읽자마자</u> 울기 시작했어요.
> "(She) started crying as soon as (she) read the letter."
> 소식을 <u>듣자마자</u> 밖으로 뛰쳐 나갔어요.
> "(He) ran outside as soon as (he) heard the news."
> 야근이 없는 날에는 보통 <u>퇴근하자마자</u> 집으로 가는 편이요.
> "On the days without overtime work to do, (I) usually tend to go home as soon as (I) get off work."

19.1.7 ~다가 "while doing, do and then"

The one-form conjunctive ~다가 is used to express a shift in action or state. First, when it is attached to a verb stem, it indicates that the subject shifts his/her action to another. Consider the following examples:

> 5분 전까지 여자 친구를 <u>기다리다가</u> 사무실로 돌아갔어요.
> "(He) waited for (his) girlfriend until five minutes ago and then returned to the office."
> 병원에 <u>가다가</u> 꽃집에 들렀어요.
> "On my way to the hospital, (I) stopped by the flower shop."

Notice in the previous examples that the subjects shifted certain actions (i.e., waiting, going to the hospital) to another actions (i.e., returning to the office, stopping by the flower shop).

Second, when ~다가 is attached to an adjective stem, it indicates a shift from one state to another. Consider the following example:

> 맛이 <u>맵다가</u> 싱거워요.
> "The taste was spicy and now (it) is bland."

Notice in the previous example that there was a shift in the state (i.e., from "being spicy" to "being bland"). The first state is no longer in effect in favor of the second state. Here are more examples:

> 오전까지 날씨가 <u>춥다가</u> 오후부터는 많이 따뜻해졌습니다.
> "The weather was cold until the a.m. and then (it) became much warmer from the afternoon."
> 기름 값이 지난 달까지 <u>싸다가</u> 이번 달부터 비싸졌어요.
> "The price of gasoline was cheap until last month but then (it) became expensive (starting) from this month."

The use of the past tense marker 었/았 is optional for the conjunctive ~다가. If the speaker wishes to highlight the past action rather than the shift in the action, he/she can optionally use the past tense marker. For instance, compare the following two sentences:

> 슈퍼에 <u>가다가</u> 변 교수님하고 마주쳤어요.
> "On my way to the supermarket, (I) ran into Professor Byon."
> 슈퍼에 <u>갔다가</u> 변 교수님하고 마주쳤어요.
> "(I) went to the supermarket and then (I) ran into Professor Byon."

The meanings of the previous sentences are similar. However, notice that there is a subtle meaning difference: whereas the first sentence simply indicates the shift in the action, the second sentence highlights that the past action was completed before the shift of the action took place.

19.2 Clausal conjunctives (option)

19.2.1 ~거나 "or"

The one-form conjunctive ~거나 is used to list two or more actions or states. It is equivalent to "or" in English, as shown in the following examples:

> 주로 도서관에 <u>가거나</u> 커피숍에 가서 공부해요.
> "Usually, (I) go to the library or the coffee shop to study."
> 이메일을 <u>보내거나</u> 전화를 하세요.
> "Give (him) a call or send (him) an e-mail."
> <u>아프거나</u> 피곤할 때 집 생각이 많이 나지요?
> "When (you) are sick or tired, (you) think about (your) home a lot, right?"

The use of the conjunctive ~거나 multiple times may imply that the actions or states listed by the conjunctive are trivial, whereas the predicate or the content of the main clause is essential.

CLAUSAL CONJUNCTIVES IV   19.3

In such cases, ~거나 is translated as "whether . . . or" in English. Consider the following example:

어렵<u>거나</u> 쉽<u>거나</u> 열심히 배울래요.
"Whether (it) is hard or easy, (I) will learn (it) enthusiastically."

Notice that the two states denoted by two adjectives, 어렵다 "difficult" and 쉽다 "easy," are trivial, whereas the predicate of the main clause, 배우다 "learn," is important. Here are more examples:

맛이 있<u>거나</u> 없<u>거나</u> 배 고프면 다 먹어요.
"Whether (it) is delicious or not, (we) eat anything if (we) are hungry."
비가 오<u>거나</u> 눈이 오<u>거나</u> 매일 운동합시다.
"Whether (it) rains or snows, (let's) exercise every day."

19.2.2 ~든지 "or, regardless"

The clausal conjunctive ~든지 is a one-form ending, and it is used to list a series of selections or to imply an unenthusiastic or indifferent attitude toward the selections. It can be translated in English as "or," "no matter," or "regardless." Consider the following example:

도서관에서 공부를 <u>하든지</u> 공원에서 조깅을 <u>하든지</u> 합시다.
"(Let's) study at the library or go jogging at the park"

Notice in the previous example that ~든지 enumerates two activities (i.e., studying at the library and jogging at the park). However, it also implies that the speaker does not care which activity is chosen. Here are more examples:

<u>살든지 죽든지</u> 당신만을 믿고 따르겠어요.
"Whether (I) live or die, (I) will believe and follow only you."
어디를 <u>가든지</u> 무엇을 <u>하든지</u> 항상 최선을 다해라.
"Wherever (you) go and whatever (you) do, always do (your) best."
<u>싫든지 좋든지</u> 부모님을 위해서 돈을 벌어야 했어요.
"Whether (I) like (it) or not, (I) had to earn money for (my) parents."
저 친구는 누가 <u>보든지</u> 안 <u>보든지</u> 항상 성실히 일해요.
"As for that fellow, (he) works diligently whether someone sees (him) or not."

19.3 Clausal conjunctives (comparison)

19.3.1 ~듯이 "like, as, as if"

The one-form conjunctive ~듯이 is used to compare the action/event/state of the first clause to that of the main clause. It corresponds to "like" or "as if" in English.

모두들 <u>뛰듯이</u> 기뻐했습니다.
"Everyone rejoiced as if jumping for joy."
정말 <u>모르듯이</u> 이야기 하던데요.
"(He) talked as if (he) really did not know (about it)."
정말 맥주를 물 <u>마시듯이</u> 마셨나요?
"Did (they) really drink beer as if (they) were drinking water?"
인간은 모두 한 번 <u>태어나듯이</u> 한 번 죽는다.
"All humans die once like (they) are born once."

Clausal conjunctives (comparison)

19.3.2 ~다시피 "just as, as if"

The conjunctive ~다시피 is a one-form ending that means "just as" or "as if," as shown in the following examples:

우리 집에서 <u>살다시피</u> 거진 매일 왔었어요.
"(He) used to stop by our house almost every day as if (he) lived here."
너도 <u>알다시피</u> 이번 달은 정신없이 바쁘잖아.
"As you also know, (I) am extremely busy this month (you see)."
<u>보다시피</u> 여기에는 아무것도 없습니다.
"As (you) can see, there is nothing here."
수업에 늦지 않기 위해서 거의 <u>뛰다시피</u> 학교에 갔다.
"(I) went to school almost as if (I) was running in order not to be late for class."

20
Negation

This chapter discusses various ways of expressing negation in Korean. Korean has two ways of negating. The first is to use the negatives 안 "not" and 못 "cannot," which have a short form and a long form. The second is to use the auxiliary verb 말다 "stop" or "avoid."

20.1 The short-form negation [안/ 못 + predicate]

The negative 안 is an abbreviated form of 아니 "no," as in 아니에요 "no," or 한국사람이 아니에요 "(I) am not a Korean." In addition, it is used for general negation. The negative 못 means "cannot" or "unable," and it is used for negation where one's volition or ability is involved.

One can make a short-form negation by placing one of these negatives in front of the predicate, as shown in the following examples:

[안 + verb]

안 떠나요	"does not leave"
안 숨어요	"does not hide"
안 울어요	"does not cry"

[안 + adjective]

안 괜찮아요	"is not fine"
안 더워요	"is not hot"
안 밝아요	"is not bright"

[못 + verb]

못 만들어요	"cannot make"
못 자요	"cannot sleep"
못 읽어요	"cannot read"

Since the negative 못 refers to one's ability or volition, it cannot be used with the adjectives that describe states or quantity. For instance, the following are ungrammatical in Korean:

바쁘다	"busy"	못 바빠요 (X)
좋다	"good"	못 좋아요 (X)
즐겁다	"happy"	못 즐거워요 (X)

The long-form negation: ~지 않아요 and ~지 못해요

The short-form negation is used for declarative and interrogative sentence types but not for imperative and propositive sentence types. For instance, consider the deferential speech level that has four different endings for each sentence type:

Declarative	버스를 안 기다립니다. "(I) do not wait for the bus."
Interrogative	버스를 안 기다립니까? "Don't (you) wait for the bus?"
Imperative	버스를 안 기다리십시다 (X)
Propositive	버스를 안 기다리십시오 (X)

Declarative	피아노를 못 칩니다. "(I) cannot play piano."
Interrogative	피아노를 못 칩니까? "(You) can't play piano?"
Imperative	피아노를 못 치십시다 (X)
Propositive	피아노를 못 치십시오 (X)

Meanwhile, not all verbs and adjectives can be used in the short negation form. A few verbs and adjectives that have corresponding negation verbs cannot take the short negation forms. For instance, 알다 "know" has the corresponding negation verb 모르다 "do not know." Consequently, the short-form negations with 알다 such as 안 알다 or 못 알다 are grammatically wrong. Other verbs that have corresponding negation verbs include 있다 "exist/have," 없다 "not exist/not have," and 맛있다 "delicious"/맛없다 "tasteless."

When negating compound verbs that are made of [noun + 하다], one needs to place the negative 안 or 못 in front of 하다 "do," not the whole compound verb.

공부하다	= 공부 안 해요 "(I) do not study." (not 안 공부해요)
	= 공부 못 해요 "(I) cannot study." (not 못 공부해요)
기대하다	= 기대 안 해요 "(I) do not expect (it)."
	= 기대 못 해요 "(I) cannot expect (it)."
대답하다	= 대답 안 해요 "(I) do not answer."
	= 대답 못 해요 "(I) cannot answer."
운동하다	= 운동 안 해요 "(I) do not exercise."
	= 운동 못 해요 "(I) cannot exercise."
찬성하다	= 찬성 안 해요 "(I) do not approve of (it)."
	= 찬성 못 해요 "(I) cannot approve of (it)."
퇴근하다	= 퇴근 안 해요 "(I) do not leave work."
	= 퇴근 못 해요 "(I) cannot leave work."

20.2 The long-form negation: ~지 않아요 and ~지 못해요

The long-form negation has the following constructions:

[stem + 지 않다]	수잔이 고기를 <u>먹지 않아요</u>	"Susan does not eat meat."
[stem + 지 못하다]	수잔이 고기를 <u>먹지 못해요</u>	"Susan cannot eat meat."

As seen in the previous constructions, the long-form negation is created by adding 지 to the stem, which is followed by a negative auxiliary, 않다 or 못하다. Here are examples:

[verb stem + 지 않다]

가지 않아요	"does not go"
마시지 않아요	"does not drink"
먹지 않아요	"does not eat"

NEGATION

[adjective stem + 지 않다]

높지 않아요	"is not high"
비싸지 않아요	"is not expensive"
크지 않아요	"is not big"

[verb stem + 지 못하다]

만들지 못해요	"cannot make"
자지 못해요	"cannot sleep"
읽지 못해요	"cannot read"

There is no major meaning difference between the long-form negation and the short-form negation. Consequently, they are used interchangeably. However, the long-form negation sounds more formal, indirect, and bookish than the short-form negation.

Meanwhile, it was noted that the negative 못 is not used with the adjectives in the short-form negation since 못 involves one's ability or volition. However, in the long-form negation, 못 can be used with a few adjectives that denote one's desire, such as 안전하다 "safe," 정확하다 "accurate," 똑똑하다 "smart," 분명하다 "clear," 충분하다 "abundant," 행복하다 "happy," 건강하다 "healthy," and 유능하다 "competent." When 못 is used with these adjectives, the negative 못 expresses a sense of disappointment rather than inability.

계획이 <u>완벽하지 못했어요</u>.
"(It is too bad that) the plan was not perfect."
그 가정은 <u>평안하지 못했어요</u>.
"(It is too bad that) for that family, (they) were not in peace."

Notice that the negative 못 in the previous sentences is not translated as ". . . could not" but ". . . was/were not." In other words, the negative 못 is used like 안 but with an emphatic meaning (or a sense of disappointment).

Moreover, negative predicates, such as 없다, 모르다, and 재미없다, can be used only in the long-form negation form, as shown in the following examples:

음식이 <u>맛없지는 않았어요</u>.
"It was not that the food was tasteless."
돈이 <u>없지는 않아요</u>.
"It is not that (he) does not have money."
아빠가 네 마음을 <u>모르지는 않으실 거야</u>.
"It is not that Dad does not know your true feeling."

Just like the short-form negation, the long-form negation is used only for declarative and interrogative sentence types but not for imperative and propositive sentence types, as shown here:

Declarative	매운 음식을 먹지 않습니다. "(I) do not eat spicy food."
Interrogative	매운 음식을 먹지 않습니까? "Don't (you) eat spicy food?"
Imperative	매운 음식을 먹지 않으십시오 (X)
Propositive	매운 음식을 먹지 않으십니다 (X)

Declarative	술을 마시지 못합니다. "(I) cannot drink alcohol."
Interrogative	술을 마시지 못합니까? "(You) can't drink alcohol?"
Imperative	술을 마시지 못합시다 (X)
Propositive	술을 마시지 못하십시오 (X)

To change the long-form negation into the past, one needs to add the past tense marker 었/았 to the negative auxiliary verbs 않다 or 못하다.

너무 미안해서 부탁을 거절하지 않았어요.
"(I) did not turn down (his) request because (I) was very sorry."
너무 미안해서 부탁을 거절하지 못했어요.
"(I) could not turn down (his) request because (I) was very sorry."

20.3 The negative auxiliary verb ~지 말다

For imperative and propositive sentences, the negative auxiliary verb 말다 is used instead, as shown in the following examples:

[stem + 지 말다]

걱정하지 말아요.	"Don't worry" or "(Let's) not worry."
걱정하지 마십시오.	"Don't worry."
걱정하지 마십시다.	"(Let's) not worry."

Notice that the stem 말 changes to 마 (as in 마십시오) and to 맙 (as in 맙시다). This is due to the fact that 말다 is a ㄹ irregular verb. In ㄹ-irregular, the stem loses ㄹ when the stem is followed by one of the following consonants: ㄴ, ㅂ, or ㅅ. Consequently, the stem 말 loses ㄹ, as it is conjugated with the formal imperative ending ~십시오 and ~십시다 (since the ending begins with ㅅ). However, with the polite speech level 어/아요, the ㄹ of the ㄹ-irregular verb is retained. Here are more examples.

그 분 이야기를 믿지 말아요.
"Don't believe his story" or "(Let's) not believe his story."
그 분 이야기를 믿지 마십시오.
"Don't believe his story."
그 분 이야기를 믿지 맙시다.
"(Let's) not believe his story."
담배를 피우지 말아요.
"Don't smoke" or "(Let's) not smoke."
담배를 피우지 마십시오.
"Don't smoke."
담배를 피우지 맙시다.
"(Let us) not smoke."
더 이상 망설이지 말아요.
"Don't hesitate anymore" or "(Let's) not hesitate anymore."
더 이상 망설이지 마십시오.
"Don't hesitate anymore."
더 이상 망설이지 맙시다.
"(Let's) not hesitate anymore."

Meanwhile, Korean has a number of expressions that typically co-occur with verbs in a negative form. Here are some examples:

결코 "definitely (not)"	꼼짝 "budging"
그다지 "(not) much"	다시는 "(not) again"
도무지 "(not) at all"	도저히 "by no means"
미처 "(not) up to that"	밖에 "except for"
별로 "(not) in particular"	아무도 "nobody"
여간 "a little"	전혀 "(not) at all"
절대로 "absolutely (not)"	조금도 "(not) in the least"
추호도 "(not) a bit"	통 "(not) at all"

이거 절대로 만지지 말아요!
"Do not ever touch this!"

NEGATION

다시는 술 마시고 운전하지 마세요.
"Don't ever drink and drive again."

20.4 Sino-Korean negative prefixes

Korean has a number of Sino-Korean negative prefixes that attach to the front of words to indicate negative meaning, such as 무 (無) "nothingness, un-, -less"; 미 (未) "not yet, un-, in-"; 부/불 (不) "not, in-, un-, non-, dis-"; and 비(非) "non-, un-, not, anti-." For instance, consider how the prefix 부/불 (不) indicates negative meaning to the nouns it attaches to.

가능 "possibility"	불가능 "impossibility"
경기 "economy"	불경기 "recession"
공평 "fairness"	불공평 "unfairness"
규칙 "rule"	불규칙 "irregularity"
균형 "balance"	불균형 "unbalance"
구속 "imprisonment"	불구속 "indictment without detention"
명예 "honor"	불명예 "dishonor"
복종 "obedience"	불복종 "disobedience"
만족 "satisfaction"	불만족 "dissatisfaction"
안정 "stability"	불안정 "instability"
이익 "profit"	불이익 "disadvantage"
친절 "kindness"	불친절 "unkindness"
투명 "transparency"	불투명 "opacity"
평등 "equality"	불평등 "inequality"
필요 "necessity"	불필요 "unnecessariness"
합격 "passing an exam"	불합격 "disqualification"
합리 "rationality"	불합리 "irrationality"
확실 "certainty"	불확실 "uncertainty"

21

Modifiers

The typical examples of English modifiers are adjectives and relative clauses. English modifiers can occur before the word they modify (e.g., in the case of adjectives, as in "intelligent Daniel") or after the word (e.g., in the case of relative clauses, as in "Daniel who is intelligent" or "Daniel who studies math").

However, in Korean, modifiers (or noun-modifying clauses) always come before the word they modify. Moreover, any predicate can be changed into a modifier by attaching a noun-modifying ending to the predicate stem. This chapter introduces four Korean noun-modifying endings: ~는, ~(으)ㄴ, ~(으)ㄹ, and ~던.

21.1 The noun-modifying ending ~는

The noun-modifying ending ~는 is used with verbs, and it carries the present tense. Consider the following examples:

Verb	Verb stem + 는
오다 "come"	도서관에 <u>오는</u> 학생 "the student who comes to the library"
찾다 "find"	언니가 <u>찾는</u> 반지 "the ring (my) older sister looks for"
마시다 "drink"	맥주를 <u>마시는</u> 남자 "the man who drinks beer"
읽다 "read"	내가 <u>읽는</u> 서류 "the document that (I) read"

Notice in the previous examples that ~는 attaches to the verb stem and changes the predicate into the present form of a relative clause.

Although ~는 is primarily used with verbs, the adjectives that end with 있다/없다 take ~는:

맛있다 "delicious"　　　　　맛있는 샐러드 "delicious salad" (맛있 + 는)
맛없다 "tasteless"　　　　　맛없는 국수 "tasteless noodles"
멋있다 "stylish"　　　　　　멋있는 넥타이 "stylish necktie"
재미있다 "interesting"　　　재미있는 이야기 "interesting story"

21.2 The noun-modifying ending ~(으)ㄴ

The noun-modifying ending ~(으)ㄴ is used with adjectives, verbs, and copulas. When ~(으)ㄴ is used with adjectives or copulas, it indicates the present tense; when it is used with verbs, it carries the past tense.

~(으)ㄴ with adjectives and copulas

MODIFIERS

One can change an adjective or a copula into a noun-modifying unit by attaching ~(으)ㄴ to its stem: ~은 is used after a stem that ends in a consonant; ~ㄴ is used after a stem that ends in a vowel. Consider the following examples:

Adjective	Adjective stem + (으)ㄴ
안전하다 "safe"	안전한 여행 "safe trip"
좋다 "good"	좋은 성격 "good personality" (좋 + 은)
예쁘다 "pretty"	예쁜 디자인 "pretty design" (예쁘 + ㄴ)
조용하다 "quiet"	조용한 집 "quiet house"
어렵다 "difficult"	어려운 일 "difficult matter"

Copula	Copula stem + (으)ㄴ
이다 "be"	훌륭한 과학자인 에디슨 "Edison who is a brilliant scientist"
아니다 "not be"	한국 사람이 아닌 사람 "the person who is not a Korean"

~(으)ㄴ with verbs

When ~(으)ㄴ is attached to a verb stem, it changes the predicate into the past form of a relative clause, as shown in the following examples:

Verb	Verb stem + (으)ㄴ
먹다 "eat"	아침을 먹은 직원 "the employee who ate breakfast" (먹 + 은)
찾다 "find"	형이 찾은 지갑 "the wallet that (my) brother found"
보다 "see"	네가 본 드라마 "the drama that you saw" (보 + ㄴ)
배우다 "learn"	수영을 배운 아이 "the child who learned swimming"

Since ~(으)ㄴ denotes the past tense, the use of past tense marker 었/았 along with ~(으)ㄴ is grammatically incorrect. For instance, saying a phrase like "the pasta that I ate" in Korean should be "내가 먹은 파스타" not "내가 먹었은 파스타."

21.3 The noun-modifying ending ~(으)ㄹ

The noun-modifying ending ~(으)ㄹ indicates that the action or state denoted by the predicate has not yet been actualized. ~을 is attached to a stem that ends in a consonant (e.g., 누나가 먹을 음식 "the food that my older sister will eat"), and ~ㄹ is attached to a stem that ends in a vowel (e.g., 우리가 볼 영화 "the movie that we will see").

읽다	나중에 읽을 보고서 "the report that (I) will read later"
가르치다	영어를 가르칠 사람 "the person who will teach English"
공부하다	내일 공부할 부분 "the part that (we) will study tomorrow"
쉽다	요리하기 쉬울 음식 "food that will be easy to cook"

As shown in the previous examples, the ending ~(으)ㄹ mainly indicates the prospective meaning. However, since the action or state has not been realized, the ending can also imply the meaning of intention or conjecture. This is particularly true when the ending is used with the past tense. Compare the following examples:

우유를 마신 사람
"the person who drank milk"
우유를 마시는 사람
"the person who drinks milk"
우유를 마실 사람
"the person who will drink milk"
우유를 마셨을 사람
"the person who might have drunk milk"

Placing a noun-modifying unit in a sentence

The first example is the past form of a relative clause as indicated by ~은; the second example indicates the present action as indicated by ~는, and the third example is about a prospective action as indicated by ~을. However, notice that the predicate of the fourth example has the past tense marker ~었 and ~(으)ㄹ (e.g., 먹 + 었 + 을). The ~(으)ㄹ ending in the fourth example does not indicate the prospective meaning but conjecture. Here are more examples:

내가 <u>탔을</u> 기차
"the train that (I) might have taken"
같이 <u>기뻐했을</u> 소식
"the news that (we) might have rejoiced about together"
너무 <u>뜨거웠을</u> 커피
"the coffee that might have been too hot"
내가 <u>좋아했을</u> 사람
"the person that I might have liked"

21.4 The noun-modifying ending ~던

The retrospective noun-modifying ending ~던 indicates a speaker's past experience or observation of the action or state. When it is used with a verb stem, the ending ~던 indicates a habitual action in the past. When it is used with an adjective stem, it implies that the past state no longer exists.

Verb	*Verb stem* + 던
만나다 "meet"	<u>만나던</u> 남자 "the man that (I) used to meet"
먹다 "eat"	<u>먹던</u> 음식 "the food that (I) used to eat"
읽다 "read"	<u>읽던</u> 신문 "the newspaper that (I) used to read"

Adjective	*Adjective stem* + 던
좋다 "good"	<u>좋던</u> 성격 "the personality that used to be good"
유명하다 "famous"	<u>유명하던</u> 가수 "the singer who used to be popular"
어렵다 "difficult"	<u>어렵던</u> 공부 "the study that used to be difficult"

One can make the past action or state even more temporarily remote by using it with the past tense marker ~었/았, as in ~었/았던. Compare the following two examples:

클라식 기타를 잘 <u>치던</u> 사람
"the person who used to play classical guitar well"
클라식 기타를 잘 <u>쳤던</u> 학생
"the person who played classical guitar well (a long time ago)"

Here are more examples:

이 가게에서 <u>일하던</u> 사람
"the person who used to work in this store"
이 가게에서 <u>일했던</u> 사람
"the person who worked in this store (a long time ago)"

21.5 Placing a noun-modifying unit in a sentence

When a predicate is changed into a noun-modifying unit, it becomes part of a new noun phrase, as shown in the following examples:

샌드위치를 먹어요.
"(I) eat a sandwich."

MODIFIERS

샌드위치를 먹은 사람
"the person who ate a sandwich"
샌드위치를 먹는 사람
"the person who eats a sandwich"
샌드위치를 먹을 사람
"the person who will eat a sandwich"
샌드위치를 먹었을 사람
"the person who might have eaten a sandwich"
샌드위치를 먹던 사람
"the person who used to eat a sandwich"

These newly transformed noun phrases (or noun-modifying clauses) can be used as a subject, object, or indirect object depending on the particle that attaches to them, as shown in the following examples:

샐러드를 먹은 사람이 제 여자 친구예요.
"The person who ate salad is my girlfriend."
샐러드를 먹은 사람을 찾았어요.
"(I) looked for the person who ate salad."
샐러드를 먹은 사람한테 물어 봤어요.
"(I) asked the person who ate salad."

22
Expressions with modifier clauses I

Korean has a number of idiomatic expressions that are built on one of the four noun-modifying endings (i.e., ~는, ~은, ~을, ~던) and a noun, such as 길, 적, 동안, and so forth. Since these nouns always appear after the noun-modifying endings (e.g., ~는 길 or ~은 적), they are called "post modifiers." This chapter introduces special expressions that are made by combining one of four noun-modifying endings with one of the following post modifiers: 것, 겸, 곳, 길, 김, 다음, 대로, 덕분, 동안/사이, 듯, and 때.

22.1 ~는/(으)ㄴ/(으)ㄹ/던 것 같다 "it seems"

The form ~는/(으)ㄴ/(으)ㄹ/던 것 같다 "it seems/looks like" is the combination of one of the four noun-modifying endings (i.e., ~는, ~(으)ㄴ, ~(으)ㄹ, and ~던), the bound noun 것 "the fact/the one/the being" (or 거 for colloquial settings), and the adjective 같다 "be the same." The selection of ~는, ~(으)ㄴ, ~(으)ㄹ, and ~던 follows the same mechanism of the noun-modifying patterns: ~는 is used after a verb stem for the present tense; ~(으)ㄴ is used after a verb stem for the past tense or after an adjective/copula stem for the present tense; ~(으)ㄹ is used after a verb or adjective stem for the prospective tense; and ~던 is used after a verb or adjective stem for the past tense/restrospective meaning.

~는 것 같다
주말마다 운동을 하는 것 같아요.
"(It) seems that (she) exercises every weekend."
이 회사에서 일하는 것 같아요.
"(It) looks like (he) works at this firm."
~(으)ㄴ 것 같다
음식이 좀 짠 것 같아요.
"The food seems to be a bit salty."
부인이 일본 사람인 것 같아요.
"(His) wife seems to be Japanese."
빵을 너무 많이 먹은 것 같아요.
"(It) seems that (he) ate too much bread."
~(으)ㄹ 것 같다
오늘은 날씨가 더울 것 같아요.
"As for today, (it) seems that the weather will be hot."
이것이 더 비쌀 것 같아요.
"(It) seems that this will be more expensive."
~던 것 같다
전에는 매운 음식을 잘 먹었던 것 같아요.
"(It) seems that (he) used to eat spicy food well."
작년 겨울은 매우 추웠던 것 같아요.
"As for last winter, (it) seems that (it) was very cold."

EXPRESSIONS WITH MODIFIER CLAUSES I

미국 시민권자이었던 것 같아요.
"(It) seems that (they) were American citizens."

For the past tense, the past tense marker 었/았 is used after 같다. Consider the following examples:

어머니가 일본 사람인 것 같았어요.
"The mother seemed to be a Japanese person."
감기에 걸린 것 같았어요.
"(It) seemed that (she) caught a cold."
이 영화가 재미있을 것 같았어요.
"(It) seemed that this movie would be interesting."
그 날 눈이 많이 왔던 것 같았어요.
"(It) seemed that it had snowed a lot on that day."

22.2 ~는/(으)ㄴ 것이다 "the fact is"

~는/(으)ㄴ 것이다 is used to give an account of events or states of affairs. It can be translated as "the fact is" or "what happened is that." This form combines the noun-modifying ending ~는 (for verbs in the present tense) or ~(으)ㄴ (for verbs in the past tense or for adjectives/copulas in the present tense), the dependent noun 것 (or 거 for colloquial usage) "fact/thing," and the copula 이다.

~는 것이다
이제부터 매일 30분씩 같이 운동하는 거예요.
"The fact is that (we will) exercise 30 minutes a day together every day from now on."
오늘 저녁 식사는 같이 하기로 한 거예요.
"The fact is that (we) decided to have dinner together tonight."
~(으)ㄴ 것이다
형이 담배를 끊은 거예요.
"The fact is that (my) older brother quit smoking."
오늘 날씨가 추운 거예요.
"The fact is that today's weather is cold."
에반이 이제 대학생인 거예요.
"The fact is that Evan is now a college student."

22.3 ~(으)ㄹ 겸 "to do A and to do B"

The bound noun 겸 means "and also" or "at the same time," as in 이 방은 서재 겸 침실로 쓰고 있어요 "(We) are using this room as a bedroom and also a study." ~(으)ㄹ 겸 is constructed from the noun-modifying ending ~(으)ㄹ and 겸, and it is used when enumerating multiple purposes for a single action, denoted by the verb.

책도 빌리고 시험 공부도 할 겸 도서관에 갔어요.
"(I) went to the library to borrow books and study for the test."
너도 보고 점심도 같이 먹을 겸 해서 왔다.
"(I) came to see you and have lunch together at the same time."
바닷가 구경도 하고 쉴 겸 지난 주에 제주도에 갔다 왔어요.
"Last week, (we) went to Jeju Island to see beaches and to rest."

22.4 ~(으)ㄹ 계획이다 "plans to"

~(으)ㄹ 계획이다 is built on the noun-modifying ending ~(으)ㄹ, the noun 계획 "plan," and the copula 이다. It is used to express one's plan.

다음 달부터 요가를 배울 계획이에요.
"(I) plan to learn yoga starting next month."

~(으)ㄴ 다음에 "after"

학교 근처에 새 가게를 열 계획이에요.
"(We) plan to open a new store near the school."

Meanwhile, you can create similar expressions replacing 계획 with other nouns such as 생각 "thought," 예정 "intention," 작정 "decision," and 마음 "mind."

앞으로 뭘 공부할 생각이세요?
"What do (you) plan to study?"
태권도를 열심히 배울 생각이에요.
"(I) plan/intend to learn Taekwondo earnestly."

22.5 ~는/(으)ㄴ 김에 "since/while you are at it/doing it"

~는/(은)ㄴ 김에 is made with the noun-modifying ending ~는 or ~(으)ㄴ, the bound noun 김 "occasion," and the particle 에. It is used to express "since/while you are at it/doing it."

한국어를 배우는 김에 한국 역사도 공부하려고요.
"Since (I) am learning the Korean language, (I) intend to study Korean history too."
부산에 온 김에 형님한테도 꼭 연락하세요.
"While (you) are in Busan, please contact (your) older brother."
뉴욕에 가는 김에 뮤지컬도 봅시다.
"Since (we) are going to New York City, (let's) also watch a musical."

22.6 ~는/던 길에 "on the way to/from"

~는/던 길에 is built on the noun-modifying ending ~는 or ~던, the noun 길 "way/road/street," and the particle 에. This form means "on the way to/from" and it is normally used with a verb of movement, such as 가다 "go" (e.g., 가는 길 "on the way to") and 오다 "come" (e.g., 오는 길 "on the way from").

보스톤으로 가는 길이에요.
"(I) am on (my) way to Boston."
공항에서 오는 길에 선물을 살 거예요.
"(I) will buy the present on (my) way from the airport."
가게에 나가던 길에 어머니를 만났어요.
"(I) met (my) mother on the way out to the store."

22.7 ~(으)ㄴ 다음에 "after"

~(으)ㄴ 다음에 means "afterward" or "later." It consists of the noun-modifying ending ~(으)ㄴ, the noun 다음 "next," and the particle 에.

집에 돌아온 다음에 샤워를 먼저 했습니다.
"(I) took a shower first after coming back home."
새집으로 이사한 다음에 살 거지요?
"(You) will buy (it) after moving in to the new house, right?"
손님이 돌아간 다음에 설거지를 하세요.
"Please do the dishes after the guests return."
일을 다 마친 다음에 운동합시다.
"(Let's) exercise after finishing all the work."

The use of the noun 후 "after" or 뒤 "behind" (instead of 다음) indicates a similar meaning, as shown in the following examples:

3과를 읽은 후에 4과를 공부하세요.
"After reading chapter 3, please study chapter 4."

EXPRESSIONS WITH MODIFIER CLAUSES I

> 보통 운동을 한 후에 샤워를 해요.
> "(I) usually take a shower after exercising."
> 영화를 본 뒤에 감상문을 쓰세요.
> "After watching the movie, please write a reaction paper."

22.8 ~(으)ㄴ 덕분에 "thanks to, by (someone's) favor"

~(으)ㄴ 덕분에 is made of the noun-modifying ending ~(으)ㄴ, the noun 덕분 "indebtedness," and the particle 에. This form is used to express "thanks to" or "by someone's favor."

> 도와 주신 덕분에 일을 빨리 마칠 수 있었습니다.
> "Thanks to your (your) help, (I) was able to finish (my) work quickly."
> 교수님이 추천서를 잘 써 주신 덕분에 장학금을 받을 수 있었습니다.
> "Through (my) professor's great recommendation letter, (I) was able to receive the scholarship."

22.9 ~는/(으)ㄴ 대로 "as soon as"

~는/(으)ㄴ 대로 means "as soon as" or "in accordance with." It is constructed from the noun-modifying ending ~는 (for a verb stem) or ~(으)ㄴ (for an adjective stem) and the bound noun 대로 "according to/the same/just as."

> 날이 밝는 대로 떠날 거예요.
> "(We) will leave as soon as the dawn breaks."
> 주는 대로 다 먹었어요.
> "(I) ate everything (she) gave (me)."
> 약속한 대로 점심을 사 주셨어요.
> "(He) bought (me) a lunch as promised."
> 내가 시키는 대로 행동하겠어요?
> "Will (you) behave according to what I ask (you to)?"
> 사무실에 도착하는 대로 전화 주세요.
> "Give (me) a call as soon as (you) arrive at the office."
> 날씨가 좋아지는 대로 시작합시다.
> "(Let's) begin as soon as the weather becomes better."

22.10 ~는 동안 /사이에 "while"

The noun 동안 means "a while/an interval," as in 오랫 동안 "for a long time," and 사이 means "interval" as in 3년 사이 "for three years." The combination of 동안/사이, the noun-modifying ending ~는, and the particle 에, as in ~는 동안/사이에, expresses two situations or activities that overlap in time. The expression ~는 동안/사이에 is equivalent to "while" or "during."

> 아내가 자고 있는 동안에 저녁을 만들었어요.
> "While (my) wife was sleeping, (I) cooked dinner."
> 제가 없는 동안에 남동생을 돌봐 주세요.
> "While I am away, please take care of (my) younger brother."
> 친구한테 전화하는 사이에 기차를 놓쳤네요.
> "(I) missed (my) train, while making a phone call to (my) friend."

22.11 ~는/(으)ㄴ/(으)ㄹ 듯하다/듯싶다 "seems"

~는/(으)ㄴ/(으)ㄹ 듯하다/듯싶다 "seems/appears to/looks like" is made of one of the noun-modifying endings, the bound noun 듯 "seeming appearance," and the dependent adjective 하다 "really/indeed" (or 싶다 "wish/seem").

봄이 온 듯해요.
"(It) seems that the spring has come."
자고 있는 듯합니다.
"(He) seems to be asleep."
아직 살아 있는 듯싶어요.
"(He) seems to be alive still."
그 소문이 사실인 듯싶어요.
"That rumor seems to be true."

For the past tense, the past tense marker ~었/았 is used after 듯하다/듯싶다, as shown in the following examples:

재즈를 좋아하는 듯했어요.
"(It) seemed that (they) like jazz."
중국 역사를 전공한 듯했어요.
"(It) seemed that (he) majored in Chinese history."
음식이 매운 듯싶었어요.
"The food appeared to be spicy."

22.12 ~(으)ㄹ 때 "when"

~(으)ㄹ 때 means "when." It combines the noun-modifying ending ~(으)ㄹ and the noun 때 "time/occasion."

밖에 나갈 때 로션을 꼭 얼굴에 꼭 바르셔야 돼요.
"(You) should apply lotion on (your) face when (you) go outside."
시간 있을 때 연락하세요.
"Contact (them) when (you) have time."
배가 아플 때 이 약을 드세요.
"Take this medicine when (your) stomach aches."
날씨가 좋을 때 떠납시다.
"(Let's) leave when the weather is good."
싱글일 때 여행을 많이 하고 싶어요.
"While (I) am a single, (I) want to travel a lot."

There are two things to remember when using ~(으)ㄹ 때 with verbs in the past tense. When only the main clause is conjugated for the past tense, the action of the 때 clause co-occurs with that of the main (or second) clause. Consider the following example:

뉴욕시에 갈 때 버스를 탔어요.
"While (I) was going to New York City, (I) took a bus."

Notice in the previous example that the action of the first clause "going" co-occurred with the action of the second clause "taking the bus," and the tense is marked only in the main clause.

However, when both clauses are conjugated for the past tense, the actions of both clauses do not co-occur: the action of the first clause happened prior to that of the main clause. Consider the following example:

뉴욕시에 갔을 때 앤드류를 처음 만났어요.
"When (I) went to New York City, (I) met Andrew for the first time."

EXPRESSIONS WITH MODIFIER CLAUSES I

Notice that the first clause "going to New York City" happened prior to the action of the main clause "meeting Andrew." Here are more examples:

일본인 친구하고 <u>대화할 때</u> 일본어를 했어요.
"While conversing with (my) Japanese friend, (I) talked in Japanese."
도서관에 <u>갈 때</u> 지하철을 탔어요.
"While going to the library, (I) took a subway."
파리에 <u>갔을 때</u> 날씨가 추웠어요.
"When (I) went to Paris, the weather was cold."
하와이에 <u>갔을 때</u> 어느 호텔에 있었어요?
"When (you) went to Hawaii, which hotel did (you) stay at?"

23

Expressions with modifier clauses II

This chapter introduces special expressions that are made by combining one of three noun-modifying endings with one of the following post modifiers: 리, 모양, 바에, 바람에, 반면에, 뻔하다, 뿐, 수 있다, 이상, and 일/적.

23.1 ~(으)ㄹ 리가 없다 "it is not possible that"

~(으)ㄹ 리가 없다 is built on the noun-modifying ending ~(으)ㄹ, the bound noun 리 "possibility," the subject particle 가, and the verb 없다 "not have/not exist." ~(으)ㄹ 리가 없다 indicates that the content of the ~(으)ㄹ 리 ending clause is not true or far from reality. It can be translated as "it is not possible that . . ." or "there is no possibility that . . ." in English.

> 그 친구들이 나를 싫어할 리가 없어요.
> "(It) is not possible that those friends hate me."
> 그가 범인일 리가 없어요.
> "There's no way that he is a criminal."
> 날씨가 추울 리가 없어요.
> "(It) is not possible that the weather is cold."
> 그들이 가난했을 리가 없어요.
> "(It) is not possible that they were poor."
> 결혼 생활이 불행했을 리가 없어요.
> "(It) is not possible that (their) marriage life was unhappy."

23.2 ~(으)ㄹ 만하다 "worth"

~(으)ㄹ 만하다 is made of the noun-modifying ending ~(으)ㄹ and the adjective 만하다 "worth."

> 결혼은 한 번 해 볼 만해요.
> "Marriage is worth trying once."
> 저 학생이 아주 믿을 만해요.
> "That student is worthy of every confidence."
> 정치인들이 비난 받을 만하네요.
> "The politicians deserve blame."
> 볼 만한 영화 좀 추천해 주세요.
> "Please recommend a movie worthy of watching."

EXPRESSIONS WITH MODIFIER CLAUSES II

23.3 ~는/(으)ㄴ/(으)ㄹ 모양이다 "appears to"

~는/(으)ㄴ/(으)ㄹ 모양이다 "appears to/looks like" consists of one of the noun-modifying endings, the noun 모양 "appearance/form/sign," and the copula 이다.

~는 모양이다
팝콘을 만드는 모양이에요.
"(It) appears that (he) makes (some) popcorn."
열쇠가 없는 모양이에요.
"(It) seems that (she) does not have the key."
영화가 재미있는 모양이에요.
"(It) appears that the movie is interesting."
~(으)ㄴ 모양이다
아침을 못 먹은 모양이에요.
"(It) appears that (they) could not eat breakfast."
친구가 그리운 모양이에요.
"(It) appears that (he) longs for (his) friend."
~(으)ㄹ 모양이다
담배를 끊을 모양이에요.
"(It) appears that (he) will quit smoking."
오늘 집에 안 올 모양이에요.
"(It) appears that (he) will not come home today."

23.4 ~(으)ㄹ 바에 "rather . . . than"

~(으)ㄹ 바에는 is constructed from the noun-modifying ending ~(으)ㄹ, the bound noun 바 "thing," and the particle 에. This expression is used to connect two clauses. However, it indicates that the speaker rejects the action of the first clause but opts for the action of the main clause. It can be translated as "rather . . . than" in English.

국수를 또 먹을 바에 차라리 굶을래요.
"(I) would rather starve than eat noodles again."
집에 아무것도 안 하고 있을 바에 밖에 나가서 운동이나 해라.
"Go out and exercise or something rather than staying home, doing nothing."
이 대학에 들어갈 바에는 유학을 가는 게 낫지 않겠니?
"Wouldn't it be better to study abroad rather than entering this university?"

23.5 ~는/(으)ㄴ 바람에 "because of"

~는/(으)ㄴ 바람에 is built on the noun-modifying ending ~는/(으)ㄴ, the noun 바람 "wind," and the particle 에. It means "as a result of" or "because of," and the effects for which ~는 바람에 is used are generally negative and incidental. Consider the following example:

늦게 일어나는 바람에 직장에 못 갔어요.
"(I) could not go to work because (I) got up late."

Notice that the ~는 바람에 indicates the cause (e.g., getting up late) of the negative or unpleasant consequence of the main clause (e.g., not being able to go to work). Here are more examples:

눈이 많이 오는 바람에 회사에 못 갔어요.
"(I) could not go to work because (it) snowed a lot."
서두르는 바람에 차 사고가 났어요.
"(I) had a car accident because (I) hurried up."
제 차 열쇠를 잃어 버리는 바람에 약속을 못 지켰어요.
"(I) could not keep the promise because (I) lost my car key."

~(으)ㄹ 법하다 "be likely"　　　　　　　　　　　　　　　23.8

날씨가 싸늘한 바람에 일찍 헤어졌어요.
"(We) departed early because of the chilly weather."

23.6　~는/(으)ㄴ 반면에 "on the other hand"

~는/(으)ㄴ 반면에 combines the noun-modifying ending ~는/(으)ㄴ, the noun 반면 "other side," and the particle 에. This expression means "on the other hand" or "in contrast," and it is usually used in writing or formal speech.

대학 졸업생 수는 증가하는 반면에 대졸 취업자 수는 줄고 있다.
"The number of college graduates is on the rise, but on the other hand, the number of college graduates who get employed is on the decline."
디자인은 심플한 반면에 기능은 많습니다.
"The design is simple, but on the other hand, (it) has many functions."
많은 한국 사람들이 매운 음식을 좋아하는 반면에 싫어하는 한국 사람도 많다.
"Many Koreans like spicy food, but on the other hand, there are many Koreans who do not like (it)."
이 가게는 20–30대 젊은 고객이 많은 반면에 저 가게는 40–50대 손님들이 주를 이룬다.
"As for this store, there are many young customers in their 20s and 30s, but on the other hand, as for that store, customers in their 40s and 50s are the majority."

23.7　~는/(으)ㄴ 법이다 "it's certain that..."

~는/(으)ㄴ 법이다 consists of the noun-modifying ending ~는/(으)ㄴ, 법 "a rule," and the copula 이다. This form is used to mean "it's bound to..." or "it's certain that...."

기대가 크면 실망도 큰 법이에요.
"If (you) get (your) hopes up, (you) are bound to be more disappointed."
싸고 맛있으면 음식이 잘 팔리는 법이에요.
"Inexpensive and delicious foods are certain to sell well."
서두르면 실수하는 법이니까 조심하세요.
"If (you) rush, (you) are certain to make a mistake, so be careful."
외로울 때 헤어진 여자 친구에 대한 생각이 나는 법이에요.
"When (you) are lonely, (you)'re bound to think about (your) ex-girlfriend."

23.8　~(으)ㄹ 법하다 "be likely"

~(으)ㄹ 법하다 is built on the noun-modifying ending ~(으)ㄹ, the noun 법 "a rule," and the verb 하다. This expression is used to indicate "probability" or "possibility" and can be translated as "be likely" or "it is possible that...."

지금쯤 도착할 법한데요.
"It's likely that (they) will arrive (there) by now."
오늘은 눈이 내릴 법한 날씨예요.
"As for today, it is probable that snow will fall."
이제 형이 집에 와 있을 법해요.
"It's likely that (my) older brother is home by now."

EXPRESSIONS WITH MODIFIER CLAUSES II

23.9 ~(으)ㄹ 뻔했다 "almost"

~(으)ㄹ 뻔했다 is made of the noun-modifying ending ~(으)ㄹ, the noun 뻔 "almost/about to," and the verb 했다 "did." The form ~(으)ㄹ 뻔했다 indicates that some event almost happened. It corresponds to "almost" or "to be nearly" in English.

날씨가 추워서 감기에 걸릴 뻔했어요.
"(I) almost caught a cold, since the weather was cold."
공항에 늦게 도착해서 비행기를 놓칠 뻔했어요.
"(I) almost missed the flight since (I) arrived in the airport late."
피곤해서 아침에 못 일어날 뻔했어요.
"(I) almost could not get up in the morning because (I) was tired."

23.10 ~(으)ㄹ 뿐 "only"

~(으)ㄹ 뿐 is constructed from the noun-modifying form ~(으)ㄹ and the bound noun/particle 뿐 "only." As a particle, 뿐 is attached to a noun to indicate meaning "only" (e.g., 한국어를 공부한 사람이 제임스뿐이에요 "The person who studied Korean is only James").

The expression ~(으)ㄹ 뿐 also means "only." However, ~(으)ㄹ 뿐 is usually used with the copula 이다/아니다 as in ~(으)ㄹ 뿐이에요 "it is only . . ." or ~(으)ㄹ 뿐만아니다 "it is not just/only."

저는 단지 당신의 말만을 믿을 뿐이에요.
"It is only your word that I believe."
내게 주어진 일만을 열심히 할 뿐이에요.
"(I) do only the task given to me."
운동을 잘할 뿐만 아니라 공부도 잘해요.
"(He) is not only good at sports but studies hard too."
이 동네는 깨끗할 뿐만 아니라 조용해요.
"As for this neighborhood, (it) is not only clean but also quiet."

23.11 ~(으)ㄹ 수 있다/없다 "can, cannot"

~(으)ㄹ 수 있다/없다 is used to indicate an ability or possibility of doing something. This form consists of the noun-modifying ending ~(으)ㄹ, the bound noun 수 "means/way," and the verb 있다 "have/exist." For negation, 없다 "not have/not exist" is used instead of 있다.

~(으)ㄹ 수 있다 is equivalent to the English translation "one can do/be" or "it is possible to," as shown in the following examples:

베이스 기타를 칠 수 있어요.
"(I) can play bass guitar" or "(It) is possible to play bass guitar."
중국어를 말할 수 있어요.
"(I) can speak Chinese" or "(It) is possible to speak Chinese."

On the other hand, ~(으)ㄹ 수 없어요 is used to express "cannot do/be" or "it is not possible to."

집에서 공부할 수 없어요.
"(I) cannot study at home" or "(It) is not possible to study at home."
파티에 갈 수 없어요.
"(I) cannot go to the party" or "(It) is not possible to go to the party."

The meaning of ~(으)ㄹ 수 없어요 is similar to that of the negative expression with 못 "cannot/unable." For instance, compare the following two sentences:

김치를 못 먹어요 (or 김치를 먹지 못해요).
"(I) cannot eat kimchi."

김치를 먹을 수 없어요.
"(I) cannot eat kimchi" or "(It) is not possible to eat kimchi."

Notice that whereas the first sentence with the negative 못 simply emphasizes one's inability (i.e., whether one can eat kimchi or not), the second sentence with ~(으)ㄹ 수 없어요 indicates one's ability as well as the possibility of the action (i.e., whether eating the kimchi is possible or not).

When ~(으)ㄹ 수 있다/없다 is used with adjectives, it indicates the possibility of the state or quality, as shown in the following examples:

금요일 시험이 어려울 수 있어요.
"(It) is possible that the test on Friday will be difficult."
내일 날씨가 추울 수 있어요.
"(It) is possible that tomorrow's weather will be cold."

Meanwhile, some particles, such as 는, 도, 만, and 밖에, can appear after the noun 수 to indicate additional meanings. Consider the following examples:

내일의 날씨가 더울 수도 있어요.
"(It) is possible that tomorrow's weather can also be hot."
뉴욕에서 살 수만 있다면 좋겠어요.
"(It) would be wonderful only if (I) could live in New York."

Notice that the particle 도 adds a special meaning of "also" to the first sentence, and the particle 만 adds a meaning of "only" to the second sentence.

When the noun 수 is followed by the particle 밖에, which means "except/but," as in ~(으)ㄹ 수 밖에 없어요, it creates an expression of "have no other way to/can't help (doing)."

이 차를 팔 수밖에 없어요.
"(I) can't help selling this car."
가격을 깎아 줄 수밖에 없었어요.
"(I) couldn't help giving discounts."

23.12 ~는/(으)ㄴ 이상 "since, unless"

~는/(으)ㄴ 이상 is the combination of the noun-modifying form ending 는 (for verbs in the present tense) or ~(으)ㄴ (for verbs in the past tense or for adjectives/copulas in the present tense), and the noun 이상 "more than." This expression means "since" or "unless," depending on if the verb of the first clause is a positive or negative one, as shown in the following examples:

결혼한 이상 이제 둘은 한 몸이에요.
"Since you are married, now both of you are one body."
날씨가 따뜻한 이상 오늘 스키는 못 타겠네요.
"Since the weather is warm, (we) may not be able to ski today."
여러 번 생각하며 신중하게 결정한 이상 더 이상 걱정하지 마세요.
"Since you made a decision after thinking seriously multiple times, do not worry about (it) any more."
열심히 연습하지 않는 이상 이길 생각하지 마세요.
"Unless (you) practice hard, do not think of winning."
약을 먹지 않는 이상 수술을 받아야 돼요.
"Unless (I) take the medicine every day, (I) must receive surgery."

23.13 ~(으)ㄴ 일/적/경험이 있다/없다 "ever, never"

~(으)ㄴ 적/일/경험 is built on the noun-modifying ending ~(으)ㄴ and the noun 적, 일, or 경험 "experience." Typically, ~(으)ㄴ 적, ~(으)ㄴ 일, or ~(으)ㄴ 경험 are followed by 있다 "exist/have"

EXPRESSIONS WITH MODIFIER CLAUSES II

or 없다 "not exist/not have," and they are used to indicate whether the subject "has an/no experience (of doing something)." Consider the following examples:

엘에이를 <u>방문한 적이 있어요</u>.
"(I) have an experience of visiting L.A."
태권도를 <u>배운 적이 없어요</u>.
"(I) have never learned Taekwondo."

The auxiliary verb ~어/아 보다 "try (doing) something" is often used with the expression ~(으)ㄴ 적/일이 있다/없다, as shown in the following examples:

서울에 <u>가 본 적이 있어요</u>.
"(I) have been to Seoul."
변 선생님을 <u>만나 본 일이 없어요</u>.
"(I) have never met Professor Byon."
일본에서 <u>일해 본 경험이 있어요</u>?
"Have (you) ever worked in Japan?"
멕시코 음식을 <u>먹어 본 일이 있어요</u>?
"Have (you) ever tried Mexican food?"

Notice that ~어/아 본 적/일/경험이 있다/없다 highlights whether the subject has an/no experience of doing something. In addition, when it is used in an interrogative sentence, the pattern expresses "Have you ever?"

24

Expressions with modifier clauses III

This chapter introduces special expressions that are made by combining one of three noun-modifying endings with one of the following post modifiers: 정도로, 줄 알다/모르다, 도중에, 지 알다/모르다, 채로, 척하다, 탓/통에, 편이다, or 한에.

24.1 ~(으)ㄹ 정도로 "to the extent that"

~(으)ㄹ 정도로 is constructed from the noun-modifying form ending ~(으)ㄹ, the noun 정도 "degree" or "extent," and the particle 로. This expression means "to the extent."

배가 <u>터질 정도로</u> 많이 먹었어요.
"(I) ate so much to the extent that (my) stomach might burst."
눈이 <u>부실 정도로</u> 아름답다.
"(She) is beautiful to the extent that (my) eyes are dazzled."
전화도 <u>못 할 정도로</u> 바빴어요?
"Were (you) busy to the degree that (you) could not even call?"
귀신이 <u>나올 정도로</u> 집이 오래됐어요.
"The house has been around so long to the extent that ghosts can appear."

24.2 ~는/(으)ㄴ/(으)ㄹ 줄 알다/모르다 "know, think"

~는/(으)ㄴ/(으)ㄹ 줄 알다/모르다 is the combination of one of the noun-modifying endings, the bound noun 줄 "the way," and the verb 알다 "know" or 모르다 "not know." The selection of ~는, ~(으)ㄴ, and ~(으)ㄹ follows the same mechanism of the noun-modifying patterns: ~는 is used after a verb stem for the present tense, ~(으)ㄴ is used after a verb stem for the past tense or after an adjective/copula stem for the present tense, and ~(으)ㄹ is used after a verb or adjective stem for the prospective tense.

~는/(으)ㄴ 줄 알다/모르다 is used to express what the speaker thinks or knows (or does not think/know) about the subject of the first clause.

오늘 수업이 <u>있는 줄 몰라요</u>.
"(They) don't know that there is class today."
엄마는 내가 화학을 <u>전공하는 줄 아세요</u>.
"As for (my) mom, (she) thinks that I major in chemistry."
시험이 <u>쉬운 줄 알아요</u>.
"(He) thinks that the test is easy."
그 사람들은 믿음이 얼마나 <u>귀한 줄 몰라요</u>.
"As for those people, (they) do not know how precious faith is."

EXPRESSIONS WITH MODIFIER CLAUSES III

24.4

~(으)ㄹ 줄 알다/모르다 is used to express a specific ability of the subject, equivalent to "know how to" in English.

> 넥타이를 맬 줄 알아요.
> "(I) know how to wear a tie."
> 영어를 할 줄 알아요?
> "(Do you) know how to speak English?"
> 한국 음식을 만들 줄 몰라요.
> "(I) do not know how to make Korean food."
> 돈을 쓸 줄 몰라요.
> "(I) do not know how to spend money."

When the expression is used in the past tense, as in ~는/(으)ㄴ/(으)ㄹ 줄 알았다/몰랐다, it indicates the speaker's presumed thought.

> 한국어를 하는 줄 몰랐어요.
> "(I) did not think that (he) speaks Korean."
> 너무 아파서 죽는 줄 알았어요.
> "(It) was so painful that (I) thought that (I) would die."
> 와인을 마신 줄 알았어요.
> "(I) thought that (they) drank wine."
> 일을 일찍 끝낸 줄 알았어요.
> "(I) thought that (they) finished the work early."
> 음식이 매운 줄 몰랐어요.
> "(I) did not think that the food would be spicy."
> 날씨가 더울 줄 알았어요.
> "(I) thought that the weather would be hot."
> 여기에 쓰레기를 버릴 줄 몰랐어요.
> "(I) did not expect that (they) would throw the garbage away here."

24.3 ~는 도중에 "in the middle of"

~는 도중에 consists of the noun-modifying ending ~는, the bound noun 도중 "on the road," and the particle 에. This form is used to express "in the middle of" or "while."

> 슈퍼에서 오는 도중에 차 사고가 있었어요.
> "(I) had a car accident on (my) way from the supermarket."
> 유도를 배우는 도중에 다리를 다쳤어요.
> "In the middle of learning judo, (I) hurt (my) leg."
> 인터뷰를 하는 도중에 화장실에 갈 수 있습니까?
> "Can one go to the restroom in the middle of conducting an interview?"
> 시험을 치는 도중에 질문이 있으면 저한테 물어 보세요.
> "If (you) have questions in the middle of taking the test, please ask me."
> 이야기하는 도중에 잡생각 하지 마세요.
> "Don't let your mind wander in the middle of conversation."
> 시험 공부하는 도중에 잠들었어요.
> "(I) fell asleep in the middle of studying for an exam."

24.4 ~는 중이다 "be in the middle of"

~는 중이다 means "be in the process/middle of (doing something)." This form is built on the noun-modifying ending ~는, the noun 중 "middle," and the copula 이다.

> 저희 모두 요리를 배우는 중입니다.
> "We are all in the middle of learning cooking."

도서관에서 그 책을 찾는 중이에요.
"(I) am in the middle of looking for that book in the library."
아마 운전하는 중일 거예요.
"(I guess that he) is in the middle of driving."
나 지금 샤워하는 중이니까 10분 후에 다시 전화해.
"I am in the middle of taking a shower, so call me again after 10 minutes."
지금 말씀하시는 중이세요.
"(He) is in the middle of a conversation."
지금 운전하는 중이니까 10분 후에 전화해 줘요.
"(I) am in the middle of driving, so please call me back in 10 minutes."

The meaning of ~는 중이다 is similar to that of the progressive ~고 있다 since both involve progressive actions. Compare the following examples:

친구하고 이야기하고 있어요.
"(I) am talking to (my) friend."
친구하고 이야기하는 중이에요.
"(I) am in the middle (or process) of talking to (my) friend."

However, while ~고 있다 simply indicates the progressive meaning, ~는 중이다 tends to highlight the process.

24.5 ~(으)ㄴ 지 되다/지나다 "it's been . . . since"

The form ~(으)ㄴ 지 되다/지나다 is constructed from ~(으)ㄴ 지 "whether" and the verb 되다 "become," (or the verb 지나다 "pass"). ~(으)ㄴ 지 . . . 되다/지나다 is used to express the amount of time that has elapsed since a certain temporal point, and it can be translated as "it's been . . . since" in English.

집에 전화를 한 지 삼 주가 됐어요.
"(It) has been three weeks since (I) called home."
봄 학기가 시작한 지 이틀이 지났어요.
"(It) has been two days since the spring semester began."
서울에 한국어를 공부하러 온 지 1년이 지났어요.
"(It) has been a year since (I) came to Seoul to study Korean.
스키를 배운 지 얼마나 됐어요?
"How long has (it) been since (you) learned skiing?"

24.6 ~(으)ㄴ 채로 "just as it is, while"

~(으)ㄴ 채로 combines the noun-modifying ending ~(으)ㄴ, the bound noun 채 "just as it is," and the particle 로. This form means "just as it is," or "while."

너무 피곤해서 안경을 낀 채로 잠들었어요.
"(I) was so tired, so (I) fell asleep wearing glasses."
토끼를 산 채로 잡읍시다.
"(Let's) catch the rabbit alive."
코트도 안 입은 채로 뛰어 나갔어요.
"(He) ran out without even wearing (his) coat."
회사 유니폼을 입은 채로 퇴근했습니다.
"(He) left work wearing (his) company uniform."
제 설명도 듣지 않고 화가 난 채로 돌아갔습니다.
"(He) went back being angry, without hearing my explanations."
양복을 입은 채로 잠이 들었어요.
"(He) fell asleep, wearing (his) suit."
안경을 그냥 쓴 채로 자고 있네요.

EXPRESSIONS WITH MODIFIER CLAUSES III | **24.9**

"(She) is asleep wearing (her) glasses."
신발을 신은 채로 집에 들어오면 안 돼요.
"(You) should not enter the house with (your) shoes on."

24.7 ~는/(으)ㄴ 척/체하다 "pretend"

~는/(으)ㄴ 척/체하다 is the combination of the noun-modifying ending ~는 or ~(으)ㄴ, the noun 척 (or 체) "pretense," and the verb 하다 "do." This form means "pretend."

그녀가 나를 모르는 척해요.
"She pretends that (she) does not know me."
열심히 공부한 척해요.
"(He) pretends that (he) studied hard."
소파에서 자는 척하세요.
"Please pretend that (you) are asleep on the sofa."
아는 척하지 말아요.
"Do not pretend that (you) know."
우리는 술을 못 마시는 척합시다.
"Let's pretend that we cannot drink alcohol."
엄마가 돌아오면 열심히 공부하는 척할 거예요.
"When (my) mom returns, (I) will pretend that (I) study hard."
영화를 안 본 척할 거예요.
"(I) will pretend that (I) did not see the movie."
그 부부는 늘 행복한 척해요.
"As for that couple, (they) always pretend to be happy."
목이 아픈 척했어요.
"(I) pretended that (my) throat was sore."

24.8 ~는/(으)ㄴ 탓/통에 "because of"

~는/(으)ㄴ 통에 is built on the noun-modifying ending ~는 or ~(으)ㄴ, the noun 탓 "excuse/reason" (or the bound noun 통 "consequence"), and the particle 에. This form means "because of," and it is used when the reason/excuse provided in the first clause causes something negative or unpleasant in the main clause.

눈이 너무 많이 오는 통에 출발시간이 지연될 것 같아요.
"It seems that the departure time may be delayed because of the heavy snow."
친구하고 대화가 길어진 탓에 늦었습니다.
"(I) was late because my conversation with (my) friend was prolonged."
어제 뷔페에서 너무 많이 먹은 탓에 얼굴이 부었어요.
"(My) face got swollen because (I) ate too much yesterday at the buffet."
술을 매일 마시는 통에 매일 밤 싸운대요.
"(I heard that they) fight every night because (he) drinks every day."
날씨가 추운 탓에 손님이 별로 없네요.
"There are not many customers because of the cold weather."

24.9 ~는/(으)ㄴ 편이다 "tends to"

~는/(으)ㄴ 편이다 is made of the noun-modifying ending ~는/(으)ㄴ, the noun 편 "side/way/party," and the copula 이다. ~는/(으)ㄴ 편이다 means "tends to" or "kind of" in English, as shown in the following examples:

유니스가 저보다 수영장에 더 자주 가는 편이에요.
"Eunice tends to go to the swimming pool more often than I do."

동생이 영어를 더 잘하는 편이에요.
"(My) younger brother kind of speaks English better (than I)."
주말에는 골프를 치는 편이에요.
"(I) tend to play golf on the weekend."
리사가 한국말을 잘하는 편이에요.
"Lisa tends to speak Korean well."
제 차가 작은 편이에요.
"My car is kind of small."
도서관이 제 집에서 먼 편이에요.
"The library is kind of far from my house."
나보다 형이 키가 더 큰 편이에요.
"(My) older brother is kind of taller than me."
이 가게 물건들이 비싼 편이에요.
"The items in this store are kind of expensive."

24.10 ~는/(으)ㄴ 한 "as long as"

~는/(으)ㄴ 한 consists of the noun-modifying ending ~는/(으)ㄴ and the noun 한 "limit." This form means "as long as" or "as much as."

내가 살아있는 한 절대로 그 사람을 잊지 않을 거다.
"(I) will never forget that person as long as I am alive."
제가 할 수 있는 한 열심히 돕겠습니다.
"(I) will help (her) as much as I can earnestly."
가능한 한 빨리 와 주세요.
"Please come as soon as possible."
제가 아는 한 그런 말을 할 친구가 아니에요.
"As far as I know, (he) is not the type of friend who can say such things."
모두가 나를 믿어 주는 한 난 절대로 포기하지 않을 것이다.
"As long as everyone believes in me, I will never give up."
특별한 반대 의견이 없는 한 회의는 예정대로 진행하겠습니다.
"As long as there is no particular opposing opinion, (we) will proceed the conference as planned."

25

Sentence endings I

Typical sentence-final endings are speech level endings, such as the formal, polite, intimate, and plain endings. However, in spoken communication, various sentence-final suffixes (e.g., 지, 군, and 네) as well as clausal conjunctives (e.g., ~거든, ~는/(으)ㄴ데, and ~어서/아서) can also serve as sentence endings. In addition, to make the sentence honorific, one can add 요 "the politeness marker" to these endings (e.g., ~지요, ~군요, ~네요, ~거든요, and ~어서/아서요).

For instance, in a delicate or face-threatening communicative situation, such as expressing disagreement, requesting, complaining, and refusing, people often opt out of saying the main clause as a strategy to be indirect and polite (e.g., so that they may reduce the degree of imposition when requesting or do not hurt the addressee's feelings when refusing or complaining). Consider the following dialogue:

> A: 오늘 밤 생일 파티에 올 수 <u>있지요</u>?
> "(You) can come to (my) birthday party tonight, right?"
> B: 미안해요. 내일 중요한 시험이 <u>있는데요</u>.
> "(I) am sorry. (I) have an important test tomorrow so. . . (I will not be able to make it)."

Notice that speaker A asks the question using the sentence-final suffix ~지요 (rather than ~어/아요). When responding to speaker A's inquiry, speaker B uses the ellipsis, leaving the main clause out ("I will not be able to make it"). In a similar manner the English conjunctive "so," which ends the first clause in the example, the conjunctive ~는데요 can serve as a sentence ender. This chapter as well as the next chapter discuss some major sentence-final endings.

25.1 ~거든(요) "you see"

In spoken communication, the conjunctive ~거든 "if" is often used as a sentence ending. The ending ~거든 (or 거든요) expresses an emphatic meaning, and it can be translated as "you know," "you see (because)," and "indeed" in English. Consider the following dialogue:

> A: 일요일인데 도서관에는 어떻게 오셨어요?
> "(It) is Sunday, but what brought you to the library?"
> B: 내일 시험이 <u>있거든요</u>.
> "(I) have a test tomorrow, you see."

Notice that B's response ends with ~거든요. By using ~거든요, B offers a kind of follow-up explanation (i.e., having a test tomorrow) to what has been implied (i.e., being in the library on Sunday). Here are more examples:

> A: 또 마실려고?
> "(You) will drink (it) again?"
> B: 응, 내가 여기 커피를 아주 <u>좋아하거든</u>.
> "I like the coffee of this place, you know."

> A: 많이 피곤해 보인다.
> "(You) look tired."

~군(요) "oh, I see . . .!"

B: 그래? 실은 어제 밤 늦게까지 일했거든.
"Really? In fact, (I) worked until late last night, you see."

A: 어제 먹은 음식인데, 또 시키실 거예요?
"(It) is the dish (you) ate yesterday, but will (you) order (it) again?"

B: 네, 아주 맛있었거든요.
"Yes, (it) was really delicious, you know."

25.2 ~고말고(요) "of course"

The ending ~고말고 is constructed from the clausal conjunctive ~고 and 말고 (the verb 말다 "stop" + the conjunctive ~고 = 말고). This ending means "of course," as shown in the following examples:

A: 한국 드라마도 보세요?
"Do (you) also watch Korean dramas?"

B: 보고말고요. 드라마뿐만 아니라 한국 영화도 좋아해요.
"Of course, (I) watch them. Not only dramas, (I) also like Korean movies."

A: 이 식당 음식이 그렇게 맛있다면서요?
"(I heard that) the food of this restaurant is that delicious, right?"

B: 맛있고말고요. 항상 손님들이 많아서 기다려야 돼요.
"Of course, (it) is delicious. There are always many customers, so one must wait in line."

A: 이 노래를 아세요?
"Do (you) know this song?"

B: 알고말고요. 제가 제일 좋아하는 노래예요.
"Of course I know. (It) is my favorite song."

25.3 ~군(요) "oh, I see . . .!"

The ending ~군(요) is used to express the speaker's immediate realization to what he/she just perceived, and it can be translated as "Oh, I see . . . that . . ." in English. ~군요 is used after adjectives and the copula stem. However, for verb stems, ~는, the noun-modifying ending for verbs, is used along with ~군요, as in ~는군요.

A: 같이 스키 타러 오니까 좋지요?
"(It) is good to come together to ski, isn't it?"

B: 네, 그런데 좀 생각보다 날씨가 춥군요.
"Yes, but (I see that) the weather is colder than (I) thought."

A: 좀 맵지 않으세요?
"Isn't (it) a bit spicy?"

B: 아니요. 전혀요. 음식이 정말 맛있군요.
"No. Not at all. (Oh, I see that) the food is delicious."

결국 한국으로 돌아가는군요.
"(Oh, I see that they) finally return to Korea."
여기서 일하는군요.
"(Oh, I see that they) work here."
전혀 맵지 않군요.
"(Oh, I see that it) is not spicy at all."

SENTENCE ENDINGS I   25.4

For immediate realization about a past event, ~었/았군요 is used for verbs, adjectives, and the copula.

    A: 어제 아카데미 시상식을 봤는데 Birdman이 상을 받았어요.
        "(I) watched the Academy Awards yesterday, and 'Birdman' received the award."
    B: 와 그 영화가 결국 받았군요.
        "Wow (oh, I see that) that movie finally got (it)."

For immediate realization about a possible or guessed future event, ~겠군요 is used.

    A: 내일이 아버지 생신이라 집에 내려가려구요.
        "Since (my) father's birthday is tomorrow, (I) intend to go home."
    B: 그럼, 누나도 만나겠군요.
        "Then, (oh, I see that you) will meet (your) older sister too."

    A: 일요일에는 가게를 안 연대요.
        "(It) says that (they) do not open the store on Sunday."
    B: 그럼, 내일은 열겠군요.
        "Then, (oh, I see that they) will open (it) tomorrow."

25.4 ~네(요) "wow, I see that . . ."

The one-form sentence-final ending ~네요 is also used to indicate the speaker's spontaneous and immediate reaction, such as unexpected surprise or realization. It may be best translated as "Oh, I see/realize that. . . ." The meaning and usage of ~네요 is similar to those of ~군요 in that both indicate what the speaker just realized. However, there is one subtle difference. Whereas ~군요 simply expresses the immediate realization in a straightforward manner, ~네요 indicates that what's been realized or perceived is contrary to the expectation.

    A: 새로 산 코트인데 어때요?
        "(This) is a coat (that I) bought new, so how is (it)?"
    B: 좋아 보이네요. 어디서 사셨어요?
        "(Oh, it) looks fabulous. Where did (you) buy (it)?"

    A: 아메리카노 시키셨지요? 어때요? 괜찮으세요?
        "(You) ordered an Americano, right? How is (it)? Is (it) okay?"
    B: 생각보다 진하네요.
        "(Wow, I see that it) is stronger than (my) thought."

정말 많이 사셨네요.
"(Wow, I see that you) really bought a lot."
한국말을 아주 잘하시네요.
"(Oh, I see that contrary to my expectation, you) really speak Korean well."
날씨가 괜찮을 거라 했는데 비가 많이 오네요.
"(They said that) the weather would be nice, but (wow, I see that) it rains a lot."
주말인데 손님들이 많네요.
"(It) is the weekend, but (wow, I see that) there are many customers."

25.4.1 ~겠네요

The suffix 겠 is a pre-final ending that comes between the stem of the predicate and the final ending. The suffix 겠 denotes the speaker's conjecture or inference about what did occur, what is occurring, and what will occur, based on circumstantial evidence.

~겠네요, the combination of the suffix 겠 and the ending ~네요, is used to indicate the speaker's realization of what will happen in reaction to the surprised or unanticipated information the speaker just encountered. It is best translated as "I guess . . . something may/will. . . ." Consider the following examples:

> A: 어젯밤 세 시간밖에 못 잤어요.
> "(I) slept only three hours last night."
> B: 괜찮으세요? 정말 피곤하겠네요.
> "Are (you) okay? (You) must be really tired."

한국에 가면 한국어 실력이 많이 늘겠네요.
"When (you) go to Korea, (I bet your) Korean proficiency will improve a lot."
모두 많이 실망하겠네요.
"(I guess that) everyone may be quite disappointed."
지금쯤 비행기 안에 있겠네요.
"(I guess that they) may be inside of the airplane."

25.4.2 ~었/았겠네요

~었/았겠네요, the combination of the past tense marker ~었/았 and ~겠네요, is used to express the speaker's surprise or realization about what must have occurred. It can be translated as "I guess that something must have . . ." as shown in the following examples:

> A: 눈 때문에 어제 파티에 많이 안 왔어요.
> "Because of snow, many did not come to the party yesterday."
> B: 정말이요? 음식이 많이 남았겠네요.
> "Really? (I guess that) there must be lots of food left over."

어제 혼자 공항으로 떠났겠네요.
"(I guess that he) must have left for the airport alone yesterday."
모두 기뻐하셨겠네요.
"(I guess that) everyone must have rejoiced."
시험이 어려웠겠네요.
"(I guess that) the test must have been difficult."

26

Sentence endings II

26.1 ~(으)ㄹ걸(요) "regrets, guessing"

~(으)ㄹ걸 is a two-form ending, and it is built on ~(으)ㄹ 거 and the particle 을/를. This form is used to indicate two things depending on the subject of the sentence. First, if the subject is the first person, it is used to express a sense of regret, as shown in the following examples:

비빔밥이 맛있어 보이네요. 참, 나도 그거 시킬걸.
"The bibimbap looks so delicious. Well, (I) also should have ordered that."
미안해요. 진작 연락할걸.
"I am sorry. (I) should have contacted (you) earlier."

If the subject is not the first person, it can indicate a sense of conjecture.

지금쯤 서울에 도착했을걸.
"(I guess that he) arrived in Seoul by now."
한국 사람일걸요.
"(I guess that he) is Korean."

26.2 ~(으)ㄹ까(요)? "wondering"

The ~(으)ㄹ까? ending is used to indicate a speaker's wondering mindset or to seek the listener's opinion. ~(으)ㄹ까요? is a three-form verb ending: ~을까요? is used with stems that end in a consonant, as in 먹을까요?, and ~ㄹ까? is used with stems that end in a vowel, as in 갈까요? With ㄹ-irregular predicates, ~까요? is used, as in 알까요?

When the speaker is (or is part of) the subject, ~(으)ㄹ까요? expresses the speaker's wondering mindset. Consider the following sentences:

A: 오늘 점심은 뭘 먹을까요?
  "What shall (we) eat for lunch today?"
B: 간단하게 피자 어때요?
  "Simply, how about pizza?"
A: 어디로 갈까요?
  "(I) wonder where (I/we) should go?"
B: 일단 사무실로 돌아가지요.
  "(Let's) return to the office first."

바쁘시면 제가 인터넷으로 알아볼까요?
"(If you) are busy, shall I look into (it) through the internet?"
오늘 퇴근하고 같이 한 잔 할까요?
"After finishing work today, shall (we) have a drink?"
이 책상은 누구한테 줄까요?
"To whom shall (we) give this desk?"

~(으)ㄹ 텐데(요) "I am afraid that, I suppose that" | 26.3

물 갖다 줄까요?
"Shall (I) bring water?"

Notice that the speaker is the subject of the sentence in the previous examples. When the subject of the sentence is a third person, ~(으)ㄹ까요? is used to seek the listener's opinion.

A: 오늘 변 교수님 연구실에 <u>계실까요</u>?
"Do (you) think that Professor Byon will be in his office today?"
B: 네, 오늘 오후 2시부터 계실 거라고 하셨어요.
"Yes, (he) said that (he) will be (in his office) from 2 p.m. today."
A: 이번에 새로 전화를 사려고 하는데 뭐가 <u>좋을까요</u>?
"(I) intend to buy a new phone; what do you think will be nice?"
B: 그냥 삼성 갤럭시 노트 사세요.
"Just buy a Samsung Galaxy note."

호텔에서 공항까지 <u>멀까요</u>?
"Do (you) think that the airport is far from the hotel?"
친구들이 한국 음식을 <u>좋아할까요</u>?
"Do (you) think that (your) friends will like Korean food?"
졸업식에 모두 다 <u>올까요</u>?
"Do (you) think that everyone will come to the graduation ceremony?"

The repeated use of ~(으)ㄹ까요? can be used to express alternative questions. For instance, consider the following sentences:

A: 버스를 <u>탈까요</u>? 지하철을 <u>탈까요</u>?
"Shall (I/we) take the bus or subway?"
B: 퇴근 시간이니까 지하철이 빠르겠네요.
"Since it is rush hour, (I) guess that the subway is faster."

한국어로 <u>말할까요</u>? 일어로 <u>말할까요</u>?
"Shall (I/we) speak in Korean or Japanese?"
노래를 <u>할까요</u>? 춤을 <u>출까요</u>?
"Shall (I/we) sing or dance?"
드럼을 <u>칠까요</u>? 기타를 <u>칠까요</u>?
"Shall (I) play the drums or the guitar?"
학교로 <u>갈까요</u>? 서점으로 <u>갈까요</u>?
"Shall (I/we) go to school or the bookstore?"

Notice that whereas the predicate (e.g., shall (I/we) eat . . .) is used only once in English, the predicate is repeated in Korean.

26.3 ~(으)ㄹ 텐데(요) "I am afraid that, I suppose that"

The clausal conjunctive ~(으)ㄹ 텐데 is used to indicate background information for the main clause. However, when it is used as a sentence ending, it indicates the speaker's sense of assumption or prediction, and it can be translated as "I am afraid that . . ." or "I suppose that . . ." in English.

A: 오늘 저녁에 사러 가려구요.
"(We) intend to go there to buy (it) this evening."
B: 주말이라 길이 많이 <u>막힐 텐데요</u>.
"(I am afraid that) the road will be congested because it is the weekend."
오늘은 가지 마세요.
"As for today, please do not go (there)."

이번 주는 무척 <u>바쁠 텐데요</u>.
"(I am afraid that they) are really busy this week."

SENTENCE ENDINGS II   **26.6**

고생 많이 하셨어요. 엄청 <u>무거웠을 텐데</u>.
"Well done. (I assume that it) must have been very heavy."

26.4 ~(으)렴 "may, go ahead (giving orders)"

~(으)렴 is a two-form ending, with ~으렴 being used after a verb stem that ends in a consonant (e.g., 먹으렴) and ~렴 after a verb stem that ends in a vowel (e.g., 보렴). This ending is used when making suggestions or granting permission in an agreeable or considerate manner. It does not take the politeness marker 요, and it is usually used by a superior toward his/her status subordinates (or among intimates).

마음대로 <u>해 보렴</u>.
"Do as (you) like."
이제 푹 <u>쉬렴</u>.
"Take a good rest now."
더 <u>마시렴</u>.
"Drink more."

26.5 ~잖아(요) "you know"

~잖아요 is a one-form ending, and it is the contracted form of ~지 않아요. As an ending, ~잖아요 is used when the speaker expects that the listener is aware of the information given in the context and seeks the listener's confirmation. ~잖아요 can be translated as "you know" in English. Consider the following examples:

A: 분위기도 좋고 서비스도 최고네요!
 "The atmosphere is good, and the service is also excellent!"
B: 일류 <u>호텔이잖아요</u>.
 "(It) is a first-class hotel, you know."

Notice in the previous example that the given contextual information is both speakers are in the first-class hotel. When speaker B uses ~잖아요, he/she expects that speaker A is fully aware of this contextual understanding while further seeking speaker A's confirmation.

A: 상호가 상우보다 키가 크네요.
 "Sangho is taller than Sangwoo."
B: 쌍둥이지만, <u>형이잖아요</u>.
 "Although they are twins, (he) is the older brother, you know."

그만 들어오라고 하세요. 많이 <u>춥잖아요</u>.
"Tell them to come inside now. It is very cold, you know."
한 병만 더 삽시다. 세일 <u>하잖아요</u>.
"(Let's) buy one more bottle. It is on sale, you know."

26.6 ~지(요) "right?"

~지(요) is a one-form ending that indicates one of the following four mental states or attitudes of the speaker: (i) seeking agreement, (ii) asking a question with a belief that the listener has the answer, (iii) assuring information, and (iv) suggesting. The speaker's intonation (e.g., falling or rising) as well as contextual factors involved (e.g., referential and situational contexts) determine which among the four moods or attitudes the ending indicates.

~지(요) "right?"   **26.6**

(i) Seeking agreement (with a rising intonation)

Consider the following two examples:

매일 운동<u>해요</u>?
"Do (you) exercise every day?"
매일 운동<u>하지요</u>?
"(You) exercise every day, right?"

Notice that the ending ~어/아요 in the first sentence simply asks the question in a straightforward manner. On the other hand, the ending ~지요 in the second sentence indicates that the speaker seeks agreement while asking the same question. Here are more examples:

중국 분<u>이시지요</u>?
"(You) are Chinese, aren't you?"
그 영화 정말 <u>재미있었지요</u>?
"That movie was really interesting, wasn't it?"
도서관 앞에서 <u>만날 거지요</u>?
"(You) will meet (them) in front of the library, right?"
오늘 아침에 은행에 <u>가셨지요</u>?
"(You) went to the bank this morning, right?"

(ii) Asking a question, believing that the listener has the answer (with a rising intonation)

기차가 몇 시에 출발해요?
"What time does the train leave?"
기차가 몇 시에 <u>출발하지요</u>?
"What time does the train leave?"

Again, the ending ~어/아요 in the first sentence simply asks the question in a direct manner. However, the second sentence with the ending ~지요 implies that the speaker believes that the listener has the answer. Here are more examples:

저게 <u>뭐지요</u>?
"What is that (over there)?"
몇 시에 <u>오지요</u>?
"What time will (they) come?"
누가 <u>전화했지요</u>?
"Who called?"

(iii) Assuring information (with a falling intonation)

네, 졸업식이 이번 주 <u>토요일에 있어요</u>.
"Yes, the graduation ceremony is this week on Saturday."
네, 졸업식이 이번 주 <u>토요일에 있지요</u>.
"Yes, (I assure you that) the graduation ceremony is this week on Saturday."

The first sentence with the ending ~어/아요 simply states the message. On the other hand, the ending ~지요 in the second sentence indicates that the speaker assures the listener of the referential message. Here are more examples:

생일인데 당연히 <u>가지요</u>.
"Since it's (your) birthday, (I assure you that) of course I will be there."
전화 번호가 330–3449 <u>이지요</u>.
"(I assure you) that the cell phone number is 330–3449."
네, 어제 약속이 <u>있었지요</u>.
"Yes, (I assure you) that (we) had an appointment yesterday."

SENTENCE ENDINGS II

(iv) Suggesting (with a falling intonation)

전화 좀 받아요.
"Please answer the phone."
전화 좀 받지요?
"(How about you) answer the phone?"

The first sentence with the ending ~어/아요 is a direct request. However, the second sentence is a suggestion because of the ~지요 ending. Here are more examples:

이제 설거지 좀 하지요?
"(How about you) do dishes now?"
더운데 에어콘 좀 틀지요?
"(It) is hot, so how about turning on the air conditioner?"

The honorific suffix ~(으)시 can be optionally used along with ~지요 to make the suggestion sound more polite, as shown in the following examples:

어디 가서 한 잔 더 하시지요?
"(How about we) go somewhere for another drink?"
목사님, 이제 가시지요?
"Pastor, (how about we) go now?"
노트북 좀 빌려 주시지요?
"(How about you) please lend (me) (your) laptop?"

27

Addressee honorifics

Speech level endings

27.1 Korean honorifics

Language has two functions: (i) to convey or exchange knowledge and information and (ii) to establish and maintain human relationships by expressing various social/interpersonal meanings involved in contexts such as speakers' attitudes/feeling toward the addressee or referent (e.g., politeness, respect, intimacy, humility, formality, etc.), as well as social variables involved in interactions (e.g., age, seniority, rank, gender, education, background, etc.). The linguistic elements employed for the second function of language have been associated with the term "honorifics" or "linguistic politeness."

Korean has a sophisticated honorific system that is operated and manifested by a number of honorific elements (e.g., address/reference terms, speech levels, humble pronouns, honorific suffixes, honorific case particles, and honorific verbs/words). For example, consider the following two sentences:

(1) 정우야, 어제 우리 모임에 와 줘서 고마웠어.
    "Jungwoo, I appreciated that you came to our meeting yesterday."
(2) 선생님, 어제 저희 모임에 와 주셔서 고마웠습니다.
    "Sir, I appreciated that you came to our meeting yesterday."

The two examples are speech acts of gratitude. The referential meanings of the examples are the same; however, their social meanings are different. For example, in (1), the use of the first name 정우 with the intimate vocative particle ~야, the use of the plain first person pronoun 우리, the absence of the honorific suffix ~(으)시, and the use of an intimate speech level ~어 indicate that the speaker is likely to address a person either who has equal or lower status, whom he/she knows well.

The example in (1) can be rude if such an expression is used by a lower person (e.g., a college student) in a formal situation to a higher-status person (e.g., professor) because the utterance lacks the proper honorific elements. To make (1) socially appropriate in a formal situation where one speaks to a person with a higher status, one needs to use the appropriate address term, such as 선생님 "sir" in place of the addressee's first name and then should change 우리 to 저희 "the humble pronoun" as shown in (2). In addition, one should add the honorific suffix ~(으)시 to the verb 주다 "give," transforming 줘서 (주어서) to an honorific verb 주셔서 (주시어서), and use the formal speech level ending ~습니다 to change 고마웠어 "appreciated" to 고마웠습니다.

As illustrated earlier, the use of honorifics in the Korean language indicates different styles of speaking that reflect various social meanings and variables involved in the setting. In addition, it shows that how an utterance is said is more important than what is said during the social interaction.

ADDRESSEE HONORIFICS

When you use Korean honorifics during conversation, you need to consider whom you are talking to (e.g., the addressee) and whom you are talking about (e.g., the referent). The honorific elements that are used to indicate your social meanings with the people you are talking to are called "addressee honorifics," whereas those used for the people you are talking about are called "referent honorifics." This chapter discusses addressee honorifics, and the subsequent chapter covers referent honorifics.

27.2 Addressee honorifics: speech level endings

Speech level endings indicate your attitude toward your addressee (e.g., respect, intimacy, humility, etc.) and also signal different styles of speaking and writing (e.g., genre, setting, formality). Note that the use of speech level endings is mandatory all the time since verb or adjective stems cannot stand alone. For Korean language learners, choosing an appropriate speech level ending for every verb or adjective is challenging because its selection is determined by various contextual factors involved in interaction, such as whether the social status of an addressee (e.g., age, occupation, seniority, family relation, etc.) is higher/equal/lower than yours, how psychologically intimate/familiar you feel toward the addressee, how formal the conversation situation is, and so forth. In contemporary Korean, there are six speech levels:

(i) The formal speech level (존댓말 "honorific speech level")
(ii) The polite speech level (존댓말 "honorific speech level")
(iii) The intimate speech level (반말 "nonhonorific speech level")
(iv) The plain speech level (반말 "nonhonorific speech level")
(v) The familiar speech level
(vi) The blunt speech level

Whereas the first four speech levels are used by all Koreans in contemporary Korean, the last two speech levels, the familiar and the blunt, are used only by some older adults (at least 40 years old or older), and their use is on the gradual decline in modern Korean.

27.2.1 The formal speech level

The formal speech level is used for public or formal communication settings, such as broadcasting, public speeches, business-related meetings, conference presentations, and so forth. It has four different endings for each sentence type: ~습니다/ㅂ니다 (statement), ~습니까/ㅂ니까 (questions), ~(으)십시오 (commands), and ~(으)십시다 (proposals).

For the declarative (statement), ~습니다 is used when the stem ends in a consonant, as in 먹 + 습니다 = 먹습니다 "(someone) eats." However, when the stem ends in a vowel, ~ㅂ니다 is used, as in 가 + ㅂ니다 = 갑니다 "(someone) goes."

Because the deferential speech level indicates a sense of formality, many formulaic/fixed expressions are made of this speech level ending. Consider the following examples:

처음 뵙겠습니다.
"Nice to meet you" (literally "(I) meet you for the first time").
감사합니다.
"Thank you" (literally "(I) do gratitude").
실례합니다.
"Excuse me" (literally "(I) do discourtesy").
축하합니다.
"Congratulations" (literally "(I) congratulate").

Addressee honorifics: speech level endings 27.2

For the interrogative (question), the ending is ~습니까 for stems ending in a consonant, as in 먹습니까? "(do you) eat?" However, it is ~ㅂ니까 for stems ending in a vowel, as in 갑니까? "(do you) go?" Here are some examples:

믿다 "believe"	그 친구를 <u>믿습니까</u>? "(Do you) believe that friend?"
가르치다 "teach"	어디서 한국어를 <u>가르칩니까</u>? "Where (do you) teach Korean?"

For the imperative (command), the ending is ~으십시오 for stems ending in a consonant, as in 먹으십시오 "eat." However, the ending is ~십시오 for stems ending in a vowel, as in 가십시오 "go." Here are some examples.

읽다 "read"	한국어 책을 <u>읽으십시오</u>. "Read the Korean book."
보다 "see"	코메디 영화를 <u>보십시오</u>! "See the comedy movie!"

For the propositive (suggestion), the ending is ~으십시다 for stems ending in a consonant, as in 먹읍시다 "(let's) eat." However, it is ~십시다 for stems ending in a vowel, as in 갑시다 "(let's) go." Here are some examples:

가다 "go"	지금 <u>가십시다</u>. "(Let's) go now."
끊다 "quit"	담배를 <u>끊읍시다</u>. "(Let's) quit smoking."

27.2.2 The polite speech level

The polite speech level is the informal counterpart of the formal speech level. As the most commonly used speech level regardless of age or gender, the polite speech level is broadly used in any situation where polite language is called for. It is used when addressing someone of senior status in casual, nonformal, and everyday types of conversations; it is used with friends if their friendship began in adulthood, and it is the most common speech level used with strangers.

The polite speech level endings have two forms: ~어요 and ~아요. When the verb or adjective stem ends in either 아 or 오, ~아요 is used (e.g., 보아요). On the other hand, ~어요 is used with stems that end in any other vowels (e.g., 먹어요).

Dictionary form	*The polite speech level endings*
가다 "go"	가요 (가 + 아요 but contracted to 가요)
보다 "see"	봐요 (보 + 아요 but contracted)
오다 "come"	와요 (오 + 아요 but contracted)
살다 "live"	살아요 (살 + 아요)
기다리다 "wait"	기다려요 (기다리 + 어요 but contracted to 기다려요)
배우다 "learn"	배워요 (배우 + 어요 but contracted)
넣다 "put (something) in"	넣어요 (넣 + 어요)
먹다 "eat"	먹어요 (먹 + 어요)

The ~어/아요 ending is used for all sentence types: statement, questions, commands, and proposals. For instance, consider the following:

아이스크림 먹어요.
"(I) eat ice cream."

ADDRESSEE HONORIFICS

아이스크림 먹어요?
"(Do you) eat ice cream?"
아이스크림 먹어요!
"Have (some) ice cream!"
아이스크림 먹어요.
"(Let's) have (some) ice cream."

Koreans use contextual elements as well as intonation (e.g., rising intonation for a question) to figure out for what sentence type the ending is used for.

Koreans frequently use the formal speech level as well as the polite speech level together even in formal conversational settings. One possible scenario is when you meet a person for the first time. The speakers may introduce themselves using the formal speech level endings (e.g., 처음 뵙겠습니다. 만나서 반갑습니다). However, once identified, they may switch to the polite speech level (e.g., 그런데 성함이 뭐라고 하셨지요?). The use of the polite speech level ending generates an effect of making a dialogue sound less formal, even in formal conversational contexts.

27.2.3 The intimate speech level

The intimate speech level is in general used in the following situations: by adults when addressing children, by parents when addressing their kids, by children when addressing their peers, and by adult friends when addressing their childhood friends (or friends whose relationships are close enough to switch to the intimate speech level from the polite speech level).

The intimate speech level ending is ~어/아. The choice of ~어 or ~아 is the same with that of the polite speech level ending ~어요/아요. ~아 is used after a stem that ends in a bright vowel, 오 or 아 (e.g., 찾아 "find" = 찾 + 아), while ~어 is used with a stem that ends in any other vowels (e.g., 배워 "learn" = 배우 + 어). Just like the polite speech level ending ~어요/아요, the intimate speech level ending ~어/아 is used for all sentence types.

오후에 운동해.
"(I) exercise in the afternoon."
오후에 운동해?
"Do (you) exercise in the afternoon?"
오후에 운동해!
"Exercise in the afternoon!"
오후에 운동해.
"(Let's) exercise in the afternoon."

Again, Koreans use contextual elements as well as intonation (e.g., rising intonation for a question) to figure out what intimate speech level ending ~어/아 is used for a specific sentence type.

27.2.4 The plain speech level

The plain speech level ending sounds more blunt and direct than the other speech level endings. The plain speech level is primarily used in the following three contexts: when one addresses a child, his/her childhood friends, or younger siblings; when the speaker talks to himself/herself or wants to draw the listener's attention to information that is noteworthy or provoking; when one writes (e.g., essay, prose, journals, magazines, newspapers, academic papers, and so forth).

Unlike the intimate and the polite speech levels that use the same endings for different sentence types, the plain speech level has four different endings for each sentence type:

Statement: ~는/ㄴ다/~다
Questions: ~니/(으)냐? (or ~는가/(으)ㄴ가? for impersonal writing)
Command: ~어/아라 (or ~라/으라 for impersonal writing)
Proposal: ~자

Addressee honorifics: speech level endings

Declarative

~는/ㄴ다 (for verb stems)

보다 "see"	본다
믿다 "believe"	믿는다
말하다 "study"	말한다

~다 (for adjective and copula stems)

쉽다 "easy"	쉽다
따뜻하다 "warm"	따뜻하다
이다 "be"	이다

~었/았다 (for verb, adjective, and copula stems in the past tense)

친구가 시카고에서 <u>왔다</u>.
"(My) friend came from Chicago."
한국에서 영어를 <u>가르쳤다</u>.
"(He) taught English in Korea."
점심이 <u>맛있었다</u>.
"The lunch was delicious."
사무실이 <u>조용했다</u>.
"The office was quiet."
성실한 학생<u>이었다</u>.
"(She) was a sincere student."

Interrogative

~니/(으)냐? (or ~는가/(으)ㄴ가? for impersonal writing) for all predicate stems.

보다 "see"	보니?/보냐? (or 보는가?)
믿다 "believe"	믿니?/믿냐? (or 믿는가?)
말하다 'speak"	말하니?/말하냐? (or 말하는가?)
쉽다 "easy"	쉽니?/쉽냐? (or 쉬운가?)
따뜻하다 "warm"	따뜻하니?/따뜻하냐? (or 따뜻한가?)
이다 "be"	이니?/이냐? (or 인가?)

~었/았니/(으)냐? (for all predicate stems in the past tense)

친구가 시카고에서 <u>왔니</u>?
"Did (your) friend come from Chicago?"
한국에서 영어를 <u>가르쳤니</u>?
"Did (he) teach English in Korea?"
점심이 <u>맛있었니</u>?
"Was the lunch delicious?"
사무실이 <u>조용했니</u>?
"Was the office quiet?"
성실한 학생<u>이었니</u>?
"Was (she) a sincere student?"
아침은 뭐 좀 <u>먹었냐</u>?
"As for breakfast, did (you) eat something?"

Imperative (applies only to verbs)

~어/아라 (or ~라/으라 for impersonal writing)

보다 "see"   보아라 (or 보라)
믿다 "believe"   믿어라 (or 믿으라)
말하다 "speak"   말해라 (or 말하라)

떠나기 전에 꼭 <u>전화해라</u>.
"Before leaving, make sure (you) call (me)."
자기 전에 꼭 <u>숙제해라</u>.
"Before going to bed, do (your) homework."
밥 먹기 전에 손 <u>씻어라</u>.
"Wash (your) hands before eating (your) meal."
학교 정문 앞에서 6시에 <u>만나라</u>.
"Meet (her) at six in front of the school's main gate."

Propositive (applies only to verbs)

~자

보다 "see"   보자
믿다 "believe"   믿자
말하다 "speak"   말하자

떠나기 전에 꼭 <u>전화하자</u>.
"Before leaving, (let's) make sure (we) call (her)."
자기 전에 꼭 <u>숙제하자</u>.
"Before going to bed, (let's) do (our) homework."
밥 먹기 전에 손 <u>씻자</u>.
"(Let's) wash (our) hands before eating a meal."
학교 정문 앞에서 6시에 <u>만나자</u>.
"(Let's) meet at six in front of the school's main gate."

Note in the previous examples that the plain speech level imperative ending ~어라/아라 and propositive ending ~자 are used only for verb stems and are not conjugated for the tense.

27.2.5 The familiar speech level and the blunt speech level

The familiar speech level has four different endings for each sentence type: ~네 (statements), ~는가/나? (questions), ~게 (commands), and ~세 (proposals). It is primarily used among older male adults (say those who are at least in their early 40s) or by older adults to younger adults (e.g., parent-in-law speaking to son-in-law; older professor speaking to young college students).

시장에 가고 지금 <u>없네</u>.
"(She) went to the market and is not here now."
자네 점심 <u>먹었는가</u>?
"Did you eat lunch?"
이러다가 늦겠네. 어서 <u>가게</u>.
"(You) will be late. Leave promptly."
다음 주말에 또 <u>만나세</u>.
"(Let us) meet next weekend again."

Meanwhile, the blunt speech level has four different endings for each sentence type: ~소/(으)오 (statements), ~소/(으)오? (questions), ~(으)오/구려 (commands), and ~읍시다/ㅂ니다

Addressee honorifics: speech level endings

(proposals). It is mainly used among some older married couples or older adults speaking to younger adults who are either of equal or lower status.

> 내가 집 <u>주인이오</u>.
> "I am the owner of the house."
> 언제 집에 <u>도착했소</u>?
> "When did (you) arrive at home?"
> 빨리 <u>돌아오구려</u>.
> "Return in a hurry."
> 국이 식겠소. 어서 <u>먹읍시다</u>.
> "The soup will be cold. (Let's) eat promptly."

Both the familiar and the blunt speech levels are on their way out of use in contemporary Korean. In fact, these speech levels are now heard only in historical TV dramas or in the aforementioned restricted contexts.

28

Referent honorifics

28.1 The subject honorific suffix ~(으)시

When Koreans wish to show respect toward the referent of the subject, they make a predicate form honorific by attaching the honorific suffix ~(으)시 to the stem of the predicate. The honorific suffix ~(으)시 is a pre-final ending that comes between the stem of the predicate and the final ending. ~(으)시 is added after a stem that ends in a consonant, as in 찾으시다 (찾 + 으시 + 다) "look for," and 시 is added after a stem that ends in a vowel, as in 가시다 (가 + 시 + 다) "go."

Dictionary form	Polite speech level	Formal speech level
가다 "go"	가요	갑니다
가시다 "go"	가세요 (가 + 시 + 어요)	가십니다 (가 + 시 + ㅂ니다)
입다 "wear"	입어요	입습니다
입으시다 "wear"	입으세요 (입 + 으시 +어요)	입으십니다 (입+ 으시 + ㅂ니다)

Various social variables that are ascribed (e.g., age, kinship relations) or achieved (e.g., occupation, seniority, rank) determine the honorific suffix usage. For instance, Koreans use the honorific suffix when they talk to or talk about their older family members, older people in general, people of esteemed occupations (e.g., doctors, lawyers, teachers, etc.), senior-rank personnel, customers/guests (in a service or commercial setting), and so forth.

Note that the referent of the subject can be whom they are talking to or whom they are talking about. Thus, when using the honorific suffix ~(으)시, you should consider that the referent of the subject and the addressee can be the same person or different people. For example, consider the following two examples:

김 교수님 지금 어디에 가세요?
"Professor Kim, where are you going now?"

In this case, the person you are talking to and talking about are the same person.

철원 씨, 김 교수님 지금 어디에 가세요?
"Chulwon, where is Professor Kim going?"

However, in this example, your addressee and the referent of the subject are different people.

28.2 Honorific verbs/adjectives

As for the following limited number of Korean predicates, you do not have to add the suffix ~(으)시 to generate honorific predicate forms since these predicates have their own corresponding honorific forms:

먹다 "eat" (not 먹으시다)   잡수시다/드시다
자다 "sleep"   주무시다

Object honorification by using "humble verbs" | **28.4**

있다 "exist/stay"	계시다 (stay)/있으시다 (have)
죽다 "die"	돌아가시다
말하다 "speak"	말씀하시다
배고프다 "be hungry"	시장하시다
아프다 "be ill"	편찮으시다 (entire body)/아프시다 (specific area)

Meanwhile, note that Koreans do not use the honorific suffix when the subject of the sentence is the speaker him/herself. In other words, one does not show honor toward him/herself. Consider the following example:

> A: 어디에 가<u>세</u>요?
> "Where are (you) going?"
> B: 집에 가요.
> "(I) am going home."

Notice that Speaker A uses the suffix when asking the question to B. However, Speaker B does not use the suffix in the reply.

28.3 The honorific particles 께 and 께서

Korean has two honorific particles 께 and 께서. The honorific particle 께서 (the honorific form of the subject particle 이/가) is used when expressing subject honorification.

> 남동생<u>이</u> 자고 있어요.
> "(My) younger brother is asleep."
> 할아버지<u>께서</u> 주무시고 계세요.
> "(My) grandfather is asleep."

Meanwhile, 께 (which is the honorific form of the particle 한테/에게) is used when expressing object honorification.

> 남동생<u>한테</u> 연락할 거예요.
> "(I) will contact (my) younger brother."
> 할아버지<u>께</u> 연락 드릴 거예요.
> "(I) will contact (my) grandfather."

28.4 Object honorification by using "humble verbs"

The following small number of Korean verbs have the corresponding humble forms.

Plain	Humble
주다 "give"	드리다
묻다 "ask"	여쭙다
보다 "see"	뵙다
데리다 "accompany"	모시다
말하다 "speak"	말씀드리다

Koreans use these humble verbs when they honor the object of the sentence (i.e., the person affected by the action of the verb). For instance, consider the following sentences.

(1) 정한아, 내가 이따가 영규한테 <u>줄게</u>.
    "Junghan, I will give (it) to Youngkyu later."
(2) 정한아, 내가 이따가 선생님께 <u>드릴게</u>.
    "Junghan, I will give (it) to teacher later."

REFERENT HONORIFICS

In both examples, the addressee is the speaker's childhood friend, Junghan. However, in (1), the object of the sentence is their mutual friend Youngkyu, while in (2), the object is their teacher. Notice that in (2), the speaker uses 드리나 instead of 주나 in order to honor the object 선생님 (which is also marked by the honorific object particle 께 rather the plain particle 한테).

28.5 Honorific nouns

A limited number of Korean nouns have corresponding honorific forms:

나이 "age"   연세
말 "speech/word"   말씀
밥 "meal"   진지
병 "illness"   병환
사람 "person"   분
생일 "birthday"   생신
아내 "wife"   부인
이름 "name"   성함
자식, 아이(들) "one's children"   자제 분, 자녀
집 "house"   댁

28.6 Using the honorific elements together

Having discussed both the addressee and referent honorific elements, let's discuss how one should put these honorific elements together. Whereas the addressee honorifics (speech level endings) and referent honorifics (the honorific suffix ~으시, honorific verbs/nouns/particles, and humble verbs) are two separate systems, they work together since the addressee and the referent can be the same or different. For example, consider the following situations.

First, let's assume that your addressee and the referent are the same people:

Addressee/referent: Grandfather

할아버지, 어디에 가세요?
"Grandfather, where are you going?"

Here, you need to use both the addressee honorifics (e.g., the polite speech level ending ~어/아요) as well as the referent honorifics (e.g., ~으시).

Addressee/referent: Your junior colleague in a company setting

재석 씨, 어디에 가요?
"Jaesuk, where are you going?"

In this case, 재석 is your junior colleague from your company. Here you speak to him using the polite speech level ending ~어/아요, but do not use any referent honorific element.

Addressee/referent: Your younger brother

서진아, 어디에 가니?
"Seojin, where are you going?"

서진 is your younger brother. You will speak to him in the intimate speech level (~어/아) and do not use any referent honorific elements.

Using the honorific elements together 28.6

Secondly, how about when the addressee and the referent are different people? We can consider the following four situations:

Addressee: Father (+ power) and Referent: Grandfather (+ power)

아버지, 할아버지께서 어디에 가세요?
"Father, where does Grandfather go?"

Here, you are asking your father where your grandfather is going. You will need to use both the addressee honorifics (e.g., ~어/아요) as well as referent honorific elements (께서, 으시).

Addressee: Father (+ power) and Referent: Younger brother (− power)

아버지, 상민이는 어디에 가요?
"Father, where does Sangmin go?"

You are asking your father where your younger brother 상민 is going. Note that you still need to speak in the polite speech level (~어/아요) but without using any referent honorific elements.

Addressee: Younger brother (− power) and Referent: Mother (+ power)

상민아, 어머니는 어디에 가시냐?
"Sangmin, where does Mom go?"

In this case, you are asking your younger brother about your mother. Note that you are using the plain speech level ending ~니/냐 (nonhonorific speech level) and using the honorific suffix ~(으)시 to honor 어머니.

Addressee: Younger brother (− power) and Referent: Younger sister (− power)

상민아, 혜원이는 어디에 가나?
"Sangmin, where does Hyewon go?

Here, you are asking your younger brother about your mutual younger sister, 혜원. Since your addressee and the referent of the subject are your younger siblings anyway, you are not using any honorific elements.

Meanwhile, since the primary function of the honorific is to establish, maintain, and reinforce interpersonal relationships, you do not need to employ honorific expressions, if/when your addressee is a nonspecific general audience, or when the subject of the sentence is not related to the interlocutors involved (e.g., talking about famous celebrity, politicians, etc.). Moreover, the use of honorific elements is not necessary in impersonal writings (e.g., newspaper/magazine articles, academic papers, etc.).

29

The passive construction

You can say a sentence either in the active voice or the passive voice. In the active sentence, the subject is the "doer" of the action. For instance, consider the following two sentences:

"Evan closes the window." (active)
"The window is closed by Evan." (passive)

In the first sentence, Evan is the doer, and the situation is depicted from the doer's standpoint. However, in the second sentence, the situation is depicted from the standpoint of the object (e.g., the window) instead. In this passive sentence, the focus is not on the doer but on the object of the action. The use of passive voice is more common in English than in Korean. For instance, as seen in the example, in English, you can change a verb into the passive form by using the copula "to be" along with the past participle of the verb (e.g., ~ed), as in "the window was closed." However, in Korean, there is only a limited set of verbs that can be made passive.

29.1 The passive suffix ~이, ~히, ~리, ~기

In Korean, you can change a limited number of transitive verbs into passive verbs by attaching the suffix ~이, ~히, ~리, or ~기 to the stem of verb:

Suffix 이

놓다 "to place" 놓이다 "to be placed"
보다 "to see" 보이다 "to be seen"
쓰다 "to use/write" 쓰이다 "to be used/written"
섞다 "to mix" 섞이다 "to be mixed"
쌓다 "to pile up" 쌓이다 "to be piled up"
묶다 "to bind" 묶이다 "to be fastened"
파다 "to dig" 파이다 "to be dug"

Suffix 히

먹다 "to eat" 먹히다 "to be eaten"
잡다 "to catch" 잡히다 "to be caught"
걷다 "to lift" 걷히다 "to be lifted"
닫다 "to close" 닫히다 "to be closed"
막다 "to block" 막히다 "to be blocked"
밟다 "to step on" 밟히다 "to be stepped on"
읽다 "to read" 읽히다 "to be read"

The passive suffix ~이, ~히, ~리, ~기 29.1

Suffix 리

팔다 "to sell"   팔리다 "to be sold"
밀다 "to push"   밀리다 "to be pushed"
물다 "to bite"   물리다 "to be bitten"
열다 "to open"   열리다 "to be opened"
듣다 "to hear"   들리다 "to be heard"
걸다 "to hang"   걸리다 "to be hung"
밀다 "to push"   밀리다 "to be pushed"
풀다 "to solve"   풀리다 "to be solved"
흔들다 "to shake"   흔들리다 "to be shaken"

Suffix 기

씻다 "to wash"   씻기다 "to be washed"
뜯다 "to tear out"   뜯기다 "to be torn out"
끊다 "to disconnect"   끊기다 "to be disconnected"
뺏다 "to take away"   뺏기다 "to be taken away"
안다 "to hold"   안기다 "to be held"
쫓다 "to chase"   쫓기다 "to be chased"
바꾸다 "to change"   바꾸다 "to be changed"
찢다 "to rip"   찢기다 "to be ripped"

There are three things to remember. First, when an active sentence is changed into a passive sentence, the subject and object relationship changes. For instance, the object of the active sentence becomes the subject of the passive sentence. Consider the following two sentences:

손님들이 이 컴퓨터를 쓴다.
"Customers use this computer."
이 컴퓨터가 손님들한테 (에게) 쓰인다.
"This computer is used by customers."

In the first sentence, the subject is 손님들, whereas the subject is 컴퓨터 in the second sentence. In addition, notice in the second sentence that 손님들 is marked by 한테. When the object is an animate noun (e.g., human or animals), you need to mark it with 한테 (or 에게). However, when it is an inanimate noun (e.g., wind, car), you need to use 에. Consider the following examples:

엄마가 애기를 안아요.
"Mom holds the baby."
애기가 엄마에게 안겨요.
"The baby is held by Mom."

강한 바람이 창문을 흔들어요.
"Strong winds rattle the window."
창문이 강한 바람에 흔들려요.
"The window is rattled by strong winds."

Second, you need to memorize both the verbs that can be changed into passive verbs as well as the suffix each verb takes. Third, while the preceding explanation illustrates how passive verbs are structurally related to their active counterparts, in the contemporary Korean language, learners are usually expected to learn passive verbs as separate words, and Koreans do not usually make new passive forms.

THE PASSIVE CONSTRUCTION

29.2 Passives with ~어/아지다

As for a limited number of transitive verbs that cannot take the aforementioned passive suffixes, one can change them into passive verbs by attaching ~어/아지다 as shown in the following examples:

깨다 "to shatter/break"	깨지다 "to be shattered/broken"
밝히다 "to brighten"	밝혀지다 "come out into the open"
쓰다 "to write"	써지다 "to be written"
이루다 "to accomplish"	이루어지다 "to be accomplished"
풀다 "to untie"	풀어지다 "to be untied; to get bleary"
알리다 "to inform"	알려지다 "to become known"
만들다 "to make"	만들어지다 "to be made"
주다 "to give"	주어지다 "to be given"
막다 "to close up"	막아지다 "to be filled up"
버리다 "to throw [something] away"	버려지다 "to be abandoned; to be dumped"
끄다 "to extinguish"	꺼지다 "to be extinguished"

이 시계는 스위스 시계 기술자에 의해 <u>만들어졌다</u>.
"As for this watch, (it) was made by a Swiss watchmaker."
사실이 곧 <u>밝혀지겠지요</u>.
"(I assume) that the facts will come out into the open soon."
저는 제 소원이 꼭 언젠가 <u>이루어질</u> 거라고 믿고 싶어요.
"As for me, (I) surely want to believe that my wish will be realized someday."

29.3 Passives with "noun + 되다"

You can change some "noun + 하다" verbs into passive verbs by replacing 하다 "do" with 되다 "become," as shown here:

이해하다 "to understand"	이해되다 "to be understood"
수정하다 "to revise"	수정되다 "to be revised"
해결하다 "to solve"	해결되다 "to be solved"
개발하다 "to develop"	개발되다 "to be developed'
기대하다 "to expect"	기대되다 "to be expected"
걱정하다 "to worry"	걱정되다 "to be worried"
준비하다 "to prepare"	준비되다 "to be prepared"
사용하다 "to use"	사용되다 "to be used"
완성하다 "to complete"	완성되다 "to be completed"
선출하다 "to elect"	선출되다 "to be elected"
선택하다 "to select"	선택되다 "to be selected"
발견하다 "to discover"	발견되다 "to be discovered"
발명하다 "to invent"	발명되다 "to be invented"
발표하다 "to announce"	발표되다 "to be announced"
치료하다 "to treat/cure"	치료되다 "to be treated/cured"
방송하다 "to broadcast"	방송되다 "to be broadcasted"
판매하다 "to sell"	판매되다 "to be sold"

너무 <u>걱정돼서</u> 어젯밤 잠을 하나도 못 잤어요.
"(I) couldn't sleep at all last night because (I) was so worried."
아침은 이제 거의 다 <u>준비됐습니다</u>.
"As for breakfast, (it) is almost ready now."

29.4 Verbs with a passive-like meaning

As for some nouns, you can combine them with the verb 당하다 "suffer/undergo" or 받다 "receive" to create compound verbs that have a passive-like meaning.

For example:

거절 "rejection" + 당하다 = 거절당하다 "to be rejected"
추천 "recommendation" + 받다 = 추천받다 "to be recommended"

Noun + 당하다

사기당하다	"to be deceived/swindled"
무시당하다	"to be ignored"
실연당하다	"to be dumped/lovelorn"
왕따당하다	"to be alienated/bullied"
고소당하다	"to be sued"
배반당하다	"to be betrayed"

Noun + 받다

존경받다	"to be respected"
칭찬받다	"to be praised"
상처받다	"to be hurt"
비난받다	"to be criticized"
간섭받다	"to be interfered with"
처벌받다	"to be punished"

존경받고 싶은 남편 사랑받고 싶은 아내
"The husband wishing to be respected and the wife wishing to be loved"
미국 학생 비자를 세 번째 신청했는데 또 거절당했습니다.
"(He) applied for a US student visa for the third time, but (he) was rejected again."

30

The causative construction

The function of a causative construction is to (i) make someone or something do something or (ii) to cause a change of state (e.g., "He got me to mow the lawn"; I made the music louder").

30.1 Causative suffixes: ~이, ~히, ~리, ~기, ~우, ~구, ~추

In Korean, you can change a limited number of verbs/adjectives into causative verbs by attaching a causative suffix to the stem of the verbs or adjectives. There are seven suffixes: ~이, ~히, ~리, ~기, ~우, ~구, and ~추.

Suffix 이

붙다 "to stick"   붙이다 "to attach [one thing to another]"
속다 "to be fooled"   속이다 "to lie"
먹다 "to eat"   먹이다 "to let [someone] eat; feed"
보다 "to see"   보이다 "to show"
죽다 "to die"   죽이다 "to kill"
끓다 "to boil"   끓이다 "to [make something] boil"

Suffix 히

식다 "to get cold"   식히다 "to chill"
입다 "to wear"   입히다 "to dress [someone]"
눕다 "to lie down"   눕히다 "to make [a person] lie down"
앉다 "to sit"   앉히다 "to have [a person] sit down"
넓다 "be wide"   넓히다 "to widen"
좁다 "be narrow"   좁히다 "to make narrow"

Suffix 리

날다 "to fly"   날리다 "to make/let fly"
살다 "to live"   살리다 "to save; to make alive"
울다 "to cry"   울리다 "to make [a person] cry"
얼다 "to freeze"   얼리다 "to freeze [something]"
알다 "to know"   알리다 "to let [a person] know"

Causative suffixes: ~이, ~히, ~리, ~기, ~우, ~구, ~추 | **30.1**

Suffix 기

굶다 "to starve"   굶기다 "to make [a person] go hungry"
벗다 "to take off"   벗기다 "to take [a person's clothes] off"
웃다 "to laugh"   웃기다 "to make [a person] laugh"
신다 "to wear"   신기다 "to put [footwear] on [a person]"
남다 "to remain"   남기다 "to leave behind"
감다 "to wash one's hair"   감기다 "to wash [someone's hair]"

Suffix 우

차다 "to be full"   채우다 "to fill up"
서다 "to stand"   세우다 "to erect"
자다 "to sleep"   재우다 "to put [a person] to sleep"
타다 "to burn"   태우다 "to burn [something]"
깨다 "to wake"   깨우다 "to wake [someone] up"
끼다 "to join in"   끼우다 "to insert"

Suffix 구/추

늦다 "to be late"   늦추다 "to postpone"
돋다 "to rise"   돋구다 "to make higher"
맞다 "to be suited"   맞추다 "to make fit into"
낮다 "to be low"   낮추다 "to lower"

김 교수님이 학생들한테 책을 많이 <u>읽히기</u>로 유명해요.
"Professor Kim is known for making (his) students read many books."
지금 아이들을 <u>재우지</u> 마세요.
"Do not let the children go to bed now."
약속 시간을 좀 <u>늦춰</u> 줄래요?
"Would (you) postpone the appointment?"
누나가 동생에게 수영복을 <u>입혔어요</u>.
"The older sister made (her) younger brother wear a swimsuit."

There are some similarities between the causative and passive forms. First, you may notice that both passive and causative suffixes contain ~이, ~히, ~리, and ~기. In fact, some verbs, such as 보이다, 업히다, and 안기다, can function both as causatives as well as passives. For example, consider the following two sentences:

아이가 영희한테 <u>업혔어요</u>.
"The child was put on Younghui's back."
어머니가 영희한테 아이를 <u>업혔어요</u>.
"The mother put the child on Younghui's back."

In such cases, you can only tell whether 업혔어요 is a causative or a passive verb by its context. In addition, as with passives, only a restricted number of verbs and adjectives (e.g., like the verbs and adjectives previously listed) can take the suffixes and be changed into causative verbs. Moreover, since there is no rule that specifies which verbs can take which causative suffixes, you have to learn both the verbs that can be changed into causative verbs as well as the suffix each verb takes.

THE CAUSATIVE CONSTRUCTION

30.2 The causative constructions ~게 하다 and ~도록 하다

Besides changing a verb into a causative by adding a suffix, there are two more ways to change verbs and adjectives into causative constructions. First, you can add the causative meaning to verbs and adjectives by attaching ~게 하다 after their stems.

가다 "to go"   가게 하다 "to make [someone] go"
먹다 "to eat"   먹게 하다 "to make [someone] eat"
배우다 "to learn"   배우게 하다 "to make [someone] learn"
보다 "to watch"   보게 하다 "to make [someone] watch"
따뜻하다 "to be warm" 따뜻하게 하다 "to make [something] warm"
맛있다 "to be delicious" 맛있게 하다 "to make [something] delicious"
기쁘다 "to be happy"   기쁘게 하다 "to make [someone] happy"
쉽다 "to be easy"   쉽게 하다 "to make [something] easy"

오래 기다리게 해서 정말 미안해.
"Sorry that (I) made (you) wait long."
한약은 꼭 따뜻하게 해서 먹어라.
"Surely, take the herb medicine after warming (it) up."

The second way to add the causative meaning to a verb is to use ~도록 하다 after the stem of verbs (e.g., 먹다 "to eat" = 먹도록 하다 "to make someone eat").

약 먹고 푹 쉬도록 했어요.
"(I) let (her) take a good rest after taking the medicine."
공항에 도착하면 전화하도록 할 거예요.
"(I) will make (them) call (me) when (they) arrive at the airport."
교실에서 한국어만 쓰도록 하셨어요.
"(He) made (us) use only the Korean language in the classroom."

The meaning difference between ~게 하다 and ~도록 하다 is minimal. However, ~도록 하다 sounds more indirect and softer than ~게 하다. In addition, since ~도록 하다 is applied only to verbs (whereas ~게 하다 can be used for both verbs and adjectives), the use of ~도록 is less frequent than that of ~게 하다.

30.3 Causatives with "noun + 시키다"

As for some "Noun + 하다" verbs, you can create causative verbs by using the verb 시키다 "to force/make [a person do]" instead of 하다 "do."

말하다 "to talk"   말시키다 "to make [someone] talk"
청소하다 "to clean up"   청소시키다 "to make [someone] clean up"
공부하다 "to study"   공부시키다 "to make [someone] study"
감동하다 "to be moved"   감동시키다 "to make [someone] emotionally moved"
이해하다 "to understand"   이해시키다 "to make [someone] understand"
준비하다 "to prepare"   준비시키다 "to make [someone] prepared"
발표하다 "to announce"   발표시키다 "to make [someone] announce [something]"
연습하다 "to practice"   연습시키다 "to make [someone] practice"

화 났으니까 말시키지 마세요.
"(I) am angry, so do not make (me) talk."
곧 떠날 준비시키세요.
"Have (her) ready to leave soon."

31
Direct and indirect questions/ quotations

This chapter discusses indirect question form ~는/(으)ㄴ/(으)ㄹ지 and direct/indirect quotations.

31.1 Indirect question form ~는/(으)ㄴ/(으)ㄹ지

Questions can be either direct or indirect:

> Direct question: "Where does Joshua work?"
> Indirect question: "Do you know where Joshua works?"

In English the indirect question is often marked by the relative clause, introduced by question words such as "whether," "what," "where," and "which." Notice in the second example that the actual question is a relative clause (e.g., where Joshua works), which is marked by the question word "where."

In Korean, the indirect question form ~는/(으)ㄴ/(으)ㄹ지 is used to construct indirect questions as well as to express the speaker's uncertain or wondering mindset. The form ~는/(으)ㄴ/(으)ㄹ지 is built on one of three noun-modifying endings and the special noun 지 "whether/given the state of being/since then/until." ~는지 appears after a verb stem for the present tense (e.g., 듣다 "listen" = 듣는지); ~(으)ㄴ지 appears after an adjective stem for the present tense (e.g., 많다 "many" = 많은지); ~(으)ㄹ지 appears after a verb or adjective stem for the unrealized or prospective tense (e.g., 배우다 "learn" = 배울지; 크다 "big" = 클지). For verbs as well as adjectives in the past tense, 었/았는지 is used (e.g., 시키다 "order" = 시켰는지; 춥다 "cold" = 추웠는지).

In addition, the form ~는/(으)ㄴ/(으)ㄹ지 is often used with certain verbs or adjectives, such as 알다 "know," 모르다 "do not know," and 궁금하다 "curious." Consider the following two questions:

> 수업이 몇 시에 끝나요?
> "What time does the class end?"
> 수업이 몇 시에 끝나는지 아세요?
> "Do (you) know what time the class ends?"

The first sentence is a direct question; the second sentence is an indirect question. Notice in the second sentence that ~는지 is used after the verb stem (e.g., 끝나 + 는지).

After a verb stem in the present tense:

> 어디에서 갈아타는지 아세요?
> "Do (you) know where (they) transfer at?"

DIRECT AND INDIRECT QUESTIONS/QUOTATIONS

뭘 <u>사야 하는지</u> 아세요?
"Do (you) know what (we) need to buy?"

After an adjective stem in the present tense:

얼마나 <u>바쁜지</u> 모르세요?
"Don't (you) know how busy (he) is?"
제 형이 <u>누구인지</u> 아세요?
"Do (you) know who (my) older brother is?"

After a verb or adjective stem in the past tense:

언제 그 일을 <u>그만두었는지</u> 아세요?
"Do (you) know when (he) quit that job?"
시험이 왜 그렇게 <u>어려웠는지</u> 아세요?
"Do (you) know why the test was so hard?"

After a verb or adjective stem in the future tense:

계산서 얼마 <u>나올지</u> 아세요?
"Do (you) know how much the bill comes out to?"
그 일이 얼마나 <u>위험할지</u> 아세요?
"Do (you) know how dangerous that task will be?"

31.2 Indicating a speculative mindset

When the form ~는/(으)ㄴ/(으)ㄹ지 is used in a noninterrogative sentence, it denotes the speaker's wondering or uncertain mindset. Consider the following sentence:

우리 딸이 그 가수를 왜 그렇게 <u>좋아하는지</u> 알고 싶어요.
"(I) want to know why our daughter likes that singer so much."

Notice that 왜 그렇게 좋아하는지 implies the speaker's wondering mindset. Here are more examples:

그 영화가 어떻게 <u>끝나는지</u> 이야기해 주세요.
"Please tell (us) how the movie ends."
주말에는 <u>몇 시에 가게를 여는지</u> 전화해서 물어볼게요.
"(I) will try to call and ask (them) what time (they) open the store on the weekend."
한국 음식을 <u>좋아하시는지</u> 여쭈어 보세요.
"Ask (him) if (he) likes Korean food."
서울에 도착하면 어디를 먼저 <u>가야 할지</u> 말해 주세요.
"Please tell (me) where (I) should go first upon arriving in Seoul."
어떻게 거절을 <u>해야 할지</u> 모르겠어요.
"(I) do not know how (I) should refuse."
사무실 어디에 <u>놓았는지</u> 찾아볼게요.
"(I) will find out where (he) put (it) in the office."
결혼해서 정말로 <u>행복한지</u> 묻고 싶어요.
"(I) want to ask (them) if (they) are really happy after getting married."
그 영화가 얼마나 <u>재미있었는지</u> 모르실 거예요.
"(I) assume that (you) do not know how interesting the movie was."
<u>맛있을지</u> 모르겠어요.
"(I) am not sure whether (it) will be tasty or not."

Direct quotations

엘비스 프레슬리가 <u>누구인지</u> 몰라요.
"(They) do not know who Elvis Presley is."
새 차였는지 기억이 안 나요.
"(I) do not remember whether (it) was a brand-new car or not."

Meanwhile, you can end a sentence with the form ~는/(으)ㄴ/~(으)ㄹ지 (without the main predicate but the politeness marker 요 to make the utterance polite), as shown in the following example:

그 동안 어떻게 <u>지내셨는지요</u>.
"(I) wonder how (you) have been."

Notice that the main predicate (i.e., 모르다 or 궁금하다) is omitted here. Ending a sentence with ~는/(으)ㄴ/~(으)ㄹ지 makes the sentence sound gentle and polite. Here are more examples:

요즘도 한국어를 열심히 <u>배우시는지요</u>.
"(I) wonder if (you) study Korean hard even nowadays."
선생님, <u>건강하신지요</u>.
"Professor, (I) wonder if (you) are well?"
한국에서의 여행은 <u>즐거우셨는지요</u>.
"(I) wonder if (your) trip to Korea was pleasant."
제가 보내 드린 소포는 <u>받으셨는지요</u>.
"(I) wonder if (you) received the package that I mailed to (you)."

31.3 Direct quotations

A direct quotation conveys an exact spoken or written message. Consider the following sentence:

"Evan said that 'I will go back to school no matter what happens!'"

This sentence is a direct quotation. On one hand, it reports what has been said or written verbatim, using quotation marks. On the other hand, an indirect quotation delivers only the main message. In an indirect quotation, the speaker delivers what somebody said or wrote without using the original speaker's exact words. Consequently, an indirect quotation involves the modification of the original utterance. Consider the following example:

"Evan said that he would go back to school no matter what happens."

Notice that the personal pronoun and the tense are modified so that they represent the speaker's or reporter's voice and perspective. This chapter introduces direct and indirect quotations in Korean.

A direct quotation in Korean is constructed from the original utterance, a quotation particle (이)라고, and a quoting verb, such as 말하다 "speak," 대답하다 "answer," 묻다 "ask," 부탁하다 "request," and 제언하다 "suggest." Consider the following examples:

김 과장님이 "우리 이제 점심 먹읍시다" <u>라고</u> 했어요.
"Manager Kim said 'let's have lunch now.'"
나연이가 선생님한테 "곧 갈게요" <u>라고</u> 대답했어요.
"Nayeon replied to the teacher, '(I) promise to go (there) soon.'"
경수가 "이번 주말 내 생일 파티에 올 거예요?" <u>라고</u> 물었어요.
"Kyungsoo asked (me) 'Will (you) come to my birthday party this weekend?'"
교실 벽에 "조용히!" <u>라고</u> 써 있었어요.
"'Be quiet!' was written on the classroom wall."
성미가 "내 고향은 부산!" <u>이라고</u> 대답했어요.
"Sungmee answered 'My hometown is Busan.'"

DIRECT AND INDIRECT QUESTIONS/QUOTATIONS

When quoting mimetic expressions or when quoting the exact forms involved along with the tone and intonation of the quoted utterance, the particle 하고 is used instead of (이)라고. Consider the following examples:

> 학교 종이 "땡땡" 하고 울렸습니다.
> "The school bell rang 'ttaeng ttaeng.'"
> "똑똑" 하고 문을 두드렸어요.
> "(She) knocked on the door 'knock knock.'"
> 사람들이 "도둑이야!" 하고 소리를 질렀어요.
> "People shouted, 'It's a thief!'"
> "와, 이제 방학이다!" 하고 소리쳤습니다.
> "(He) shouted, 'Wow, it's vacation!'"
> 여자 친구에게 "우리 결혼하자" 하고 고백했습니다.
> "(He) proposed to (his) girlfriend, saying 'Let's get married.'"

31.4 Indirect quotations

Generally speaking, in Korean, the use of indirect quotations is more frequent than that of direct quotations. The function of indirect quotations in Korean is twofold: (i) to convey what somebody has said or written without using the original speaker's or writer's exact words, and (ii) to report one's own thoughts or feelings (i.e., internal speech).

Indirect quotations in Korean are constructed from the following: the quoted utterance, the indirect quotation particle 고, and a verb, such as 말하다 (or 하다) "say," 묻다 "ask," 대답하다 "answer," and the adjective 그렇다 "to be that way."

When a direct quote is converted to an indirect report, part of the original utterance (e.g., tense, personal pronouns, place pronouns and honorifics) is modified to fit the perspective of the reporter. Compare the following two sentences:

> 영규가 "제가 음료수를 가져올게요" 라고 말했어요.
> "Youngkyu said 'I will bring beverages.'"
> 영규가 자기가 음료수를 가져오겠다고 했어요.
> "Youngkyu said that he (himself) would bring beverages."

The first sentence is a direct quotation, whereas the second is an indirect quotation. Notice that the first person pronoun 저 in the first sentence was replaced by the noun 자기 "himself" in the second sentence. In addition, the polite speech level ending in the first sentence is replaced by the plain speech level ending in the second (e.g., 가져올게요 to 가져오겠다). Note that the plain speech level has different endings depending on the sentence type:

Declarative	Interrogative	Imperative	Propositive
~는/ㄴ다	~(으)니/냐	~어라/아라	~자

Consequently, depending on the sentence type of the quoted utterance, one of the four plain speech level endings is used accordingly before the quotation particle 고.

Declarative sentences

~는/ㄴ다고 하다 *(for verbs)*

> 보통 매일 두 시간 정도 텔레비전을 본다고 해요.
> "(They) say that (they) usually watch TV about two hours every day."
> 대학에서 한국 역사를 전공한다고 말했어요.
> "(He) said that (he) majors in Korean history in college."

Indirect quotations

겨울 코트를 <u>사러 왔다고 했어요</u>.
"(She) said that (she) came (here) to buy a winter coat."

~다고 하다 *(for adjectives)*

요즈음 한국 날씨가 무척 <u>춥다고 해요</u>.
"(They) say that the weather in Korea is very cold."
방이 좀 <u>지저분하다고 했어요</u>.
"(He) said that the room is messy."
이 식당 국수가 <u>맛있었다고 했어요</u>.
"(She) said that the noodles of this restaurant were delicious."

~라고 하다 *(for the copula)*

남편이 중국 <u>사람이라고 해요</u>.
"(She) says that (her) husband is Chinese."
내년 여름에 한국을 <u>여행할 거라고 했어요</u>.
"(He) said that (he) would travel to Korea next summer."

Interrogative

~(느)냐고 하다/묻다 *(for verbs)*

몇 시쯤 <u>올 거냐고 물어요</u>.
"(They) ask (her) around what time (she) will come."
캘리포니아에서 어디를 <u>여행했냐고 물었어요</u>.
"(He) asked (them) where in California (they) traveled."
오늘 몇 시쯤 <u>퇴근하냐고 물었어요</u>.
"(We) asked about (him) what time (he) gets off the work today."

~냐고 하다/묻다 *(for adjectives and the copula)*

뉴욕에서는 아직도 눈이 <u>오냐고 물었어요</u>.
"(She) asked (them) if (it) is still snowing in New York."
우리 중에서 누가 미국 <u>사람이냐고 물었어요</u>.
"(They) asked (us) who is an American among us."
서울에서 머물고 있는 호텔은 <u>어디냐고 물었어요</u>.
"(He) asked (them) in what hotel (they) are staying in Seoul."

Imperative

~(으)라고 하다 *(for verbs)*

뛰기 전에 꼭 준비 <u>운동하라고 했어요</u>.
"(She) told (him) to definitely do warm-up exercises before running."
절대로 술마시고 <u>운전하지 말라고 했어요</u>.
"(He) told (him) to never drive after drinking alcohol."
빨리 택시를 <u>잡으라고 했어요</u>.
"(He) told (me) to catch a taxi."

Note that ~(으)라 is used instead of the plain style ~어라/아라.

DIRECT AND INDIRECT QUESTIONS/QUOTATIONS

Propositive

~자고 하다 (for verbs)

아침 일찍 같이 <u>떠나자고 합니다</u>.
"(He) suggests that (we) leave together early in the morning."
이번 주말에 같이 영화 <u>보러 가자고 했어요</u>.
"(He) suggested that (we) go to see a movie this weekend."
함께 한잔 <u>하자고 했어요</u>.
"(He) suggested that (we) have a drink together."

31.5 Abbreviation of the indirect quotation endings in colloquial usages

In conversational settings, some of the aforementioned indirect quotation endings can be abbreviated, as shown in the following examples:

~는/ㄴ다고 하다 is shortened to ~는/ㄴ대요 (e.g., 다고 해요 => 대요):

남편이 타이 음식을 <u>좋아한대요</u>.
"(She) says that (her) husband likes Thai food."

~라고 하다 is shortened to ~래요 (e.g., 라고 해요 => 래요):

형이 경찰이<u>래요</u>.
"(He) says that (his) older brother is a policeman."

~(으)라고 하다 is shortened to ~(으)래요 (라고 해요 => 래요):

자기 전에 꼭 약을 <u>먹으래요</u>.
"(She) tells (us) to take the cold medicine before going to sleep."

~자고 하다 is shortened to ~재요 (자고 해요 = 재요):

내일 같이 농구 <u>하재요</u>.
"(They) suggest that (we) play basketball tomorrow together."

31.6 Reporting one's thoughts or feelings

Beside reporting the speech or writing of a third person, indirect quotation is also used to report one's own thoughts or feelings. It is constructed from the following: the quoted utterance, the indirect quotation particle 고, and a verb, such as 생각하다(or 하다) "think" or 느끼다 "feel." Consider the following example:

요즈음 한국 경제가 참 <u>어렵다고 생각한다</u>.
"(I) think that the Korean economy nowadays is very difficult."

Notice that the form reports one's thought rather than quotes someone else's idea. Here are more examples:

나는 그 들의 행동이 <u>용감했다고 생각했다</u>.
"(I) thought that their actions were brave."
아직 2월인데 날씨가 <u>따뜻했다고 느꼈다</u>.
"(I) felt that the weather was warm although it was still February."
호텔 직원들의 서비스가 참 <u>좋았다고 느꼈다</u>.
"(I) felt that the hotel employees' service was particularly nice."

32

Prenouns

This chapter discusses prenouns, which may also be termed "determiners," "unconjugated adjectives," or "adnouns," that serve to modify or delimit the meaning of the nouns that they follow.

Just like bound nouns, which cannot be used independently, prenouns also cannot be used by themselves but must always used with other nouns. There are four groups of prenouns in Korean. The first group of prenouns are those that specifically delimit the quality or status of certain nouns. Consider the following example.

    첫 직장   "one's first job"

Notice that 첫 "first" is a prenoun that delimits the quality or status of the noun 직장 "job."

첫 "first" appears to be an adjective. However, prenouns differ from adjectives. A chief distinction between prenouns and adjectives is whether they are subject to morphological variations or not. Prenouns are nouns, and they are not subject to any inflectional variation. On the other hand, adjectives are subject to variations. For example, in Korean, "a different direction" can be written with a prenoun 딴 "another" or with an adjective 다른 "different."

딴 쪽   (딴 "another" + 쪽 "direction")
다른 쪽   (다른 "different" + 쪽 "direction")

Notice that 다른 is the conjugated form of 다르다 "to be different" (다르 + ㄴ = 다른). How to change an adjective stem into a noun-modifying form is discussed in detail in Chapter 21. Here are some more examples of prenouns:

딴 생각	"different thought" (딴 "another" + 생각 "thought")
딴 방법	"another method" (딴 "another" + 방법 "method")
딴 날	"some other day" (딴 "another" + 날 "day")
맨 뒤	"at the very end" (맨 "the very" + 뒤 "last/end")
맨 앞	"at the very front" (맨 "the very" + 앞 "front")
맨 위	"at the very top" (맨 "the very" + 위 "above")
새 건물	"new building" (새 "new" + 건물 "building")
새 컴퓨터	"new computer" (새 "new" + 컴퓨 "computer")
새 전화	"new telephone" (새 "new" + 전화 "telephone")
순 자산	"net assets" (순 "pure" + 자산 "assets")
순 이익	"net profit" (순 "pure" + 이익 "profit")
순 한국식	"pure Korean style" (순 "pure" + 한국식 "Korean style")
옛 추억	"old memories" (옛 "old" + 추억 "memories")
옛 말	"old saying" (옛 "old" + 말 "word")
옛 친구	"old friends" (옛 "old" + 친구 "friend")
헌 자전거	"used bicycle" (헌 "used" + 자전거 "bicycle")
헌 책	"used books" (헌 "used" + 책 "book")
헌 집	"old house" (헌 "used" + 집 "house")

PRENOUNS

The second group of prenouns are numbers. Consider the following examples:

한 번	"once"
세 번	"three times"
다섯 번	"five times"

두 시간	"two hours"
네 시간	"four hours"
여섯 시간	"six hours"

일 년	"one year"
이 년	"two years"
삼 년	"three years"

사 초	"four seconds"
오 초	"five seconds"
육 초	"six seconds"

Notice that these numbers come before the noun (or counters) that they modify.

The third group of prenouns includes demonstratives. Appearing before the noun that they modify, demonstratives indicate the speaker's physical as well as psychological distance relative to the listener or a referent. English has two demonstratives: "this" and "that." However, Koreans make three referential locations: 이 "this (near the speaker)," 그 "that (near the listener)," and 저 "that over there (away from both the speaker and the listener)."

이 책상	"this desk"
그 책상	"that desk"
저 책상	"that desk (over there)"

Differing from English demonstratives, which can be used independently, as in "I like this," the Korean demonstratives cannot be used alone and must be followed by a noun. In other words, Korean demonstratives are always used with nouns, as in 이 손님 "this customer," 이 열쇠 "this key," and so on.

Meanwhile, Korean has two bound nouns that are often used with the demonstratives: 것 (or 거 in colloquial situations) "thing" and 곳 "place."

    이 것 (or 이 거 for colloquial usages) "this (thing)"
    그 것 (or 그 거 for colloquial usages) "that (thing)"
    저 것 (or 저 거 for colloquial usages) "that (thing over there)"
    이 곳 (or 여 기 for colloquial usages) "here"
    그 곳 (or 거 기 for colloquial usages) "there"
    저 곳 (or 저 기 for colloquial usages) "over there"

Since 것 (or 거) is a bound noun that cannot be used by itself, it is always used with a modifier (i.e., a prenoun or an adjective).

The fourth group of prenouns includes question prenouns such as 어느 "which," 무슨 (or 어떤) "what kind of," and 웬 "what kind of, what/why on earth."

    무슨 색을 좋아하세요?
    "What kind of color (do you) like?"
    어떤 사람을 사귀고 싶으세요?
    "What kind of person (do you) wish to date?"

PRENOUNS

<u>어느</u> 가게에 가세요?
"Which store (do you) go to?"
갑자기 <u>왠</u> 비야?
"All of sudden, why rain?"

Notice that these question prenouns cannot be used by themselves, and they modify the nouns that they appear before.

33

Adverbs

This chapter discusses adverbs (or adverbials) and mimetic/onomatopoetic words.

33.1 Adverbs

The primary function of adverbs is to modify verbs, adjectives, or sentences. That is, they provide extra information regarding an action, state, or event, such as time, degree, manner, and the speaker's assessment regarding the action/state. Consider the following examples:

(1) 어제는 <u>일찍</u> 퇴근했어요.
  "(I) left work early yesterday."
(2) <u>매우</u> 무거워요.
  "(It) is very heavy."
(3) <u>보통</u> 6시에 일어나서 7시에 출근합니다.
  "Normally, (I) get up at 6 and leave for work at 7."

In (1), 일찍 "early" modifies the verb 퇴근했어요 "left work." In (2), 매우 "very" modifies the adjective 무거워요 "heavy." In (3), 보통 "usually/normally" modifies the entire sentence respectively.

33.1.1 Semantic categorization of adverbs

Korean adverbs can be grouped into three types according to their meaning: sentential adverbs, conjunctional adverbs, and componential adverbs. Sentential adverbs modify the whole sentence. Conjunctional adverbs are those that connect two different sentences. Componential adverbs modify a specific part of the sentence such as the verbs or adjectives. Consider the following example:

물론 월급은 <u>아주</u> 적어요. <u>그렇지만</u> 일이 재미있어요.
"Of course the pay is very small. But the work is interesting."

물론 "of course" is a sentential adverb since it modifies the entire sentence, 월급은 아주 적어요 "the pay is very small." 아주 "very" is a componential adverb since it specifically modifies the adjective 적어요 "is small." 그렇지만 "but" is a conjunctional adverb since it links two sentences.

Examples of sentential adverbs include the following:

가령 "if, supposing"   과연 "indeed"
기어이 "by all means"   다행히 "fortunately"
당연히 "naturally"   만일/만약 "if"
물론 "of course"   반드시 "certainly"
보통 "normally"   사실은 "in fact"
설령 "even if"   설마 "surely (not)"
아마 "perhaps"   역시 "as expected"
제발, 부디 "please"   하마터면 "almost"
하여튼 "anyway"   혹시 "by any chance"

Adverbs 33.1

Examples of conjunctional adverbs include:

그래서 "so"
그러니까 "therefore"
그런데 "by the way"
그렇지만 "however"
더구나 "moreover"
더우기 "furthermore"
또 "also"
또한 "moreover"
오히려 "rather"
즉 "in other words"
그러나 "but"
그러므로 "since it is so"
그럼 "if so"
그리고 "and"
더군다나 "besides"
따라서 "accordingly"
또는 "or"
아니면 "otherwise"
왜냐하면 "if that is why"
혹은 "alternatively"

There are three groups of componential adverbs depending on what kind of relation they modify, such as manner, temporal relations, and degree. First, manner adverbs express some relation of manner.

가까이 "shortly, nearly"
가장 "most"
너무 "too much"
많이 "much"
멀리 "far"
아주 "quite, very (much)"
열심히 "diligently"
잘 "well, often"
천천히 "slowly"
함부로 "recklessly"
가만히 "silently"
각각 "respectively"
달리 "differently"
매우 "very, exceedingly"
빨리 "fast, early, soon"
안녕히 "at peace"
일부러 "intentionally"
제일 "the first"
함께 "together"
혼자서 "alone"

Time adverbs that concern temporal relations include the following:

가끔 "sometimes"
내일 "tomorrow"
늘 "always"
드디어 "finally"
막 "just at the moment"
모래 "the day after tomorrow"
방금 "right now"
보통 "usually"
아직 "yet, still"
요즈음 (요즘) "recently"
이미 "already"
지금 "now"
항상 "at all times"
갑자기 "suddenly"
냉큼 "immediately"
당분간 "for a while"
마침내 "at last"
먼저 "ahead"
밤낮 "night and day"
벌써 "long ago"
아까 "some time ago"
언제나 "all the time"
이따 "later"
일찍 "early"
줄곧 "all the time"
현재 "present"

Degree adverbs include the following:

가장 (제일, 최고) "most"
겨우 "hardly"
꽤 "relatively"
다 "all"
더 "more"
덜 "less"
몹시 "terribly"
별로 "not particularly"
아주 "very"
전혀 "totally [not]"
주로 "mainly"
참 "really"
거의 "almost"
그리 "not so much"
너무 "so much"
대단히 "much"
더욱 "all the more"
매우 "greatly"
무척 "exceedingly"
심히 "extremely"
약간 "slightly"
조금 "a bit"
지극히 "extremely"
훨씬 "by far more"

ADVERBS 33.1

Meanwhile, when there is more than one componential adverb in a sentence, the adverbs tend to occur in the following sequence: time, degree, and manner, as shown in the following example.

아버지가 언제나 가장 열심히 운동하세요.
"(My) father always exercises the most diligently."

Notice that the first adverb is a time adverb 언제나 "always," followed by the degree adverb 가장 "most," and the manner adverb 열심히 "diligently."

33.1.2 Structural categorization of adverbs

Structurally speaking, adverbs in Korean can be classified into two groups depending on whether they take morphological variations or not. The first group includes adverbs that are not derived from other word classes or do not take morphological variations. These adverbs are also called "proper adverbs," and some examples include:

가끔 "sometimes"	곧 "soon"
늘 "the whole time"	더 "more"
덜 "less"	매우 "very"
먼저 "first"	바로 "straight"
아마 "perhaps"	아주 "very"
언제나 "all the time"	이미 "already"
조금 "a bit"	즉시 "immediately"
퍽 "awfully"	항상 "always"

The second group of adverbs includes adverbials (a word or phrase functioning as an adverb). Adverbials are derived from other word classes by taking morphological variations, and there are several sets. The first set includes those that take the one-form ending ~게. Consider the following examples:

(1) 햄버거를 맛있게 먹었어요.
    "(I) ate a hamburger deliciously."
(2) 방을 아름답게 꾸몄어요.
    "(We) decorated (our) room beautifully."

In (1), notice that 맛있게 "deliciously" modifies the verb 먹었어요 "ate," and 아름답게 "beautifully" modifies 꾸몄어요 "decorated" in (2). However, 맛있게 and 아름답게 are not proper adverbs but adverbials in Korean since they are the results of the morphological variations:

맛있다 "delicious"	=맛있게 (맛있 + 게) "deliciously"
아름답다 "beautiful"	=아름답게 (아름답 + 게) "beautifully"

Notice in the preceding example that the adverbial form ~게 is attached to the adjective's stems. In Korean, one can change an adjective into an adverbial form by attaching ~게 to the adjective stem. Here are some examples:

간단하다 "simple"	간단하게 "simply"
그렇다 "like that"	그렇게 "in that way"
넓다 "wide"	넓게 "widely"
늦다 "late"	늦게 "late"
쉽다 "easy"	쉽게 "easily"
싱겁다 "mild (taste)"	싱겁게 "insipidly"
싸다 "cheap"	싸게 "at a low price"
이렇다 "like this"	이렇게 "in this way"
작다 "small"	작게 "tinily"
재미있다 "interesting"	재미있게 "in a fun way"
춥다 "cold"	춥게 "in a cold way"

Mimetic/onomatopoetic words   **33.2**

크다 "big" 크게 "hugely"
행복하다 "happy" 행복하게 "happily"

The second set includes a small number of adverbial forms that are built on an adjective and the suffix ~이 (or ~히), as shown here:

같다 "the same" 같이 "alike"
곱다 "beautiful" 고이 "beautifully"
넉넉하다 "ample" 넉넉히 "amply"
높다 "high" 높이 "highly"
많다 "many" 많이 "many"
부지런하다 "diligent" 부지런히 "diligently"
빠르다 "fast" 빨리 "fast"
조용하다 "quiet" 조용히 "quietly"

The third set includes adverbial forms that are made of a noun and the instrumental particle (으)로. Some examples are as follow:

강제 "coercion" 강제로 "forcibly"
겉 "exterior" 겉으로 "outwardly"
다음 "the next" 다음으로 "next"
속 "inside" 속으로 "inwardly"
앞 "the front" 앞으로 "forwardly"
진심 "sincerity" 진심으로 "truly"
최후 "the last" 최후로 "lastly"

The fourth set includes a limited number of nouns that can be transformed into adverbial forms by attaching the suffix ~껏 "as much as possible" and 상 "for the sake of." Examples include:

능력 "ability" 능력껏 "to the best of one's ability"
마음 "heart" 마음껏 "to one's heart's content"
성의 "sincerity" 성의껏 "sincerely"
욕심 "greed" 욕심껏 "as much as one desires"
사정 "situation" 사정상 "due to circumstances"
양심 "conscience" 양심상 "for conscience's sake"
예의 "courtesy" 예의상 "as a matter of courtesy"
형식 "form" 형식상 "for form's sake"

33.2 Mimetic/onomatopoetic words

Korean makes an extensive use of mimetic words and onomatopoetic words. Mimetic words (의태어) mimic manner, and onomatopoetic words (의성어) mimic sounds. These mimetic and onomatopoetic words typically serve as adverbs, as they can precede and modify verbs. For instance, consider the following examples:

눈이 펑펑 내려요.
"It's snowing hard."
혼자서 찬물을 벌컥벌컥 마셨어요.
"(He) chugged cold water by himself."

Notice that the mimetic word 펑펑 modifies the verb 내려요, and the onomatopoetic word 벌컥벌컥 modifies the verb 마셨어요. Here are more examples:

길이 꽁꽁 얼었어요.
"The road is frozen all the way through."

ADVERBS 33.2

거리가 <u>미끌미끌</u>해요.
"The street is slippery."
너무 피곤해서 교실에서 <u>꾸벅꾸벅</u> 졸았어요.
"(I) was so tired, so (I) was nodding off in the classroom."
누가 <u>낄낄</u> 웃니?
"Who is giggling?"
코를 <u>드르렁드르렁</u> 골면서 자더라구요.
"(He) was sleeping, snoring loudly."
바람이 <u>쌩쌩</u> 불고 추워요.
"The wind is blowing hard, and it is cold."

Although English also has its mimetic as well as onomatopoetic words, its number as well as usage are much more limited when compared to Korean. For instance, some Korean onomatopoetic words have their corresponding English words, such as 멍멍 "bowwow," 음메 "moo," 두근두근 "pit-a-pat," and 빵빵 "toot, toot." However, many Korean mimetic and onomatopoetic words do not have direct equivalents in English.

Part B
Functions

34
Ability

This chapter examines expressions that are used to indicate one's abilities or capabilities.

34.1 Using words that indicate "ability"

The Korean words that denote "ability" or "capability" include 능력, 솜씨, 재능, 실력, 기량, and 수완.

능력
밥 한끼 사 줄 <u>능력</u>은 있어요.
"I have the ability to buy you a meal."

솜씨
여자 친구 음식 <u>솜씨</u>가 좋은데.
"Your girlfriend's cooking skill is good."

재능
음악에는 <u>재능</u>이 전혀 없는 사람이에요.
"He is a man who has no talent in music whatsoever."

실력
운전 <u>실력</u>이 많이 늘었네요.
"Your driving skill improved a lot."

기량
이번 경기에서 <u>기량</u>을 충분히 발휘했습니다.
"He showed his ability fully in this game."

수완
우리는 모두 그의 정치적 <u>수완</u>을 높이 평가했었습니다.
"We used to have a very high opinion of his political ability."

Among the preceding words, the last two, 기량 and 수완, tend to be used in limited contexts.

34.2 ~(으)ㄹ 줄 알다/모르다 "know how to" (see 24.2)

A: 인테넷으로 기차표를 <u>예매할 줄 알아요</u>?
"Do you know how to purchase a train ticket in advance online?"
B: 아니요, 한 번도 안 해 봤는데요.
"No, I have never done that before."

A: 이 세탁기 어떻게 <u>쓸 줄 아세요</u>?
"Do you know how to use this washing machine?"
B: 아니요, 저도 몰라서 좀 물어보려구요.
"No, I don't know either, so I intend to ask someone."

ABILITY

A: 스키 탈 줄 아세요?
"Do you know how to ski?"
B: 그럼요. 제가 가르쳐 드릴게요.
"Sure, I will teach you."

유투브에 동영상을 올릴 줄 아세요?
"Do you know how to upload a video file on YouTube?"
혹시 자동차 엔진 오일 갈 줄 아세요?
"By any chance, do you know how to change engine oil?"
아직 한글로 이메일을 칠 줄 몰라요.
"I do not know how to type an e-mail in Hangul yet."
한국어를 할 줄 몰라요.
"I do not know how to speak Korean."

34.3 ~(으)ㄹ 수 있다/없다 "can/cannot" (see 23.11)

A: 무슨 외국어를 할 수 있으세요?
"What foreign languages can you speak?"
B: 영어는 물론이고 일본어도 할 수 있습니다.
"I can speak English, of course, and Japanese too."

A: 수영 할 수 있으시지요?
"You can swim, right?"
B: 그럼요. 제가 하와이 출신이잖아요.
"Of course, I am from Hawaii, you know."

A: 한국 드라마 보실 때 자막이 없어도 이해할 수 있으세요?
"When you watch Korean dramas, can you understand without subtitles?"
B: 네, 드라마는 대충 이해할 수 있는데 뉴스는 아직 이해할 수 없어요.
"Yes, I can understand dramas roughly, but I can't understand the news yet."

너무 매워서 먹을 수가 없네요.
"I can't eat it because it is too spicy."
선약이 있어서 오늘은 갈 수 없을 것 같습니다.
"I do not think that I can go there because I have a previous engagement."

34.4 ~다 못해(서) "unable to"

This form is made of the conjunctive ~다가 "do and then" (see 19.1.7), the negative 못, and the verb 해서 (하다 + 어/아서). The expression means "unable to," as shown in the following examples:

A: 왜 그 좋은 회사를 그만두었대요?
"What did he say about why he quit that great company?"
B: 업무에 관한 스트레스를 견디다 못해서 결국 사표를 냈대요.
"I heard that he was unable to cope with the stress from work, so he finally submitted his resignation."

그들의 불평을 듣다 못해 그냥 나와 버렸어요.
"Unable to hear their grumbling, I just went out."
배가 불러서 주신 음식을 다 먹다 못해 남기고 말았어요.
"I was so full that I was unable to eat all the food that she prepared for me, so I ended up leaving the rest."
보다 못해 결국 나도 화를 냈다.
"Unable to remain a mere spectator, I also got mad."
아내 잔소리에 참다 못해 화를 내고 말았다.
"Unable to hear my wife's nagging, I ended up expressing my anger."

35

Addressing someone

Choosing an appropriate address (or reference) term is crucial not only for communicating successfully but also for maintaining smooth personal relationships. For instance, suppose that you address your company president by his first name on the very first day of work at the company. This is likely to bring forth a negative impression if the president does not know you well and is the type of CEO who believes in the chain of command and formal etiquette.

One's choice of address term or reference term is contingent upon the speaker's relationship with the person he/she is speaking/referring to. There are several social factors that may affect or determine one's relationship with him/her, such as power (e.g., who is older, who is the subordinate or boss, what kind of occupation he/she holds, and so forth) and psychological distance (e.g., how familiar or interpersonally close one feels toward the addressee). The use of inappropriate address terms may have serious consequences in Korea as well. The Korean language makes use of an extensive and intricate list of address terms.

35.1 Address terms in Korean

Here are examples of Korean address terms, arranged in decreasing deference (e.g., less difference in the power relationship) or distance (e.g., less psychological distance or more familiar/intimate).

Honorific title ~님

교수님 (professional title + nim) "Honorable professor"
김 사장님 (last name + professional title + nim) "Honorable Kim"
아버님 (kinship term + nim) "Honorable father"

Professional titles (e.g., 교수, 기사, 과장, 부장, 실장)

박 선생 (last name + professional title) "Teacher Park"
이 팀장 (last time + professional title) "Team chief Lee"

Rank terms (선배, 후배)

최정운 선배 (full name + rank term) "Senior Choi Jungwoon"
김 선배 (last name + rank term) "Senior Kim"
후배 (as a reference term) "Junior"

Sibling terms (형, 오빠, 누나, 언니)

정호 형 (first name + sibling term) "older brother Jungho"
기주 언니 (first name + sibling term) "older sister Keejoo"

ADDRESSING SOMEONE

Neutral title 씨

변상필 씨 (full name + neutral title) "Mr. Sangpil Byon"
종규 씨 (first name + neutral title) "Mr. Jongkyu"

Loanword titles (e.g., 미스타, 미스)

미스타 김 (Mr. + Kim) "Mr. Kim"
미스 박 (Ms. + Park) "Ms. Park"

Junior titles 양, 군

최 군 (last name + junior title) "Mr. Choi"
이선희 양 (full name + junior title) "Ms. Sunhee Lee"

Familiar vocative ~이 (after a consonant)/none (after a vowel)

상필이 (first name + vocative particle) "Sangpil"
종규 (first name) "Jongkyu"

Intimate vocative ~아 (after a consonant)/~야 (after a vowel)

상필아 (first name + intimate vocative) "Sangpil"
종규야 (first name + intimate vocative) "Jongkyu"

Consequently, a businessman 김현우, "Kim Hyunwoo" can be addressed in his work place at least in the following ways:

과장님	"Section chief" (when his junior colleagues address him)
김 과장	"Section chief Kim" (when his boss addresses him)
김 선배	"Senior Kim" (when his junior colleague who happens to have graduated from the same high school addresses him)
김현우 씨	"Mr. Hyunwoo Kim" (when adult distant friends who are of equal or higher status address him)
미스타 김	"Mr. Kim" (when an older boss addresses him)

In his personal life, his college friend who may be two or three years younger may call him 현우 형. His high school friends who are the same age can call him 현우 or 현우야. Meanwhile, his wife may call him 여보 "darling," 당신 "dear," 오빠 "older brother" (if she is younger than he) or 수미 아빠 "Soomee's dad" (the father of their child).

As shown in the preceding list, notice that the difference in status (e.g., who has the higher status or power between the speaker and the addressee), the familiarity (e.g., how close or familiar the speaker is with the addressee/referent), and also the contextual factors (e.g., professional/private, formal/informal) determine the choice of address term.

It is beyond this chapter's scope to cover all possible address/reference terms since one's choice of address terms is determined by the complex interplay of various factors. However, the following sections describe some basic rules of thumb (with sample address terms) that you may use in various situations.

35.2 How to address a family member

Due to the collectivistic and hierarchical values rooted in the Korean language and culture, Korean has a list of highly stratified and extensive family terms. The Korean family terms signal

How to address a family member

35.2

how one is related to others in intricate manners (e.g., whether the relative is a male or female, whether the relative is older or younger, whether the relative is on the mother's or father's side, whether the relative is the husband's or wife's, and so on). Koreans use family terms as both address terms and reference terms for their family members. For instance, it is rare for younger brothers or sisters to address their older siblings by their first name.

Korean family terms can fall into two groups. The first group has two family term sets depending on the gender of the person related.

For a female speaker:

Spouse	당신, 남편, 여보, 자기야
Older brother	오빠
Older sister	언니
Brother's wife	새언니 (older brother's wife)
	올케 (younger brother's wife)
Sister's husband	형부 (older sister's husband)
	제부 (younger sister's husband)
Husband's father	아버님, 시아버지
Husband's mother	어머님, 시어머니
Husband's brother	아주버님 (husband's older brother)
	도련님, 삼촌 (husband's younger, unmarried brother)
Husband's sister-in-law	형님 (husband's older brother's wife)
	동서 (husband's younger brother's wife)
Husband's sister	형님 (husband's older sister)
	아가씨 (husband's younger sister)
Husband's brother-in-law	고모부님, 아주버님 (husband's older sister's husband)
	고모부, 서방님 (husband's younger sister's husband)

For a male speaker:

Spouse	당신, 아내 (부인), 여보, 자기야
Older brother	형
Older sister	누나
Brother's wife	형수님 (older brother's wife)
	제수씨 (younger brother's wife)
Sister's husband	자형, 매형 (older sister's husband)
	매부, 매제 (younger sister's husband)
Wife's father	아버님, 장인어른
Wife's mother	어머님, 장모님
Wife's brother	형님 (wife's older brother)
	처남 (wife's younger brother)
Wife's sister-in-law	처남댁, 아주머니 (wife's older brother's wife)
	처남댁 (wife's younger brother's wife)
Wife's sister	처형 (wife's older sister)
	처제 (wife's younger sister)
Wife's brother-in-law	형님 (wife's older sister's husband)
	동서 (wife's younger sister's husband)

The second group includes the family terms used by both genders.

Grandparents	조부모님
Paternal grandfather	할아버지
Paternal grandmother	할머니
Maternal grandfather	외할아버지

ADDRESSING SOMEONE   35.4

	Maternal grandmother	외할머니
	Parents	부모님
	Father/dad	아버지/아빠
	Mother/mom	어머니/엄마
	Son	아들, first name
	Daughter	딸, first name
	Grandchild(ren)	손주, first name
	Grandson	손자, first name
	Granddaughter	손녀(딸), first name
	Younger brother	남동생, 아우, first name
	Younger sister	여동생, first name
	Paternal uncle	큰아버지, 백부님 (an older brother of one's father)
		작은아버지, 숙부님 (a married younger brother of one's father)
		삼촌 (an unmarried younger brother of one's father)
		고모부 (the husband of the sister of one's father)
	Paternal aunt	고모 (both older or younger sister of one's father)
		큰어머니 (the wife of an older brother of one's father)
		작은어머니, 숙모 (the wife of a married younger brother of one's father)
	Maternal uncle	외삼촌 (both older or younger brother of one's mother, regardless of their marital status)
		이모부 (the husband of a sister of one's mother)
	Maternal aunt	이모 (both older or younger sister of one's mother)
		외숙모 (the wife of both older or younger brother of one's mother)
	Son-in-law	사위, last name + 서방 (e.g., 김서방)
	Daughter-in-law	며느리, (새)아가, 어멈아
	Cousin	사촌

35.3 How to address a friend/familiar person

Koreans frequently use some family terms when addressing or referring to non-kin members as well (e.g., friends, friends' family members). For instance, Korean males often use 형 "older brother" when addressing or referring to an older male friend. They may use 어머니 "mother" when addressing or referring to their friend's mother. When addressing a stranger who appears apparently old (say over 60), Koreans use 할아버지 "grandfather" or 할머니 "grandmother."

Address term	Person being addressed
상필아	Close friend of same age (e.g., your elementary school friend)
상필이	Close friend of same age
형(님), 오빠	Close male friend who is somewhat older
누나, 언니	Close female friend who is somewhat older
선배(님)	Close friend who is somewhat older and a senior at school
자기야, 상필 씨	Boyfriend/girlfriend
상필이 어머님	Friend's mother
할아버지/할머니	Older adults (over 60)

35.4 How to address a colleague at your workplace

Korean makes extensive use of professional titles as address and reference terms. It is beyond this chapter's limit to enumerate them all. However, here are some address terms commonly used within a company setting.

How to address an unfamiliar person/stranger

Address term	Person being addressed
회장님	Chairman
사장님	Company president
부사장님	Vice president
전무님	Executive director
상무님	Director
이사님	Member of board of directors
실장님/부장님	Department head
팀장님	Team head
차장님	Deputy department head
최 차장	Deputy department head Choi
과장님	Section head
김 과장(님)	Section manager Kim (your subordinate)
대리님	Deputy section chief
박 대리(님)	Deputy section chief Park
선배(님)	Senior member (who has more seniority than you)
변상필 씨/상필 씨	Equal colleague at workplace
미스타 변	Subordinate at workplace

35.5 How to address an unfamiliar person/stranger

The most common and proper way to address someone who is a stranger is not to use any address term at all. For instance, even when you have to get attention from someone in a store or restaurant setting, the most common way is to get his/her attention by using expressions, such as 저어, 여기요 "Well, here,"; 실례지만 "excuse me"; and 죄송합니다만 "I am sorry but." However, if unavoidable, one can use one of the following:

Address term	Person being addressed
애(야), 꼬마야	(e.g., child)
학생	(e.g., college student/younger looking adolescent)
총각/젊은이	(e.g., younger looking male)
언니	(e.g., female server or hair dresser)
아주머니/아줌마	(e.g., older female, 40s to 50s)
아저씨	(e.g., older male, 40s to 50s)
사모님, 선생님	(e.g., older female, socially superior, 40s to 70s)
선생님, 사장님	(e.g., older male, socially superior, 40s to 70s)
할아버지, 할머니	(e.g., very old adult, beyond 60)
기사님, 기사 아저씨	(e.g., bus/taxi driver)
아저씨	(e.g., male store clerk, janitor, technician, plumber, etc.)
손님, 고객님	(e.g., customers)

Note that the address terms listed here are just examples. Depending on who the speaker is, the address term can differ. For instance, if you are a college student in your early 20s, you will not call someone who is about your age by 총각/젊은이 (terms that are used by an older adult when addressing a young man). Moreover, if you are a male in your 60s, you will not call a young male clerk/technician 아저씨, but maybe by 총각 or 젊은이.

36
Advice

This chapter discusses various expressions associated with seeking, giving, and responding to advice.

36.1 Seeking advice

36.1.1 ~(으)ㄹ까요? "wondering" (see 26.2)

뭘 준비해 가는 게 <u>좋을까요</u>?
"I wonder what would be nice to prepare and bring?"
어디 가서 먹는 게 <u>좋을까요</u>?
"Where do you think we should eat?"
어떻게 <u>하면 될까요</u>?
"What I should do?"
어떤 색이 <u>괜찮을까요</u>?
"What color do you think will be nice?"
뭘 사는 게 <u>좋을까요</u>?
"I wonder what will be good to buy?"

36.2 Giving advice

36.2.1 ~지 그래요? "why don't you . . .?"

This form is constructed from the sentence ending ~지 (see 26.6) and the adjective 그렇다 "be so." It means "why don't you?" in English.

A: 요즘 일 때문에 스트레스가 많은데 어떻게 하면 좋을까요?
"Lately, I am under stress because of work, so what should I do?"
B: 조깅같은 가벼운 운동을 <u>시작해 보시지 그래요</u>?
"Why don't you start a light exercise like jogging?"

친구한테 <u>물어보지 그래요</u>?
"Why don't you ask your friend?"
약을 좀 <u>먹어 보지 그래요</u>?
"Why don't you take some medicine?"
정말 맛있는데 더 <u>드시지 그래요</u>?
"It is really tasty, so why don't you help yourself to more?"
인터넷으로 <u>예매하지 그래요</u>?
"Why don't you make a reservation via the internet?"
플로리다에 왔는데 디지니월드라도 <u>가 보지 그래요</u>?
"You came all the way to Florida, so why don't you visit Disney World or something?"
다른 전공을 좀 <u>생각해 보지 그래요</u>?
"Why don't you think of other majors?"

Seeking and giving advice **36.3**

부모님을 찾아뵙고 <u>인사 드려 보지 그래요</u>?
"Why don't you pay a visit to your parents?"

36.2.2 ~도록 하세요 "do" (see 18.1.6)

This form is built on the conjunctive ~도록 (see 18.1.6) and the verb 하세요 "do." The form literally can be translated as "do so that he . . ." However, it is often used when giving advice in a rather authoritative manner (e.g., a boss to a subordinate; a medical doctor to a patient).

A: 과장님, 호텔로 내일 몇 시에 모시러 가야 할까요?
   "Sir, what time should I go pick him up at the hotel?"
B: 호텔 로비로 8시 50분 전까지 가서 룸으로 <u>전화 드리도록 하세요</u>.
   "Please go to the hotel lobby by 8:50 and give a call to the room."

담배를 꼭 <u>끊도록 하세요</u>.
"Please quit smoking by all means."
연고를 상처에 자주 <u>바르도록 하세요</u>.
"Please put the ointment on the scar often."
너무 늦게 <u>자지 않도록 하세요</u>.
"Please make sure they do not go to sleep late."
꼭 선물을 잊지 말고 사 가지고 <u>오도록 하세요</u>.
"By all means, please do not forget to buy and bring the gift."
며칠 동안 푹 <u>쉬도록 하세요</u>.
"Please rest for a few days."

36.3 Seeking and giving advice

The following can be used for either seeking or giving advice depending on context and intonation:

36.3.1 어때요/어떨까요? "How about?"

<u>어떠세요</u>?
"How is it?"
이 색은 <u>어떻습니까</u>?
"How about this color?"
먼저 어떤 회사인지 신중하게 알아보고 결정하는 게 <u>어떨까요</u>?
"How about making a decision after seriously investigating what kind of company it is?"
인터넷으로 저널을 써 보는 건 <u>어때요</u>?
"How about writing a journal using the internet?"

36.3.2 ~지 않을까요? "Don't you think . . .?"

This structure is made with the long negation form ~지 않다 (see 20.2) and ~(으)ㄹ까 (see 26.2).

이 정도로 <u>충분하지 않을까요</u>?
"Don't you think these will be enough?"
병원에 가서 진단을 받아 보는 게 <u>좋지 않을까요</u>?
"Don't you think that going to the hospital for a check up will be better?"
대신 한국 역사 수업을 들어 보는 게 <u>좋지 않을까요</u>?
"Don't you think that taking a Korean history course instead will be better?"
좀 어렵더라도 계속 공부하는 게 <u>도움이 되지 않을까요</u>?
"Although it may be a bit hard, don't you think that continuing your studies would be helpful?"

ADVICE

36.3.3 ~것이 어떨까 싶네요 "how about . . ." (see 15.4)

이번 주말에 사러 가는 게 어떨까 싶어요?
"How about we go to buy the gift together this weekend?"
당장 기차표를 예매하는 게 어떨까 싶네요?
"How about we purchase the train ticket in advance right now?"
좀 더 기다려 보는 게 어떨까 싶네요?
"How about we wait for a little longer?"
오늘 저녁은 한식으로 하시는 게 어떨까 싶네요?
"How about we have Korean food for dinner tonight?"

36.3.4 ~(으)ㄹ 만하다 "worth . . ." (see 23.2)

여기 음식들 대부분 먹을 만해요?
"Are most of the dishes here worth trying?"
어느 영화가 볼 만하셨어요?
"Which movie was worth watching?"
근처에 추천할 만한 곳이 있으면 소개해 주세요.
"Please tell me if there are any places worth recommending around this area."
볼 만한 영화 좀 추천해 주세요.
"Please recommend movies that are worth watching."
그랜드캐년은 일생 꼭 한번 가 볼 만한 곳이에요.
"The Grand Canyon is a place worth visiting at least once in a lifetime."
새로 산 컴퓨터가 좀 비쌌지만 그래도 쓸 만했어요.
"Although the computer that I bought was a bit expensive, it was worth it."
동대문시장은 물건이 다양하고 비교적 가격도 저렴해서 쇼핑할 만해요.
"The items at Dongdaemun Market are diverse and prices are also relatively reasonable, so it is worth shopping there."

36.4 Responding to advice

What follow are some sample responses to advice:

네, 감사합니다. 그리 하도록 하겠습니다.
"Yes, thank you. I will do so then."
선생님 조언을 따르도록 하겠습니다.
"I will take your advice."
좀 더 신중히 생각해 볼게요.
"I will seriously think about it more."
좀 더 생각해 보고 결정할게요.
"Let me think about it more and decide."
선배 덕분에 걱정이 많이 줄었어요. 조언 감사드립니다.
"Thanks to you, I feel much less worried. Thanks for your advice."
조언이 많은 도움이 되었습니다.
"Your advice helps a lot."
형 말이 힘이 되었어요. 고마워요.
"Your advice helps. Thanks."
자세히 알려 주셔서 많은 도움이 됐습니다.
"Because you informed me in detail, it has become a big help."
친절하게 설명해 주셔서 감사합니다.
"Thanks for explaining it nicely."

37
Causes

What follow are expressions that are often used for asking about/expressing cause.

37.1 Asking about cause

To ask about the cause of an event/state, it is common to use the word 원인 "cause" or question words such as 왜 "why" and 어떻게 "how," as shown in the following examples:

    A: 그 화재 사고의 <u>원인</u>이 뭐라고 합니까?
        "What do they say is the cause of the fire accident?"
    B: 건조한 날씨 때문이래요.
        "They say that it is because of the dry weather."

뭐가 <u>원인</u>이에요?
"What's the cause?"
무엇이 산불의 <u>원인</u>입니까?
"What is the cause of the mountain fire?"
<u>왜</u> 산불이 났어요?
"Why did the mountain fire occur?"
<u>어떻게 해서</u> 산불이 일어났어요?
"How did the mountain fire occur?"

37.2 Expressing cause

To indicate cause, the following expressions can be used.

37.2.1 N의 원인은 N이다 "N's cause is N."

<u>폐암의 원인은 흡연</u>으로 밝혀졌습니다.
"It became known that the cause of lung cancer is smoking."
<u>비만의 원인은 스트레스와 불규칙한 식사 습관</u>이다.
"Some causes of obesity are stress and irregular eating habits."
<u>매일 밤 늦게 먹고 잤던 것이 원인</u>이었어요.
"Eating late at night and then going to bed every day was the cause."

37.2.2 N때문에 "because of N"

<u>나쁜 날씨 때문에</u> 취소했어요.
"We canceled it due to the bad weather."
<u>두통 때문에</u> 공부를 할 수가 없네요.
"Because of the headache, I can't study."

CAUSES

봄에는 계절성 알러지 때문에 고생해요.
"I suffer due to seasonal allergies in the spring."
일찍 퇴근할 생각이었는데 갑자기 생긴 중요한 회의 때문에 나올 수가 없었어요.
"I was thinking of taking off early, but because of the urgent meeting that was just scheduled, I was not able to come out."

37.2.3 ~기 때문에 "because of ~ing" (see 4.1.9)

금요일에는 수업이 없기 때문에 늦게 일어나요.
"I get up late on Fridays because I don't have a class."
음식 값이 비교적 싸고 맛있기 때문에 자주 들릅니다.
"Because it is delicious with a relatively cheap price, I stop here often."
저녁에 커피를 마시면 잠을 못 자기 때문에 늦은 오후부터는 안 마시려고 해요.
"Because I can't sleep if I drink coffee in the evening, I try not to drink it in the late afternoon."

37.2.4 N으로 말미암아(서) "owing to N"

This form is made of the particle ~(으)로, the verb 말미암다 "arise from," and the conjunctive 어서/아서. The form is used to express "owing to," "in consequence of," and "because of." It is usually used for written or formal communication.

지구 온난화로 말미암아 자연 재해가 더 심해지고 있습니다.
"Because of global warming, natural disasters are becoming more severe."
비싼 학자금으로 말미암아 학업을 포기하는 학생들도 늘고 있습니다.
"Because of expensive tuition, the number of students who quit school is on the rise."
동료들과의 불화로 말미암아 결국 사표를 내게 되었습니다.
"Because of conflict with my colleagues, I ended up submitting my resignation."
오래된 음주 문화로 말미암아 알콜 중독자 수가 많다고 합니다.
"Because of a drinking culture with a long history, the number of alcoholics is large."
나쁜 식습관으로 말미암아 위암 발병률이 높다고 합니다.
"Because of bad eating habits, it is said that the frequency of stomach cancer is high."
바쁜 일상으로 말미암아 가족하고 시간을 보내기가 더 쉽지 않아졌습니다.
"Because of people's busy daily life, it has become increasingly more difficult to spend time with family."

37.2.5 N으로 인해서 "due to N"

This form is built on the particle ~(으)로, the verb 인하다 "to be caused by," and the conjunctive 어서/아서. It is often used in formal communication.

A: 그곳 도로 사정은 어떻습니까?
    "How are the road conditions there?"
B: 어제 폭설로 인해서 아직도 교통이 마비된 상태입니다.
    "Due the heavy snow yesterday, the traffic is still blocked."

스트레스로 인해서 머리가 빠지는 환자가 늘고 있습니다.
"Due to stress, the number of patients who lose their hair is on the rise."
전쟁으로 인해서 고아의 수가 많이 늘었습니다.
"Due to the war, the number of orphans increased."
지나친 음주로 인해서 간암에 걸리는 사람들의 수가 늘고 있습니다.
"Due to excessive drinking, the number of people who get liver cancer is on the rise."
춥고 건조한 날씨로 인해서 증상이 더 심해지고 있습니다.
"Due to the cold and dry weather, his symptoms are getting worse."

38
Changes

In English, one can indicate a change with verbs/adjectives, such as "turn," "become," "get," "grow," and so forth. This chapter covers various expressions that can be used to indicate a change in action or state in Korean.

38.1 Expressing a change in action/state

38.1.1 ~게 되다 "to turn out" (see 15.8)

This form is made of the adverbial form ~게 and the auxiliary verb 되다 "become." The form is used to indicate a change in action or state (which you have no control over), and it can be translated as "it turned out that . . ." as shown in the following examples.

    A: 여자 친구하고 다시 사이가 좋아졌나 봐요.
        "It appears that your relationship with your girlfriend has gotten better again."
    B: 네, 여러 번 다투고 나서 서로를 더 잘 이해하게 됐어요.
        "Yes, we came to understand each other better after we argued several times."

상황이 아주 복잡하게 됐어요.
"The situations turned out to be very complicated."
치아가 하얗게 됐어요.
"My tooth became white."
다이어트 때문에 술을 끊게 됐습니다.
"Because of the diet, I ended up quitting drinking."
미국에 가서 맥주를 잘 마시게 됐습니다.
"After I went to America, it turned out that I was a beer drinker."
중국 북경으로 출장을 가게 됐어요.
"It turned out that I am going to Beijing China for a business trip."
원래 국수를 안 좋아했었는데 남자 친구 때문에 좋아하게 됐어요.
"Originally, I did not like noodles, but because of my boyfriend, I came to like them."

38.1.2 ~(으)ㄹ수록 "the more . . . the more" (see 18.2.6)

This conjunctive ~(으)ㄹ수록 indicates a change caused by evolving events or situations, as shown in the following examples:

    A: 한국어 어때요?
        "How is Korean?"
    B: 배울수록 어려운 것 같아요.
        "It seems that the more you learn, the more difficult it is."

이 동네는 살수록 좋은 것 같아요.
"As for this neighborhood, the longer you live here, the more you like it."

CHANGES

노트북은 작으면 작을수록 더 비싸요.
"As for a laptop, the smaller it is, the more expensive it is."
도와주는 사람이 많을수록 빨리 끝낼 수 있잖아요.
"The more people help us, the faster we can finish our task."
술은 마시면 마실수록 더 마실 수 있게 된대요.
"As for alcohol, they say that the more you drink, the more you will be able to drink."
골프는 치면 칠수록 재미있어요.
"The more you play golf, the more interesting it becomes."

38.1.3 ~어/아지다 "become" (see 14.6)

A: 곧 날씨가 많이 싸늘해질 거예요.
   "Soon, it will become chillier."
B: 그래요? 그럼 이제 우리도 정리하고 들어가십시다.
   "Is that so? Then, let's clean up and get going."

너 정말 예뻐졌다.
"You really became pretty."
2년 전에 비해서 체격이 좋아졌어요.
"When compared to my body two years ago, it became better."
이제 질이 많이 나빠졌어요.
"Now, the quality has become substantially worse."
이 상가도 재개발로 없어질 거예요.
"This business sector will be gone soon because of the redevelopment."
책상 서랍에 들어 있던 돈이 없어졌어요.
"My money that was in the drawer of the desk disappeared."
성격이 많이 달라졌어요.
"His personality changed a lot."
리모델링한 후로 방도 넓어지고 분위기가 많이 고급스러워졌어요.
"After remodeling, the room became larger, and the atmosphere has become much more sophisticated."

38.2 Verbs that express a change

The following are some typical verbs used to express change:

변하다 *"change"*
사람의 감정은 상황에 따라서 변해요.
"People's moods change according to situations."
하나도 안 변하셨네요.
"You haven't changed a bit."
20대 후에 목소리가 많이 변하는 바람에 가수의 꿈을 버렸어요.
"Because my voice changed a lot after my 20s, I gave up my dream of becoming a singer."
바뀌다 *"change"*
마음이 바뀌면 언제든지 연락 주세요.
"Please contact me if you change your mind."
제 집 주소가 바뀌었습니다.
"I have changed my home address."
해가 바뀌면서 허리를 다쳤어요.
"At the turn of the year, he hurt his back."
변화하다/변화를 겪다 *"change"*
지난 3년간 우리 회사는 많은 변화를 겪었다.
"Over the past three years, our company went through a lot of changes."
환자의 상태에는 아무런 변화도 없었습니다.
"The condition of the patient remains the same."

Verbs that express a change

좀 더 좋게 <u>변화된 모습</u>으로 다시 돌아오겠습니다.
"I will come back in better shape."
지난 1년간 건강에 많은 <u>변화를 겪었습니다.</u>
"My health underwent many changes in the past year."
저희 학교도 지난 3년간 많은 <u>변화를 겪었습니다</u>.
"Our school also experienced many changes these last three years."

39

Choices

This chapter looks into various expressions that can be used to indicate choices.

39.1 A하고 B하고 어느 쪽으로 하시겠어요? "Which would you prefer, A or B?"

A: <u>복도 쪽하고 창문 쪽하고 어느 쪽</u> 자리로 하시겠어요?
"Which would you prefer an aisle seat or a window seat?"
B: 복도 쪽으로 부탁드립니다.
"An aisle seat please."

A: 디저트로 <u>아이스크림하고 커피가 있는데 뭘로</u> 하실래요?
"As for desert, we have ice cream and coffee, which would you like?
B: 커피로 할게요.
"Coffee please."

A: <u>한식하고 양식하고 뭘로</u> 할래요?
"Between Korean or Western food, which would you like?"
B: 한식이 좋겠어요.
"I would like Korean food."

39.2 ~거나 "or" (see 19.2.1)

A: 점심은 주로 뭘 드세요?
"What do you usually have for lunch?"
B: 주로 도시락을 <u>먹거나</u> 학교 식당 음식을 먹어요.
"I usually eat a box lunch or eat the school cafeteria food."

A: 결혼기념일에 뭐 하실 거예요?
"What will you do on your wedding anniversary?"
B: 근사한 레스토랑에서 <u>외식을 하거나</u> 가까운 곳으로 여행을 갈까 생각 중 이에요.
"We are thinking of eating out at a nice restaurant or having a trip to a place nearby."

디저트로 커피를 <u>마시거나</u> 과일을 먹어요.
"For dessert, I drink coffee or eat fruits."
<u>가거나 말거나</u> 네 마음대로 해라.
"Whether you go or not, do whatever you like."
날씨도 좋은데 자전거를 <u>타거나</u> 산책하러 나가십시다.
"It is beautiful outside, so let's go out to ride bikes or walk."

39.3 ~건 ~건 "whether . . . or not"

The conjunctive ~건 denotes "whether," and the repetitive use of this conjunctive as ~건 ~건 is equivalent to "whether . . . or not" in English.

> A: 다른 차가 있건 없건 교통 신호는 지켜야 해요.
> "Whether there are cars or not, one must observe the traffic signal."
> B: 죄송합니다. 다음부터는 꼭 조심하겠습니다.
> "I am sorry. I will certainly be careful next time."

돈이 많건 적건 상관없이 베풀고 살아야지요.
"Regardless of whether you are rich or not, you should live giving of yourself."
승낙을 하시건 안 하시건 상관없이 일단 여쭈어 보십시다.
"Regardless of whether he gives his approval or not, let's ask him anyway."
회사가 좋건 싫건 열심히 하세요.
"Whether you like or dislike the company, do your best."

39.4 ~느니 "rather, instead of doing X" (see 17.2.13)

> A: 곧 올 텐데 어디 가세요?
> "They will be here shortly, so where are you going?"
> B: 여기서 기다리느니 차에 가서 있을게요.
> "Rather than waiting here, I will be in my car."

또 국수를 먹느니 굶을래요.
"I would rather starve myself than eat noodles again."
그 사람하고 계속 일을 같이 하느니 그만두고 싶어요.
"I would rather quit than continue to work with that person."
조건만 보고 결혼해서 사느니 독신으로 남고 싶어요.
"I would rather remain single than marry someone under his terms."
이런 데서 일하느니 차라리 다 때려치우고 떠날 거예요.
"I would rather quit and leave instead of working in such a place."
그 사람한테 부탁을 하느니 차라리 포기하는 게 낫겠어요.
"Rather than asking for a favor from that person, it would be better just to give it up."

39.5 N 대신에 "instead of N"

This form is made of the noun 대신 "back up, substitution" and the particle 에.

> A: 생각보다 빨리 오셨네요.
> "You arrived earlier than we expected."
> B: 택시 대신에 지하철 타고 왔어요.
> "We took the subway instead of a taxi."

편지 대신에 이메일로 보내 주세요.
"Please send it to me via e-mail instead of a letter."
현금 대신에 카드로 지불해도 될까요?
"I wonder if I can pay by card instead of cash?"
표가 매진돼서 연극 대신에 영화를 보려구요.
"The tickets were sold out, so we intend to see a movie instead of a play."
항공편 대신에 배편으로 보내 드릴게요.
"I will send it to you via ship instead of air."

CHOICES

39.6 ~는/(으)ㄴ 대신에 "in place of ~ing"

This form consists of the noun-modifying ending ~는/(으)ㄴ, the noun 대신 "substitution," and the particle 에.

A: 반품하셨어요?
"Did you return it?"
B: 네. 그런데 환불을 받는 대신에 다른 사이즈로 받아왔어요.
"Yes, but in place of receiving a full refund, I got a different size."

소고기를 먹는 대신에 닭고기를 드셔 보시면 어때요?
"In place of eating beef, how about trying chicken?"
커피를 사 주시는 대신에 점심을 사 주셨어요.
"In place of treating us to coffee, he bought us lunch."
안경을 쓰는 대신에 콘택트렌즈를 써 보세요.
"In place of wearing eye glasses, please try contact lenses."
비싼 대신에 맛이 좋아요.
"Even though it is costly, it is tasty."

39.7 ~든지 ~든지 "or else" (see 19.2.2)

A: 가격이 생각보다 좀 비싸면 어떻게 할까요?
"What shall I do if the price is more expensive than I thought?"
B: 싸든지 비싸든지 상관하지 말고 사세요.
"Do not be concerned whether it is cheap or expensive, just buy it."

연필로 쓰든지 펜으로 쓰든지 빨리 적어요.
"Whether you're writing with a pencil or pen, write it down quickly."
커피를 마시든지 아이스크림을 먹든지 다 괜찮아요.
"Whether we drink coffee or have ice cream, they are both fine with me."
내일 박물관에 가든지 도서관에 가든지 할 거예요.
"Tomorrow, we will either go to the museum or the library."
집으로 가든지 학교로 가든지 빨리 서두르세요.
"Whether you go home or school, please hurry."
토요일 아침에 만나든지 오후에 만나든지 빨리 정하세요.
"Whether we meet on Saturday morning or afternoon, please decide soon."
샌드위치를 시키든지 파스타를 시키든지 어서 결정하세요.
"Please hurry up and decide, whether you order a sandwich or pasta."

39.8 ~(으)ㄹ 바에(야) "rather . . . than" (see 23.4)

A: 옆집 부부 이혼할지도 모른대요.
"I heard that the couple next door may divorce."
B: 매일 싸울 바에 차라리 헤어지는 게 나을 것 같아요.
"It would be better to be separated, rather than fighting every day."

그렇게 비싼 가격에 살 바에 차라리 안 사고 말 거예요.
"Rather than buying it at that expensive price, I would rather not buy it."
걱정만 할 바에(야) 차라리 다른 일을 찾아 보는 게 낫지 않을까요?
"Instead of just worrying about it, wouldn't it be better to look for alternative work?"
이제와서 그만둘 바에(야) 아예 시작이나 하지 말지 그랬어요.
"You should not have even begun if you would quit at this point anyway."
굶으면서 다이어트를 할 바에야 차라리 조금씩 먹고 운동하는 게 낫지 않을까요?
"Exercising and eating smart would be better than starving on a diet?"

39.9 N(이)나 "or" (see 8.2.2)

A: 무슨 과일을 사 가지고 갈까요?
 "What kind of fruits should I bring?"
B: 오렌지나 사과 사 오시면 돼요.
 "All you need to do is to buy either oranges or apples."

서점이나 가십시다.
"Let's go to the bookstore or something."
어디 가서 커피나 한잔 하면서 이야기 할까요?
"Shall we go somewhere and talk while having coffee or something?"
배고픈데 햄버거나 먹자.
"I'm hungry, so let's eat a hamburger or something."

39.10 N이라도 "even if it is" (see 17.2.4)

A: 혹시 시원한 주스 있나요?
 "By any chance, do you have cold juice?"
B: 주스는 없고요. 레모네이드가 있는데 그거라도 드실래요?
 "We do not have juice, but we have lemonade, and would you like to try it?"

앞에는 자리가 없는데 뒷자리라도 괜찮으시겠어요?
"There is no seat available in the front, but would the seats in the back be okay?"
아침에 바쁘시면 오후라도 연락 주세요.
"If you are busy in the morning, please give me a call even in the afternoon."
6시 영화는 매진됐는데 8시 영화라도 볼까요?
"The movie at six is sold out, so shall we see a movie at eight?"
오렌지 주스 없으면 사과 주스라도 주세요.
"If you do not have orange juice, please give me apple juice."

40

Comparing

This chapter presents various expressions associated with making comparisons in Korean.

40.1 N보다 더/덜 "more/less than noun" (see 7.3.1)

A: 오늘 저녁으로 뭐 드실래요?
"What would you like to eat for dinner tonight?"
B: 중국 음식<u>보다</u> 한식이 <u>더</u> 먹고 싶은데요.
"I want to eat Korean food more than Chinese food."

A: 하숙집하고 기숙사하고 어디에서 지내기가 <u>더</u> 편하셨어요?
"Between the boarding house and dormitory, where was it more comfortable to stay?"
B: 저는 하숙집<u>보다</u> 기숙사가 <u>더</u> 좋았었어요.
"As for me, the dorm was a lot better than the boarding house."

A: 여름이 겨울<u>보다</u> <u>덜</u> 좋으세요?
"Do you like summer less than winter?"
B: 네, 더운 거<u>보다</u> 추운 게 <u>더</u> 좋아요.
"Yes, I like the cold more than the heat."

잠<u>보다</u> 운동이 낫지요.
"Exercising is better than sleeping."
버스<u>보다</u> 지하철로 가는 게 <u>더</u> 빠를 것 같아요.
"Going by subway seems to be faster than by bus."
중국의 인구는 인도의 인구<u>보다</u> <u>더</u> 많습니다.
"The population of China is more than that of India."
와인<u>보다</u> 맥주를 <u>더</u> 좋아합니다.
"I like beers more than wine."
이게 그거<u>보다</u> <u>덜</u> 매워요.
"This is less spicy than that."
생각했던 것<u>보다</u> 치료비가 <u>덜</u> 나왔어요.
"The medical expense was less than what I thought."

40.2 ~는/ㄴ다기보다(는) "rather than"

The form is built on the plain speech level ending (~는/ㄴ다 for verb stem or ~다 for adjective and the copula stems) (see 27.2.4), the nominalizing ending ~기 (see 4.1), and the particle 보다 (see 7.3.1).

A: 운동을 원래 싫어하세요?
"Do you naturally dislike exercise?"
B: 운동을 <u>싫어한다기보다는</u> 바빠서 못 하고 있어요.
"It is not that I dislike it, but rather I am unable to exercise because I am too busy."

N 만큼 "as . . . as" (see 7.3.3)

A: 김치를 아주 좋아하시나 봐요.
"You seem to like kimchi very much."
B: 김치를 <u>좋아한다기보다는</u> 그냥 자주 먹는 편이에요.
"Rather than saying that I like kimchi, I tend to eat it often."
A: 오늘은 어제보다 더 더운 것 같아요.
"It seems that it is hotter today than yesterday."
B: <u>덥다기보다는</u> 날씨가 습하네요.
"Rather than saying it is hot, it is humid."

<u>싫어한다기보다는</u> 그냥 관심이 없는 거예요.
"Rather than saying that I hate it, I am just not interested in it."
<u>애완동물이라기보다</u> 가족이라 할 수 있어요.
"Rather than saying he is a pet, he is more like a family member."
일이 <u>힘들다기보다</u> 단지 급여가 작아서 그만둘까 생각 중이에요.
"It is not that the work is hard, but rather the pay is small, so I am thinking of quitting."
커피를 <u>싫어한다기보다</u> 오후에 안 마실 뿐이에요.
"It's not that I dislike coffee, but I just don't drink it in the afternoon."
<u>고맙다기보다는</u> 미안하지요.
"Saying that I am sorry would be more appropriate than thankful."
마음에 <u>안 들다기보다는</u> 비싸서 사기 망설여지네요.
"It's not that I don't like it, but I am hesitating to buy it because it's expensive."
<u>잘생겼다기보다는</u> 호감이 가는 형인 것 같아요.
"It is not that he is handsome, but rather he is the type of person who has a favorable impression."

40.3 N와/과 비교해서 and N에 비해서 "when compared to"

N와/과 비교해서 is made of the particle 과/와 (see 6.3.1), the verb 비교하다 "compare," and the conjunctive 어서/아서. In addition, N에 비해서 consists of the particle 에 (see 6.1.1), the verb 비하다 "compare," and 어서/아서. Both forms have similar meanings and usage, as shown in the following examples:

A: 서울 날씨는 <u>뉴욕 날씨와 비교해서</u> 어떤가요?
"How is the weather in Seoul, compared with the weather in New York?"
B: 비슷해요.
"It is about the same."
A: <u>나이에 비해서</u> 젊어 보이세요.
"You look younger compared to your age."
B: 별말씀을요. 하지만 감사합니다.
"Not at all. But thank you."

<u>공부한 것에 비해서</u> 점수가 잘 나왔어요.
"Compared to how much I studied, my score turned out well."
동경의 여름은 <u>서울의 여름과 비교해서</u> 습하고 더워요.
"Summer in Tokyo is humid and hot when compared to summer in Seoul."
<u>처음에 비해서</u> 많이 익숙해졌습니다.
"Compared to the beginning, I accustomed myself to it a lot."
<u>과거에 비해서</u> 세상 정말 편해졌어요.
"Compared to the past, the world has become really convenient."

40.4 N 만큼 "as . . . as" (see 7.3.3)

A: 화학도 <u>물리학만큼</u> 어렵나요?
"Is chemistry as difficult as physics?"

COMPARING

B: 저는 화학이 좀 더 어려운 것 같아요.
"As for me, chemistry seems to be more difficult."
A: 일본 음식도 한국 음식만큼 맵나요?
"Is Japanese food as spicy as Korean food?"
B: 아니오, 전혀요.
"No, not at all."

수학은 영어만큼 쉽지 않아요.
"Math is not as easy as English."
서울의 겨울은 제가 있는 올바니 겨울만큼 춥지 않습니다.
"Winter in Seoul is not as cold as winter in Albany where I live."
여자 친구를 하늘만큼 땅만큼 사랑해요.
"I love my girlfriend as much as the sky and earth."
서울의 야경도 홍콩의 야경만큼 아름다워요.
"The night view of Seoul is also as beautiful as that of Hong Kong."

40.5 ~는 것보다 ~는 게 낫다 "Doing X is better than doing Y."

This form is constructed from ~는 것 (see 4.4), the particle 보다, and the adjective 낫다 "better."

A 더 증상이 심해지기 전에 빨리 병원에 가보세요.
"Before the symptoms get worse, you should go to the hospital immediately."
B: 병원에 가는 것보다 집에서 푹 쉬는 게 나을 것 같아요.
"It seems that taking a good rest at home is better than going to the hospital."
A: 생일 파티를 집에서 하는 게 좋을까요? 식당에서 하는 게 더 나을까요?
"Would it be better to have the birthday party at home or at the restaurant?"
B: 괜히 많은 돈 들여서 식당에서 하는 것보다 그냥 친한 사람들만 불러서 집에서 하는 게 더 낫지 않을까요?
"Wouldn't it be better just inviting close friends and having it at home instead of at a restaurant and spending lots of money?"

혼자 사는 것보다 둘이 사는 게 나아요.
"Living with someone is better than living alone."
기숙사에서 사는 것보다 하숙집에서 지내는 것이 더 나아요.
"Staying in a boarding house is better than staying in a dormitory."
단지 굶는 것보다 운동을 하면서 다이어트를 하는 게 낫지요.
"Dieting while exercising is better than simply starving."
혼자서 공부하는 것보다 여럿이 같이 공부하는 게 더 나을 거 같네요.
"Rather than studying alone, studying with several others seems to be more effective."

40.6 N중에서 N가 최고로/제일

When comparing three or more things, you can use 중에서 "among" with adverbs like 제일 "the most" or 최고로 "the best."

A: 삼형제 중에서 누가 키가 제일 커요?
"Among the three brothers, who is the tallest?"
B: 둘째요.
"It's the second one."
A: 이 네가지 디자인 중에서 뭐가 제일 마음에 드시나요?
"Among these four designs, which one do you like the best?"
B: 저는 두 번째 디자인이 제일 좋은데요.
"As for me, the second design is the best."

N중에서 N가 최고로/제일

한국어, 중국어, 일본어 중에서 뭐가 제일 어려웠나요?
"Among Korean, Chinese, and Japanese, which one was the most difficult?"
스케이트, 스키, 스노우보딩 중에서 스키가 제일 재미있어요.
"Among skating, skiing, and snowboarding, skiing is the most fun."
넷 중에서 막내가 제일 똑똑해요.
"Among the four, the youngest child is the brightest."
대한민국의 산 중에서 아마 한라산이 최고로 유명하지 않을까요?
"Don't you think that among the mountains in South Korea, perhaps, Halla Mountain may be the most famous?"

41

Complaining

What follow are expressions that are often used for complaining, disapproving, or criticizing.

41.1 ~(으)면서 ... 해요 "while" (see 19.1.4)

공부는 안 하면서 A를 받고 싶어해요.
"While he does not study, he wants to receive an A."
제일 높은 봉급을 받으면서 실력은 전혀 없어요.
"While he receives the highest salary, he does not have any skill at all."
직업도 없으면서 비싼 차만 찾아요.
"While he does not even have a job, he only looks for expensive cars."
휴가도 적으면서 연봉도 완전 짜요.
"While the number of vacation days is small, the salary is also very tiny."

41.2 아무리 ~기로서니 "no matter how ... you may be ..." (see 17.2.14)

아무리 바쁘기로서니 여자 친구 생일을 잊어버리면 어떻게 해요?
"Regardless of how busy you may be, how can you forget your girlfriend's birthday?"
아무리 시간이 없기로서니 전화 한 통 못 해요?
"No matter how busy you may be, can't you give me at least one phone call?"
아무리 피곤하기로서니 늦게 오면 어떻게 해요?
"No matter how tired you may be, how can you be late?"
아무리 선물이 마음에 안 들기로서니 얼굴에 그렇게 티를 내면 되겠어요?
"No matter how much you don't like your present, how could you show your feelings on your face like that?"
배가 아무리 고프기로서니 먼저 먹으면 어떻게 하니?
"No matter how hungry you are, how can you eat first?"
한 번 실수를 좀 했기로서니 어떻게 해고할 수 있겠어요?
"Yes, I understand you made a mistake, but how can they fire you?"
좀 힘들기로서니 포기하면 안 되지요.
"I understand that you are having difficulties, but you shouldn't give up."
아무리 화가 나기로서니 그냥 나가면 어떻게 해요?
"No matter how angry you are, how can you go out like that?"

41.3 ~어/아 빠지다 "is extremely" (see 14.2)

게을러 빠져가지고 어떻게 할 거니?
"You are extremely lazy, so how will you handle this?"

~었/았어야지요 "should have"   41.7

현정부는 완전히 <u>썩어 빠졌어요</u>.
"The current government is rotten to the core."
아주 <u>약아 빠졌어요</u>.
"She is so cunning."

41.4 ~기 일쑤이다 "prone to" (see 4.1.19)

제 동생은 열쇠를 집에다가 <u>두고 나오기 일쑤예요</u>.
"My younger brother is prone to coming out of the house leaving his keys inside."
월요일마다 회사에 <u>지각하기 일쑤예요</u>.
"He is prone to being tardy at work every Monday."
실수가 잦아서 선생님한테 <u>혼나기 일쑤예요</u>.
"He is prone to getting reprimanded by the professor for making errors frequently."

41.5 ~어/아 대다 "do frequently" (see 13.4)

하루 종일 집에서 컴퓨터 <u>게임만 해 대요</u>.
"He repeatedly plays only computer games at home all day long."
자꾸 전화를 <u>해 대서</u> 귀찮아요.
"He repeatedly calls me, so I am bothered."
옆 집 사람들이 너무 <u>떠들어 대서</u> 잠을 잘 수가 없네요.
"I can't go to sleep because my neighbors next door are noisy."
밥은 안 먹고 <u>과자만 먹어 대면</u> 어떻게 하니?
"If you continue to eat only snacks and not meals, will it be good for you?"

41.6 ~(으)려고 들다 "rush to" (see 18.1.2)

너무 자기 것만 <u>챙기려 들지 마세요</u>.
"Do not rush to take care of only yourself."
형이 하는 것은 <u>다 따라하려고 들어요</u>.
"He tries to imitate everything his older brother does."
<u>따지려 들지</u> 말고 먼저 이야기를 들어 보세요.
"Try not to nitpick, but listen to my story first."
급히 <u>해결하려 들지 말고</u> 천천히 생각해 보십시다.
"Don't rush to solve it, but let's think about it calmly."
남이 하는 것만 <u>흉내 내려고 들지</u> 말고 네 것을 만들어 봐.
"Try not to copy what others do, but try to make your own."

41.7 ~었/았어야지요 "should have"

This form is constructed from the past tense ~었/았 (see 11.1), the auxiliary verb ~어야 하다 (see 15.9), and the sentence ending 지요 (see 26.6). It is the shortened form of ~었/았어야하지요.

이메일을 <u>확인했어야지요</u>.
"You should have checked your e-mail."
미리 <u>예약했어야지요</u>.
"You should have reserved it in advance."
눈이 오면 더 조심히 <u>운전했어야지요</u>.
"When it snowed, you should have driven more carefully."

COMPLAINING

신용카드를 분실하셨을 때 바로 카드회사에 <u>연락하셨어야지요</u>.
"When you lost your credit card, you should have contacted the credit card company immediately."
집을 나서기 전에 가스불은 껐는가 확인하고 <u>나갔어야지요</u>.
"Before leaving home, you should have checked whether you turned off the gas or not."
다른 사람에게 <u>도와 달라고 했어야지요</u>.
"You should have asked others for help."

41.8 Examples of complaining remarks

A: 도대체 왜 그래? 만날 때마다 번번이 늦고.
  "What's wrong with you? You are late all the time."
B: 미안해. 오늘도 차가 좀 밀려서.
  "Sorry. The traffic was jammed today too."

또야!
"Not again!"
아이고 망했다.
"Oh, I am screwed."
정말 한심하구만.
"You are really pathetic."
마음에 안 들어.
"I don't like it."
왜 하필 나예요?
"Why me?"
그만 좀 해!
"Just stop!"
매번 실수를 하잖아.
"You make mistakes every single time."
모두 네 탓이야!
"It's all your fault!"
정말 이해가 안 돼요.
"I really cannot understand him."
정말 기가 막혀요.
"It's really outrageous."
세상에 너무 해요.
"Oh my, that's too much."
징징대지 말아요!
"Stop whining!"
죽을 맛이에요./ 죽겠어요.
"I feel like dying."
완전 최악이에요.
"Totally the worst."
이건 완전히 불공평해요!
"This is completely unfair!"
언제라도 그만두고 싶어요.
"I am ready to quit anytime."
그냥 때려 치우고 싶어요.
"I just want to quit."
할 일이 태산이에요.
"I have mountains of work to do."
해도 해도 끝이 보이지 않네요.
"No matter how much I do, it never ends."

Examples of complaining remarks   **41.8**

요즘 눈 코 뜰 사이 없이 바빠요.
"I am incredibly busy nowadays."
정말 하기 싫어 죽겠어요.
"I really hate to do this."
왜 나만 미워하는지 모르겠어요.
"I don't know why he only hates me."
자꾸 이럴래?
"Here you go again."
너무 심한 거 아니에요?
"Aren't you being a little too nasty?"
왜 이렇게 맨날 늦니?
"Why are you late all the time like this?"
어떻게 그렇게 무심하실 수 있어요?
"How can you be so indifferent?"
저한테 좀 심하신 거 아니에요?
"Don't you think you're a little cruel to me?"
그렇다고 그렇게 사람들 다 있는데 큰소리로 윽박지르시면 어떻게 해요?
"Even so, how can you talk down to me like that in front all these people?"
늦으면 늦는다고 전화라도 하지 그랬어요?
"If you knew that you would be late, why not at least call?"
문자 메세지라도 보내 주면 좋잖아요.
"It would be better if you could at least text me."
그 날 휴가를 내면 너무 무책임한 거 아닙니까?
"How irresponsible are you that you took that day off?"
그 때 꼭 가야 해요?
"Do you really have to go at that time?"
사람들을 초대할 때마다 이렇게 실수를 하면 어떻게 해요?
"How can you keep making mistakes every time we invite people over?"
제 남자 친구는 도대체 왜 그러는지 모르겠어요.
"I can't understand why my boyfriend does that."
월급이 너무 적어서 별로예요. (불만이에요/힘들어요)
"It is not to my liking since the salary is too low."
일이 너무 많고 근무 환경도 별로 좋지 않아요.
"It's not good since the workload is huge and the work environment is not good."
휴가도 거의 없을 뿐만 아니라 월급도 별 볼일 없어요.
"They offer almost no vacation days, and to make things worse, the pay is not good either."

42

Conditions

In English, one can express a condition by using expressions such as "if," "unless," "in case," "supposing," and so forth. Korean also has a number of expressions to state conditions about actions or states, as described in the following sections.

42.1 Expressing conditions by conjunctives

The most common way to express a condition in Korean is the use of the following conjunctives:

42.1.1 ~거든 "when, if" (see 18.2.4)

A: 꼭 만나야 돼요?
   "Do I really have to meet her?"
B: 만나기 싫거든 만나지 마세요.
   "If you hate meeting her, then don't meet her."

바쁘지 않거든 저녁에 잠깐 만납시다.
"If you are not busy, let's get together for a while this evening."
마음에 안 들거든 다시 바꾸면 돼요.
"If you don't like it, all you need to do is to exchange it again."
할 말이 있거든 이따 퇴근 후에 하십시다.
"If you have something to say, let's talk about it after work later."
멧돼지가 또 나타나거든 곧바로 연락 주세요.
"If boars show up again, please contact us immediately."

42.1.2 ~(으)면 "if, when" (see 18.2.1)

A: 첫 월급을 받으시면 뭐 하실 거예요?
   "What will you do when you receive your first paycheck?"
B: 전부 부모님께 드릴 거예요.
   "I will give it all to my parents."

내일 비가 많이 오면 집에서 모이는 것으로 합시다.
"If it rains a lot tomorrow, let's meet at home."
결혼하시면 어디에서 사실 거예요?
"If you get married, where will you live?"
오늘 저녁 바쁘지 않으시면 시간 좀 내 주실 수 있으신지요?
"If you are not busy this evening, would you please spare some time for me?"
내년에 졸업하면 한국에 나가 보려구요.
"When I graduate next year, I intend to go to Korea."

Expressing conditions by conjunctives

42.1.3 ~(으)면 몰라도 "unless"

This form is constructed from the conjunctive ~(으)면 (see 18.2.1), the verb 모르다, and the conjunctive ~어도/아도 (see 17.2.4).

A: 이 일 제가 한 번 맡아서 해보면 안 될까요?
"I wonder if I can take this job?"
B: 이 일에 사전 경험이 많으면 몰라도 아무나 하면 안 돼요.
"Unless you have a lot of previous experiences regarding this job, it is not something that anyone can do."

친구들하고 같이 가면 몰라도 혼자 여행하는 것은 위험할 거예요.
"Unless you go there with your friends together, traveling alone may be dangerous."
날씨가 추우면 몰라도 이런 날씨에 스키타면 안 좋아요.
"Unless the weather is cold, it is not good for skiing (under this kind of weather)."
잘 아는 사람이면 몰라도 그런 부탁하는 것은 실례인 것 같아요.
"Unless he is a person that you know well, asking such a favor may be discourteous."

42.1.4 ~(으)려면 "if you intend to" (see 18.2.2)

A: 시청으로 가려면 몇 호선을 타야 합니까?
"If I intend to go to City Hall, what subway line should I take?"
B: 지하철 2호선을 타시면 돼요.
"All you need to take is line number two."

밥을 잘 지으려면 물의 양을 적당히 맞추셔야 돼요.
"If you intend to cook rice well, you need to put in the appropriate amount of water."
한국 식당을 찾으시려면 여기서 30분을 더 가셔야 해요.
"If you intend to find a Korean restaurant, you need to go 30 more minutes from here."
이 회사에 취직하려면 2개의 외국어에 능통해야 한다고 합니다.
"They say that if one intends to get a job in this company, one needs to be fluent in two foreign languages."

42.1.5 ~어/아야 "only if" (see 18.2.5)

A: 어떻게 하면 골프를 잘 칠 수 있을까요?
"How can I play golf well?"
B: 매일 연습을 많이 해야 실력이 늘겠지요.
"I assume that you can improve your skill only if you practice a lot every day."

국제운전면허가 있어야 차를 빌릴 수 있대요.
"They say that you can rent a car only if you have an international driver's license."
신용카드가 있어야 신청할 수 있다고 합니다.
"They say that you can apply only if you have a credit card."
등록비 $100를 내야 멤버가 될 수 있어요.
"Only if you pay a 100 dollar registration fee, can you become a member."
신분증이 있어야 대출 가능합니다.
"Only with your ID, can you receive a loan."
영어를 유창하게 해야 취직할 수 있어요.
"You can get a job here only if you speak English fluently."
꾸준히 약을 먹어야 병이 낫지요.
"Only if you take the medicine steadily, will your illness get better."
부부 관계가 좋아야 가정이 행복해질 수 있습니다.
"Only if the spousal relationship is good, can the family be happy."

CONDITIONS

42.2 Other ways to express conditions

42.2.1 ~할 경우 "in the event that"

This form is made of the verb 하다, the noun-modifying ending ~(으)ㄹ (see 21.3), and the noun 경우 "case."

    A: 또 고장날 경우 어떻게 해야 하나요?
        "In the event that it breaks down again, what should I do?"
    B: 가지고 오시면 새것으로 바꿔 드리겠습니다.
        "If you bring it here, we will exchange it with a new one."

또 음주운전을 할 경우 체포 당할 수 있습니다.
"In the event that you drink and drive again, you can be arrested."
급하게 도움이 필요할 경우에는 저한테 언제든지 연락 주세요.
"In the event that you need urgent help, contact me any time."
드물지만 수술이 필요할 경우도 있습니다.
"Even though it is rare, there may be cases where you need surgery."

42.2.2 ~지 않는 한/이상 "unless"

This form consists of the long-form negation ~지 않다 (see 20.2), the noun-modifying ending ~는 (see 21.1), and the noun 한 "limit" (or 이상 "above, beyond").

    A: 오늘 저녁 그 일식집으로 가고 싶은데 자리가 있을까요?
        "I want to go to that Japanese restaurant tonight, but I wonder if they will have tables?"
    B: 아마 없을 거예요. 그 집은 미리 예약하고 가지 않는 한 항상 앉을 데가 없어요.
        "Perhaps not. They never have any tables unless you go there after making a reservation."

담배를 끊지 않는 한 절대로 건강해질 수 없어요.
"Unless you quit smoking, you can't expect to become healthy."
48시간 이전에 미리 취소를 하지 않는 한 환불을 받을 수 없어요.
"Unless you cancel it 48 hours in advance, you can't receive a refund."
100불 이상 구입하지 않는 한 무료 배송 서비스를 받을 수 없습니다.
"Unless you spend more than 100 dollars, you can't receive the free delivery service."
내가 죽지 않는 한 절대로 허락하지 않을 거다.
"Unless I die, I will never give my approval."
제품에 하자가 있지 않는 이상 교환은 불가능합니다.
"Unless there is something wrong with the product, an exchange is not possible."
가격을 내리지 않는 이상 사지 않을 거예요.
"Unless they lower the price, I will not buy it."

42.2.3 ~(느)냐에 달려 있다 "it depends on"

This form is built on the plain speech level question ending ~(느)냐 (see 27.2.4), the particle 에 (see 6.1.1), and the verb 달리다 "depend on, hang on" (달려 있다 = 달리어 + 있다).

    A: 이번에는 체중 감량에 성공할까요?
        "Do you think that he will succeed to lose weight this time?"
    B: 어떤 음식을 먹느냐에 달려 있겠지요.
        "I guess that it depends on what kind of food he eats."

어떻게 생각하고 행동에 옮기느냐에 달려 있다고 생각합니다.
"I think that it depends on how you think and put that thought into action."
얼마나 열심히 노력하느냐에 달려 있어요.
"It depends on how much effort you put in."

Other ways to express conditions

얼마나 좋은 재료를 <u>쓰느냐에 달려 있습니다</u>.
"It depends on what kind of materials you will use."
뭘 먹고 어떻게 <u>운동하느냐에 달려 있어요</u>.
"It depends on what you eat and how you exercise."

42.2.4 ~기 나름이다 "it depends on" (see 4.1.3)

A: 이 전화기 배터리는 한 번 충전하면 얼마나 오래 가나요?
"How long does the battery of this phone last once fully charged?"
B: 손님이 <u>사용하시기 나름입니다</u>.
"It depends on how you use it."

우리가 <u>실천하기 나름입니다</u>.
"It depends on our action."
학교 성적은 교수가 <u>평가하기 나름이에요</u>.
"School grades depend on how the professor evaluates them."
자식은 부모가 <u>가르치기 나름이에요</u>.
"As for kids, it depends on how parents teach them."
모든 일에 긍정적으로 <u>생각하기 나름이에요</u>.
"It depends on how positively one thinks."
다 공부하는 습관을 <u>들이기 나름이에요</u>.
"It all depends on what kind of study habits one gets."

43

Congratulations, condolence, and gratitude expressions

What follow are some common expressions associated with expressing congratulations, condolence, and gratitude.

43.1 Congratulating someone

축하합니다!
"Congratulations!"
생일 축하합니다.
"Happy birthday."
졸업 축하해.
"Congratulations on your graduation."
두 분의 결혼을 진심으로 축하드립니다.
"My heartfelt congratulations on your wedding."
늘 평생 행복하시길 바랍니다.
"I pray that you have a happy life."
취직한 것 진심으로 축하합니다.
"Congratulations on your employment."
정말 잘됐다. 축하해.
"That's really great. Congratulations."

43.2 Expressing good wishes for special occasions

새해 복 많이 받으세요.
"Happy New Year."
즐거운 성탄절 맞이하세요.
"Have a merry Christmas."
메리 크리스마스!
"Merry Christmas!"
행복한 성탄절과 따뜻한 연말 보내세요.
"Hope you have a merry Christmas and a warm end of year."
생일 축하합니다.
"Happy Birthday."
합격을 진심으로 축하드립니다.
"Congratulations on passing."
승진하신 것 축하드립니다.
"Congratulations on your promotion."
사랑스런 아기의 탄생을 축하드리며 산모와 아기의 건강을 기원합니다.

Expressing concerns and condolences

"Congratulations on the birth of your lovely baby, and best wishes for the health of both mother and baby."
아기의 첫돌을 축하드리며 귀엽고 튼튼하게 키우시길 바랍니다.
"Congratulations on your baby's first birthday and may you continue to raise him cute and strong."
결혼을 축하드리며 두 분의 앞날에 사랑과 행복이 늘 가득하시길 기원합니다.
"Congratulations on your wedding, and may both of your futures be filled with love and happiness."
개업을 축하드리며 사업 번창하시길 기원합니다.
"Congratulations and wishing you great luck in your new business."

43.3 Expressing concerns and condolences

43.3.1 When you express concern

괜찮으세요?
"Are you OK?"
좀 어떠세요?
"How are you doing?"
무슨 일 있으세요?
"What's the matter?"
안색이 안 좋아보이시네요. 어디 불편하세요?
"Your face does not look well. Are you OK?"
몸조리 잘 하세요.
"Please take care of yourself."
힘내십시오.
"Cheer up."
빨리 쾌유하시기 바래요.
"I hope for a fast recovery."
푹 쉬고 빨리 나아라.
"Take a good rest and get well soon."

43.3.2 When you express condolences in person

충격이 크셨겠어요.
"It must be a shock for you."
상심이 크시겠습니다.
"You must be really sad."
불행 중 다행이네요.
"You are lucky in that its isn't worse."
정말 고생이 많으십니다.
"You have been really through a lot."
뭐라고 위로의 말씀을 드려야 할지 모르겠네요.
"I am not sure how to console you."
제가 도움이 될 수 있다면 언제든지 말씀해 주세요.
"If I can be of any help, please tell me anytime."

43.3.3 When you express condolences in formal speech or writing

하루빨리 건강을 되찾으시기 바랍니다.
"Best wishes for a speedy recovery."
속히 나으셔서 건강한 모습으로 돌아오시길 기도합니다.
"Hoping you will return to us in good health following a speedy recovery."

CONGRATULATIONS, CONDOLENCE, AND GRATITUDE EXPRESSIONS

뭐라고 위로해 드릴 말씀이 없습니다.
"I wish there was something that I could say to console you."
삼가 고인의 명복을 빕니다.
"I pray that his soul will be blessed."
삼가 애도의 뜻을 (조의를) 표합니다.
"I express my deepest condolences."

43.4 Gratitude

43.4.1 In casual conversations

고맙다/고마워요/고마워.
"Thanks."
감사합니다.
"Thank you."

43.4.2 In formal speech or writing

대단히 감사합니다.
"Thank you very much."
다시 한 번 감사드립니다.
"Thank you again."
그동안 신세 많이 졌습니다.
"I am much indebted to you."
진심으로 감사합니다.
"My heartfelt gratitude to you."
덕분에 잘 놀다 갑니다.
"We had great fun, thanks to you."
폐를 끼쳤습니다.
"Much obliged."
덕분에 좋은 시간 보냈습니다.
"We had a great time, thanks to you."
뭐라고 감사의 말씀을 드려야 할지 모르겠습니다.
"I am not sure how to express my gratitude to you."

43.4.3 When you receive a gift

보내 주신 선물 잘 받았습니다. 잘 쓰도록 하겠습니다.
"Thanks for the present that you sent me. I will use it well."
선물 고마워요. 잘 입을게요.
"Thanks for the gift. I will wear it well."
마음에 꼭 들어요. 고마워요.
"I like it so much. Thanks."
괜히 미안하네. 나까지 챙겨 주지 않아도 되는데.
"Ah, sorry. You did not really have to buy it for me too."
그냥 오셔도 되는데 뭘 이런 걸 갖고 오셨어요? 비쌀 텐데.
"You could have come without it. Why did you bring it? It must be costly."
고마워. 근데 과용한 거 아니지?
"Thanks, but you didn't go over your budget, right?"

43.4.4 Before being treated to a meal/drink

A: 잘/감사히/맛있게 먹겠습니다.
   "Thanks for the meal."

Replying to expressions of gratitude | **43.5**

B: 네, 많이 드세요.
"Yes, please help yourself."

43.4.5 After being treated to a meal/drink

너무 맛있었습니다.
"It was so tasty."
잘 먹었습니다.
"Thank you for the meal."
미안해서 어쩌지요? 번번이 이렇게 신세를 져서요.
"I feel bad that I am indebted to you each time."
오늘 신세 많이 졌습니다. 폐만 끼치고 가네요.
"I am indebted to you. I guess I was a bother."

43.5 Replying to expressions of gratitude

괜찮아요.
"It's fine."
아니에요.
"No problem."
뭘요. 제가 오히려 더 감사하지요.
"Don't mention it. It is me who is grateful."
고맙기는요. 별거 아닌데요.
"What you mean? It is nothing."
별말씀을요.
"Don't mention it. (lit. What kind of talk is that?)"
천만에요.
"Not at all."

44

Conjecture

In English, one's conjecture is indicated by expressions such as "right off the top of my head, I think it's 10 dollars," "I guess that she's 25," "I bet I got a good grade," and so forth. This chapter examines some common expressions that are used to indicate one's conjecture or supposition.

44.1 ~겠네요/겠어요 "you must be . . ." (see 12.1.4)

A: 많이 드세요. 많이 <u>시장하셨겠어요</u>.
"Please eat a lot. You must be hungry."
B: 아, 네. 감사합니다.
"Oh, yes. Thank you."

늦게 <u>일어나셨겠네요</u>.
"You must have gotten up late."
정말 많이 <u>피곤하시겠어요</u>.
"You must be really tired."
일문학을 전공했으니까 일본어는 <u>잘하겠네요</u>.
"Since she majored in Japanese literature, she must be fluent in Japanese."
아드님이 많이 <u>자랑스러우시겠어요</u>.
"You must be really proud of your son."
많이 <u>불안하시겠어요</u>.
"You must be very nervous."
고향이 <u>서울이겠네요</u>.
"His hometown must be Seoul."

44.2 ~나/(으)ㄴ가 보다 "it looks like" (see 15.7)

A: 밖이 많이 <u>추운가 봐요</u>.
"It looks like it is very cold outside."
B: 말도 마세요. 길이 다 얼었어요.
"Cold? Oh yes. All the roads are frozen."

A: 부인이 <u>일본 사람인가 봐요</u>.
"His wife seems to be a Japanese person."
B: 좀 그런것 같지요? 발음도 좀 이상하고요.
"You thought so too? Her pronunciation sounds a bit strange too."

요새도 요리학원에 <u>다니나 봐요</u>.
"It looks like she still attends cooking school these days."
이제 <u>퇴근하나 봐요</u>.
"It appears that they get off of work now."
무슨 좋은 일이 <u>있나 봐요</u>.
"It appears that they have some good news."

~는/(으)ㄴ/(으)ㄹ 것 같다 "I think/guess that" (see 22.1)

한국어가 유창한 걸 보니 한국에서도 오래 <u>살았나 봐요</u>.
"Seeing that she is fluent in Korean, I assume that she lived in Korea for a long time."
수업 시간에 꾸벅꾸벅 조는 걸 보니 어젯밤에 <u>잠을 설쳤나 봐요</u>.
"Seeing that he dozed off during class time, he probably did not sleep well last night."
사고가 크게 <u>났나 봐요</u>.
"It appears that it was a big accident."
옷이 다 젖은 걸 보니 우산이 <u>없었나 봐요</u>.
"Looking at your completely soaked clothes, you probably didn't have an umbrella."
많이 <u>슬픈가 봐요</u>.
"It seems that he is really sad."
많이 사는 거 보니까 상당히 <u>싼가 봐요</u>.
"Seeing that he buys them a lot, they must be really inexpensive."
빈 접시를 가져온 걸 보니 내 음식이 <u>맛있었나 봐요</u>.
"Seeing that they brought empty plates, my food must have been delicious."
아버지가 <u>의사신가 봐요</u>.
"It seems that his father is a doctor."

44.3 ~나/(으)ㄴ가 했다 "I thought/guessed that"

This form is built on the ending ~나/(으)ㄴ가 (see 27.2.4) and the verb 했다 "did."

A: 영어가 유창해서 미국에서 오래 <u>공부하셨나 했어요</u>.
   "Since your English is so good, I thought that you studied in the states for long time."
B: 별말씀을요.
   "Oh, not really."

A: 서로 좋아하는 사이<u>인가 했어요</u>.
   "I thought that you guys were a couple."
B: 네? 무슨 말씀하시는 거예요?
   "What? What are you talking about?"

집에서 학교까지 5분 걸린다고 해서 기숙사에서 <u>사나 했어요</u>.
"Since you said that it would take only five minutes from your home to school, I thought that you lived in the dorm."
요즘 통 안 보여서 집에 <u>갔나 했어요</u>.
"Since I have not seen you around at all lately, I thought that you went back home."
살이 많이 빠져서 <u>다이어트 했나 했어요</u>.
"Since you lost a lot of weight, I thought that you were on a diet."
새로운 프로젝트 때문에 많이 <u>바쁘신가 했어요</u>.
"I thought that you must be really busy because of the new project."
안경이 꽤 두꺼워서 눈이 많이 <u>나쁜가 했어요</u>.
"Since your eye glasses look so thick, I thought that you had really bad vision."
약속 시간에 <u>늦었나 했어요</u>.
"I thought that I was late for the appointment."
하도 어려 보여서 고등학생<u>인가 했어요</u>.
"You looked so young, so I thought that you were a high school student."

44.4 ~는/(으)ㄴ/(으)ㄹ 것 같다 "I think/guess that" (see 22.1)

A: 앤드류 씨가 지금쯤 호텔에 도착했을까요?
   "Do you think that Andrew arrived at the hotel by now?"
B: 지금 퇴근 시간이라 아마 <u>아직일 것 같아요</u>.
   "Since it is a rush hour now, I guess not yet."

A: 한국어하고 일본어하고 뭐가 더 어려워요?
   "Between Korean and Japanese, which one is more difficult?"

CONJECTURE

B: 일본어보다 한국어가 더 <u>어려운 것 같아요</u>.
 "I think that Korean is more difficult than Japanese."

주말마다 요가를 <u>배우는 것 같아요</u>.
"It seems that she learns yoga every weekend."
시험이 많이 어렵고 경쟁이 꽤 <u>치열할 것 같아요</u>.
"It seems that the test is hard, and the competition is quite severe."
경험도 쌓고 돈도 벌고 <u>일석이조일 것 같아요</u>.
"It seems that it will be like killing two birds with one stone, getting experience and earning money at the same time."
아무리 돈이 많더라도 그런 결심을 하기는 <u>쉽지 않을 것 같아요</u>.
"No matter how rich he is, making such a decision is probably not easy."
다음 학기에는 한국 역사 수업도 <u>들을 것 같아요</u>.
"It seems that he will take a Korean history class as well next semester."
지갑을 식당에 <u>두고 온 것 같아요</u>.
"It seems that I left my wallet at the restaurant."
집안이 많이 <u>후덥지근한 것 같아요</u>.
"I think that the inside of the house is too muggy."

44.5 ~는/(으)ㄴ/(으)ㄹ 듯하다 "it seems that . . ." (see 22.11)

A: 버스가 곧 <u>도착할 듯합니다</u>.
 "It looks like the bus will arrive soon."
B: 그래요? 그럼 일단 나가서 기다립시다.
 "Really? Then, let's go out and wait."

오늘 밤은 어제보다 <u>추울 듯해요</u>.
"Tonight appears to be colder than yesterday."
밖에 눈이 <u>내리는 듯합니다</u>.
"It looks like it is snowing outside."
못해도 한 시간은 <u>기다린 듯해요</u>.
"It seems that he waited at least one hour."
아직 <u>싱글인 듯합니다</u>.
"It seems that she is still unmarried."
열쇠를 <u>잃어버린 듯합니다</u>.
"It seems that he lost his keys."

44.6 ~는/(으)ㄴ/(으)ㄹ 모양이다 "it appears that . . ." (see 23.3)

A: 지금 몇 시인데 아직 안 오지요?
 "What time is it now that he has not shown up yet?"
B: 회의가 아직 안 <u>끝난 모양이에요</u>.
 "It appears that the meeting has not ended yet."

아직 <u>자고 있는 모양이에요</u>.
"It appears that she is still sleeping."
오늘이 여자 친구 <u>생일인 모양이에요</u>.
"It seems that today is his girlfriend's birthday."
아직도 컴퓨터 게임을 <u>하고 있는 모양이에요</u>.
"It appears that he is still playing a computer game."
와인은 비싸서 <u>안 산 모양이에요</u>.
"It appears that he did not buy the wine because it was expensive."
아직도 친구를 <u>기다리는 모양이에요</u>.
"It seems that he still waits for his friend."

44.7 ~는/(으)ㄴ/(으)ㄹ 줄 알았다/몰랐다 "knew/thought" (see 24.2)

A: 서울 물가가 이렇게 비싼 줄 몰랐어요.
"I did not know that the cost of living in Seoul would be expensive like this."
B: 그래도 동경보다는 쌀걸요.
"But, I assume that it is cheaper than that of Tokyo."

네가 좋아할 줄 알았어.
"I thought that you would like it."
희연이가 춤을 잘 추는 줄 몰랐어요.
"I did not know that Hui-Yeon is good at dancing."
시험에 합격한 줄 알았어요.
"I thought that he passed the exam."
인터넷에서 사진으로 봤을 때는 방이 넓은 줄 알았어요.
"When I just looked at the photo of the room on the internet, I thought that the room was wide."
모텔이 아니고 호텔에서 묵는 줄 알았어요.
"I thought that I would stay at a model not a hotel."
기차가 아니고 버스로 가는 줄 몰랐어요.
"I didn't know that we would go by bus instead of by train."
한국 분이신 줄 알았어요.
"I thought that you were Korean."

44.8 ~어/아 보이다 "appears to be" (see 14.1)

This form is usually used to indicate one's conjecture on the appearance of a person, thing, or event, as shown in the following examples:

A: 많이 피곤해 보이세요. 어디 아프세요?
"You look very tired. Are you feeling OK?"
B: 아, 네. 어제 잠을 좀 설쳤더니 오늘 몸이 좀 안 좋네요.
"Oh, yes. I didn't have a good night's sleep last night. So, I am not feeling well today."
A: 기분이 나빠 보이네요. 무슨 일 있으셨어요?
"You look unhappy. What's the matter?"
B: 아, 예. 집에 좀 일이 있어서요.
"Oh yes. Something happened at home."

두 분 너무나도 행복해 보이세요.
"Both of you look so happy."
다 맛있어 보인다. 뭐 먼저 먹을까?
"They all look delicious. What shall I eat first?"
너무 슬퍼 보여요. 좀 웃으세요.
"You look so sad. Please smile."

44.9 ~(으)ㄹ 거예요 "I think/guess" (see 12.1.1)

A: 아직 사무실에 계실까요?
"Do you think that he is still in his office?"
B: 아니요. 벌써 퇴근했을 거예요.
"No. He probably left work already."

마음에 드셨을 거예요.
"I guess that he liked it."

CONJECTURE

지금쯤이면 수술이 다 끝났을 거예요.
"By now, the operation is probably over."
오늘은 수영하기에 좀 싸늘할 거예요.
"I assume that it is a bit chilly for swimming today."
그 분 생각은 아마 제 생각하고는 많이 다를 거예요.
"His opinion will probably be a lot different from mine."

44.10 ~(으)ㄹ걸요 "I bet/think" (see 26.1)

A: 집에 오는 길에 제가 사가지고 올게요.
  "I will buy it and bring it on my way back home."
B: 서두르셔야 돼요. 아마 주말이라 일찍 닫을걸요.
  "You need to hurry. Since it is the weekend, I bet that it will be closed soon."

지금쯤 회의가 끝났을걸요.
"I assume that the meeting ended by now."
물가가 올랐으니 등록금도 오를걸요.
"Since the price of living increased, the tuition will probably increase too."
기름값이 올라서 한국 경기도 좋아지기 힘들걸요.
"Since the price of oil went up, it may be difficult to expect the Korean economy to get better."
금년 겨울은 작년에 비해서 눈도 많이 오고 더 추울걸요.
"Winter this year will probably be colder with heavier snow than last year's."
저보다 훨씬 잘 벌걸요.
"I assume that he earns much more than I."

44.11 ~(으)ㄹ까요 "Do you think . . .?" (see 26.2)

This form is used to indicate a speaker's wondering mindset or to seek the listener's opinion.

A: 생일 선물로 이 가방이 어떨까요?
  "As a birthday present, how about this bag?"
B: 그 가방보다는 이 드레스를 더 좋아할 것 같은데요.
  "She may like this dress more than that bag, I think."

지금쯤 서울에 도착했을까요?
"I wonder if they arrived in Seoul by now?"
내일까지 이 일을 마칠 수 있을까요?
"Do you think that they can finish this work by tomorrow?"
주말인데 길이 많이 막히지 않을까요?
"It is weekend, so I wonder if the roads are congested."
이 사이즈가 저한테 맞을까요?
"Do you think this size will fit me?"

44.12 ~(으)ㄹ지도 모르다 "not sure if"

This form is made of the noun-modifying ending ~(으)ㄹ, the special noun 지, the particle 도, and the verb 모르다 "not know." It is used to indicate the speaker's wondering or speculative mindset, and is equivalent to "not sure if . . ." "who knows . . ." and "it may be possible that. . . ."

A: 많이 늦으시네요.
  "He is really late."
B: 퇴근 길이라 길이 많이 막힐지도 몰라요.
  "Since it is rush hour, the traffic may be really congested."

~(으)ㄹ 테니까 "I suppose . . . so" (see 16.2.3)

출근했을지도 모르겠네요.
"It may be possible that he left for work."
시간이 많이 걸릴지도 몰라요.
"It may take longer."
머리를 짧게 잘랐을지도 모르겠네요.
"It may be possible that she had her hair cut really short."
지금 집으로 오고 있을지도 몰라요.
"He may be on his way back home."
10년안에 북한과 한국이 통일될지도 몰라요.
"Who knows? North and South Korea may be unified within ten years."
올 여름은 작년 여름보다 더 더울지도 몰라요.
"Who knows? Summer this year might be hotter than last summer."
가까운 미래에 누구나 쉽게 우주여행을 할 수 있을지도 몰라요.
"Who knows? Maybe, in the near future, anyone will be able to travel to space easily."
내년 봄에는 저도 한국에 없을지도 몰라요.
"I also may not be in Korea in spring next year."
계속 약을 먹어야 될지도 몰라요.
"I may continue to take the medicine."
환경오염 때문에 100년안에 북극곰이 멸종될지도 몰라요.
"Because of environmental pollution, polar bears may go extinct within 100 years."
계속 했더라면 아마 유명한 피아니스트가 되었을지도 몰라요.
"If he continued to do so, he might have become a famous pianist."

44.13 ~(으)ㄹ 텐데 "I guess that" (see 17.1.2)

A: 많이 피곤하실 텐데 여기 좀 앉아서 쉬세요.
   "You must be really tired; please have a seat and rest here."
B: 네. 감사합니다.
   "Yes. Thank you."

하루 종일 시험 공부했을 텐데 잠깐 쉬어라.
"You must have studied the whole day for the test, take a rest for a while."
아직 아무것도 못 먹었을 텐데 우유라도 마시고 하세요.
"You have not been able eat at all, so why don't you have a cup of milk and continue?"
어제도 일 때문에 늦게 들어가셨을 텐데 오늘은 일찍 퇴근하세요.
"I assume that you returned home late due to work even yesterday, so please leave the office early today."
배고플 텐데 이거라도 좀 드세요.
"You must be hungry, please help yourself to this."
가방이 무거울 텐데 제가 들어 드릴게요.
"I assume that the bag must be heavy, so let me help you carry that."

44.14 ~(으)ㄹ 테니까 "I suppose . . . so" (see 16.2.3)

A: 선영이 전화 번호는 누가 알지요?
   "Who knows Sunyoung's telephone number?"
B: 정우가 알 테니까 물어보세요.
   "I suppose that Jungwoo knows it, so ask him."

설탕을 많이 넣으면 달 테니까 두 숟갈만 넣으세요.
"If you put too much, it will be too sweet, so put only two tablespoons."
저녁 값은 우리 형이 낼 테니까 많이 드세요.
"My older brother will pay for dinner, so eat a lot."
아침에는 날씨가 쌀쌀할 테니까 코트를 준비해 놓으세요.

CONJECTURE

"It will be chilly in the morning, so prepare coats in advance."
길이 많이 <u>막힐 테니까</u> 지하철 타세요.
"The roads must be really congested, so please take the subway."
밖에 눈이 많이 와서 <u>미끄러울 테니까</u> 운전 조심하시구요.
"It must be really slippery because of the heavy snow outside, so please drive carefully."

45

Contrast

This chapter discusses a number of forms that can express contrast.

45.1 Expressing contrasts with clausal conjunctives

The following clausal conjunctives express contrast.

45.1.1 ~고도 "although, even after" (see 17.2.8)

A: 담배를 끊겠다고 다짐을 <u>하고도</u> 아직 못 끊었대요.
"I heard that even after he made a resolution to quit smoking, he has not quit yet."
B: 그래요? 제가 직접 만나서 다시 한번 이야기해 볼게요.
"Really? I will try to talk to him again in person."

약속 장소에 늦게 <u>오고도</u> 사과 한마디도 안 했어요.
"Although he came late to the meeting place, he did not say a single word of apology."
네 눈으로 직접 <u>보고도</u> 아직도 못 믿겠니?
"Even after you saw it with your own eyes, you still can't believe it?"
그렇게 <u>혼나고도</u> 또 하고 싶었니?
"Even after you were scolded like that, you wanted to do that again?"
공인회계사 시험까지 <u>합격하고도</u> 아직 취직을 못 하고 있어요.
"Although he passed the CPA exam, he has not found a job yet."

45.1.2 ~건만 "despite"

This form is a contracted form of ~건마는 "though/despite."

A: 법학 대학원까지 <u>졸업했건만</u> 아직도 취직을 못 하고 있대요.
"Even though he graduated from law school, I heard that he is still unemployed."
B: 워낙 요즘 변호사들이 너무 많아서 그런가 봐요.
"Perhaps it is because there are too many lawyers nowadays."

<u>최선을 다했건만</u> 낙선했다.
"He did his best, but he lost the election."
여러 번 <u>연락했건만</u> 답장이 없었어요.
"Though I contacted her several times, there was no response."
둘 다 내년이면 나이가 벌써 <u>서른 다섯이건만</u> 아직 결혼할 생각을 안 하네요.
"Though both of them will be 35 years old by next year, they do not think of getting married yet."

45.1.3 ~지만 "although" (see 17.2.1)

A: 한국어 수업 어때요?
"How is your Korean language class?"

CONTRAST   **45.1**

B: 조금 <u>어렵지만</u> 재미있어요.
"It's a bit difficult, but fun."

이 식당 음식은 좀 <u>비싸지만</u> 맛있다고 소문났어요.
"Although food in this restaurant is a bit pricey, it is known for its great taste."
기숙사 생활이 <u>편할 수 있지만</u> 기숙사비가 만만치 않아요.
"Although living in a dorm can be convenient, the dorm fee is formidable."
오늘의 날씨는 대체적으로 <u>맑겠지만</u> 오후부터는 쌀쌀해지겠습니다.
"As for today's weather, overall it is expected to be clear, but it will be chilly starting from the afternoon."
서울 사람들은 성격이 <u>급하지만</u> 에너지가 넘치는 것 같아요.
"People in Seoul seem to be impatient but full of energy."
<u>박사 학위는 없지만</u> 그 분야에서는 최고의 학자다.
"Although he does not have a PhD degree, he is the most esteemed scholar in his field."

45.1.4 ~기는 ~지만 "indeed ... but"

This form is made of ~기는 하다 (see 4.1.6) and the conjunctive ~지만 (see 17.2.1).

A: 점심 드셨지요?
"You ate lunch, right?"
B: <u>먹기는 했지만</u> 아직도 좀 출출하네요.
"I did indeed eat lunch, but I am still a bit hungry."

골프를 <u>배우기는 배웠지만</u> 잘 못 쳐요.
"Although I did indeed learn golf, I am not good at it."
그 영화를 <u>보기는 봤지만</u> 스토리가 하나도 생각이 안 나네요.
"I did see that movie, but I cannot remember its story at all."
시골에 살면 <u>불편하기는 하지만</u> 공해가 없어서 좋아요.
"It is indeed a bit inconvenient to live in rural area, but I like it because there is no pollution."

45.1.5 ~어/아도 "although" (see 17.2.4)

A: 좀 맵지요?
"It's a bit spicy, right?"
B: <u>매워도</u> 맛있네요.
"Though it is spicy, it is delicious."

아무리 <u>피곤해도</u> 매일 아침 7시 전에는 일어나요.
"Regardless of how tired I am, I get up before 7 in the morning every day."
배가 <u>고파도</u> 항상 천천히 드시도록 하세요.
"No matter how hungry you are, always make sure to eat slowly."
시간이 <u>없어도</u> 하루에 꼭 세 끼 챙겨 드세요.
"Even if you have no time, please make sure to have three meals a day."

45.1.6 ~더라도 "even though" (see 17.2.6)

A: 가방이 좀 <u>무겁더라도</u> 꼭 가지고 오세요.
"Though the bag may be a bit heavy, please make sure you bring it."
B: 네, 알겠습니다.
"Sure, I will."

별로 <u>안 좋아하시더라도</u> 갖다 드리세요.
"Even though he does not like it much, please bring it to him."
스트레스가 <u>많더라도</u> 담배는 다시 피우지 마세요.
"Even if you feel a lot of stress, please do not smoke again."

Expressing contrast with conjunctional adverbs (see 33.1.1)

비용이 많이 <u>들더라도</u> 금년에는 꼭 새 차를 장만하려고요.
"Even if it costs a lot, I intend to purchase a new car this year."
아무리 <u>바쁘더라도</u> 꼭 정기적으로 건강 검진을 받는 것이 중요합니다.
"No matter how busy you are, it is important to receive a regular physical check up."

45.1.7 ~으나 "but" (see 17.2.3)

A: 아이들이 좋아할 텐데 주말에 가족 분들하고 갔다오세요?
    "Kids will love it, so why not visit there with your family this weekend?"
B: <u>가고 싶으나</u> 시간이 없습니다.
    "I would like to go, but I have no time."

개인 레슨을 <u>받고 있으나</u> 실력이 늘지 않아요.
"She is receiving private lessons but does not improve much."
별로 차린 것은 <u>없으나</u> 많이 드시기 바랍니다.
"It's not much, but I hope that you please help yourself to a lot."
생활 습관도 <u>중요하나</u> 유전적 요인도 무시할 수 없겠지요.
"Your daily routine is important, but you cannot ignore genetic factors."
제품의 양도 물론 <u>중요하겠으나</u> 질도 생각해야지요.
"Of course, the quantity of the product is important, but you need to consider its quality as well."
제가 사는 시골은 대중교통이 <u>불편하나</u> 공해가 적고 경치가 좋습니다.
"The public transportation in the rural area where I live is inconvenient, but the area has less pollution and beautiful scenery."
백화점이나 쇼핑센터가 <u>많지 않으나</u> 생활비가 덜 드는 편입니다.
"There are not many department stores or shopping malls, but the cost of living tends to be low."

45.1.8 ~는/(으)ㄴ데(도) "even after" (see 17.2.5)

A: 오늘은 <u>주말인데도</u> 손님이 별로 없네요.
    "Today is the weekend, but there are not many customers."
B: 글쎄 말이에요. 요즘 경기가 안 좋아서 죽을 지경이에요.
    "Well, that's right. The economy is so bad nowadays that I am on the verge of dying."

어제 오래 <u>잤는데도</u> 피곤하다.
"Even though I slept for a long time yesterday, I am tired."
가방이 이렇게 <u>많은데</u> 더 사고 싶니?
"You have so many bags, but you want to buy more?"
<u>한국 사람인데도</u> 매운 음식을 싫어해요.
"He is Korean, but he still dislikes spicy food."

45.2 Expressing contrast with conjunctional adverbs (see 33.1.1)

Beside the above clausal conjunctives described in section 45.1, the following conjunctional adverbs also indicate contrast.

그러나 "but"

보기에는 얌전해요. <u>그러나</u> 성격은 활발해요.
"She is gentle in appearance. But as for her personality, she is active."
제 친한 친구 중 한 명이었어요. <u>그러나</u> 제가 제일 힘들 때 옆에 있어 주지 않았어요.
"He was one of my close friends. But, he was not next to me when I underwent my most difficult times."

CONTRAST

그런데 "by the way"

착하고 예뻐요. 그런데 주위에 친구가 별로 없어요.
"She is nice and pretty. But, she does not have many friends around her."
얼굴이 낯이 익네요. 그런데 이름이 생각나지 않아요.
"His face looks familiar. But, I can't think of his name."

그렇지만 "however"

지금까지는 괜찮았어요. 그렇지만 다음 달부터 걱정이에요.
"So far, it has been fine. But, I am worried from next month."
비쌌어요. 그렇지만 정말 맛있었어요.
"It was expensive. But, it was really delicious."

45.3 Expressing contrast with the particle 은/는 (see 7.2.1)

When two sentences, marked by the topic particle 은/는, are used in parallel, the particle 은/는 serves to compare and contrast the two topics of the sentences. Consider the following two examples:

저스틴은 캐나다 사람이에요.
"As for Justin, he is Canadian."
그렇지만 치에꼬는 일본 사람이에요.
"However, as for Chieko, she is Japanese."

Notice that both Justin and Chieko are the topics of each sentence. Since these sentences are used in parallel, these two topics are compared and contrasted (e.g., one is Canadian whereas the other person is Japanese).

저는 고기를 좋아하는데 저희 집 사람은 채식주의자예요.
"As for me, I like meat, but as for my wife, she is a vegetarian."
저는 형만 둘 있는데 수잔은 언니만 셋이에요.
"As for me, I have two older brothers, but as for Susan, she only has three sisters."
저는 아빠를 많이 닮았는데 제 동생은 엄마를 많이 닮았어요.
"As for me, I resemble my dad a lot, but as for my younger brother, he resembles my mom."
형은 안경을 쓰는데 동생은 시력이 좋아요.
"As for my older brother, he wears eye glasses, but as for my younger brother, he has good vision."

45.4 Other expressions of contrast

45.4.1 ~는/(으)ㄴ가 하면 "on the other hand"

This form is the combination of the ending ~나/(으)ㄴ가 (see 27.2.4), and the verb 하다 "do," and the conjunctive ~(으)면 "if."

A: 오늘은 손님이 아주 많네요. 매일 바쁘신가 봐요.
  "There are many customers today. You seem to be busy every day."
B: 어떤 날은 아주 바쁜가 하면 어떤 날은 한가해요.
  "On certain days, I am busy, but on certain days, I am free."

혼자 먹는 손님이 있는가 하면 단체로 와서 먹는 손님들도 있어요.
"There are customers who eat alone, but on the other hand, there are customers who come and eat in groups."

For writings and formal contexts　　　　　　　　　　　　　　　　　　**45.5**

집으로 가는 사람이 <u>있는가 하면</u> 호텔로 가는 사람들도 있어요.
"There are people who go back home, but there are people who return to their hotels."
사람을 사귈 때 외모를 보는 사람이 <u>있는가 하면</u> 성격을 중요시 하는 사람도 있어요.
"When making friends, there are people who consider one's appearance, but on the other hand, there are people who consider one's personality."
전공을 선택할 때 본인의 적성에 맞는 전공을 찾는 학생이 <u>있는가 하면</u> 취업하기 쉬운 전공만을 택하는 학생들도 있어요.
"When deciding one's major, there are students who look for majors that fit their aptitudes, but there are students who only choose majors that are good for getting jobs."

45.4.2　~는/(으)ㄴ 반면에 "on the other hand" (see 23.6)

A:　대형 로펌에 다니면 연봉을 많이 받겠네요. 그렇지요?
　　"As an employee of a big law firm, I assume that he gets a high salary, right?"
B:　높은 연봉을 <u>받는 반면에</u> 업무가 엄청나게 많아요.
　　"He receives a high annual salary, but on the other hand, the workload is awfully overwhelming."

노래는 <u>잘하는 반면에</u> 춤은 잘 못 춥니다.
"She sings well, but on the other hand, she can't dance well."
하와이는 집값이 <u>비싼 반면에</u> 세금이 비교적 낮아요.
"In Hawaii, home prices are high, but on the other hand, the taxes are relatively low."
공무원은 월급이 <u>적은 반면에</u> 의료보험 등 혜택이 많아요.
"Government employees' salary is low, but there are many benefits like health insurance."
이 새 전화기는 기능이 <u>많은 반면에</u> 가격이 좀 비싼 것 같아요.
"This new phone has many functions, but on the other hand, it is a bit pricey."

45.4.3　~(으)ㅁ에도 불구하고 "even after, in spite of"

This form is built on the nominalizing ending ~(으)ㅁ (see 4.2), the particle 에도, and 불구하고 "regardless" (불구하다 "disregard" + 고 "and").

<u>최선을 다했음에도 불구하고</u> 시험에 또 떨어졌습니다.
"Even after he put forth his best efforts, he failed the exam again."
<u>공부를 많이 한 사람임에도 불구하고</u> 예의범절을 잘 몰라요.
"In spite of the fact that he is an educated man, he does not know the rules of etiquette."
부모님의 강한 반대가 <u>있었음에도 불구하고</u> 결국 우린 결혼했다.
"Even though there were severe oppositions from her parents, we got married in the end."
<u>어려운 부탁임에도 불구하고</u> 제 요청을 들어주셨습니다.
"In spite of the fact that it was a big favor, he agreed to my request."

45.5　For writings and formal contexts

The following expressions mean "in contrast," and these are primarily used for formal and written communication.

Noun 와/과 달리

모두가 기대했던 것과는 달리 4강 진출에 결국 실패했다.
"In contrast to what everyone expected, the team failed to advance to the semifinals after all."

CONTRAST

Noun 와/과 다르게

저희가 미리 생각했던 것과는 다르게 조건과 가격이 아주 적절했었습니다.
"In contrast to what we thought beforehand, the conditions and price were very appropriate."

Noun 와/과 대조적으로

방송에서 보도됐던 것과 대조적으로 실종자 수가 더 많은 것으로 나왔습니다.
"In contrast to what was reported in the broadcast, it turned out that the number of missing persons was more numerous."

46
Deciding

To ask about or express decisions, you can use the following expressions.

46.1 결정 + verb "decide"

The Korean word for "decision" is 결정. This noun is commonly used with verbs, such as 하다, 내리다, and 되다 to express decisions:

결정하다 "decide"
결정 내리다 "decide"
결정짓다 "determine"
결정나다 "be determined"
결정되다 "be decided"
결정을 따르다 "follow a decision"

A: 언제 부모님 뵈러 갈지 결정하셨어요?
  "Have you decided when to visit your parents?"
B: 아니요. 아직 아무것도 결정된 게 없어요.
  "No. Nothing has been decided yet."

이건 우리가 결정할 문제가 아니다.
"As for this, it is not a problem for us to decide."
결정은 형한테 달렸어요.
"It's up to my older brother to decide."
어디로 갈 것인지 결정할 수가 없었어요.
"We couldn't decide where to go."
결국 한국을 떠나지 않기로 결정했습니다.
"Finally, they've decided not to leave Korea."

46.2 결심하다 "make a resolution"

A 오늘부터 금연하기로 결심했어요.
  "I made a resolution to quit smoking starting today."
B: 아, 그러세요? 이번에는 꼭 성공하길 빌어요.
  "Oh, is that so? I wish you the best this time."

나는 그녀와 금년 안으로 꼭 결혼하기로 결심했다.
"I am set on marrying her within this year."
그 친구는 한 번도 새해마다 결심한 것을 실천한 적이 없었어요.
"He has never lived up to his New Year's resolution in the past."

DECIDING

46.3 정하다 "decide on, choose, set"

A: 어느 식당으로 갈지 정하셨어요?
"Have you decided on which restaurant you will go to?"
B: 아직이요. 과장님하고 상의하고 정하려구요.
"Not yet. I am thinking of deciding after I discuss it with the chief."

지금 약속 장소를 정하세요.
"Decide where to meet now."
아직 출발 날짜를 정하지 못했어요.
"I have not been able to fix a date for departure."
먼저 우선순위를 정하고 행동에 옮기세요.
"Set your priorities first, and then put them in action."

46.4 ~기로 하다 "decide to" (see 4.1.10)

A: 어떻게 하실 거예요?
"What will you do about it?"
B: 일단 기다려 보기로 했습니다.
"I decided to wait for their answer first."

건강 때문에 술을 끊기로 했어요.
"Because of health reasons, I decided to quit drinking alcohol."
주말에 친구들하고 한잔 하기로 했습니다.
"I decided to have drinks with my friends this weekend."
다음 주 금요일에 부모님을 찾아뵙기로 했습니다.
"I decided to pay a visit to my parents on Friday next week."
가구는 우선 살 집부터 알아보고 천천히 사기로 했어요.
"As for furniture, we decided to look for a house to live in first, and then buy it."
오후 3시에 도서관 앞에서 만나기로 했어요.
"We decided to meet them at 3 p.m. in front of the library."
주말 아침마다 동생하고 조깅하기로 했는데요.
"Every weekend morning, I decided to jog with my younger brother."
이번 목요일 저녁은 회사 동료들하고 식사하기로 했는데요.
"As for this Thursday's dinner, I decided to have a meal with my company colleagues."

47

Degree and extent

This chapter covers a variety of expressions used to indicate degree or extent.

47.1 Expressing degree and extent

47.1.1 N만 "only" (see 8.1.5)

    A: 한국에 가족이 많으세요?
        "Do you have many family members in Korea?"
    B; 아니요. 형제들 모두 미국에 있는데 <u>부모님만</u> 한국에 계세요.
        "No. All of my brothers are in the states; only my parents are in Korea."

저희 가족 모두 키가 작은데 <u>저만</u> 키가 유난히 커요.
"Everyone in my family is short, but only I am unusually tall."
저희 중에서 <u>나오꼬 씨만</u> 결혼했어요.
"Among us, only Naoko is married."
친구 중에서 <u>성민이만</u> 학생이고 다 직장에 다녀요.
"Among my friends, only Sungmin is a student, while everyone works full time."

47.1.2 N만하다 "be as . . . as"

만하다 is an adjective meaning "be the extent of," "worth," and "worth of."

    A: 집이 얼마나 컸나요?
        "How big was his house?"
    B: 집이 <u>체육관만했어요</u>.
        "The house was as big as a gym."

얼굴이 <u>주먹만해요</u>.
"Her face is as small as a fist."
수박이 <u>사과만하게 작아요</u>.
"The watermelon is as small as an apple."
<u>형만한</u> 동생이 없다.
"No younger brother is better than his older brother."
월급이 <u>쥐꼬리만해요</u>.
"My salary is as small as the size of a rat tail."

47.1.3 N만 해도 "just talking about . . ."

This form is made of the particle 만 (see 8.1.5), the verb 하다 "do," and the conjunctive ~어/아도 (see 17.2.4).

    A: 회사가 큰가요?
        "Is your company big?"

DEGREE AND EXTENT

B: 그럼요. 종업원만 해도 100명이 넘어요.
"Of course. Just talking about employees, there are over 100."
학교 등록금만 해도 일년에 4만불이 넘습니다.
"Just talking about the school tuition, it is over 40,000 dollars per year."
우리 동네만 해도 피자 가게가 5개나 있어요.
"Just talking about our town, there are as many as five pizzerias."
어제만 해도 손님이 많았는데 오늘은 가게가 한가하네요.
"Yesterday, there were many customers, but as for today, the store is not busy."

47.1.4 N뿐 "only" (see 8.1.7)

이제 우리 둘뿐이에요.
"Now, it is only the two of us."
인생은 한 번뿐이에요.
"You only have one life."
그렇게 믿는 사람은 너뿐이야.
"Nobody believes so except yourself."

47.1.5 N밖에 "nothing but, only" (see 8.1.6)

이제 우리밖에 없어요.
"There is nobody except us now."
사과밖에 안 샀어요.
"I bought only apples."
다 팔고 남은 것은 이 집밖에 없어요.
"I have nothing but this house after selling all of my belongings."

47.1.6 ~기 짝이 없다 "beyond measure" (see 4.1.21)

정말 한심없기 짝이 없어요.
"He is extremely deplorable."
우리 모두 기쁘기 짝이 없었어요.
"We all were happy beyond measure."
정말 유치하기 짝이 없네요.
"It is childish beyond measure."

47.1.7 ~도록 "to the extent that . . ." (see 18.1.6)

A: 오래 기다리셨나요?
"Did you wait a long time?"
B: 눈이 빠지도록 기다렸습니다.
"We waited to the extent that my eyes would pop out."
저희 모두 목이 쉬도록 응원했어요.
"We all cheered until our voices were hoarse."
배가 터지도록 먹었어요.
"I ate until I was about to burst."
골치가 아프도록 시끄러웠어요.
"It was noisy to the extent that my head ached."

47.1.8 ~(으)ㄹ 정도로 "to the extent that . . ." (see 24.1)

A: 지난 주에 많이 바쁘셨나 봐요.
"I guess you were very busy last month."

Expressing degree and extent

47.1

B: 네. <u>정신을 못 차릴 정도로</u> 바빴어요.
"Yes. I was busy to the extent that I lost my senses."

<u>눈이 부실 정도로</u> 아름다우세요.
"You are beautiful to the extent that my eyes are dazzled."
<u>형 옷을 입을 정도로</u> 많이 컸네요.
"He grew up a lot to the extent that he can now wear his older brother's clothes."
<u>앞이 잘 안 보일 정도로</u> 비가 많이 오고 있어요.
"It is raining to the extent that you can't really see right in front of you."
<u>기절할 정도로</u> 피곤하다.
"I am tired to the extent that I might pass out."

47.1.9 ~(으)리만치 (similar to ~을 정도로)

A: 파리의 야경 어땠나요?
"How was the night view of Paris?"
B: 뭐라고 <u>표현할 수 없으리만치</u> 아름다웠어요.
"It was beautiful beyond description."

<u>믿겨지지 않으리만치</u> 충격이었어요.
"It was shocking to the extent that it was unbelievable."
<u>상상할 수 없으리만치</u> 어려웠어요.
"It was difficult to the extent that one cannot even imagine it."
<u>조금도 움직일 수 없으리만치</u> 아프더라구요.
"It was painful to the point that I couldn't move a bit."
<u>누구인지 못 알아보리만치</u> 많이 늙었어요.
"He aged to the extent that one can't discern who he is."

47.1.10 ~는/(으)ㄴ/(으)ㄹ 만큼 "to the extent that . . ."

This form is the combination of one of the noun-modifying endings ~는/(으)ㄴ/(으)ㄹ (see Chapter 21) and the bound noun 만큼 "extent" (see 1.3).

A: 많이 드셨어요?
"Did you eat a lot?"
B: <u>배가 터질 만큼</u> 먹었어요.
"I ate to the extent that I was about to burst."

누구랑 <u>데이트할 만큼</u> 한가하지 않아요.
"I don't have enough free time to date someone."
많은 <u>버는 만큼</u> 많이 쓰게 돼요.
"It turns out that you will end up spending as much as you earn."
각자 <u>먹은 만큼</u> 내자.
"Let's pay individually according to how much each person eats."
사람은 <u>아픈 만큼</u> 성숙해져요.
"As for people, they mature as much as they suffer."
<u>눈물이 날 만큼</u> 웃었어요.
"I laughed to the extent that I was tearing."
열심히 <u>노력한 만큼</u> 대가가 있을 거예요.
"There will be rewards to the extent of your effort."
많이 있으니까 <u>가지고 싶은 만큼</u> 가지세요.
"We have a lot, so take as much as you want."

DEGREE AND EXTENT

47.2 Expressing the degree of satisfaction

Here are some typical expressions that indicate one's degree of satisfaction, arranged from least to most enthusiastic.

최악입니다.
"It is a nightmare."
형편없어요.
"It is terrible."
별로예요.
"I don't like it much."
그저그래요.
"It's so so."
괜찮았어요.
"It was fine."
나쁘지 않네요.
"It's not bad."
괜찮은 편이에요.
"It is kind of nice."
좋네요.
"It's nice."
만족합니다.
"It is satisfying."
아주 좋습니다.
"It's really wonderful."
최고입니다.
"It's the best."
강추입니다.
"I strongly recommend it."
아주 아주 대만족입니다.
"I'm totally satisfied."
끝내줘요.
"I can't ask for anything more."

48

Describing people, places, weather, color, and taste

This chapter introduces a number of expressions used to describe people, places, weather, color, and the taste of food.

48.1 Describing people

Here are some expressions used to describe people (i.e., physical features, personality):

    A: 누가 언니세요?
         "Who is your older brother?"
    B: 긴 머리에 청바지를 입고 있는 사람이 제 언니예요.
         "The person wearing blue jeans with long hair is my older sister."

김영규 씨는 키가 커요.
"Mr. Kim Youngkyu is tall."
제 여동생은 머리가 길고 눈이 예뻐요.
"My younger sister has long hair and pretty eyes."
임경찬 씨는 성실하고 성격도 아주 좋아요.
"Mr. Kyungchan Lim is diligent and has a very good personality."
저기 하얀 티셔츠를 입고 선글라스를 쓰고 있는 사람이 제 남동생이에요.
"The person wearing a white T-shirt and sunglasses over there is my younger brother."
형은 성격이 활발하고 외향적이지만 동생은 얌전하고 내성적인 편이에요.
"My older brother is active and extroverted, but my younger brother is kind of gentle and introverted."

48.2 Describing places

To describe places, you can use the following expressions:

    A: 올바니는 어떤 도시예요?
         "What kind of city is Albany?"
    B: 뉴욕의 주도로 전형적인 행정 교육 도시예요.
         "As the capital of New York State, it is a typical educational and administrative city."

파리는 에펠탑으로 유명합니다.
"Paris is famous for the Eiffel Tower."
서울은 물가가 비싸고 교통이 복잡합니다.
"As for Seoul, the price of living is high, and the traffic is bad."
그 호텔은 시내에 있고 기차역에서 가까워요.
"That hotel is located near the train station downtown."

DESCRIBING PEOPLE, PLACES, WEATHER, COLOR, AND TASTE

48.4

라스베가스는 도박의 도시로 유명하지요.
"Las Vegas is famous as the city of gambling."

48.3 Describing the weather

Here are some typical expressions associated with weather:

    A: 밖의 날씨 어때요?
        "How is the weather outside?"
    B: 조금 쌀쌀하지만 하늘은 맑고 화창해요.
        "It is a bit chilly, but the sky is clear and sunny."

날씨가 고르지 않아요.
"The weather is not consistent."
지금 예측할 수가 없네요.
"It's unpredictable now."
아침내내 흐렸어요.
"It's been cloudy all morning."
바람이 세게 불었어요.
"There was a strong wind."
날씨가 많이 풀렸어요.
"The weather became warmer."
이제 날씨가 개었어요.
"The weather cleared up now."
비가 갠 뒤의 좋은 날이었어요.
"The weather was nice just after the rainfall."
하늘을 봐서는 내일 비가 올 것 같아요.
"Judging from the look of the sky, it will rain tomorrow."
아직 5월인데 여름같이 후덥지근하네요.
"It is only May, but it is as humid as summer."
아직 9월인데 이맘때 치고는 날씨가 꽤 춥지요?
"It's only September, but it's a little too cold for this time of the year, right?"
해가 점점 짧아지고 있네요.
"The days are getting shorter."
서울은 지금 눈이 오고 있어요.
"It is snowing in Seoul right now."

48.4 Describing color

When describing the color of things, the following expressions can be used:

    A: 차가 무슨 색인가요?
        "What is the color of your car?"
    B: 저기 보이는 하얀 SUV가 제 차입니다.
        "The white SUV that you see over there is my car."

방이 너무 어두워요.
"The room is too dark."
저기 남색 티셔츠 주세요.
"Please give me that T-shirt in blue."
저희 집 기와는 갈색이에요.
"The color of the roof tiles of our house is brown."
어두운 색보다는 밝은 색이 더 잘 어울리실 것 같아요.
"It seems that bright colors rather than dark colors fit better."

Describing the taste of food

48.5 Describing the taste of food

To describe the taste of food, you can use the following expressions:

    A: 입에 맞으세요?
          "Does it suit your taste?"
    B: 네, 느끼하지도 않고 아주 맛있네요.
          "Yes, it is not greasy and very delicious."

너무 싱겁네요.
"It's too bland."
음식 맛이 맵고 짜기도 해요.
"The food tastes spicy and salty too."
좀 짠 맛이 있는 것 같아요.
"It seems that it is a bit salty."
조금 달콤하네요.
"It's a bit sweet."
조금 쓴 맛이 나요.
"It has a bitter taste."
식초같이 맛이 몹시 시네요.
"It's too sour like vinegar."
조금 떫은 맛이 나요.
"It has a little bit of a bitter flavor."
음식이 산뜻하고 시원합니다.
"The food is fresh and refreshing."

49

Discoveries

In English, one can indicate a sense of discovery by using verbs or phrases such as "I realize/ discover that," "come up," "learn of," "find out," "notice," and so forth. This chapter examines various expressions that are used to indicate discovery or surprise.

49.1 ~군/네(요) "oh, I see . . ." (see 25.3 and 25.4)

The sentence ending ~군/네(요) (see 25.3 and 25.4) can indicate both surprise or discovery, as shown in the following examples:

    A: 12시인데 점심 식사 안 하세요?
          "It is 12 o'clock, so aren't you going to have lunch?"
    B: 아, 벌써 점심 시간이네요.
          "Oh, it is already lunch hour."

많이 아프셨군요.
"Oh, you have been really sick."
눈이 많이 나쁘시네요.
"Oh, your vision is really bad."
형이 경찰관이시군요.
"Oh, I see that your older brother is a police officer."

49.2 ~(으)니까 "when" (see 16.2.2)

The primary function of the conjunctive ~(으)니까 is to indicate a reason, as translated as "since, because, so." However, it has an additional function of indicating a sense of discovery, translated as "when." For instance, consider the following conversation:

    A: 정말 싸게 사셨네요. 어디서 사셨어요?
          "You bought it at a really cheap price. Where did you buy it?"
    B: 백화점에 가니까 세일을 하고 있던데요.
          "When I went to the department store, sales were going on."

Notice in B's response that the first clause (백화점에 가니까) indicates a sense of discovery or a realization that is expressed in the second clause (세일을 하고 있던데요).

사무실에 가니까 모두들 저를 기다리고 있었어요.
"When I went to the office, everyone was waiting for me."
집에 전화하니까 엄마가 전화를 받으셨어요.
"When I called home, my mom answered the phone."
아침에 일어나니까 침대 옆에 선물이 놓여 있었어요.
"When I woke up in the morning, I noticed that a gift was put next to my bed."

49.3 ~고 보니(까) "after having tried doing . . . and then realize"

This form is made of the auxiliary verb ~고 보다 "do and then realize" (see 15.2) and the conjunctive ~으니까 (see 16.2.2). The form is used when the speaker learned something new (by doing something first and then seeing how things turned out from there).

    A: 어렵지 않았어요?
           "Wasn't it hard?"
    B: 배우고 보니까 재미있더라구요.
           "After I tried learning it, I found it fun."

계속 사귀고 보니까 좋은 사람 같았어요.
"After I tried dating her for a while, I realized that she appeared to be a nice person."
인턴으로 일하고 보니 외국어 능력이 얼마나 중요한가를 깨닫게 되었어요.
"After I tried working as an intern, I realized how critical a foreign language ability is."
기차를 타고 보니까 편하더라구요.
"After I tried riding a train, I realized it was convenient."
요가를 하고 보니까 건강이 좋아졌어요.
"After I tried doing yoga, my health got better."
골프를 치고 보니까 어렵더라구요.
"After I tried playing golf, I realized it was hard."

49.4 ~다(가) 보니(까) "after tried doing X . . . and then realize"

This form is constructed from the conjunctive ~다가 (see 19.1.7), the verb 보다 "see, try" and the conjunctive ~(으)니까 (see 16.2.2). The meaning of ~다가 보니까 is similar to that of ~고 보니까 since both forms are used when the speaker comes upon something new by having tried doing something. But there is a slight meaning difference between them. That is, you use ~다가 보니까 when you learn something new after you have tried doing something, which you have done continuously for long time in the past.

    A: 집에서 자주 해 드세요?
           "Do you cook often at home?"
    B: 아니요. 혼자 살다 보니까 주로 밖에서 먹게 돼요.
           "No. Since I have lived alone for a long time, I usually end up eating out."

매운 음식도 자주 먹다 보니 잘 먹게 되었어요.
"After I tried eating spicy foods often, I have become able to eat them well."
매일 조깅을 하다 보니까 체중을 많이 줄일 수 있었어요.
"After I tried jogging every day, I was able to lose a lot of weight."
정신없이 일하다 보니까 벌써 시간이 이렇게 됐네요.
"While I worked frantically, it has become this late."
계속 먹다 보니까 괜찮던데요.
"While I continued to eat, I thought it was not that bad."
한국 드라마를 자주 시청하다 보니까 한국어 실력이 늘었어요.
"While I watched Korean dramas frequently, my Korean proficiency improved."
외국에서 혼자 살다 보니까 음식 솜씨가 많이 좋아졌어요.
"While I lived alone abroad, my ability to cook food got a lot better."

49.5 ~다(가) 보면 "if/when continue to do something . . . then . . . will"

This form consists of the conjunctive ~다가 (see 19.1.7), the verb 보다 "see, try" and the conjunctive ~(으)면 "if, when" (see 18.2.1). Its meaning is equivalent to "if/when you continue to do something, you will come upon something new" in English.

    A: 너무 어려워서 힘드네요.
         "I am struggling because it is too hard."
    B: 계속 공부를 하다 보면 요령이 생기니까 너무 걱정하지 마세요.
         "If you continue to study, you will acquire 'know-how,' so don't worry too much."

아이들이 놀다 보면 서로 싸울 수도 있지요.
"When kids are playing with each other, they may easily fight."
살다 보면 좋은 일도 나쁜 일도 겪기 나름이지요.
"In life, it is natural that one faces both good times and bad times."
공원에서 산책하다 보면 철새도 쉽게 볼 수 있을 거예요.
"When you take a walk at the park, you can easily see migratory birds too."
같이 지내다 보면 서로 다툴 일도 있을 거예요.
"When you live together, I assume that there will be matters of conflict."

49.6 ~(었/았)더니 "since, seeing as" (see 16.2.6)

This form is used when a speaker remembers past events and then describes an immediate discovery.

    A: 열심히 공부하더니 합격했구나. 축하한다.
         "After studying hard, you finally passed the exam. Congratulations."
    B: 운이 좋았지요. 감사합니다.
         "I was lucky. Thank you."

    A: 안 주무세요?
         "Won't you go to bed?"
    B: 오늘 커피를 많이 마셨더니 잠이 안 오네요.
         "I drank a lot of coffee today, so I can't fall asleep."

다이어트를 하더니 날씬해졌어요.
"She became slim after dieting."
성공하더니 교만해진 것 같아요.
"It seems that he became arrogant after succeeding."
어렸을 때부터 운동을 잘하더니 결국 프로 골퍼가 됐네요.
"Ever since he was a kid, he was good at sports, and now I see that he eventually became a professional golfer."
돈이 없다고 하더니 결국 아르바이트를 시작했군요.
"He said that he didn't have money, and now I see that he started working a part-time job."
약을 먹었더니 이제 좀 괜찮아졌어요.
"I took some medicine, so I feel much better now."
며칠 계속 야근을 했더니 몸살이 났어요.
"In the past few days, I worked until late at night, so I ache all over."
어제 늦게 잤더니 오늘 아침에 못 일어나겠더라구요.
"I went to bed late last night, so I could not get up this morning."

50
Emphasizing strategies

In Korean, there are a number of expressions one can use to make your utterance more emphatic or explicit (e.g., often by highlighting or intensifying the degree of a particular state of affairs, situations, or activity). This chapter discusses several expressions that you can use to indicate emphasis.

50.1 ~거든요 "you see, you know" (see 18.2.4)

~거든 is a clausal conjunctive meaning "if/when." However, you can use this as a sentence ending when giving a response to a question or providing an explanation for a preceding context. When doing so, it makes your utterance sounds more emphatic. Compare the following examples:

> 내일 시험이 있어서 오늘 바빠요.
> "Since I have a test tomorrow, I am busy today."
> 내일 시험이 있어서 오늘 바쁘거든요.
> "Since I have a test tomorrow, I am busy today, you see."

Notice that the basic meanings of both sentences are similar, but the second sentence with ~거든요 sounds more emphatic.

> A: 천천히 드세요. 많이 시장하신가 봐요."
>   "Please eat slowly. You must be very hungry."
> B: 저 아직 아침도 안 먹었거든요.
>   "I did not have breakfast either yet, you know."

새벽 5시까지 공항에 가야 하거든요.
"We need to get to the airport by five in the morning, you see."
나 어제 잠 한 숨도 못 잤거든!
"I couldn't sleep at all last night, you know!"
인턴으로 일할 곳이 없을까 찾고 있거든요.
"I am searching for a place to work for as an intern, you know."
저도 갈까 생각 중이었거든요.
"I was also thinking of going there, you see."

50.2 ~잖아요 "you know" (see 26.5)

The meaning of ~잖아요 is similar to the sentence ending ~지요 (see 26.6) in that it is used when seeking the listener's confirmation. However, it sounds more emphatic than ~지요.

> 영화가 재미있잖아요.
> "The movie is interesting, you know."
> 다음부터 조심한다고 하잖아요!
> "He says that he will be more careful from now on, you see."

EMPHASIZING STRATEGIES

우리 딸이 워낙 한국 드라마를 좋아하잖아요.
"My daughter likes Korean dramas so much, you see."
서울이 부산보다 춥잖아요.
"Seoul is colder than Busan, you see."

50.3 ~기가 이를 데 없다 (~기가 그지없다/~기 짝이 없다) "extremely"

This form is constructed from the nominalizing ending ~기, the subject particle 가, the verb 이르다 "arrive," the noun-modifying ending (으)ㄹ, the dependent noun 데 "place" and the verb 없다 "does not have/exist." This pattern is used to emphasize the degree of state of being, denoted by the nominalized adjective. For example, compare the following:

배우들의 연기가 훌륭했어요.
"The actors' performances were great."
배우들의 연기가 훌륭하기가 이를 데 없었어요.
"The actors' performances were so great." (lit. The actors' performances defy the description of just being great.)

Whereas the basic meaning of both previous sentences is the same, the second sentence with this form sounds more emphatic than the first one.

이 곳 호텔 직원들이 친절하기가 이를 데 없네요.
"The hoteliers here are extremely kind."
뷔페 음식 종류가 다양하기가 이를 데 없었어요.
"The food at that buffet restaurant was extremely diverse."
선생님의 새 책 내용이 유익하기 이를 데가 없었습니다.
"The content of your new book was so instructive."

Meanwhile, expressions like ~기가 그지없다 (~기가 + the noun 그지 "the end" + 없다 "not exist/have") and ~기(가) 짝이 없다 (~기가 + the noun 짝 "pair" + 이 없다) have similar meanings, as shown in the following examples:

부끄럽기가 이를 데 없어요.
부끄럽기가 그지없어요.
부끄럽기 짝이 없어요.
"I am terribly embarrassed."

50.4 ~기는 커녕 "far from ~ing" (see 4.1.7)

자주 만나기는 커녕 바빠서 전화로 목소리도 못 들어요.
"Far from meeting frequently, I can't hear her voice even by phone because we are busy."
택시를 타기는 커녕 버스 타고 다닐 돈도 없네요.
"Far from taking a taxi, I don't have enough money even for the bus."
좋아하시기는 커녕 쓸데없이 돈 썼다고 혼내셨어요.
"Far from liking it, he scolded me by saying that I wasted money."
고마워하기는 커녕 오히려 화를 내던데요.
"Far from being grateful, instead he got angry at me."

50.5 여간 ~지 않다 "exceedingly"

This form is made of the adverb 여간 "normally" or "usually" and the negation form ~지 않다 (see 20.2). Although this form is used in a negative form (e.g., ~지 않다, 이/가 아니다),

its meaning is not negative. Instead, it makes the assertion stronger. Compare the following sentences:

> 그 영화가 정말 재미있어요.
> "That movie is really interesting."
> 그 영화가 여간 재미있지 않아요.
> "That movie is so interesting." (lit. That movie is not JUST interesting.)

The basic meaning of both of the previous sentences is similar. However, the second sentence with 여간 ~지 않다 sounds more emphatic than the first sentence.

> 규현이가 여간 피아노를 잘 치지 않아요.
> "Kyuhyun really plays piano well."
> 시험이 여간 어렵지 않았어요.
> "The exam was really difficult."
> 김 목사님이 여간 친절하신 분이 아니세요.
> "Pastor Kim is such a kind person."
> 변 교수님은 여간 부지런한 분이 아니세요.
> "Professor Byon is really a diligent person."

50.6 얼마나/어찌나 ~은/는지 (모르다) "don't know ... how ..." (see 31.1)

This form is used to emphasize the degree of a particular state or situation. Compare the following two sentence:

> 시험이 아주 어려워요.
> "The exam is very difficult."
> 시험이 얼마나 어려운지 몰라요.
> "The exam is so difficult." (lit. I don't know how difficult the exam is.)

Note that the basic meaning of both sentences is similar. However, the degree of difficulty of the exam in the second sentence with the pattern sounds more emphatic than the first one.

> 매일 얼마나 열심히 공부하는지 몰라요.
> "He studies extremely hard every day."
> 작년 겨울에 얼마나 눈이 많이 왔는지 몰라요.
> "It snowed so much last winter."
> 취직했다는 소식을 듣고 얼마나 기뻤는지 몰라요.
> "We were so happy to hear the news that he got the job."
> 어제는 어찌나 피곤한지 회의 시간에 졸았어요.
> "I was so tired that I dozed off during the meeting."
> 어찌나 월급이 적은지 저축할 돈이 없어요.
> "My salary is so little that I have no money to save."
> 어찌나 해외 출장이 잦은지 한달의 반은 집에 없어요.
> "His overseas business trips are so frequent that he is not home for half of each month."
> 어찌나 손님들이 까다로운지 일하기가 힘들어요.
> "Customers are so finicky that it is difficult to work there."
> 어찌나 경쟁이 심한지 취업하기가 하늘의 별따기예요.
> "The competition is so severe that getting a job is like catching a star."

EMPHASIZING STRATEGIES

50.7 ~(으)ㄹ 뿐이다 "only, just" (see 8.1.7, 23.10)

The noun 뿐 means "only/just," and ~(으)ㄹ 뿐이다 is used to emphasize that there is only one available course of action or state. Compare the following sentences:

집 주소는 모르고 전화번호만 알아요.
"I don't know her home address; I know only her telephone number."
집 주소는 모르고 전화번호만 알 뿐이에요.
"I don't know her home address; I know only her telephone number."

Although the meaning of both sentences is similar, the second sentence with ~(으)ㄹ 뿐이다 sounds more assertive.

남자 친구가 아니구요. 단지 동료일 뿐이에요.
"He is not my boyfriend. He is just a colleague."
아프지는 않고 좀 피곤할 뿐이에요.
"I am not sick; I just feel tired."
학교에서 답변이 오기만을 기다리고 있을 뿐이에요.
"We are just waiting to hear the response from school."

50.8 ~(으)ㄹ 수밖에 없다 "have no choice but" (see 23.11)

This form is used to highlight a situation where you have no other choice but to do the action denoted by the preceding verb.

진통제를 또 먹을 수밖에 없어요.
"I have no other choice but to take a painkiller again."
제 가족일이라 집에 곧 내려갈 수밖에 없어요.
"Since it is about a family matter, I have no other choice but go back home soon."
세일 가격이 너무 좋아서 살 수밖에 없었어요.
"Since the sale price was so good, I had no other choice but to buy it."
열쇠가 없어서 집 밖에서 기다릴 수밖에 없었어요.
"Since I had no key, I had no choice but to wait outside of my home."

50.9 ~(으)ㄹ래야 ~(으)ㄹ 수가 없다 "though I try . . . I can't"

This form consists of ~(으)ㄹ래야, which is a contracted form of ~으려고 하여도 (see 18.1.2 and 17.2.4), and ~(으)ㄹ 수가 없다 "cannot" (see 23.11). The pattern is used to highlight the fact that no matter how hard you intend to do something, you are unable to do so due to some unavoidable circumstance.

웃을래야 웃을 수가 없었어요.
"Though I tried to smile, I couldn't."
약이 너무 써서 마실래야 마실 수가 없어요.
"The medicine is so bitter, so I can't drink it even if I want to."
좋게 생각할래야 좋게 생각할 수가 없다.
"Though I try to think positively about it, I can't think positively."
상대편 팀이 너무 강해서 이길래야 이길 수가 없었어요.
"Since the opposing team was so strong, we could not win even if we tried."

50.10 N(이)야말로 "indeed" (see 7.2.3)

건강이야말로 무엇보다 소중해요.
"Health is indeed more precious than anything else."

Using exclamatory remarks

피라미드야말로 이집트를 대표하는 관광지예요.
"Pyramids are indeed the landmark that represents Egypt."
이 집이야말로 제가 원했던 집이에요.
"This house is the exact house that I wanted to have."

50.11 ~는/(으)ㄴ 데다가 "besides"

This form is constructed from the noun-modifying ending ~는/(으)ㄴ, the bound noun 데 "place," and the particle 에다가 "in/on/addition to" (see 6.1.2).

어제는 비가 오는 데다가 바람도 많이 불었어요.
"Besides being rainy, it was windy yesterday."
등록금도 비싼 데다가 기숙사비도 만만치 않아요.
"Besides tuition being expensive, the dorm expense is also formidable."
아직 아침도 못 먹은 데다가 어제 잠도 잘 못 잤어요.
"Besides not being able to have breakfast yet, I couldn't sleep well last night."
워낙 불경기인 데다가 취업난이 심해서 모두 힘들어해요.
"Everyone is having a hard time because the economic situation is extremely bad, and the unemployment rate is high."
경험을 쌓을 수 있는 데다가 약간의 보수도 받을 수 있어요.
"You can accumulate experiences and can receive a small amount of money."
업무량도 많은 데다가 출장도 잦아요.
"Besides the heavy workloads, business trips are frequent too."

50.12 Using exclamatory remarks

Besides the expressions in the previous section, one can use and add various exclamatory expressions (or interjections) to make his/her utterance or message more emphatic. These are some commonly used exclamatory expressions in informal conversational Korean.

Cheers! = 건배, 원샷, 위하여
Come on! = 자, 빨리, 자 빼지 말고
Damn it = 제기랄, 젠장
Gee = 에이
Give me a break = 흥
Go to hell = 엄병할, 얼어죽을, 빌어먹을
Gross = 징그러
Hooray = 아싸
How dare you = 아쭈
Hurrah! = 우와, 만세
Let's go! Good luck! = 아자아자 화이팅!
Look at you = 얼씨구
No way = 아, 참
Oh; oh by the way = 아참, 아차
Oh dear, oh boy = 이런, 어휴, 어이, 저런, 어떻해, 어머나, 에그
Oh my goodness = 아이고, 어머나, 아니, 어? 원 세상에, 맙소사, 내 원 참
Oh yeah? = 어쭈구리?
Oops = 아이고, 엄마야
Ouch = 아야, 아이쿠
Shhhh = 체, 치, 피
So little = 애개
Ta-dah = 짠

EMPHASIZING STRATEGIES

What a bastard/bitch = 망할 놈/년, 미친 놈/년, 못된 놈/년
What the heck = 까짓것
Whew = 아휴, 휴우
Wow, yeah = 야, 와, 어쩜, 아싸
Yikes = 으

51

Establishing a sequence

Here are some major expressions that are used both in speaking and writing to link or indicate the logical relationship between sentences/paragraphs.

Above all, first (e.g., 우선, 먼저, 일단)

우선 점심부터 먹어요.
"Let's eat lunch first."

According to (e.g., N에 의하면)

들리는 소문에 의하면 작년에 이미 이혼했대요.
"Rumor had it that she already divorced him last year."

Against one's will (e.g., 본의 아니게)

본의 아니게 걱정을 끼쳐 드렸네요. 죄송합니다.
"My apologies. I caused anxiety to you all against my will."

As I said (e.g., 앞서 말씀드렸듯이)

앞서 말씀드렸듯이 처음 듣는 이야기인데요.
"As I said earlier, it is the first time that I have heard about it."

As mentioned earlier (e.g., 앞서 언급/말씀드린 바와 같이)

앞 장에서도 특별히 앞서 언급했던 바와 같이 이것은 중요한 사실입니다.
"As I mentioned in the last chapter, this is an important fact."

As you know (e.g., 아시다시피)

아시다시피 원래 모든 운동을 좋아했었고 또 잘했었어요.
"As you know, he used to like all kinds of sports and also was good at them."

As you mentioned (e.g., 네 말따나)

네 말따나 여기 맛이 별로다.
"As you mentioned, it is not tasty here."

ESTABLISHING A SEQUENCE

At any rate, anyway (e.g., 아무튼, 어쨌든, 하여튼, 여하튼, 하여간)

아무튼 신경써 줘서 고마워요.
"Anyway thank you for your concern."

After all (e.g., 어차피, 어쨌든, 결국에는, 필경)

어차피 제가 해야 했을 일인데요.
"In any case, that's a job that I had to do."

By the way (e.g., 그런데, 그건 그렇고)

그런데 준기에 관한 소식 들었니?
"By the way, have you heard the news about Junki?"

Come to think of it (e.g., 그러고 보니까)

그러고 보니까 그의 얼굴이 좀 창백해 보였던 것 같아요.
"Come to think of it, his face seemed to look a little pale."

Consequently (e.g., 그 결과, 따라서)

오늘은 국경일이다. 따라서 우체국은 닫는다.
"Today is a national holiday. Consequently, the post office is closed."

First (e.g., 제일, 먼저, 첫째로)

먼저 계약서를 좀 봐도 되겠습니까?
"Could I take a look at the contract first?"

For example (e.g., 예를 들면, 예컨데)

예를 들면 한국어와 일본어에 비슷한 표현들이 있어요.
"For example, there are similar expressions in Korean and Japanese."

Frankly speaking (e.g., 솔직히 말해서, 툭 까놓고 말해서)

솔직히 말해서 저는 부모님 재산에 관심이 없어요.
"Franking speaking, I am not interested in my parents' wealth."

Furthermore (e.g., 게다가, 더구나, 더군다나, 더욱이, 또한, 뿐만 아니라)

값도 싸고 맛도 있고 게다가 서비스도 최고예요.
"The price is cheap, the taste is great, and furthermore, their service is also the best."

In all likelihood (e.g., 십중팔구)

십중팔구 또 지각할 거예요.
"In all likelihood, she will be late."

ESTABLISHING A SEQUENCE

In contrast (e.g., 그에 반해서, 대조적으로)
그에 반해서 강원도는 춥고 눈이 많이 와요.
"In contrast, in Kangwon Province, it is cold and snows a lot."

Indeed/really (e.g., 과연, 그야말로, 실로, 실제로, 아주, 정말로, 진짜로, 참으로)
실로 충격적인 뉴스였어요.
"It was indeed shocking news."

In fact (e.g., 실은, 사실, 사실상, 안 그래도, 그렇지 않아도)
여름 방학은 사살상 끝난 것이나 다름없었어요.
"As for summer vacation, in fact, it is the same as being over."

In my opinion (e.g., 내 생각에는, 제 의견으로는, 내가 보기엔)
제 의견으로는 더 이상 허비할 시간이 없습니다.
"In my opinion, there is no time to lose."

In sequence (e.g., 순서대로)
순서대로 책들을 정리해 놓으세요.
"Please arrange the books in sequence."

In short (e.g., 간단히 말하자면, 요약하면, 요컨대, 한마디로 말해서)
간단히 말하자면 제 전공을 바꾸고 싶어요.
"In short, I want to change my major."

In some respects (e.g., 어떤 면에서는, 어떻게 보면)
어떻게 보면 제 잘못이기도 해요.
"In some respects, it is also my fault."

In the end, finally (e.g., 결국, 마침내)
마침내 시험에 합격할 수 있었어요.
"Finally, I was able to pass the exam."

In other words (e.g., 다시 말해서, 즉)
즉 그의 생각이 옳았다.
"In other words, his ideas were right."

Lastly (e.g., 끝으로, 마지막으로)
끝으로 졸업 후 계획에 대해 여쭙고 싶습니다.
"Lastly, I'd like to ask you about your plans after graduation."

ESTABLISHING A SEQUENCE

Nevertheless (e.g., 그럼에도 불구하고, 그래도, 그렇다 하더라도)
   떠나지 말라고 했는데 그럼에도 불구하고 한국으로 가 버렸어요.
   "I told her not to leave, and nevertheless, she ended up leaving for Korea."

No wonder, as expected (e.g., 아니나 다를까, 역시, 그럼 그렇지)
   아니나 다를까 또 늦었어요.
   "Sure enough, he was late again."

On the one hand (e.g., 한편으로는)
   기쁘지만 한편으로는 좀 불안하기도 해요.
   "I am glad, but on the one hand, I am also a little nervous."

On the other hand (e.g., 반면에)
   어떤 사람들은 마늘을 좋아하지만, 반면에 다른 사람들은 아주 싫어한다.
   "Some people like garlic, while others really hate it."

Otherwise (e.g., 그렇지 않으면)
   이번에 꼭 이야기하세요. 그렇지 않으면 후회하게 될 거예요.
   "Please do tell her this time. If not, you will regret it."

Rather, on the contrary (e.g., 오히려, 도리어)
   오히려 제가 더 죄송합니다.
   "On the contrary, I am more sorry."

So-called (e.g., 소위)
   그는 소위 음악의 천재다.
   "He is a so-called musical genius."

So to speak (e.g., 말하자면)
   말하자면 그는 저에게 아버지같은 분이세요.
   "He is, so to speak, like a father figure to me."

Speaking of which (e.g., 말이 나온 김에, 말이 나왔으니까 말인데)
   말이 나왔으니까 말인데, 그 사람 완전 사기꾼이에요.
   "Speaking of which, he is a real swindler."

Therefore, so (e.g., 그러므로, 고로, 그러니까, 그래서)
   그러므로 이 프로젝트를 지원하기로 했습니다.
   "Therefore, we decided to support this project."
   저 오늘도 야근이에요. 그러니까 저녁 먼저 드세요.
   "I have to work overtime tonight too. So, please eat dinner first."

52

Experiences

This chapter looks into expressions that can be used to ask and talk about one's own past experiences.

52.1 Nouns and verbs that indicate one's experience

경험 "experience"

경험이 많으세요?
"Do you have a lot of experiences?"
20대에 이미 많은 실패를 경험했어요.
"He already experienced several failures in his 20s."
전에는 느끼지 못했던 성취감을 경험했습니다.
"I experienced a sense of accomplishment that I had never felt before."
형은 미국에서 살면서 겪은 경험을 들려줬다.
"My older brother shared his experience living in America."

체험 "experience"

아버지는 한국 전쟁을 체험한 세대세요.
"My father belongs to the generation that experienced the Korean War."
말로만 듣던 가난을 직접 체험했습니다.
"I experienced poverty that I had only heard about."
한국 전통 문화를 체험할 수 있는 좋은 기회입니다.
"It is a great opportunity for you to experience traditional Korean culture."
나에게 그 기숙사에서의 일주일은 잊지 못할 체험이었다.
"To me, the week at that dorm was an unforgettable experience."

경력 "career or work experience"

자동차 경비사로 오랜 경력이 있습니다.
"He has a long career of experience as an auto mechanic."
트럭 운전사로 경력이 짧습니다.
"My work experience as a truck driver is short."
현재 회계사로서의 경력을 쌓고 있습니다.
"Currently, I am accumulating work experience as an accountant."
프로 골퍼의 경력을 가진 사람이에요.
"She is a person with work experience as a professional golfer."

EXPERIENCES

겪다 "to experience/undergo"

이런 더위는 처음 겪어 봐요.
"I've never experienced hot weather like this."
겪어 보니 좋은 사람이었어요.
"On further acquaintance, she turned out to be a good person."
모든 학생들이 이 학교에 다니면서 한 번씩 겪는 문제예요.
"It is a problem every student in our school experiences during his/her stay here."
이별을 겪어 보지 않은 사람은 그 외로움을 몰라요.
"Those who never experienced separation don't know the depth of that loneliness."

52.2 ~(으)ㄴ 적/일이 있다/없다 "have/don't have an experience of ~ing" (see 23.13)

A: IT 회사에서 일한 적이 있으십니까?
   "Do you have experience working at an IT company?"
B: 네. 작년 여름에 3개월 동안 인턴으로 일했었습니다.
   "Yes. I worked as an intern for three months last summer."

서울에 간 적이 있어요.
"I have been to Seoul."
보스톤에 한 번도 간 적 없어요.
"I have never been to Boston even once."
북경을 여행한 적이 있으세요?
"Do you have an experience of traveling to Beijing?"

52.3 ~어/아 보다 "try (doing something)" (see 13.6)

A: 혹시 나이아가라 폭포에 가 보셨나요?
   "By any chance, have you been to Niagara Falls?"
B: 아니오. 아직 못 가 봤는데요.
   "No. I have not been able to go there yet."

전에 인턴으로 일해 봤어요.
"I tried working as an intern before."
그 식당 음식을 드셔 보셨어요?
"Have you tried that restaurant's food?"
한 번 써 봤는데 저는 별로던데요.
"I tried using it once, but I did not like it much."

52.4 ~어/아 본 적/일이 있다/없다 "have/don't have an experience of trying"

This form is the combination of ~어/아 보다 and ~(으)ㄴ 적/일이 있다.

A: 제주도에 가 보신 적이 있으세요?
   "Have you tried visiting Jeju Island?"
B: 아니요, 아직이요.
   "No, not yet."

담배를 피워 본 적이 있습니까?
"Have you ever tried smoking?"
한국에서 유학할 때 전통주를 마셔 본 적이 있었어요.
"While I studied abroad in Korea, I tried drinking traditional alcohol."

~어/아 본 적/일이 있다/없다 "have/don't have an experience of trying"

누구를 가르쳐 본 적이 없어요.
"I have never tried teaching anyone before."
대학 다닐 때 A를 받아 본 일이 없어요.
"I have never received an 'A' while attending college."
미국 사람이지만 샌프란시스코에 가 본 적이 없어요.
"Although he is American, he has never been to San Francisco."

53

Greetings and leave taking

This chapter presents numerous formulaic expressions for greetings and leave taking.

53.1 Greetings

53.1.1 Greetings as phatic expressions

In general, greetings are common phrases or expressions that are used as whole units rather than individual words. In addition, frequently, they are phatic questions, serving as attention-getting or ice-breaking expressions.

안녕하세요?
"How are you?"
건강하시지요?
"You are well, right?"
요즈음 어떻게 지내세요?
"How have you been lately?"

The topics of Korean greetings often concern not only the listener's well-being but also other personal issues, such as his/her business, children, family, and so on. Since these greetings are phatic expressions, when greeted with these questions, one does not have to answer the questions but rather reply with similar greetings or vague responses:

A: 사업은 잘되시구요?
"Is your work/business doing well?"
B: 네, 덕분예요. 선생님도 별일 없으셨지요?
"Yes, thanks to you. You have been well too, right?"

A: 아이들은 잘 크지요?
"Are your kids growing well?"
B: 네, 덕분에 잘 있습니다.
"Yes, they are thanks to you."

A: 좋은 아침입니다.
"Good morning."
B: 네, 안녕히 주무셨어요?
"Yes, did you sleep well?"

A: 어디 가세요?
"Are you going somewhere?"
B: 네, 어디 가요. 이따가 사무실에서 뵐게요.
"Yes, I am going somewhere. I will see you back in the office later."

A: 어디 다녀오세요?
"Are you coming back from somewhere?"
B: 네, 뭐 살 게 좀 있어서요. 그런데 식사하셨어요?
"Yes, because I had something to buy. By the way, did you eat?"

53.1.2 When you meet someone for the first time

처음 뵙겠습니다.
"Nice to meet you."
저는 미국 뉴욕 올바니에서 온 앤드류 변이라고 합니다.
"I am Andrew Byon from Albany, NY, USA."
만나서 반갑습니다.
"It's nice meeting you."
앞으로 잘 부탁드립니다.
"I request your guidance from now on."

53.1.3 When you greet someone who you have not seen for a long time

A: 정말 오래간만이네요. 그 동안 안녕하셨어요?
"It has been such a long time. How have you been?"
B: 글쎄 말이에요. 이게 얼마만이지요? 별일 없으셨지요?
"I know. How long has it been? Everything has been fine?"
A: 그 동안 더 젊어지셔서 못 알아보겠네요.
"You look so much younger that I couldn't recognize you."
B: 별말씀을요. 선생님도 하나도 안 변하셨어요.
"Not at all. You also have not aged/changed at all."

53.1.4 When you enter unfamiliar places

실례합니다. 아무도 안 계세요?
"Excuse me. Is anybody here/inside?"
저 누구 안 계십니까? 실례하겠습니다.
"Is no one inside? Excuse me."

53.1.5 When you return from your work, school, or an outing

A: 학교 다녀왔습니다.
"I am back from school."
B: 어 왔어? 어서 들어와라.
"You came? Come inside."

A: 여보, 나 왔어.
"Honey, I am home."
B: 오늘은 좀 늦었네요. 저녁은요?
"You are a bit late today. What about dinner?"

A: 저 왔어요.
"I am here/home."
B: 이제 오세요?
"You are here now?"

53.2 Leave taking

53.2.1 When you end a conversation

오늘은 그만 하자. 나 간다.
"Let's stop here. I am going."
미안한데, 그럼, 오늘은 여기까지.
"Sorry, but then, this is it for today."

GREETINGS AND LEAVE TAKING 53.2

죄송하지만, 그럼, 이제 일어나야겠네요 (가봐야겠습니다).
"I am sorry, but well . . . I should get going now."
오늘은 이만 끝냅시다.
"Let's call it a day."
이상입니다. 들어 주셔서 감사합니다.
"This concludes my speech. Thank you for listening."
말씀 도중에 죄송한데요. 내일 회사에 일찍 출근해야 해서 먼저 일어나 봐야 할 것 같습니다.
"I am sorry to interrupt. But I think that I will have to get going because I have to get to work early tomorrow."

53.2.2 When you leave for work/school

A: 아빠 회사 갔다 올게. 엄마 말 잘 듣고.
   "Dad is going to work. Listen to your mom well."
B: 네. 안녕히 다녀오세요.
   "Bye. Have a good day."

A: 학교 다녀오겠습니다.
   "Bye. I am going to school."
B: 그래, 차 조심하고 잘 갔다 와.
   "OK, bye. Be careful of cars and have a good day."

53.2.3 When you leave the office/work

A: 수고하셨습니다. 이만 먼저 들어가 보겠습니다.
   "Thank you for your work. I should get going first."
B: 네. 들어가세요. 내일 뵐게요.
   "Good bye. See you tomorrow."

A: 그럼, 먼저 퇴근하겠습니다.
   "Then, I am leaving now."
B: 네, 수고하셨습니다. 그럼, 조심해서 들어가세요.
   "Yes, good job. Take care, then."

53.2.4 When you say good-bye

안녕히 가세요.
"Good bye."
네 들어가세요.
"Good bye. Take care."
이렇게 만나서 반가웠어요.
"It was nice meeting/talking to you."
내일 뵙겠습니다.
"See you tomorrow."
시간을 너무 많이 빼앗었네요. 죄송해요.
"Sorry for taking your time."
다음에 또 보자.
"See you next time."
내일 학교에서 보자구.
"See you at school tomorrow."
수고하세요.
"See you later."

Leave taking   **53.2**

A: 오늘 즐거웠습니다. 저 그럼 이만 가 봐야 할 것 같은데요.
   "I had such a great time today. Well, I should get going now."
B: 그래 그럼, 운전 조심하고 도착하면 전화하고.
   "Drive safely, and give me a call when you get there."

A: 아니, 시간이 벌써 이렇게 되었네요. 저는 이만 다른 약속이 있어서요.
   "Wow, it's already this late. I have another appointment so . . ."
B: 아 예, 그러세요. 아쉽지만, 그럼 다음에 또 뵈어요.
   "Ah, Okay. I am sorry, but let's meet again next time."

A: 집에 밀린 일들이 좀 있어서요 . . . 죄송해요.
   "I have things to do at home, so. . . . Excuse me."
B: 뭘요. 괜찮아요. 안 나갈게요. 살펴 가세요.
   "It's okay. Let me just see you off here. Goodbye."

A: 그럼, 우리 언제 다 같이 한 번 모이자.
   "Okay, then, let's get together sometime."
B: 그래, 들어가고. 연락해.
   "Okay, take care, and keep in touch."

A: 나 갈게. 또 보자. 푹 쉬고.
   "Bye, I have to go. See you again. Take a good rest."
B: 그래, 전화하고, 잘 가.
   "Okay, don't forget to give me a call. Bye."

54

Hypothetical situations

In English, one can indicate a hypothetical situation (i.e., involving or based on a supposed/suggested idea) by using expressions such as "on a supposition," "assuming that," "based on the assumption that," and so forth. To express a hypothetical situation in Korean, you can use the following expressions.

54.1 ~는/ㄴ다면 "if"

This form is built on the plain speech level ending ~는/ㄴ다 (see 27.2.4) and the conjunctive ~(으)면 "if" (see 18.2.1).

> A: 타이머신이 있다면 언제로 가고 싶으세요?
> "If you have a time machine, when do you wish to go back?"
> B: 제 20대로 돌아가고 싶어요.
> "I wish to go back to my 20s."

만약 부잣집 아들로 태어났다면 어땠을까요?
"I wonder what it would be like if he were born as the son of a rich household?"
시험만 합격한다면 주저하지 않고 그녀에게 프로포즈할 거야.
"Only if I pass the bar exam, will I propose to her without hesitation."
내가 만약 돈이 많다면 부모님께 집을 사 드릴수 있을 텐데.
"If I have a lot of money, I suppose that I would be able to buy a house for my parents."
제가 복권에 당첨된다면 세계 일주를 떠날 거예요.
"If I ever win a lottery, I will leave for a tour around the world."
만약 이 회사에 취직하게 된다면 일단 마케팅 부서에서 일하고 싶습니다.
"If I end up working for this company, I want to work in the marketing department first."
10년 전으로 돌아갈 수 있다면 법을 공부하고 싶어요.
"If I can go back to ten years ago, I want to study law."
내일 지구가 멸망한다면 오늘 하루 뭘 꼭 하고 싶으세요?
"If the earth is destroyed tomorrow, what do you really want to do today?"

54.2 ~는/ㄴ다고 치다/가정하다/하다 "supposedly..."

This form consists of the indirect quotation marker ~는/ㄴ다고 (see 31.4) and the verb 치다/가정하다/하다 "suppose."

> A: 어제는 아파서 그랬다고 치고 오늘은 또 왜 늦은 거예요?
> "Suppose that you were late yesterday because you were sick, but why were you late again today?"
> B: 죄송합니다. 다시는 늦지 않겠습니다.
> "I am sorry. I will not be late again."

그냥 고장났다고 치고 새로 하나 사는 게 어때요?
"Just assuming that it is broken, how about buying a new one?"
제가 손님이라고 가정하고 설명해 보세요.
"Assuming that I am your customer, please explain it to me."
결혼을 승낙해 주신다고 쳐도 결혼 비용은 어떻게 마련할 건데요?
"Even if we assume that they will approve of your wedding, how will you come up with money for the wedding?"
싸게 준다고 쳐도 살 돈이 없어요.
"Although we suppose that they would give it to us at a cheap price, we do not have enough money to buy it."

54.3 ~는/ㄴ다고 해서 "saying we suppose"

This form consists of ~는/ㄴ다고 치다/가정하다/하다 and the conjunctive ~어/아서 "so" (see 16.2.1).

A: 우등생인데 무슨 걱정이 있겠어요?
"He is a top student, so what kind of worries would he have?"
B: 공부를 잘한다고 해서 고민이 없는 것은 아니에요.
"Saying we suppose that he is smart, it is not that he does not have worries."

경기가 안 좋다고 해서 모두가 힘든 것은 아니에요.
"Even if we suppose that the economy is bad, it is not difficult for everyone."
부자라고 해서 모두 행복하지는 않아요.
"However rich one may be, not everyone is happy."
영어를 잘한다고 해서 다 금방 취직할 수 있지는 않지요.
"However fluent one may be in English, it is not that everyone can get employment soon."

54.4 ~더라도 "even if" (see 17.2.6)

A: 좀 불편하시더라도 이해해 주세요.
"However inconvenient it may be, I ask for your understanding."
B: 불편하기는요. 저희는 괜찮으니까 신경쓰지 마세요.
"What do you mean inconvenient? We are fine, so please don't worry."
A: 지금 제일 비쌀 텐데 세일할 때까지 기다리시지요?
"It may be too expensive so why don't you wait until the sale begins?"
B: 비싸다고 하더라도 살 거예요.
"However expensive it may be, I will buy it."

시험에 떨어지더라도 실망하지 마세요.
"Even if you fail the exam, don't be disappointed."
손해 보는 일이 있더라도 어떻게든 도와 주실 거예요.
"Even if he loses money, he will help you in anyway."
어떤 결정을 내리시더라도 따르겠습니다.
"No matter what kind of decision you may make, we will follow."
실패하더라도 낙심하지 않고 끝까지 최선을 다합시다.
"Even if we fail, let's not be despaired, and do our best to the end."
돈이 아무리 좋다고 하더라도 건강을 잃으면 다 잃는 거예요.
"No matter how favorable one finds money, if one loses health, he/she loses everything."
미래가 불투명하다고 하더라도 인생은 살 만한 것입니다.
"However uncertain our future is, life is worth living."
의학이 아무리 발전한다고 하더라도 인간은 질병에서 절대로 자유스러워질 수 없을 것이다.
"No matter how far medicine advances, human beings can never be free from illness."

HYPOTHETICAL SITUATIONS

54.5 ~(으)ㄹ 뻔하다 "almost" (see 23.9)

A: 제발 일찍 좀 나오세요. 하마터면 버스를 놓칠 뻔했잖아요.
"Please come out early. We almost missed the bus, you see."
B: 죄송합니다. 번번히 저 때문에.
"I am sorry. Every time because of me."

길이 너무 미끄러워서 넘어질 뻔했어요.
"The road was so slippery that I almost fell."
잃어 버릴 뻔했어요.
"I nearly lost it."
식당에 지갑을 두고 나갈 뻔했네요.
"I almost left the restaurant, leaving my wallet there."
기차를 놓칠 뻔했어요.
"I almost missed the train."

54.6 ~(으)ㄹ지라도 "even if . . . may" (see 17.2.10)

This form is built on the indirect question form ~(으)ㄹ지 and the conjunctive ~어도/아도 (see 17.2.4).

A: 맛이 좀 없을지라도 맛있게 드세요.
"Though it may not be tasty, please enjoy yourself."
B: 별말씀을요. 아주 맛있겠는데요.
"What do you mean? It must be really delicious."

어려움이 닥칠지라도 희망을 잃지 맙시다.
"Even if we encounter hardships, let's not lose hope."
비록 나이는 어릴지라도 예의가 바르고 똑똑해요.
"Though he may be young in age, he is courteous and smart."
좀 비쌀지라도 꼭 사도록 하세요.
"Though it may be expensive, make sure you buy them."
아무리 친한 사이일지라도 돈 계산은 확실히 해야 한다.
"Though they may be close friends, they should be clear on money matters."

54.7 ~(으)ㄹ지언정 "even though . . . may" (see 17.2.11)

A: 태워 준다는데 정말 같이 안 갈 거예요?
"He is saying that he will give you a ride; you really will not go with him?"
B: 집까지 걸어갈지언정 같이 타고 싶지 않아요.
"Even though I may have to walk home, I don't want to ride with him."

취업을 포기할지언정 학업을 포기하지 않겠다.
"Even if I may have to give up employment, I will not give up my studies."
부모님께서 반대하실지언정 제 뜻을 굽히지 않을 거예요.
"Even if my parents may not approve, I will not change my mind."
차라리 굶을지언정 누구한테 달라고 하지 않을 거예요.
"Even if I may have to starve, I will not ask anyone for help."
그가 나이는 비록 어렸을지언정 생각과 행동은 어른스러웠습니다.
"Even though he was young, his thoughts and actions seemed mature."
모두에게 비난을 받을지언정 절대로 사과하지 않을 거예요.
"Even if I will receive criticism from everyone, I will never apologize."

54.8 ~(으)ㄹ망정 "even if . . . may" (see 17.2.12)

A: 많은 회사들이 요즈음 불경기로 힘들다고 하던데 경호 씨 회사는 괜찮아요?
"I heard many companies face difficulties lately due to the recession; is your company okay, Kyungho?"
B: 저희 회사가 규모는 <u>작을망정</u> 재정 상태는 견실합니다.
"Even if the size of our company may be small, its financial condition is solid."

이대로 <u>죽을망정</u> 절대로 다시 병원으로 돌아가고 싶지 않아요.
"Even if I may die like this, I don't want to go back to hospital again."
<u>굶어 죽을망정</u> 구걸하며 살고 싶지 않아요.
"Even if I may starve to death, I don't want to live begging."
좀 <u>손해를 볼망정</u> 부정한 방법으로 돈을 벌고 싶지는 않습니다.
"Even if I may lose money, I don't wish to make money by unlawful means."
서로 성격은 <u>다를망정</u> 서로 노력하며 살아야지요.
"Even if their personalities may differ, they should make best effort to live."
작고 싼 집으로 <u>이사를 갈망정</u> 더 이상 빚을 지고 싶지 않아요.
"Even if I may have to move to a smaller and cheaper house, I don't want to have debt anymore."

54.9 ~기 망정이지 "it was good that . . . otherwise . . ."

This form is made of the nominalizing ending ~기, the bound noun 망정 "fortunate event," the copula 이다, and the sentence ending ~지.

A: 오시는 길에 타이어가 펑크 났다면서요? 괜찮으셨어요?
"I heard that you had a flat tire on your way here. Were you okay?"
B: <u>스페어타이어가 있었기에 망정이지</u> 회의에 늦을 뻔했습니다.
"It was good that I had a spare tire; otherwise, I would have been late for the meeting."

USB에 <u>저장해 놨기에 망정이지</u> 다 잃어버릴 뻔했어요.
"It was good that I saved it to my USB; otherwise, I would have lost everything."
지갑에 카드가 <u>있었기에 망정이지</u> 망신당할 뻔했어요.
"It was good that the card was in my wallet; otherwise, I would have been embarrassed."
날씨가 <u>따뜻했기에 망정이지</u> 큰 일 날 뻔했어요.
"It was good that it was warm today; otherwise, we would have run into big trouble."

54.10 ~는/(으)ㄴ 셈치다 "suppose"

This form is made of the noun-modifying ending ~(는)ㄴ, the bound noun 셈 "thinking, plan" (1.3), and the verb 치다 "suppose."

A: 좀 비싼 것 같은데 어떻게 할까요?
"It seems to be a bit expensive, so what should I do?"
B: 좀 <u>손해보는 셈치고</u> 그냥 구입하는 게 어때요?
"On the supposition that you lose some money, why don't you just buy it?"

그냥 비싼 커피 <u>마신 셈칩시다</u>.
"Let's just assume that we drank expensive coffee."
<u>안 들은 셈칠 테니까</u> 다시는 그런 부탁하지 마세요.
"I will suppose that I did not hear what you said, so don't ask me for that kind of favor again."
그냥 <u>운동하는 셈치고</u> 걸어갔다 오려구요.
"On the supposition that I will exercise, I will take a walk there."

54.11 ~었/았더라면 "if/when (something had been the case)" (coo 18.2.3)

A: 모두 기다렸는데 안 오셨어요?
"Everyone waited for you; why didn't you come?"
B: 시험만 없었더라면 갈 수 있었을 텐데 어쨌든 죄송합니다.
"Only if I didn't have an exam, I could have gone there. Anyway, my apologies."

미리 예약했더라면 볼 수 있었을 거예요.
"If you would have made a reservation in advance, you would be able to see them."
늦게 자지 않았더라면 좀 더 일찍 일어날 수 있었을 거예요.
"If I did not go to bed late, I would have been able to get up earlier."
아프지 않았더라면 저도 갈 수 있었을 거예요.
"If I was not sick, I would also have been able to go there."

54.12 ~(으)나 . . . ~(으)나 "whether . . . or" (see 17.2.2)

The meaning of the ~(으)나 . . . ~(으)나 pattern is to list selections of action or states that have opposite meanings. The pattern indicates that the content of the main clause happens regardless of the selections indicated by the pattern. Consider the following example:

즐거우나 슬프나 사랑하겠습니다.
"I will love her whether I am happy or sad."

Notice that ~(으)나 lists two states that have opposite meanings (i.e., happy and sad), whereas the main clause occurs regardless of the activities of the previous clauses. Here are more examples:

앉으나 서나 그분만을 생각하십시오.
"Whether you sit or stand, think only of him."
약을 먹으나 마나 별로 차도가 없습니다.
"Whether she takes the medicine or not, there is not much improvement."
병원에 가나 마나 소용없을 거예요.
"Whether you go to hospital or not, it will be useless."

55

Initiating and maintaining conversations

This chapter discusses expressions associated with initiating and maintaining conversations, such as introducing topics, switching topics, and using various listener responses.

55.1 Initiating a conversation

The following are some typical phrases you can use when initiating a conversation:

말씀 좀 묻겠습니다?
"May I ask you a question?"
저 드릴 말씀이 있는데요?
"May I have a word with you?"
지금 10분 정도 시간 괜찮으세요? (있으세요?)
"Do you have about ten minutes now?"
지금 바쁘신가요?
"Are you busy now?"
좀 여쭈어 볼 게 있는데요.
"I have something to ask you."

55.2 Introducing topics

55.2.1 The particle 은/는 "as for" (see 7.2.1)

You can make any element of the sentence the topic of the conversation by adding the topic particle 은/는 to it and placing it in the beginning of the sentence, except the verb/adjective that appears at the end of the sentence. For example, consider the following sentences:

존은 오전 9시에 메리하고 도서관에서 한국어를 공부해요.
"As for John, he studies Korean with Mary at the library at 9:00 a.m."
오전 9시에는 존이 메리하고 도서관에서 한국어를 공부해요.
"At 9:00 a.m., John studies Korean with Mary at the library."
메리하고는 존이 오전 9시에 도서관에서 한국어를 공부해요.
"With Mary, John studies Korean at the library at 9:00 a.m."
도서관에서는 존이 오전 9시에 메리하고 한국어를 공부해요.
"At the library, John studies Korean with Mary at 9:00 a.m."

Note that as a Subject-Object-Verb (SOV) language, in Korean the most important sentential elements (i.e., predicates) tend to appear at the end of the sentence. The less important or most known information is, the more toward the beginning of the sentence it tends to appear. Notice in the previous examples that the 은/는-marked elements (topics) appear in the beginning of the

INITIATING AND MAINTAINING CONVERSATIONS

sentence. This means that the topic of the sentence in Korean tends to be a contextually understood element, which can be easily omitted during conversation.

This contrasts with the subject marked by the particle 이/가 (see 5.3). The subject particle 이/가 is used to mark a subject (which happens to be new information or has not been mentioned previously in the context). For instance, this explains why most interrogative words, such as 누구 "who," 무엇 "what," 언제 "when," and 어느 "which," are used with the particle 이/가, as in, 누구(가) and 무엇이, instead of with the topic particle 은/는.

> 어느 식당 음식은 맛있어요?
> "Which restaurant's food is delicious?" (X)
> 어느 식당 음식이 맛있어요?
> "Which restaurant's food is delicious?" (O)
> 누구는 미국 사람이에요?
> "Who is an American?" (X)
> 누가 미국 사람이에요?
> "Who is an American?" (O)

55.2.2 N에 관해서는 "regarding"

> 골프에 관해서는 전혀 아는 게 없습니다.
> "Regarding golf, I know absolutely nothing about it."
> 당신 친구들은 유난히 남의 일에 관해서 말하기를 좋아하는 것 같아요.
> "It seems that your friends particularly like talking about other people's business."
> 그 안건에 관해서는 여러 전문가들의 의견이 분분합니다.
> "Regarding that issue, the opinions of several experts are different."

55.2.3 N에 대해서 "about"

> 골프의 역사에 대해서 알고 싶습니다.
> "I would like to know about the history of golf."
> 한국의 민속놀이에 대해서 궁금합니다.
> "I am curious about Korean traditional folk games."
> 호텔 수영장에 대해서 여쭈어 볼 것이 있는데요.
> "I have something to ask about the hotel swimming pool."

55.3 Switching topics

You can use the topic particle 은/는 to switch the topic from one thing to another. For instance, consider the following conversations:

> A: 실례합니다. 이 바지 얼마예요?
>   "Excuse me, how much are these pants?"
> B: 네, 20,000원입니다.
>   "Yes, these are 20,000 won."
> A: 그럼, 이 치마는 얼마예요?
>   "Then, as for this skirt, how much is it?"
> B: 네, 32,000원입니다.
>   "Yes, it is 32,000 won."
> A: 이 청바지는요?
>   "How about these jeans?"

Let's assume that speaker A is a customer and speaker B is a saleswoman in the preceding conversation. Notice that speaker A uses the topic particle 은/는 when she changes the topic from one item to another (e.g., asking for the price of a skirt and then jeans).

55.4 Listener responses

Here are some common listener responses.

55.4.1 Paying attention

네 (응, 어)
"Yes."
아, 그래요/그러세요?
"Ah, is that so/right?"
아 그렇지요/그렇네요.
"Yes, that's right."
음
"um"

You can indicate that you are fully engaged in conversation by repeating the entire phrase or part of the phrase or word by a previous speaker:

    A: 다음 주 토요일 오후에 누나 결혼식이 있어서요.
           "My older sister's wedding is on Saturday next week, so . . ."
    B: 아, 그래요? 다음 주 토요일.
           "Oh, is that so? Saturday next week."

55.4.2 Asking for confirmation

누구/어디/언제/몇 시?
"Who/where/when/what time?"
저 혹시 변상필 씨 아니세요?
"Uh, by any chance, aren't you Mr. Sangpil Byon?"
실례지만 동아시아학과 사무실 맞지요?
"Excuse me, but this is the department office of East Asian studies, right?"
한국 역사에 관심이 많다고 들었는데요. 정말이에요?
"I heard that you are really interested in Korean history. Is that right?"
내일 2시에 도착할 거라고 하던데 맞지요?
"They said that he would arrive at two tomorrow, but is that right?"

55.4.3 Showing surprise

You can use exclamatory remarks, such as 와 "wow" and 정말 "really?" as well.

    A: 우리 동갑이거든.
           "We are the same age, you know?"
    B: 와, 정말? 너무 어려 보여서 내가 언니인 줄 알았네.
           "Wow, really? You look so young so I thought I was older."

55.4.4 Requesting a repetition

죄송하지만, 다시 한 번 말씀해 주시겠어요?
"I am sorry but could you say it again please?"
뭐라 하셨나요?
"What did you say?"
뭐라고?
"What?"

INITIATING AND MAINTAINING CONVERSATIONS 55.4

55.4.5 Making corrections

When negating or making corrections, you can use N이/가 아니고/아니라 or ~(으)ㄴ/는/(으)ㄹ 게 아니라, as shown in the following examples:

    A: 저녁 6시 예약이라고 했지요?
        "You said that the dinner reservation is at 6 p.m., right?"
    B:: 아, <u>6시가 아니고</u> 6시 반이네요. 죄송해요.
        "Oh, it is not 6 but 6:30. My apologies."

이 그림들은 <u>파는 게 아니래요</u>.
"She says that these paintings are not for sale."
수업이 <u>끝난 게 아니라</u> 쉬는 시간이에요.
"The class has not ended yet, but it is break time."
나오미 씨는 <u>일본 사람이 아니라</u> 미국 사람이래요.
"Naomi is not Japanese but an American."

55.4.6 Acknowledging what the other says

네, 맞습니다.
"Yes, that's right."
맞아요. 저도 그렇게 생각해요.
"Right, I also think so."
그런 면도 없지는 않겠네요.
"Perhaps, it may be the case."
아무래도 그렇겠네요.
"Somehow yes, it makes sense."

56

Intentions and plans

This chapter covers various words, phrases, and expressions in Korean that indicate one's intentions and plans.

56.1 ~겠어요 "will" (see 12.1.4)

A: 카드로 <u>결제하시겠어요</u>?
"Will you pay by a credit card?"
B: 아니요. 현금으로 내겠습니다.
"No. I will pay by cash."

금년에는 꼭 담배를 <u>끊겠습니다</u>.
"I will quit smoking by all means this year."
그럼, <u>주문 하시겠어요</u>?
"Then, would you like to order?"
복도 쪽 아니면 창가 쪽 어느 쪽 자리로 <u>하시겠습니까</u>?
"Aisle or window, which side would you like to sit?"

56.2 ~어야겠어요 "I think that I need to . . ."

This expression is a contracted form of ~어/아야 하겠어요, which is built on ~어/아야 하다 "must" (see 15.9), the suffix ~겠 (see 12.1.4), and the polite speech level ending ~어요 (see 27.2.2).

A: 아직도 좀 안 좋으신가 봐요.
"You still look not well."
B: 두통이 너무 심해서요. 병원에 <u>가 봐야겠어요</u>.
"My headache is really bad. I think that I need to go to hospital."

회사 근처로 아파트를 <u>알아봐야겠어요</u>.
"I think that I need to find an apartment near my company."
컴퓨터가 너무 오래돼서 이번에 새 거로 <u>사야겠어요</u>.
"My computer is fairly old, so I think that I need to buy a new one this time."
오늘 아무것도 아직 못 먹었는데 뭐 좀 <u>먹어야겠어요</u>.
"I was unable to eat anything today, so I think that I need to eat something."
오늘 저녁에 손님이 오시는데 집 <u>청소를 해야겠어요</u>.
"We have visitors tonight, so I think that I need to clean up the house."
아버지가 포도주를 좋아하셔서 좀 <u>사 놔야겠어요</u>.
"My father likes red wines, so I think that I need to buy some in advance."

INTENTIONS AND PLANS

56.3 ~(으)ㄹ 거예요 "will" (see 12.1.1)

A: 이번 여름 방학에는 뭐 하실 거예요?
"What are you going to do this summer break?"
B: 부모님 가게에서 일하면서 돈 좀 모으려구요.
"I am thinking of saving some money while working at my parents' store."

오늘 밤에 만날 거예요.
"I will meet her tonight."
내년에는 꼭 한국에 갈 거예요.
"I will go to Korea next year by all means."
오늘은 먹고 싶은 만큼 먹을 거예요.
"For today, I will eat as much as I wish to eat."

56.4 ~(으)ㄹ게요 "will (promise)" (see 12.1.3)

A: 선약이 있어서 먼저 갈게요.
"I will excuse myself first because I have a previous engagement."
B: 네, 들어가세요. 그럼, 내일 회사에서 뵈어요.
"Sure, return safely. See you then at the office tomorrow."

퇴근할 때 전화할게요.
"I will call you when leaving the office."
커피는 제가 사 드릴게요.
"I will buy you coffee."
이따가 사무실로 갖다 드릴게요.
"I will bring it over to your office later."

56.5 ~(으)ㄹ까 해요 "I am thinking of ~ing" (see 15.6)

A: 집에서 회사까지 멀지요?
"Your house is far from the company, right?"
B: 네. 그래서 가까운 곳으로 이사할까 해요.
"Yes. So I am thinking of moving to a place near the company."

주말에는 친구들하고 삼겹살이나 구워먹을까 해요.
"I am thinking of eating grilled pork belly or something with friends this weekend."
여행 중에 운전할 수 있도록 국제면허를 따 볼까 해요.
"I am thinking of getting an international license so that I can drive during my travels."
유럽은 한 번도 안 가 봤는데 결혼 기념일에 유럽을 여행할까 해요.
"I have never been to Europe, so I am thinking of traveling Europe for our wedding anniversary."

56.6 ~(으)ㄹ래요 "will (intend)" (see 12.1.2)

A: 저녁은 어디 가서 먹을래요?
"Where would you like to go for dinner?"
B: 글쎄요, 비도 오는데 국수집 어때요?
"Well, it is raining, so how about a noodle shop?"

그냥 택시 타고 갈래요.
"I will just take a cab."
저는 앞에 앉을래요.
"I will sit in the front."

호텔은 시설보다는 위치가 좋은 곳으로 <u>예약할래요</u>.
"As for the hotel, I will make a reservation for a hotel in a good location rather than the one with nice facilities."

56.7 ~어/아야지 "will, should"

This expression is a contracted form of ~어/아야 하지요, which is the combination of ~어/아야 하다 "must" (see 15.9) and the sentence ending ~지요 (see 26.6). This form is used to indicate one's intention or a sense of necessity depending on context (see 61.1.3).

A: 이번에는 집에 내려가실 거예요?
"Do you plan to visit your parents this time?"
B: 아버님 생신인데 당연히 <u>가야지요</u>.
"It's my father's birthday, so I should certainly go."

오늘은 실컷 <u>먹어야지</u>.
"I will stuff myself with food."
다음부터는 좀 더 조심히 <u>운전해야지</u>.
"I will drive more carefully starting from next time."
이번에는 꼭 살을 <u>빼야지</u>.
"I will lose some weight this time by all means."
그 영화 재미있다던데 나도 곧 <u>봐야지</u>.
"I heard that the movie was interesting, so I am also going to watch it soon."

56.8 ~(으)ㄹ 겸 ... ~(으)ㄹ 겸 "to do A and to do B" (see 22.3)

A: 어제 백화점에는 뭐 사러 가셨나요?
"Did you go to the department store to buy something?"
B: 아니요, 그냥 뭐 좀 <u>먹을 겸 구경도 할 겸</u> 갔어요.
"No, I went to the department store to eat something and also to look around."

공원에서 <u>운동도 할 겸 바람도 쐴 겸</u> 나왔어요.
"I came to the park to exercise and also to enjoy a cool breeze."
한국에는 친구도 <u>사귈 겸</u> 한국말도 <u>공부할 겸</u> 해서 왔어요.
"I came to Korea to make some friends and also to study Korean."
여기서 경험도 <u>쌓을 겸</u> 돈도 <u>벌 겸</u> 해서 일하기로 했습니다.
"I decided to work here to get experience and to earn money."
커피도 <u>마실 겸</u> 공부도 <u>할 겸</u> 커피숍에 왔어요.
"I came to the coffee shop to drink coffee and to study."

56.9 ~(으)려다가 "intending to" (see 18.1.3)

A: 어떻게 해서 다치셨어요?
"How did you hurt yourself?"
B: 요가를 배워 <u>보려다가</u> 허리를 삐걱했네요.
"While trying to learn yoga, but I hurt my back."

커피를 가지고 <u>가려다가</u> 쏟았어요.
"I tried to take coffee with me but spilled it."
방을 <u>청소하려다가</u> 피곤해서 그만두었다.
"While trying to clean up the room, I stopped because I was tired."
도서관에 공부하러 <u>가려다가</u> 피곤해서 그냥 집에 왔어요.
"On my way to the library to study, I just came home because I felt tired."

INTENTIONS AND PLANS

56.10 ~(으)리라 "will"

~(으)리라 is a sentence ending (primarily used by adults) that indicates one's strong intention or resolution. This ending is primarily used when the speaker talks to himself/herself, wants to draw the listener's attention to information that is noteworthy or provoking, or writes something (e.g., personal note, journals, and so forth).

금년에는 꼭 취직하고 결혼도 하리라.
"This year, I will get a job and get married by all means."
이번 여름에는 바쁘더라도 가족 여행을 떠나리라.
"This summer, I will have a family trip no matter how busy we are."
인정받는 배우로 성장하리라.
"I am determined to grow as a recognized actor."
오늘은 꼭 사랑한다고 고백하리라.
"Today, I will definitely confess to her that I love her."

56.11 Other ways to indicate intention or plans

You can use words, such as 계획 "plan," 예정 "schedule," and 생각 "thought" to express your intentions and plans.

A: 이번 휴가 때 무슨 계획 있으세요?
"Do you have any plan during this vacation?"
B: 하와이에 계신 부모님 집에 갈까 해요.
"I am thinking of going to my parents' house in Hawaii."

금년에는 일본을 여행할 생각입니다.
"I am thinking of traveling Japan this year."
발표 준비는 다 끝내 놓고 갈 계획입니다.
"I am planning to leave after completing my presentation preparation."
다음 주쯤에 도착할 예정입니다.
"They are scheduled to arrive here sometime next week."

57

Likes and wishes

This chapter introduces various ways to express one's likes or wishes.

57.1 좋아하다 "like"

The most common way of expressing one's likes is to use the verb 좋아하다 "like."

  A: 가장 좋아하는 과목이 뭐예요?
   "What is his favorite subject?"
  B: 수학을 좋아해요.
   "He likes math."

닭고기보다 소고기를 좋아합니다.
"I like beef more than chicken."
나오미는 키 크고 마른 남자만 좋아했어요.
"As for Naomi, she only liked tall slim men."
내 아내는 유난히 사진 찍는 것을 좋아했다.
"My wife particularly liked taking photos."
커피는 별로 좋아하지 않아요.
"I do not like coffee much."
기민이는 매운 음식을 엄청 좋아해요.
"As for Keemin, she likes spicy food very much."
내가 널 얼마나 좋아하는지 아니?
"Do you know how much I like you?"
당신을 처음 봤을 때부터 좋아했습니다.
"I've liked you since the first time I saw you."
제가 사람들하고 어울리는 것을 워낙 좋아했거든요.
"I really like to socialize with people, you know."
잔소리를 좋아하는 사람이 있을까요?
"Do you think that there are people who like to nag?"

Alternatively, you can use the adjective 좋다 "be good."

그 사람이 그렇게 좋아요?
"Do you like him that much?"
저는 한국 음식이 좋은데요.
"I like Korean food." (lit. As for me, Korean food is good.)
저는 이 색깔이 좋은 것 같아요.
"I kind of like this color." (lit. As for me, this color seems to be nice.)
좋으면 좋다고 말해.
"If you like it, say so."

Meanwhile, one can express dislikes by using 싫어하다/싫다 "dislike."

내 여자 친구는 유난히 운동하는 것을 싫어했어요.
"My girlfriend particularly disliked exercising."

LIKES AND WISHES

담배 냄새가 정말 싫어요.
"I really dislike a whiff of smoke."

57.2 ~고 싶다 "want, wish, would like to" (see 15.3)

A: 점심으로 뭐 드시고 싶으세요?
"What would you like to eat for lunch?"
B: 햄버거나 피자 어때요?
"How about hamburgers or pizza?"

저희 회사에 입사하시면 어느 부서에서 일하고 싶으십니까?
"If you do enter our company, in which department would (you) like to work?"
졸업한 후 한국에서 일하고 싶습니다.
"After graduating, I would like to work in Korea."
어딘가로 훌쩍 떠나고 싶었습니다.
"I wanted to leave for somewhere aimlessly."
생일에 교회 친구들도 초대하고 싶어서요.
"It's because I want to invite my friends from church on my birthday."
그는 나에게 무언가를 말하고 싶어했다.
"He wanted to say something to me."
광고 홍보 관련 일을 하고 싶습니다.
"I want to do something related to PR."
저희 할아버지께서는 돌아가시기 전에 꼭 고향에 가고 싶어하셨어요.
"My grandfather really wished to visit his hometown before dying."
언제쯤 집에 오고 싶다고 했니?
"When did he say he wants to come home?"

57.3 ~(으)면 좋겠다/하다 "It'd be great if . . ."

The combination of ~(으)면 (see 18.2.1) and 하다 "do" or 좋겠다 "would/will be nice" expresses the speaker's wish or hope. ~(으)면 하다 sounds slightly more polite or formal than ~(으)면 좋겠다. However, both can be translated as "wish/hope" or "it'd be great if . . ." in English.

월급이 좀 늘면 좋겠어요.
"I hope that my salary increases."
시험에 붙으면 좋겠어요.
"It'd be great if I pass the test."
이번 겨울 방학에 스키타러 가면 좋겠어요.
"I hope we go skiing this winter break."
여기서 결혼 피로연을 하면 좋겠어요.
"It'd be nice if we can have our wedding reception here."
편찮으신 어머니께서 이제 좀 건강해지시면 좋겠어요.
"I wish that my sick mother gets healthier."
학교 근처로 이사하면 좋겠어요.
"It'd be great if I can move near my school."

Adding the past tense marker ~었/았 to ~(으)면 하다/좋겠다 makes the speaker's desire or wish sound more assertive or emphatic.

어머니께서 항상 건강하셨으면 좋겠어요.
"I wish that my mother would always be healthy."
북한과 남한이 하루속히 통일이 됐으면 좋겠어요.
"I wish that North and South Korea would be unified as soon as possible."
다음 학기에는 꼭 한국으로 교환학생으로 갔으면 좋겠어요.
"I wish that I could go to Korea as an exchange student next semester."

희망 "hope" and 소원 "wish"

이제부터 제발 병원비 걱정을 <u>안 했으면 해요</u>.
"I wish that I would not worry about the hospital expense from now on."
이제 <u>가 봤으면 합니다</u>.
"I wonder if I can be excused now." (lit. I wish that I would go now.)
어제 면접을 본 회사에 꼭 <u>취직했으면 좋겠어요</u>.
"I hope that I get the job at the company that I was interviewed at yesterday."
입사한 지 4년이나 됐는데 이제 <u>승진했으면 좋겠어요</u>.
"It has been four years since I started working for this company, so I wish to be promoted now."
아들은 있으니까 이제 딸을 <u>낳았으면 합니다</u>.
"I have a son, so I wish to have a daughter now."
좀 더 큰 집을 <u>사면 좋겠어요</u>.
"It'd be great if we bought a bigger house."

57.4 ~기 바라다 "to hope" (see 4.1.11)

금년에는 꼭 좋은 사람 만나서 <u>장가가기 바란다</u>.
"I hope that you surely meet a good person and get married this year."
이번에는 꼭 시험에 꼭 <u>합격하기를 바래요</u>.
"I hope that you surely pass the exam this time."
부디 참석하여 주셔서 <u>축복해 주시길 바랍니다</u>.
"We sincerely hope that you attend the ceremony and bless our marriage."
빨리 회사 사정이 <u>좋아지길 바랍니다</u>.
"I hope that the situation of the company gets better soon."

57.5 마음에 들다 "be to one's liking"

This idiomatic expression is made of the noun 마음 "heart, mind," the particle 에, and the verb 들다 "pick up, get [into]."

A: 어떠세요? <u>마음에 드시는지요</u>?
"How is it? I wonder if you like it."
B: 다 좋은데 색상이 <u>마음에 들지 않네요</u>.
"I like them all, but I do not like the color."

가격은 신경쓰지 말고 <u>마음에 드는 것으로</u> 고르십시오.
"Do not worry about the price, and choose the one that pleases you."
가격도 디자인도 색상도 다 <u>마음에 드네요</u>.
"I like its price, design, color, and all."
저는 저 집이 <u>마음에 들어요</u>.
"As for me, I like that house."
제 선물이 <u>마음에 드셨는지요</u>?
"I wonder if you liked my gift."

57.6 희망 "hope" and 소원 "wish"

You can also express your wishes, likes, and hopes by using the noun 희망 "hope" and 소원 "wish."

모든 <u>희망</u>이 사라졌습니다.
"All my hopes were gone."
장래 <u>희망</u>이 뭐예요?
"What do you want to be in the future?"

LIKES AND WISHES

금년 한국 경제 전망은 <u>희망적</u>이다.
"The prospects of the Korean economy this year are hopeful."
제 간절한 <u>소원</u>을 들어주셨습니다.
"He granted my earnest wishes."
할아버지의 마지막 <u>소원</u>은 고향 땅에 묻히는 것이었다.
"My grandfather's last wish was to be buried in his hometown."
여기에 동전을 던지고 <u>소원</u>을 빌면 언젠가 이루어진대요.
"They say that if you throw a coin here and make a wish, your wish will come true someday."
딸아이는 의대에 합격하기를 간절히 <u>희망하고 있다</u>.
"My daughter is hoping to enter medical school."
그들에게는 자식들이 유일한 <u>희망이었습니다</u>.
"Their children were the only hope for them."
절망하지 말고 <u>희망</u>을 한 번 가져 봅시다!
"Let's not despair but have hope!"
나는 <u>소원</u>대로 법대에 입학할 수 있었다.
"I was able to enter law school as I had wished for."

57.7 원하다 "to want"

대한민국 국민 모두 우리 팀의 승리를 간절히 <u>원했다</u>.
"Every citizen in South Korea sincerely wished/prayed for the victory of our team."
그들은 다시 미국으로 <u>돌아가기를 원했습니다</u>.
"They longed to return to the US again."
아버지는 내가 사업가로서 보다는 훌륭한 의사로서 <u>성공하기를 원하셨어요</u>.
"My father wanted me to succeed as an excellent medical doctor rather than a businessman."
<u>원하신다면</u> 내일까지 계셔도 돼요.
"You can stay until tomorrow if you wish."
저희가 <u>원했던 가격으로</u> 주셨어요.
"He gave it to us at the price we had wished for."
<u>원하던 점수</u>를 못 받아서 엄청 속상했다.
"I felt terribly disappointed, because I could not get the score that I wished for."

57.8 Expressing good wishes in writing or in person

새해 복 많이 받으세요.
"Happy New Year."
금년에는 꼭 소원하시는 모든 것 이루시길 바랍니다.
"Best wishes for this new year, hoping all your wishes come true."
건강하세요.
"Take care."
크리스마스 잘 보내세요.
"Have a merry Christmas."

58

Listing and including additional information

This chapter looks into expressions that are used to enumerate activities, states, or things or to indicate the inclusion of additional information.

58.1 Listing

58.1.1 ~고 "and" (see 19.1.1)

    A: 오후에 뭐 할 거예요?
        "What will you do this afternoon?"
    B: 도서관에 가서 책 <u>반납하고</u> 공부하고 올게요.
        "I will go to the library, return a book, study, and then come back."

    A: 남자 친구 어때요?
        "How is her boyfriend?"
    B: 키도 <u>크고</u> 잘생겼어요.
        "He is tall and handsome."

거실이 <u>춥고 어둡고</u> 좁네요.
"The living room is cold, dark, and narrow."
저 식당은 음식 값도 <u>싸고</u> 맛도 <u>있고</u> 분위기도 좋아요.
"As for that restaurant, their food price is cheap, their food is tasty, and the atmosphere is also good."

58.1.2 ~는가 하면 "while"

This form consists of the plain speech level ending ~는가 (see 27.2.4) and 하면 (하다 "do" + 면 "if").

    A: 요새 많이 힘드시지요?
        "It's been tough lately, right?"
    B: 살다 보면 행복할 때가 <u>있는가 하면</u> 힘들 때도 있지요.
        "In life, there are times of happiness, while there are also times of difficulties."

남을 도울 때가 <u>있는가 하면</u> 때론 남에게 도움을 받을 때도 있어요.
"There are times when you help others, while there are times when you receive help from others."
수업 시간에 열심히 공부하는 학생들이 <u>있는가 하면</u> 조는 학생들도 있어요.
"In class, there are students who study hard, while there are also students who doze off."
같은 주라도 가뭄으로 고생하는 사람들이 <u>있는가 하면</u> 홍수로 집을 잃은 사람들도 있어요.
"Even in the same state, there are people who suffer from drought, while there are people who lose their homes due to floods."

LISTING AND INCLUDING ADDITIONAL INFORMATION

58.1.3 ~(으)랴 ~(으)랴 "while doing X and doing X"

A: 여전히 많이 바쁘신가 봐요.
   "You seem to be very busy still."
B: 네, 가르치랴 연구하랴 엄청 바빠요.
   "Yes, I am very busy teaching and conducting research."

아이들 키우랴 일하랴 쉴 틈이 없습니다.
"I have no time to rest while taking care of my children and working."
집에서도 숙제하랴 피아노 레슨 받으랴 시간이 없어요.
"Even at home, she has no free time while doing homework and receiving piano lessons."
영어 배우랴 새로운 환경에 적응하랴 힘들어요.
"I have a hard time learning English and adjusting myself to a new environment."

58.1.4 ~(으)며 "and" (see 19.1.5)

A: 대학에서 뭐 공부하세요?
   "What do you study at college?"
B: 전공은 경영학이며 부전공은 회계학입니다.
   "My major is management, and my minor is accounting."

이 청소기는 소음이 적으며 가볍습니다.
"As for this vacuum cleaner, its noise is minimal, and it is light."
이 전화기는 기능이 다양하며 배터리가 오래갑니다.
"As for this phone, its functions are diverse, and its battery lasts long."
이 지역은 교통이 편리하며 집세가 싼 편입니다.
"As for this area, the traffic is convenient, and the house rent is kind of low."

58.1.5 N(이)며 N(이)며 "and"

A: 커피며 콜라며 카페인이 들어간 것은 절대로 드시면 안 돼요.
   "You should never take anything that has caffeine, like coffee and cola."
B: 언제까지요?
   "Until when?"

학생이며 교수며 학기말에는 모두 바빠요.
"At the end of the semester, everyone is busy, including students and professors."
알레르기 때문에 눈이며 코며 간지러워서 너무 힘들어요.
"Because of my allergy, I have a hard time because my eyes and nose are itchy."
김치며 밑반찬이며 내가 좋아하는 음식들을 가지고 오셨어요.
"She brought me food that I like, such as Kimchee and side dishes."

58.2 Expressing additional information

58.2.1 Particles and conjunctives

What follow are expressions associated with indicating additional information.

N에 "in addition to" (see 6.1.1)

커피에 케이크까지 아주 맛있었습니다.
"The coffee as well as the cake were all very delicious."

Expressing additional information | **58.2**

N에다가 "in addition to" (see 6.1.2)

스테이크<u>에다가</u> 와인까지 시켰어요.
"Besides steak, I also ordered wine."

게다가 "besides"

태권도를 배우고 있고 <u>게다가</u> 한국어도 공부하고 있어요.
"He is learning Taekwondo and is also studying Korean."

더욱이 "furthermore"

그는 먹지도 못하고 <u>더욱이</u> 걷지도 못했어요.
"He could not eat, and furthermore, he was not able to walk."

그리고 "and"

술을 끊으세요. <u>그리고</u> 운동을 시작하세요.
"Quit drinking. And start exercising."

58.2.2 ~거니와 "as well as" (see 19.1.3)

A: 이번 주말에 어디 안 가세요?
   "Aren't you going anywhere this weekend?"
B: 같이 데이트할 사람도 <u>없거니와</u> 돈도 없어요.
   "I don't have anyone to date and no money either."

노래도 잘 <u>부르거니와</u> 춤도 잘 춰요.
"She sings well and also dances well."
저와는 전공도 <u>다르거니와</u> 관심 분야도 달라요.
"Her major differs from mine, and our interests differ."
관심도 <u>없거니와</u> 능력도 안 돼요.
"I am not interested in it and do have not any talent in it."
운동도 <u>잘하거니와</u> 공부도 잘해요.
"He is good at sports and also studies well."
성공적인 다이어트를 위해서는 운동을 규칙적으로 <u>해야겠거니와</u> 건강한 음식을 먹어야 한다.
"For a successful diet, you need to exercise regularly and need to eat healthy food."

58.2.3 ~는/(으)ㄴ 데다가 "in addition to" (see 50.11)

A: 어제 그 레스토랑 어땠어요?
   "How was that restaurant yesterday?"
B: 별로였어요. 맛도 <u>없는 데다가</u> 비싸기까지 했어요.
   "Not good. It tasted terrible, and to make things worse, it was also expensive."

<u>추운 데다가</u> 비까지 와요.
"It is cold and also rainy."
<u>지하실인 데다가</u> 창문도 없어요.
"The room is in the basement and it does not even have windows."
지하철이 <u>빠른 데다가</u> 편리해서 자주 타요.
"Since the subway is fast and also convenient, I use it often."
<u>주말인 데다가</u> 날씨까지 좋아서 공원이 붐볐어요.
"On top of the fact that it was the weekend, the weather was great, so the park was crowded."
공부도 많이 <u>안 한 데다가</u> 시험까지 어렵게 나왔어요.
"I did not study much, and to make things worse, the exam turned out to be difficult."

LISTING AND INCLUDING ADDITIONAL INFORMATION

58.2.4 ~(으)ㄹ 뿐만 아니라 "not just . . . but also . . ."

This form is made of (으)ㄹ 뿐 "only" (see 23.10) and the negative copula 아니라서 (아니다 + 라서).

A: 한문 배우신다면서요. 어때요? 어려워요?
 "I heard that you are learning Chinese characters. How is it? Difficult?"
B: 말도 마세요. 배우기 어려울 뿐만 아니라 재미도 없어요.
 "Don't even bring it up. They are not only difficult but not fun to learn."

태권도를 배우면 건강이 좋아질 뿐만 아니라 자신감도 생겨요.
"If you learn Taekwondo, your health will improve and you will have confidence as well."
뉴욕시는 차가 항상 막힐 뿐만 아니라 주차할 곳도 마땅치 않아요.
"In New York City, the roads are always congested, and there are no parking spaces either."
한국에 가면 친구들을 사귈수 있을 뿐만 아니라 한국어도 배울 수 있어요.
"If you go to Korea, you will be able to make Korean friends and can also learn Korean."
제주도는 경치만 좋을 뿐만 아니라 공기도 맑습니다.
"As for Jeju Island, its scenery is beautiful, and its air is also clean."
등산을 하면 좋은 공기를 마실 수 있을 뿐만 아니라 스트레스도 해소할 수 있어요.
"If you hike, you can enjoy not only clean air but relieve your stress as well."
이 전화기는 가격이 저렴할 뿐만 아니라 디자인도 예쁘고 기능도 많아서 요즘 인기가 많아요.
"As for this phone, its price is not just cheap, but its design is also pretty with many functions, so it is very popular nowadays."

58.2.5 ~(으)ㄹ뿐더러 "not only . . . but also"

This form is built on ~(으)ㄹ 뿐 "only" (see 23.10) and the particle 더러.

A: 김치가 건강식품이라고 들었습니다.
 "I heard that Kimchee is a healthy food."
B: 그럼요. 건강에도 좋을뿐더러 다이어트에도 효능이 있습니다.
 "Sure. It is not only good for health, but it is also effective for dieting."

성격도 좋을뿐더러 얼굴도 잘생겼어요.
"Not only his personality is good, he is also handsome."
여기는 경치도 좋을뿐더러 공기도 맑아요.
"Here, its scenery is not only great but the air is also clear."
값도 비쌀뿐더러 맛도 그저그래요.
"Not only it is expensive, but it also tastes so-so."

58.2.6 N을/를 비롯해서 "including, starting with N"

This form is constructed from the particle 을/를 (see 5.4), 비롯하다 "begin," and the conjunctive ~어서/아서 "so" (see 16.2.1).

A: 어제 회의에 많이 오셨어요?
 "Did many people come to the meeting yesterday?"
B: 네. 회장님을 비롯해서 전 회원이 모두 모였어요.
 "Yes. Including the chairman, all the members gathered."

KPOP은 아시아를 비롯해서 전 세계적으로 인기가 많아지고 있습니다.
"The popularity of KPOP is spreading all over the world, starting with Asia."
할아버지를 비롯해서 집안 식구 모두 저희 집으로 갔습니다.
"All the family members including my grandfather went to my house."
한국을 비롯해서 동아시아 각국에 사업을 확장하기로 했습니다.
"We decided to expand our business all over East Asian countries, including Korea."

59

Location, direction, and distance

This chapter presents expressions used to ask and describe location, direction, and distance.

59.1 Asking and describing the location of an object

59.1.1 N에 있다 "there is ..."

When asking for the specific location of a certain object, Koreans use the question word 어디 "where" with the verb 있다 as in, 은행이 어디(에) 있어요? "Where is the bank (lit., where does the bank exist)?" Notice that the question word 어디 appears right before the verb 있어요.

One can use 이에요 with 어디, as in 은행이 어디예요? "Where is the bank?" However, notice that the question does not seek the specific location of 은행 rather it simply questions the general whereabouts of 은행. In other words, the copula 이에요 cannot be used to refer to the location of an object.

For example, for the question in the preceding paragraph, a response such as 은행이 학교 도서관 뒤에 있어요 "The bank is (lit., exist) behind the school library" is acceptable. However, 은행이 학교 도서관 뒤예요 "The bank is the back of the school library" is not acceptable since these two responses do not mean the same thing.

When indicating the precise location, such as "inside of," "above," "below," and so forth, you have to use location words, such as 아래/밑, 위, 옆, 안, 밖, 앞, and 뒤 (as in 사무실 밖 "outside the office" or 사무실 안 "inside the office").

    A: 우체국은 <u>어디에 있어요</u>?
         "Where is the post office?"
    B: 은행 바로 <u>옆에 있습니다</u>.
         "It is right next to the bank."

강아지가 집 <u>밖에 있어요</u>.
"The puppy is outside the house."
저희 학교는 시청 <u>근처에 있습니다</u>.
"Our school is located near city hall."
변 교수님 연구실은 <u>몇 층에 있어요</u>?
"On what floor is Professor Byon's office?"
커피숍이 백화점 <u>4층에 있어요</u>.
"The coffee shop is on the fourth floor of the department store."
경찰서는 지하철역 <u>건너편에 있어요</u>.
"The police station is across from the subway station."
커피숍이 학교 <u>맞은편에 있어요</u>.
"The coffee shop is on the front side of the school."
거실은 1층에 그리고 침실은 <u>2층에 있습니다</u>.
"The living room is on the first floor, and the bedroom is on the second floor."

LOCATION, DIRECTION, AND DISTANCE

59.2 Asking and indicating for directions/destination

59.2.1 N에 (see 6.1.1)

When indicating a direction toward a specific location (e.g., destination), you need to use the particle 에 "to."

    A: <u>어디에</u> 가세요?
        "Where are you going?"
    B: <u>서점에</u> 가는 길인데요.
        "I am on my way to the bookstore."

    A: <u>연세 대학교에</u> 가려면 지하철 몇 호선을 타야 돼요?
        "Which subway line should I take to get to Yonsei University?"
    B: 지하철 2번을 타세요.
        "Please take line number two."

오후에 <u>도서관에</u> 갈 거예요.
"We will go to the library in the afternoon."
저어, 실례하지만 <u>은행에</u> 어떻게 가지요?
"Well, excuse me, but how can you get to the bank?"
<u>인사동에</u> 가려면 어디서 내려야 하나요?
"Where should I get off for Insa-dong?"
실례하지만 <u>시청에</u> 가려면 몇 번 버스를 타야 됩니까?
"Excuse me, but what number bus should I take to go to the city hall?"

59.2.2 N(으)로 (see 6.2)

When indicating a general direction, you need to use the particle (으)로 "to/toward."

    A: <u>어디로</u> 갈까요?
        "Where shall we go?"
    B: 길 건너서 <u>왼쪽으로</u> 가세요.
        "Cross the street and then turn to the left."

    A: 어디에서 돌까요?
        "Where can I turn?"
    B: 다음 신호등에서 <u>오른쪽으로</u> 도세요.
        "Turn to the right at the next traffic light."

    A: 교보문고에 가려면 몇 번 출구로 나가야 합니까?
        "Which exit should I take to go to Kyobo bookstore?"
    B: <u>3번 출구로</u> 나가세요.
        "Please go out the exit three."

    A: <u>어디로</u> 모실까요?
        "Where shall I take you?"
    B: 신촌 세브란스 병원까지 부탁드립니다.
        "Shinchon Severance Hospital please."

<u>뒤로</u> 갈까요? <u>앞으로</u> 갈까요?
"Shall we move to the back or to the front?"
돌지 말고 <u>똑바로</u> 가면 돼요.
"All you need to do is to go straight without turning."
<u>집으로</u> 가고 있어요.
"I am going home."
<u>오른쪽으로</u> 가세요.
"Go toward the right side."

Asking and indicating distance

식탁은 <u>TV쪽으로</u> 움직여 주세요.
"As for the table, please move it toward the side with the TV."
<u>올림픽대로로</u> 해서 가 주세요.
"Please go via the Olympic Highway."
<u>아파트 단지 안으로</u> 들어가서 세워 주세요.
"Please let me off inside the apartment complex."

59.3 Asking and indicating distance

59.3.1 N에서 N까지 (see 6.1.3, 8.1.2)

When expressing distance from something, you need to use the particles 에서 and 까지, as shown in the following examples:

A: 학교가 <u>집에서</u> 가깝나요?
"Is school near your house?"
B: 아니요. 멀어요. 버스 타고 30분 정도 타고 가야 할 거리에 있어요.
"No. It's far. It is located in a place where you need to take a bus for about 30 minutes."

<u>서울에서 부산까지</u> 약 300 KM예요.
"Seoul is about 300 kilometers from Busan."
<u>뉴욕시에서 올바니까지</u>의 거리는 약 150 마일입니다.
"The distance from New York City to Albany is approximately 150 miles."
<u>지하철역에서 학교 정문까지</u> 걸어서 약 10분 정도 걸려요.
"From the subway station to the school's front gate, it takes about ten minutes on foot."
<u>호텔에서 회의장까지는</u> 걸어서 5분입니다.
"It takes five minutes on foot from your hotel to the conference center."

60

Means

This chapter covers expressions associated with indicating the means or what is needed to achieve a certain action.

60.1 Expressing means

You can express means of tools, instruments, transport, and materials using the particle (으)로 or (으)로써.

60.1.1 N(으)로 "as/by/with" (see 6.2.1)

    A: 어떻게 보내실 거예요?
       "How will you send this?"
    B: 항공편으로 부쳐 주세요.
       "Please send it to me via air."

    A: 수건이 없었을 텐데 뭘로 닦으셨어요?
       "I guess there was no towel, so what did you use to wipe it with?"
    B: 냅킨으로요.
       "With a napkin."

펜으로 사인하셔야 해요.
"He needs to sign it with a pen."
국수는 꼭 젓가락으로 드세요.
"As for noodles, please eat them using chopsticks."
헌 타이어를 새 거로 바꿨어요.
"I changed the old tires with new tires."
수건으로 얼굴을 가렸어요.
"He covered his face with a towel."
권력으로 엄청난 재산을 모았어요.
"With his power, he amassed huge wealth."
선거에 참여함으로 시민의 권리와 의무를 수행할 수 있습니다.
"One can pursue the duty and right of citizens by casting one's vote."
노래하고 춤으로 스트레스를 해소해요.
"I let my stress go by singing and dancing."
한국은 1988년 올림픽을 개최함으로 나라의 위상을 한층 높일 수 있었다.
"Korea was able to upgrade the national image by hosting the Olympics in 1988."

Describing means of transportation

60.1.2 N(으)로써 "as/by/with" (see 6.2.1)

The meaning of (으)로써 is similar to that of (으)로. However, the use of (으)로써 can make your message sound more emphatic than the use of (으)로.

A: 많이 힘드셨지요?
  "It must be really difficult for you, right?"
B: 정말 <u>말로써</u> 표현할 수 없을 정도로 힘들었어요.
  "It is difficult to the degree that one cannot express its severity in words."

떡은 <u>쌀로써</u> 만듭니다.
"We make Korean rice cakes with rice."
<u>보기로써</u> 이 기사를 읽어 보세요.
"As an example, take a look at this newspaper article."
이웃을 먼저 <u>배려함으로써</u> 좋은 사회를 만들어 갈 수 있습니다.
"By putting others first, we can create a better society."
다양한 일자리를 <u>마련함으로써</u> 취업 문제를 해결할 수 있습니다.
"By providing diverse jobs, we can solve unemployment issues."
<u>그렇게 함으로써</u> 문제를 해결하려고 합니다.
"By doing so, we try to solve the problem."
쓰레기를 줄이고 <u>재활용함으로써</u> 환경오염을 막을 수 있다.
"By reducing the amount of waste and recycling, we can prevent environmental problems."
하루에 10불 정도를 <u>기부함으로써</u> 세상을 변화시킬 수 있습니다.
"You can change the world by donating about ten dollars a day."

60.1.3 N(을/를) 가지고 "by/with"

This form is the combination of the verb 가지다 "have, carry" and the conjunctive ~고. It is used to mean "with" and "by means of."

A: 많이 비쌌을 텐데, 현금으로 사셨어요?
  "It must be expensive, so did you buy it with cash?"
B: 아니요. <u>신용카드 가지고</u> 샀어요.
  "No. I bought it with my credit card."

<u>공을 가지고</u> 놀았어요.
"We played with a ball."
<u>가위하고 풀 가지고</u> 만들어 보려구요.
"I intend to make it, using scissors and glue."
<u>드라이버 가지고</u> 한 번 고쳐 보세요?
"Why don't you try fixing it with a screwdriver?"
<u>나침반만 가지고</u> 찾아왔어요.
"I came all the way up here by using a compass only."

60.2 Describing means of transportation

To indicate means of transportation, you can use the following expressions:

A: 어떻게 갈까요?
  "How shall we go?"
B: 버스로 갑시다.
  "Let's go by bus."

A: 매일 학교에 어떻게 가요? 데려다 주세요?
  "How does he go to school every day? Do you give him a ride?"
B: 아니오. 걸어서 다녀요.
  "No. He goes to school on foot."

MEANS

60.2

A: 택시를 부를까요?
   "Shall I call a cab?"
B: 날씨도 좋은데 그냥 걸어서 갑시다.
   "It's nice out, so let's just go on foot."

A: 시내 쇼핑 센터까지 가고 싶은데 어떻게 가면 좋을까요?
   "I want to go to the shopping center downtown, but how can I get there?"
B: 시내까지 호텔 셔틀을 이용하실 수 있습니다.
   "You can use the hotel shuttle to go downtown."

A: 출근하실 때 주로 대중교통을 이용하시나요?
   "When you leave for work, do you primarily use public transportation?"
B: 네, 보통 지하철을 타고 출근해요.
   "Yes, I usually go to work by subway."

공항까지 지하철을 이용해서도 갈 수 있어요.
"You can also take the subway to get to the airport."
날씨가 좋을 때면 자전거 타고 학교에 가요.
"When the weather is nice, I go to school by riding my bike."

61

Obligation and necessity

This chapter introduces various ways to express a sense of obligation and a sense of necessity.

61.1 Obligation

In English, a sense of obligation is expressed by various auxiliary verbs, such as "should," "must," "ought to," "need to," and "have to." However, in Korean, a sense of obligation can be indicated by various expressions.

61.1.1 ~지 않으면 안 되다 and 안 ~(으)면 안 되다 "must"

These forms are the combinations of ~(으)면 안 되다 "if you do . . . it's not okay" (used for denying somebody permission) and the negative form. Consider the following examples:

> 병원에 <u>안 가면</u> 안 돼요.
> 병원에 <u>가지 않으면</u> 안 돼요.
> "You must go to the hospital."

Notice that the meaning of both sentences is the same. The difference between 안 ~(으)면 안 되다 and ~지 않으면 안 되다 is that while the first uses the short-form negation (see 20.1), the second uses the long-form negation (see 20.2).

> A: 나중에 가면 안 될까요?
> "I wonder if I can leave later?"
> B: 무슨 말씀을요? 지금 당장 <u>가시지 않으면</u> 안 돼요.
> "What do you mean? You must leave now immediately."

> 그 질병은 빨리 <u>치료받지 않으면</u> 안 됩니다.
> "As for that disease, one must get the treatment as soon as possible."
> 저는 아침마다 커피를 <u>안 마시면</u> 안 돼요.
> "I must drink coffee every morning."
> 건강을 위해서 금연을 <u>하지 않으면</u> 안 돼요.
> "For your health, you need to quit smoking."
> 이번 학기에 졸업을 <u>안 하면</u> 안 돼요?
> "Must I graduate this semester?"
> 내일 오전까지 <u>준비해 놓지 않으면</u> 안 돼요.
> "We must prepare them before tomorrow morning."

61.1.2 ~어/아야 되다/하다 "must/have to" (see 15.9)

The idea of obligation or necessity can be also indicated by ~어/아야 되다 (or ~어/아야 하다 for more formal usages).

> A: 공항으로 몇 시쯤 떠나실 거예요?
> "Around what time do you plan to leave for the airport?"

OBLIGATION AND NECESSITY

61.1

> B: 집에서 10시 전에는 <u>나가야 돼요</u>.
> "I must leave home before 10 o'clock."
>
> A: 꼭 본인의 <u>사인이라야 합니까</u>?
> "Does it have to be his signature?"
>
> B: 그럼요. 그러니까 꼭 <u>모시고 오셔야 해요</u>.
> "Of course. So, you need to bring him here."

매일 밤마다 자기 전에 약을 <u>먹어야 돼요</u>.
"I must take the medicine every night before going to bed."
다음 주 월요일까지는 카드를 사서 <u>보내야 합니다</u>.
"You should buy and mail out the card by Monday next week."
가장 중요한 조건으로 비흡연<u>자라야 돼요</u>.
"As the most important condition, he has to be a nonsmoker."
두 분 꼭 <u>행복하셔야 돼요</u>.
"Both of you must be happy."
일단 거실이 <u>커야 합니다</u>.
"First, the living room has to be big."
먼저 열쇠를 빨리 <u>찾아야 되는데요</u>.
"First, I need to find my key soon."
미국 시민권<u>자라야 돼요</u>?
"Does he have to be an American citizen?"
유학하기 위해서는 여러 가지 서류를 <u>준비해야 합니다</u>.
"In order to study abroad, you need to prepare various documents."

61.1.3 ~어/아야지요 "should"

The sentence ending ~어/아야지(요) is made of ~어/아야 하다 "must" (see 15.9) and the sentence ending ~지요 (see 26.6). This form denotes a necessity (or intention, see chapter 56) and can be translated as "should."

> A: 여권하고 서류는 잘 <u>챙기셔야지요</u>.
> "You should prepare your passport and the documents."
>
> B: 네, 그렇지 않아도 어제 벌써 다 준비해 놓았습니다.
> "Yes, as a matter of fact, I already prepared them all yesterday."

운동은 매일 꾸준히 <u>해야지요</u>.
"You need to exercise consistently every day."
입맛이 없더라고 식사는 꼭 챙겨서 <u>드셔야지요</u>.
"Though you lost your appetite, you should definitely have your meals."
성능하고 디자인이 둘 다 <u>좋아야지요</u>.
"Both the function and design have to be good."
돈을 좀 모으려면 먼저 가계부를 쓰는 버릇을 <u>가져야지요</u>.
"If you intend to save some money, you need to get into the habit of writing a budget."

61.1.4 ~(으)ㄹ 의무가 있다 "have an obligation to"

This form is built on the noun-modifying ending ~(으)ㄹ, the noun 의무 "duty," the subject particle 가, and the verb 있다 "have/exist."

> A: 환자로서 의사의 말을 100% 믿고 <u>따를 의무가 있습니다</u>.
> "As a patient, you have the obligation to trust and follow your doctor's advice."
>
> B: 죄송합니다. 제가 너무 걱정이 돼서.
> "I am sorry. I am just too concerned, so . . ."

배우자의 빚을 다른 배우자가 <u>갚아야 할 의무가 있나요</u>?
"Does a spouse have the obligation to pay off his/her spouse's debt?"

Necessity

대한민국의 남자마다 군복무를 <u>해야 할 의무가 있습니다</u>.
"Each man in Korea has the obligation to serve in the military."
저는 제 가정을 사랑과 헌신으로 <u>지켜야 할 의무가 있습니다</u>.
"As for me, I have the obligation to protect my family with love and dedication."

61.1.5 ~지 않아도 되다 "do not have to"

This form expresses negative obligations. It consists of the long-form negation ~지 않다, the conjunctive ~어도/아도, and the verb 되다 "become."

A: 오늘 회식에 꼭 가야 하나요?
"Do I really need to go to the company dinner today?"
B: 많이 바쁘시면 <u>가지 않으셔도 돼요</u>.
"If you are very busy, you don't have to go."

<u>사과하지 않으셔도 돼요</u>.
"You don't need to apologize."
부모님께 <u>말씀드리지 않아도 될 것 같아요</u>.
"I think that you don't need to tell your parents."
내일은 일찍 <u>오지 않으셔도 돼요</u>.
"You don't need to come early tomorrow."
<u>전화하지 않으셔도 됩니다</u>.
"You don't need to call us."

61.2 Necessity

The Korean word for "need/necessity" is 필요. This noun is commonly used with verbs, such as 있다, 없다, and 하다 to express need.

61.2.1 ~이/가 필요하다 "be necessary"

<u>소금하고 참기름이 필요한데요</u>.
"I need salt and sesame oil."
지금 저에게는 <u>휴식이 필요해요</u>.
"What I need now is rest."
당장 <u>필요한 게 뭐예요</u>?
"What is the thing that you need right now?"
은행 대출에 <u>필요한 서류</u>를 준비해 놓으세요.
"Please prepare the necessary documents for a bank loan."

61.2.2 필요 없다 "no need"

거스름 돈은 <u>필요 없습니다</u>.
"I don't need the change."
더 이상 그 프로그램은 <u>필요 없을 거 같아요</u>.
"I think that I don't need that program anymore."
헬멧은 <u>필요 없어요</u>.
"I don't need a helmet."
다른 것은 <u>필요 없으세요</u>?
"You don't need anything else?"

61.2.3 ~(으)ㄹ 필요가 있다 "it is necessary to"

다시 한 번 검사를 <u>받으셔야 할 필요가 있습니다</u>.
"It is necessary for you to receive an examination again."

OBLIGATION AND NECESSITY

일을 서두를 필요가 있습니다.
"It is necessary for you to rush."
처음부터 다시 검토할 필요가 있습니다.
"It is necessary to reconsider that from the beginning."
다시 연락 드릴 필요가 있는 것 같아요.
"I think that it is necessary to contact them again."

61.2.4 ~(으)ㄹ 필요가 없다 "there is no need for"

A: 내일도 와야 합니까?
 "Do I need to come here tomorrow as well?"
B: 아니오. 내일은 오실 필요 없으세요.
 "No. As for tomorrow, there is no need for you to come."

걱정하실 필요 없어요.
"There is no need to worry."
서로 동갑이니까 존댓말을 쓰실 필요는 없을 것 같아요.
"Since you guys are the same age, I think there is no need to use honorifics."
그냥 파티니까 정장을 입으실 필요는 없을 것 같아요.
"It is just a party, so I don't think that you need to wear a suit."
주말에는 입장료를 내실 필요 없어요.
"There is no need to pay an admission fee on the weekend."

62

Permission and prohibition

This chapter introduces major expressions that are associated with seeking/giving/denying permission or forbidding someone from doing something.

62.1 Seeking and giving permission

62.1.1 ~어/아도 되다 "you may"

Seeking or giving permission in Korean is typically carried out by the form ~어/아도 되다. This form is constructed from ~어/아도 "even if" and the verb 되다 "become/get/turn into." Some other adjectives, such as 괜찮다 "be fine" or 좋다 "be good," can be used instead of 되다 to indicate a similar meaning. Consequently, the construction ~어/아도 되다 (or 괜찮다/ 좋다) literally means "it is all right even if. . . ."

~어/아도 되다 in an interrogative sentence is used to ask for permission. On the other hand, ~어/아도 되다 in a declarative sentence is used to give permission, as shown in the following examples:

    A: 이제 집에 <u>가도 될까요</u>?
         "May I go home now?" (lit. Is it all right even if I go home now?)
    B: 네. 이제 <u>가셔도 됩니다</u>.
         "Yes. You may go now."

    A: 좀 <u>빌려 가도 괜찮으시겠어요</u>?
         "Would it be fine even if we borrow some?"
    B: 필요하신 만큼 <u>가져 가셔도 돼요</u>.
         "You can take as much as you need."

    A: 전화 좀 <u>써도 될까요</u>?
         "May I use your phone, please?"
    B: 아, 예. 여기 있습니다.
         "Oh, sure. Here it is."

    A: 여기 <u>앉아도 되겠습니까</u>?
         "May I sit here?"
    B: 네. 그럼요.
         "Yes, of course."

    A: 좀 <u>들어가도 되겠습니까</u>?
         "May I enter, please?"
    B: 예. 들어오십시오.
         "Yes. Please come in."

    A: 더운데 에어컨을 좀 <u>켜도 될까요</u>?
         "It's hot, so may I turn on the air conditioner, please?"
    B: 아, 예. 그럼요.
         "Oh, yes. Sure."

PERMISSION AND PROHIBITION 62.2

> A: 여기에 있는 물 좀 <u>마셔도 될까요</u>?
> "May I drink the water here?"
> B: <u>그럼요</u>.
> "Certainly."
>
> A: 저희가 먼저 <u>먹어도 괜찮을까요</u>?
> "May we eat first?"
> B: 네, 먼저 드세요.
> "Yes, help yourself first."
>
> A: 좀 <u>매워도 괜찮아요</u>?
> "Is it okay even if it is a bit spicy?"
> B: 네. 저 매운 거 좋아해요.
> "Sure. I like spicy food."

Meanwhile, ~어/아도 되다 in a negative sentence (e.g., 안 ~어/아도 되다 or ~지 않아도 되다) means ". . . do not have to . . ." as shown in the following examples:

> A: 이번 주는 좀 바쁜데 다음 주에 가도 될까요?
> "I am kind of busy this week, so would it be OK if I go there next week?"
> B: 바쁘면 <u>안 가셔도 괜찮아요</u>.
> "If you are busy, you do not have to go."
>
> A: 꼭 양복을 입고 가야 하나요?
> "Do I have to go there wearing a suit?"
> B: 불편하면 양복을 <u>입지 않아도 괜찮아요</u>.
> "If you feel uncomfortable, you do not have to put on a suit."
>
> A: 지금 좀 비싸던데 다음에 세일할 때 사는 게 어떨까요?
> "It's a bit expensive now. How about buying them later when they are on sale?"
> B: 너무 비싸면 당장 <u>안 사셔도 돼요</u>.
> "If it is too expensive, you do not have to buy them now."

62.2 Denying permission/expressing prohibition

62.2.1 ~(으)면 안 되다 "must not"

For denying permission, prohibiting some action, or giving a warning, you can use ~(으)면 안 되다. This form is the combination of ~(으)면 "if" (see 18.2.1), 안 "not" (see 20.1), and the verb 되다 "become/get/turn into." It can be translated as "it is not all right if . . ." or "you should/must not" in English.

> A: 선생님, 수업 시간에 영어 해도 돼요?
> "Professor, can we speak in English during class?"
> B: 아니요. 수업 시간에는 영어를 <u>쓰면 안 돼요</u>.
> "No. You must not use English in class."

거짓말 <u>하면 안 돼요</u>.
"You should not lie."
결혼식 때 <u>울면 안 돼요</u>.
"You should not cry during the wedding ceremony."
먼저 <u>떠나면 안 돼요</u>.
"You should not leave first."
여기서 담배 <u>피우시면 안 됩니다</u>.
"You should not smoke here."
여기에 쓰레기를 <u>버리시면 안 됩니다</u>.
"You should not throw away garbage here."

Denying permission/expressing prohibition

운전 중에 전화기를 <u>쓰시면 안 돼요</u>.
"You must not use a phone while driving."
지금은 길을 <u>건너면 안 돼요</u>.
"You must not cross the street now."
도서관 안에서는 크게 음악을 <u>들으시면 안 됩니다</u>.
"You must not listen to music aloud inside of the library."
탄산 음료와 인스턴트 식품은 <u>드시면 안 됩니다</u>.
"You must not intake carbonated drinks or instant food."
절대로 <u>과로하시면 안 됩니다</u>.
"You must not overwork yourself."
옷이 너무 <u>비싸면 안 돼요</u>.
"It would not be all right if the dress is too expensive."
날씨가 <u>흐리면 안 돼요</u>.
"It would not be all right if the weather is cloudy."
수업에 <u>늦으면 안 돼요</u>.
"It would not be all right if you are late for class."
룸메이트가 <u>남학생이면 안 돼요</u>.
"It would not be all right if your roommate is a male student."

62.2.2 ~지 마세요 "do not" (see 20.3)

A: 그 영화 어땠어요? 볼 만해요?
  "How was that movie? Was it worth watching?"
B: <u>보지 마세요</u>. 정말 별로였어요.
  "Don't watch it. It was really bad."

담배를 <u>피우지 마십시오</u>.
"Do not smoke."
수업 시간에 <u>떠들지 마세요</u>.
"Do not talk aloud in class."
음악을 너무 크게 <u>틀지 마세요</u>.
"Do not play music too loud."
담배는 입에도 <u>대지 마십시오</u>.
"Don't even try smoking."

62.2.3 Formal written words that specify prohibited activities

금연
"No smoking"
주차 금지
"No parking"
출입 금지
"Off limits"
촬영 금지
"No photography"
통행 금지
"No passing"
횡단 금지
"No crossing"
보행 금지
"No walking"
우회전 금지
"No right turn"

PERMISSION AND PROHIBITION

좌회전 금지
"No left turn"
유턴 금지
"No U-turn"
건너지 마시오.
"Do not cross the street."

63
Personal information

This chapter discusses various ways to ask and give personal information, such as one's name, age, place of origin/hometown, occupation, and so forth.

63.1 Name

To ask a person's name, you can use the following expressions, ranged from formal to informal/intimate.

실례지만 성함이 어떻게 되세요?
"Excuse me, but what is your name?" (lit. How does your name become?)
이름이 어떻게 돼요?
"What is your name?"
이름이 뭐라고 했지?
"What did you say your name was?"
이름이 뭐니?
"What is your name?"

In Korean, one's last/family name comes first, and then the first/given name follows. When giving your name, you can use the following expressions.

저는 김대성이라고 합니다.
"As for me, I am Dae Sung Kim."
제 이름은 변상필입니다.
"My name is Sangpil Byon."
안녕하세요? 신입사원 장기철이라고 합니다.
"How are you? I am Ki Chul Chang, the new employee."

63.2 Age

As the first step to open up an interpersonal relationship with an unfamiliar person, Koreans often ask each other's age. Foreigners may find this strange. However, note that the main reason they ask each other's age is not because they are simply curious about other's age, but to find out who is older/younger so that they can determine a ground where they can start their interpersonal relationship. Note that age is one of the most influential social variables that affects the interpersonal relationship. Words that are commonly associated with one's age include 나이 "age," 연세 "age (honorific)," 학번 "class of," 띠 "Chinese zodiac sign," and 학년 "year, grade." Here are some common expressions for asking and giving one's age, ranged from the most formal to most informal:

A: 연세가 어떻게 되시나요?
"How old are you?" (lit. How does your age become?)
B: 올해로 쉰아홉입니다.
"I am 59 years old this year."

PERSONAL INFORMATION

A: 실례지만 무슨 띠세요?
"Excuse me, what is your zodiac sign?"
B: 70년 개띠입니다.
"Mine is the year of the dog, 1970."
A: 나이가 어떻게 되세요?
"How old are you?" (lit. How does your age become?)
B: 스물다섯입니다.
"I am 25 years old."
A: 저는 97학번인데 어떻게 되시나요?
"I am in the class of '97; how about you?"
B: 저보다 위시네요. 저는 99학번입니다.
"You are older than I. I am in the class of '99."
A: 학번이 어떻게 되세요?
"What is the year you entered college?"
B: 88 학번인데요.
"I am in the class of '88."
A: 몇 학년이야?
"What grade are you?"
B: 중 1인데요.
"I am in the seventh grade."
A: 너 몇 살이니?
"How old are you?"
B: 열 살이에요.
"I am ten years old."

63.3 Place of origin

Words that are commonly associated with one's place of origin include 출신 "a native of," 국적 "nationality," and 고향 "one's hometown." To talk about your place of origin, you can say the following:

A: 고향이 어디신가요?
"Where is your hometown?"
B: 서울이에요.
"Seoul is my hometown."
A: 태어나신 곳이(출생지가) 어디세요?
"Where were you born?"
B: 대전에서 태어나서 자랐어요.
"I was born and raised in Daejon."
A: 어디 출신이세요?
"Where are you from?"
B: 부산이요.
"I am from Busan."

63.4 Nationality

To ask and talk about one's nationality, you can say the following:

A: 어느 나라 사람이세요?
"Where are you from?" (lit. Which country are you from?)

Marital status

 B: 저는 일본 사람인데요.
   "I am Japanese."
 A: 어디 (어느 나라)에서 오셨습니까?
   "Where (what country) are you from?"
 B: 미국에서 왔습니다.
   "I am from the US."
 A: 국적이 어떻게 되세요?
   "What is your nationality?"
 B: 미국 시민권자입니다.
   "I am a US citizen."

63.5 Occupation

Words that are associated with one's occupation include 일, 직업, and 직종. The following are commonly used expressions for asking about the occupation of a person:

 A: 무슨 일을 하세요?
   "What kind of work do you do?"
 B: IT에 관련한 일을 하고 있습니다.
   "My work is related to IT."

 A: 어떤 일을 하시나요?
   "What kind of work do you do?"
 B: 대학에서 근무하고 있습니다.
   "I am employed at a college."

 A: 어떤 직종에 종사하고 계세요?
   "In what occupation are you engaged?"
 B: 대기업에 다니고 있습니다.
   "I am working for a large enterprise."

 A: 하시는 일이 무엇인지 여쭤 봐도 될까요?
   "May I ask you what kind of work you do?"
 B: 초등학교 교사입니다.
   "I am an elementary school teacher."

 A: 그 사람 직업이 뭐예요?
   "What is the occupation of that person?"
 B 공무원입니다.
   "He is a government employee."

63.6 Marital status

Words related to one's marital status include 결혼 "marriage," 이혼 "divorce," 기혼 "married," 미혼 "unmarried," 독신 "single," 싱글맘 "single mom," and 부부 "couple." The following are common expressions for saying one's marital status.

 A: 결혼은 하셨나요?
   "Are you married?"
 B: 아니오. 아직 싱글이에요.
   "No. I am still single."

 A: 결혼하셨지요?
   "You are married, right?"
 B: 네. 결혼 3년차입니다.
   "Yes. I am in my third year."

PERSONAL INFORMATION

63.7 Family

The Korean word for family is 가족 or 식구. Here are some typical expressions you can use to ask and answer about your/other's family:

    A: 가족이 몇 분이세요?
         "How many people are in your family?"
    B: 제 아내하고 아들 딸 그리고 저까지 넷입니다.
         "There are four altogether, including my wife, my son, my daughter, and myself."

    A: 자녀 분은 계신가요?
         "Do you have children?"
    B: 딸 하나 있습니다.
         "I have one daughter."

    A: 식구가 어떻게 되세요?
         "How many are there in your family?"
    B: 아버지하고 어머니가 계시고 누나가 한 명 있어요.
         "There are my father and mother, and I have one older sister."

64

Possibility

Here are some major expressions that Koreans use to indicate possibility and impossibility.

64.1 가능하다 "be possible"

The Korean word for "possibility" is 가능성, and the adjective "possible" is 가능하다.

    A: 언제 시간 괜찮으세요?
        "When is a convenient time for you?"
    B: 다음 주 중 저녁이라면 언제든지 가능합니다.
        "Any evening next week is possible."

가능하면 빨리 오세요.
"If possible, come quickly."
신용카드가 있어야 신청이 가능합니다.
"You can apply only if you have a credit card."
이 계획은 충분히 실현 가능합니다.
"This plan is quite practicable."

The word for impossibility is 불가능성, and the adjective "impossible" would be 불가능하다.

그 프로젝트는 실현 불가능합니다.
"That project cannot possibly be done."
그는 불가능한 일을 해 냈습니다.
"He performed an impossible act."
이 작전은 사실상 불가능한 일이라고 생각합니다.
"I think that this operation is a virtual impossibility."

64.2 ~(으)ㄹ 수(도) 있다 "possible" (see 23.11)

    A: 아직도 세일하고 있을까요?
        "I wonder if the sale is still going on."
    B: 글쎄요. 세일 기간이 끝났을 수도 있어요.
        "Well. It is possible that the sale ended."

교회 문이 잠겨 있을 수 있으니까 열쇠를 가지고 가세요.
"It is possible that the church door is locked, so take the key with you."
날씨가 좋으면 야외에서 먹을 수도 있어요.
"If the weather is nice, it is possible that we can eat outside."
비행기가 늦게 도착할 수 있다고 합니다.
"They say that the plane might arrive late."
증상이 더 나빠지면 오늘 수술 날짜를 잡을 수도 있어요.
"If the symptoms get worse, it is possible that they will schedule an operation date today."

POSSIBILITY

눈 때문에 강의가 취소될 수도 있으니 학교에 가기 전에 꼭 확인해 보세요.
"It is possible that class will be cancelled due to snow, so please check before going to school."
지금 가면 아무도 없을 수 있어요.
"If you go there now, it is possible that there may be no one there."

64.3 ~(으)ㄹ지도 모르다 "may" (see 31.2)

This form is built on the indirect question form ~(으)ㄹ지 (see 31.1), the particle 도 "also" (see 8.1.3), and the verb 모르다 "do not know."

A: 점심 먹고 오후에 도서관에 갔다 올게요.
"After eating lunch, I will go to the library in the afternoon."
B: 이따가 눈이 올지도 모르니까 지금 갔다 오세요.
"It may snow later, so why not go there now."

소포가 내일 도착할지도 몰라요.
"The package may arrive here tomorrow."
이번 시험은 어려울지도 모르겠어요.
"I think that the exam may be difficult this time."
학생증을 보여 주면 할인을 받을 수 있을지도 몰라요.
"By showing your student ID, you may receive a discount too."

64.4 ~(으)ㄹ 리가 없다 "it's hardly possible" (see 23.1)

A: 빈방이 하나도 없대요.
"She says there are no rooms available."
B: 비성수기인데 방이 없을 리가 없어요.
"It is a slow season, so it is hardly possible that the rooms are sold out."

예약을 안 했을 리가 없어요.
"It is hardly possible that he did not make a reservation."
이렇게 많이 나올 리가 없어요.
"It is hardly possible that the charge comes out to this much."
새로 산 것이라 벌써 고장날 리가 없을 텐데요.
"Since this is a newly purchased one, it is hardly possible that it is broken already."
지갑이 없을 리가 없어요.
"It is hardly possible that the wallet is lost."
액수가 틀릴 리가 없는데요.
"It's hardly possible that the amount is incorrect."
10불이 부족할 리가 없어요.
"It is hardly possible that it lacks ten dollars."
미치지 않은 이상 그런 말을 했을 리가 없어요.
"Unless he is crazy, he would never say such things."

65

Probability and inevitability

This chapter looks into various expressions that Koreans use to indicate probability or inevitability.

65.1 Expressing probability

65.1.1 ~(으)ㄹ 거예요 "will probably" (see 12.1.1)

A: 언제쯤 올까요?
"When do you think they will come?"
B: 아마 오후 늦게 도착할 거예요.
"They will probably arrive here in the late afternoon."

비 때문에 어디 안 나가고 집에 있을 거예요.
"Because of rain, they will probably stay home and not go anywhere."
퇴근 시간이라 길이 막힐 거예요.
"Since it is rush hour, the roads will be likely congested."
다음 달부터 주말마다 테니스를 배우기 시작할 거예요.
"I will probably start learning tennis every weekend, starting from next month."

65.1.2 ~(으)ㄹ 법하다 "be likely" (see 23.8)

A: 금전적으로 힘들 법한데 잘 버티고 있네요.
"It is likely that he has a hard time financially, but he is hanging in there well."
B: 한국에 계신 아버지가 엄청 부자이신 거 모르셨어요?
"You didn't know that his father in Korea is really rich?"

눈치를 챘을 법한데 계속 모른 척하네요.
"It is likely that he found out about it, but he continuously pretends that he does not know about it."
어제 야근 때문에 피곤할 법한데 오늘 아침도 조깅하러 나갔어요.
"Because of working late last night, he is likely to be tired, but he went out to jog this morning too."
도움을 받았으니 커피라도 한잔 살 법한데 지금까지 전혀 연락이 없어요.
"Since he got my help, it is likely that he will at least buy me a cup of coffee, but I haven't heard anything so far."
이제 많이 익숙해졌을 법도 한데 여전히 실수 투성이에요.
"It is likely that he is used to it by now, but he still frequently makes mistakes."

PROBABILITY AND INEVITABILITY

65.2 Expressing inevitability

65.2.1 ~(으)ㄹ 게 뻔하다 "bound to"

This form is made with the noun-modifying ending ~(으)ㄹ, the bound noun 게 (the contracted form of 것이), the noun 뻔 "almost/about to," (see 23.9) and the verb 하다 "do." This expression indicates that some events are bound to happen.

    A: 이번에는 시험에 합격할 수 있을까요?
        "Do you think that he will pass the bar this time?"
    B: 합격이요? 이번에도 공부를 열심히 안 해서 떨어질 게 뻔해요.
        "Pass? No way. He did not study hard, so he is bound to fail this time as well."

어젯밤 잠을 하나도 못 자서 피곤해할 게 뻔해요.
"Since he could not sleep at all last night, he is bound to be tired."
지금 나가면 비 때문에 신발이 젖을 게 뻔해요.
"If you go out now, it is inevitable that your shoes will become wet because of the rain."
목이 부어서 못 먹을 게 뻔해요.
"It is obvious that he will be unable to eat because his throat is swollen."

65.2.2 ~기 십상이다 "it is easy to" (see 4.1.14)

    A: 좀 출출한데 지금 시간에 뭐 먹으면 안 되겠지요?
        "I am kind of hungry, but I should not eat at this hour, right?"
    B: 그럼요. 밤 늦게 먹고 자면 살찌기 십상이에요.
        "Of course. If you eat and sleep late, it is easy to gain weight."

지금 팔면 손해보기 십상이에요.
"If you sell it now, you are most likely to lose money."
담배를 끊지 않으면 건강을 잃기 십상이에요.
"If you don't quit smoking, it is easy to lose your health."
미리 준비 운동을 하지 않고 조깅을 하면 다치기 십상이에요.
"If you jog without stretching in advance, it is easy to hurt yourself."

65.2.3 ~기 마련이다 "bound to" (see 4.1.12)

    A: 남자 친구 생긴 뒤 예원이가 요즘 많이 변했지요?
        "After getting a boyfriend, Yewon has changed a lot lately, right?"
    B: 연애를 하면 누구나 예뻐지기 마련이에요.
        "One is bound to become pretty if he/she falls in love with someone."

꾸준히 노력하면 좋은 결과를 얻기 마련이다.
"If you continue to make an effort, you are bound to get good results."
베풀고 살면 존경받기 마련이에요.
"If you love giving, you are bound to be respected."
언젠가는 진실이 밝혀지기 마련이니까 기다려 봅시다.
"Someday, the truth is bound to be revealed, so let's try to wait."

65.2.4 ~는 법이다 "it is certain that . . ." (see 23.7)

    A: 우리 아이들은 거진 매일 싸워서 속이 상해요.
        "I am upset because my children argue almost every day."
    B: 아이들은 싸우면서 크는 법이니까 너무 걱정하지 마세요.
        "It is certain that children grow up fighting, so don't worry too much."

정직하지 못한 사람은 결국 실패하는 법이에요.
"It is certain that the person who is not honest will fail at the end."

Expressing inevitability   **65.2**

꾸준히 노력하는 사람만이 <u>성공하는 법이에요</u>.
"It is certain that only those who strive steadily succeed."
사람의 욕심은 <u>끝이 없는 법이에요</u>.
"It is certain that people's greed is limitless."
집 떠나서 생활하면 <u>고생하는 법이에요</u>.
"It is certain that you will have a hard time while living away from your home."
추운 겨울이 지나면 <u>따뜻한 봄이 오는 법이에요</u>.
"It is certain that when the cold winter passes, warm spring comes."
충분히 쉬어야 <u>힘이 나는 법인데</u> 너무 무리하는 거 아니에요?
"It is certain that you need to rest to get strength, but don't you overwork yourself?"

65.2.5 ~(으)ㄹ 수 밖에 없다 "have no choice but" (see 23.11)

A: 영화 본다면서 왜 일찍 들어왔니?
"You said that you would watch the movie, but why did you come back so early?"
B: 표가 매진돼서 그냥 집에 <u>돌아올 수 밖에 없었어요</u>.
"Since the tickets were all sold out, we had no choice but just return home."

지갑을 집에 두고 와서 사무실까지 <u>걸어 갈 수 밖에 없었어요</u>.
"Because I left my wallet at home, I had no choice but to walk to the office."
감기에 걸려서 집에서 <u>쉴 수 밖에 없어요</u>.
"Since I caught a cold, I have no choice but to rest at home."
제가 공항에 <u>나갈 수 밖에 없을 것 같아요</u>.
"It seems that I have no choice but to go to the airport."

65.2.6 안 ~(으)ㄹ 수 없다 "have no choice but" (see 23.11)

A: 내일 모임에 참석하실 거예요?
"Will you participate at the meeting tomorrow?"
B: 그럼요. 엄청나게 중요한 모임인데 <u>안 갈 수 없지요</u>.
"Of course. It is an extremely important meeting, so I have no choice but to go there."

형 부탁인데 <u>안 도와 줄 수 없지요</u>.
"It's my older brother's request, so I have no choice but to help out."
내일 시험을 <u>안 볼 수 없지요</u>.
"I have no choice but take the exam tomorrow."
제 제일 친한 친구가 졸업하는데 <u>안 갈 수 없지요</u>.
"My best friend will graduate, so I have no choice but to go to the commencement."

65.2.7 ~는/(으)ㄴ 마당에 "in this situation"

This form is constructed from the noun-modifying endings ~는/(으)ㄴ (see 21), the noun 마당 "occasion," and the particle 에 (se 6.1.1).

A: 일단 어디가서 이야기 좀 하면서 생각해 봅시다.
"Let's go somewhere, talk, and think about it more."
B: <u>이 위급한 마당에</u> 그게 무슨 말이에요?
"In this urgent situation, what do you mean by that?"

<u>함께 늙어 가는 마당에</u> 그게 무슨 소리예요?
"In this situation where both of us are getting old, what are you talking about?"
<u>떠나는 마당에</u> 무슨 할 말이 있겠어요?
"What should I say at this time of departure?"
<u>너무 급한 마당에</u> 실수를 하고 말았다.
"I ended up making mistakes because of this urgent situation."
일이 다 <u>이렇게 된 마당에</u> 포기하면 안 되지요.
"In this situation where things turned out this way, you should not give up."

66

Purpose

What follow are some major expressions that Koreans use to indicate purpose.

66.1 Asking about purpose

To ask about purpose, you can use the following expressions:

무슨 일로 오셨습니까?
"What brought you here?"
뭐 때문에 만나셨나요?
"Why did you meet him?"
뭐 하시려구요?
"What do you intend to do?"
무엇을 위해서 그렇게 열심히 준비하십니까?
"For what do you prepare so passionately?"
도서관에는 왠 일이세요?
"What brought you to the library?"

66.2 Expressing purpose

66.2.1 ~고자 "intending to" (see 18.1.4)

A: 어떻게 저희 연극영화과에 관심을 가지게 되었지요?
"What made you become interested in our Department of Theatre?"
B: 배우로서의 꿈을 펼쳐 보고자 지원하였습니다.
"I applied so that I can start my dream of becoming an actor."

부탁을 좀 드리고자 전화 드렸습니다.
"I called because I have a favor to ask you."
이웃들과 좋은 관계를 유지하고자 노력하고 있습니다.
"We are trying our best to maintain good relationships with our neighbors."
스트레스를 풀고자 운동을 하고 있습니다.
"I am exercising to relieve stress."
오늘은 한국의 직업난에 대해서 이야기하고자 합니다.
"Today, I intend to talk about Korea's unemployment issue."

66.2.2 ~으러 "in order to" (see 18.1.1)

A: 어디 가세요?
"Where are you going?"
B: 빌린 책을 반납하러 도서관에요.
"To the library to return some borrowed books."

Expressing purpose

66.2

남자 친구 <u>만나러</u> 한국에 가려구요.
"I intend to go to Korea to meet my boyfriend."
중국어를 <u>배우러</u> 학원에 다니고 있어요.
"I am attending a foreign language institute to learn Chinese."
친구를 <u>마중하러</u> 공항에 가는 길이에요.
"I am on my way to the airport to greet my friends."

66.2.3 ~(으)려고 "to" (see 18.1.2)

A: 도서관에는 웬 일이세요?
   "What brought you to the library?"
B: 보고서 자료를 <u>찾아보려고요</u>.
   "I intend to search for the report data."

건강을 <u>되찾으려고</u> 규칙적인 생활을 하고 있습니다.
"I am living a well-regulated life to get my health back."
네 목소리 좀 <u>들으려고</u> 전화했다.
"I called to listen to your voice."
의대에 <u>들어가려고</u> 준비하고 있어요.
"I am preparing to get admitted to a medical school."
살을 좀 <u>빼려고</u> 하루에 두 끼만 먹고 있어요.
"I am eating only twice a day to lose some weight."
친구하고 영화 <u>보려고</u> 왔어요.
"I came to watch a movie with friends."
여자 친구에게 <u>주려고</u> 목걸이를 하나 샀어요.
"I bought a necklace to give it to my girlfriend."
새벽에 <u>일어나려고</u> 알람을 두 개나 맞춰 놓았어요.
"I set up two alarms to get up at daybreak."
<u>잊지 않으려고</u> 메모해 두었어요.
"I took some memos in advance not to forget."

66.2.4 ~도록 "so that" (see 18.1.6)

A: 지금 몇 시예요?
   "What time is it now?"
B: 죄송합니다. 다시는 <u>늦지 않도록</u> 조심하겠습니다.
   "I am sorry. I will be careful so that I will never be late again."

감기에 <u>걸리지 않도록</u> 꼭 조심하세요.
"Please take care of yourself so that you do not catch a cold."
증상이 더 <u>심해지지 않도록</u> 약은 꼭 제시간에 드세요.
"Make sure that you take the medicine in time so that your symptoms do not worsen."
푹 잘 <u>수 있도록</u> 커피같이 카페인이 들어 있는 것은 드시지 마시구요.
"Do not drink things like coffee that contain caffeine so that you can sleep well."
제가 부장님과 <u>상의하도록</u> 이야기해 놓겠습니다.
"I will tell him so that he will discuss it with the department manager."
다른 달로 <u>옮기도록</u> 요청해 놓겠습니다.
"I will request it in advance so that they can move the schedule to the next month."

66.2.5 ~게 "so that" (see 18.1.5)

A: 지금 깨울까요?
   "Shall I wake him up now?"
B: 아니요. 더 <u>자게</u> 내버려 두세요.
   "No. Leave him alone so that he can sleep longer."

PURPOSE

쉽게 찾을 수 있게 식탁 위에 올려 놓았어요.
"I put it on the table so that you can find it easily."
목욕하게 물 좀 받아 주세요.
"Please prepare hot water so that I can take a bath."
라면 좀 먹게 물 좀 끓여 줄래요?
"Can you please boil some water so that I can eat Ramen?"
그 DVD 나도 좀 보게 빌려주세요.
"Please lend it to me so that I can also watch that DVD."
내가 잘 볼 수 있게 글자를 크게 복사해 주세요.
"Please copy it in a bigger letter size so that I can read it easily."

66.2.6 N위해서 "for the sake of N"

This form is made of 위하다 "treat with care" and the conjunctive ~어서/아서 (see 16.2.1).

A: 금연하신다면서요.
   "I heard that you quit smoking."
B; 아이들을 위해서라도 꼭 끊어야 할 텐데 잘될까 모르겠어요.
   "At least for the sake of my children, I should definitely quit, but I am not sure if I can succeed."

건강을 위해서 매일 아침마다 30분쯤 걷기 시작했습니다.
"For the sake of my health, I started walking about 30 minutes every day."
잊어버리지 않기 위해서 메모하려구요.
"I intend to take a memo in order not to forget about it."
좀 더 좋은 물건을 싸게 구입하기 위해서 나왔습니다.
"We are out here so that we can purchase better items at a better price."

67

Reasons

Korean has a number of expressions to express reasons.

67.1 Asking about reasons

The following are some typical expressions used to ask about or express reasons.

뭐 때문에 "for what?"

> 뭐 때문에 안 왔어요?
> "Why didn't you come?"
> 뭐 때문에 화가 나셨어요?
> "Why were you upset?"
> 이유가 뭐예요?
> "What's the reason?"

어떻게 "how?"

> 어떻게 된 거예요?
> "What happened?"
> 어떻게 한국어에 관심을 가지게 되셨어요?
> "What made you become interested in the Korean language?"
> 어떻게 되었는지 설명 부탁드립니다.
> "Please explain how it turned out."

왜 "Why?"

> 왜요?
> "Why?"
> 왜 그러세요?
> "What's wrong?"
> 하다가 왜 그만두셨어요?
> "Why did he quit in the middle of working on it?"
>
> A: 왜 안 오셨어요?
>   "Why didn't you come?"
> B: 피곤해서요.
>   "Because I was tired."
>
> A: 뭐 때문에 이리 늦었어요?
>   "Why are you so late?"
> B: 미안해요. 갑자기 눈이 오는 바람에 길이 엄청 막혔어요.
>   "Sorry. Because it started snowing all of a sudden, the road was really congested."

REASONS

67.2 Expressing reasons

67.2.1 ~고 해서 "so"

This form is made of the conjunctive ~고 (see 19.1.1), the verb 하다 "do," and the conjunctive ~어서/아서 (see 16.2.1).

    A: 앤드류 씨는 뭐 드실 거예요?
        "Andrew, what are you going to drink?"
    B: 날씨도 덥고 해서 아이스 커피 시키려구요.
        "It is hot, so I am thinking of ordering ice coffee."

눈도 오고 해서 집에 일찍 들어가려구요.
"It is also snowing, so I intend to go home early."
기분도 우울하고 해서 산책 나왔어요.
"I am feeling depressed, so I came out for a walk."
월급도 타고 해서 밥 사 주려고 나왔어요.
"I received my monthly pay check, so I came out to buy her dinner."
돈도 없고 해서 그냥 집에 있으려구요.
"I don't have much money left, so I am just thinking of staying home."
아침도 늦게 먹고 해서 점심은 별로 생각이 없는데요.
"I ate my breakfast late, so I am not really hungry for lunch."

67.2.2 ~기에 "since"

This form consists of the nominalizing ending ~기 (see 4.1) and the particle 에 (see 6.1.1).

    A: 왜 이리 많이 사셨어요?
        "Why did you buy so much?"
    B: 오늘로 세일이 끝난다기에 많이 샀지요.
        "I bought a lot of them since the sales end today."

기름 값이 많이 내렸기에 좀 더 큰 차를 구입하려고요.
"Since the gas price went down a lot, I am thinking of buying a bigger car."
업무도 많고 출장도 많기에 그만두려고 합니다.
"Since my job has a heavy workload and many business trips, I am thinking of quitting."
정말 열심히 준비해 왔기에 합격 소식에 더욱 기뻤어요.
"Since I have worked really hard, I was extremely happy to hear that I got accepted."
아직 지금 회의 중이시기에 기다리고 있습니다.
"Since he is in the middle of a meeting, I am waiting."

67.2.3 ~길래 "since" (see 16.2.7)

    A: 히터 틀었어요?
        "Did you turn on the heater?"
    B: 네. 집이 좀 춥길래 켰는데요.
        "Yes. I turned it on since the house was a bit chilly."

그렇게도 디즈니랜드에 가고 싶어하길래 이번 여름 방학 때 가기로 했어요.
"Since they want to go to Disney Land so much, we decided to go there this summer vacation."
무슨 실수를 했길래 그렇게 화가 나셨어요?
"What did you do wrong that he was so angry at you?"
얼마나 어렵길래 이렇게 열심히 공부하세요?
"How difficult is it that you study this hard?"
어떤 사람이길래 그렇게 욕을 하세요?
"What kind of person is he that you swear at him like that?"

Expressing reasons

얼마나 집이 좋길래 그렇게 부러워하세요?
"How great is his house that you envy it so much?"

67.2.4 ~느라고 "as a result of" (see 16.2.4)

A: 왜 이렇게 늦게 나와요?
"Why do you come out so late?"
B: 열쇠 찾느라고요. 미안해요.
"Because I was looking for my keys. Sorry."

다른 생각을 하느라고 못 들었어요.
"I could not hear it for I was thinking about something else."
제 동생하고 수다 떠느라고 깜박했네요.
"I forgot because I was chatting with my younger sister."
야근을 하느라고 전화를 못 드렸습니다.
"I could not give you a call because I was working late at night."
아이를 맡기고 오느라고 늦었어요.
"I was late because I dropped the child off at the daycare."

67.2.5 ~는/(으)ㄴ 바람에 "because of" (see 23.5)

A: 아이구, 어떻게 다치셨어요?
"Oh my, how did you get hurt?"
B: 축구하다가 넘어지는 바람에요.
"Because I fell while playing soccer."

여자 친구 생일을 잊어버리는 바람에 다퉜어요.
"Because I forgot when my girlfriend's birthday was, we argued."
제 컴퓨터가 바이러스에 걸리는 바람에 파일을 열 수 없었어요.
"Because my computer was infected with a virus, I could not open the file."
버스가 늦게 오는 바람에 늦었습니다.
"Because the bus arrived late, I was late."
갑자기 소나기가 내리는 바람에 옷이 흠뻑 젖었네요.
"Because a shower came suddenly, my clothes are soaked."
열쇠를 사무실에 놓고 오는 바람에 밖에서 기다리고 있었어요.
"Because I left my keys in my office, I was waiting outside."
약속 시간을 착각하는 바람에 늦었습니다.
"Because I was confused with the appointment time, I was late."
집에 다시 들어갔다가 나오는 바람에 버스를 놓치고 말았어요.
"Because I went in and out of the house again, I missed the bus."

67.2.6 ~는/(으)ㄴ 이상 "since"

This form consists of the noun-modifying ending ~는/(으)ㄴ (see 21) and the noun 이상 "above, beyond."

A: 좀 더 생각해 보고 결정하고 싶은데 어떻게 안 될까요?
"I want to decide after giving it some more thought; is there any way I can do so?"
B: 죄송합니다. 계약서에 사인을 하신 이상 바꿀 수가 없네요.
"I am sorry. Since you signed it, you can't change it."

이 사실을 알게 된 이상 가만히 있을 수는 없어요.
"Since I found out about this fact, I can't just remain silent."
회원 대부분이 찬성한 이상 모두 열심히 해 봅시다.
"Since the majority of the members agreed on this, let's do our best."
그 사람과 이미 결혼한 이상 평생 같이 살아야 해요.
"Since you are already married to that person, you must live with him for your whole life."

REASONS

67.2

내가 <u>선장인 이상</u> 모든 일에 책임을 져야 돼요.
"Since I am the captain of the ship, I need to take responsibility for all matters."

67.2.7 ~는/(으)ㄴ 탓/통에 "because" (see 24.8)

A: 잠자리가 불편하셨나요?
   "Was your bed uncomfortable?"
B: 룸메이트가 <u>코를 심하게 골아 대는 통에</u> 잠을 설쳤습니다.
   "I could not sleep well because my roommate snored loudly."

A: 지금쯤 어디세요?
   "Where are you?"
B: 아직 회사 근처요.
   "Still near the company."
   비가 많이 <u>오는 탓에</u> 길이 엄청 막히네요.
   "Because of the heavy rain, the traffic is really congested."

<u>경기가 안 좋은 탓에</u> 취직하기가 어려운 거겠지요.
"I guess it has been difficult to get a job because business is not good."
담배를 평생 <u>피웠던 탓에</u> 결국 폐암으로 죽었어요.
"Because he smoked all of his life, he eventually died of lung cancer."
아이가 밤새 <u>우는 통에</u> 한숨도 못 잤어요.
"Because the child cried all night long, I could not sleep at all."
성격이 <u>급한 탓에</u> 실수가 잦은 편이에요.
"Because of my quick temper, I tend to make mistakes often."
배가 심하게 <u>흔들리는 통에</u> 멀미할 뻔했어요.
"Because the ship rolled terribly, I almost vomited."
회사 화장실을 <u>수리하는 통에</u> 좀 불편해요.
"Because the toilet is under construction, it is a bit in convenient."
어제 친구들하고 맥주를 너무 많이 <u>마신 탓에</u> 머리가 아프네요.
"Because I drank a lot of beers with my friends yesterday, my head aches."
인터뷰 <u>점수가 낮았던 탓에</u> 떨어진 것 같아요.
"Because my interview score was low, I think that I didn't make it."
아직 <u>미성년자인 탓에</u> 부모가 같이 가야 한대요.
"They say that since he is a minor still, his parents must go with him."
계속 <u>사달라고 조르는 통에</u> 엄청 짜증이 났었어요.
"Because he continued to nag me to buy it, I was very annoyed."

67.2.8 ~어/아서 "so" (see 16.2.1)

A: 서울 생활은 어떠세요?
   "How is your life in Seoul?"
B: 아는 사람이 별로 <u>없어서</u> 심심해요.
   "There are not many people that I know, so it is boring."

갑자기 <u>회의가 생겨서</u> 일찍 나올 수가 없었어요.
"Since there was an urgent meeting, I could not come out earlier."
바쁘지만 일이 <u>재미있어서</u> 견딜 만해요.
"It is busy, but since the work itself is fun, I can somehow hang in there."
학교 일이 너무 <u>많아서</u> 어쩔 수가 없었어요.
"Since there was too much school work, I could not do anything about it."
중요한 손님이 갑자기 <u>방문하셔서</u> 정신없이 바빴어요.
"Since important visitors visited me suddenly, I was really busy."
부장님이 <u>이야기 좀 하자고 하셔서</u> 늦었어요.
"The department chief asked to have a conversation, so I was late."

Expressing reasons   67.2

과장님이 오늘까지 보고서를 끝내라고 하셔서 야근해야 돼요.
"The section chief asked me to complete the report by today, so I need to work all night."
시차 때문에 자지 못 해서 피곤하네요.
"I couldn't sleep due to the time difference, so I am tired."
잠자리가 바뀌어서 푹 못 잤어요.
"Since the bed changed, I couldn't sleep well."
차를 오래 타서 멀미를 했어요.
"I got carsick because I rode in the car for a long time."

67.2.9 ~어/아서 그런지 "perhaps … so"

집이 낡아서 그런지 고칠 곳이 많아요.
"Perhaps, the house is old, so there are many places to fix."
창문이 없어서 그런지 공기가 탁하네요.
"Maybe, since there is no window, the air is stuffy."
성격이 좋아서 그런지 친구가 많아요.
"Perhaps his personality is good, so he has many friends."
매일 운동해서 그런지 피곤하지 않네요.
"Maybe because I exercise every day, I am not tired."
평일이라서 그런지 손님이 별로 없네요.
"Perhaps it is a weekday, so there are not many customers."
하와이라서 그런지 항상 관광객이 엄청 많아요.
"Perhaps, since it is Hawaii, there are so many tourists all the time."

67.2.10 ~(으)니까 "since" (see 16.2.2)

A: 여기는 구경할 것이 별로 없으니까 시내로 나갑시다.
    "Since there are not many things to see, let's go downtown."
B: 네, 그럼, 그럴까요?
    "OK, then, shall we?"

길을 잘 모르니까 꼭 GPS를 쓰세요.
"Since I do not know the way well, please use the GPS at any cost."
오전에는 수업이 있으니까 오후 2시쯤 들르세요.
"Since I have a class in the morning, please stop by around 2 p.m."
이번 금요일에 쉬니까 그때 오세요.
"I am off this Friday, so please come at that time."
비싸니까 지금 사지 말고 금년 말까지 좀 기다리세요.
"Since it is expensive, don't buy it now but wait until the end of the year."
추우니까 스웨터 잊지 말고 입고 나가세요.
"It's cold, so don't forget to wear your sweater when you go out."

67.2.11 ~(으)므로 "because, since" (see 16.2.5)

재능도 있고 성실하므로 분명히 성공할 거예요.
"Since he has talents and is diligent, I am sure he will succeed."
다음 주부터는 세일이 끝나므로 가능하면 미리 사 두시는 게 좋을 것 같습니다.
"The sale period will end starting from next week, so if possible, I think it would be nice to buy them in advance."
요즘 독감이 유행하는 시기이므로 건강에 특히 조심하십시오.
"Since it is the flu season these days, pay extra attention for your health."
어린이의 생각하는 방식은 어른들과 다르므로 아이의 관점에 맞춰서 이야기하셔야 해요.
"Since children's way of thinking differs from that of adults, you need to talk to them by adjusting your perspectives with theirs."

68

Recollecting

This chapter examines various expressions related to recollection or retrospection.

68.1 Some verbs, words, or phrases related to recollection

The typical words or verbs for remembering or recollecting in Korean include 기억, 추억, 기억하다, 기억나다, 생각이 나다, and 생각해 내다.

    A: 작년 선우 결혼식에서 봤었는데 저 <u>기억하세요</u>?
        "We met at Sunwoo's wedding last year; do you remember me?"
    B: 아, 예, <u>생각납니다</u>. 선우 고등학교 친구이시지요?
        "Oh, yes, I remember you. You are Sunwoo's high school friend, right?"

<u>생각이 잘 안 나네요</u>.
"I can't really remember that."
<u>기억이 안 나요</u>.
"I don't remember that."
그때가 <u>그립네요</u>.
"I long for those days."
그 <u>추억은 잊을 수가 없어요</u>.
"I can't forget that memory."
아직도 <u>기억이 생생해요</u>.
"Even now, my memory is vivid."
그때 정말 <u>재미있었는데</u> . . .
"It was really fun back then . . ."
많이 <u>그립고 그때로 돌아가고 싶다</u>.
"I miss those days and wish to go back."
단발 머리에 웃는 미소가 예뻤던 네 모습이 <u>생각난다</u>.
"I remember you with bobbed hair and a pretty smile."
안 잊고 <u>추억</u> 속에 간직할게요.
"I will never forget but cherish it in my memory."

68.2 The use of past tense marker ~었/았

68.2.1 ~었/았었어요 (see 11.2)

    A: 여기 음식 어때요?
        "How is the food here?"
    B: 작년에 한 번 <u>왔었는데</u> 그때 정말 <u>맛있었었어요</u>.
        "We came here once last Christmas, and it was really delicious back then."

그때 정말 <u>좋았었어요</u>.
"It was so great back then."

The use of retrospective suffix ~더 (see 11.3)

그랜드캐년에 갔었는데 너무 <u>감동적이었었어요</u>.
"I visited the Grand Canyon, and it was really moving back then."

68.2.2 ~었/았을 때 "when"

The form is made of the past tense ~었/았, the noun-modifying ending ~(으)ㄹ (see 21.3), and the noun 때 "time."

A: 한국에 <u>갔을 때</u> 독감 때문에 엄청 고생했어요.
"When I went to Korea, I suffered a lot because of the flu."
B: 아이구 그럼 많이 구경 못 하셨겠네요.
"Oh my . . . then I guess that you could not see much."

처음 남자 친구하고 <u>헤어졌을 때</u> 무척 힘들었었어요.
"When I first broke up with my boyfriend, it was really hard."
새로 산 컴퓨터가 <u>고장났을 때</u> 좀 황당했어요.
"When my new computer broke, I was in a panic."
그 노래를 <u>들었을 때</u> 네 생각이 났었다.
"When I heard that song, I remembered you."

68.2.3 ~곤 했다 "used to"

This form consists of the conjunctive ~고 (see 19.1.1), the topic particle 은/는 (see 7.2.1), the past tense marker ~었/았 (see 11.1), and the verb 하다 "do." It is used to recollect one's habitual actions in the past.

A: 여기가 처음이 아니신가 봐요.
"It seems that it is not your first time being here."
B: 어렸을 때 할머니하고 이 곳 성당에 일요일마다 <u>오곤 했어요</u>.
"When I was a kid, I used to attend this Catholic Church with my grandmother every Sunday."

눈이 오는 날이면 그 사람이 <u>생각나곤 했어요</u>.
"On every snowy day, I used to remember that person."
스트레스를 받을 때면 자주 머리가 <u>아프곤 했어요</u>.
"Whenever I felt stressed, I used to have a headache."
주말에는 남편이 <u>요리를 해 주곤 했어요</u>.
"On the weekend, my husband used to cook for me."
너무 바쁠 때는 점심도 못 먹고 <u>일하곤 했어요</u>.
"When I was too busy, I used to work without even eating lunch."
가끔 네 <u>이야기를 하곤 했다</u>.
"From time to time, she used to talk about you."

68.3 The use of retrospective suffix ~더 (see 11.3)

68.3.1 ~데요 "I notice/remember that . . ."

The form is made of the retrospective suffix ~더 (see 11.3) and the polite speech level ~어/아요 (see 27.2.2).

A: 아는 분이셨어요?
"Was she a person you know?"
B: 듣고 보니까 <u>제 누나 동창이데요</u>.
"Hearing her story, I noticed that she was my older sister's school friend."

모두 맛있게 <u>먹데요</u>.
"I noticed that everyone ate deliciously."

RECOLLECTING

정말 직접 보니까 <u>신기하데요</u>.
"Seeing it with my own eyes, I noticed that it was really marvelous."
다들 <u>눈물을 흘리시네요</u>.
"I noticed that everyone was in tears."
그 일도 못 할 짓이데요.
"I remember that the job was also a difficult task."
그 학교 들어가기 정말 <u>어렵데요</u>.
"I noticed that getting admitted to that school was really hard."

68.3.2 ~더라고(구)요 "I'm telling you, you know" (see 11.3)

A: 왜 창문을 닫았어요?
   "Why did you close the window?"
B: 창문을 여니까 모기가 많이 <u>들어오더라구요</u>.
   "When I opened the window, a lot of mosquitos entered the room, you know."

입어 보니까 너무 <u>크더라구요</u>.
"When I tried it on, it was too big, you know."
커피가 싸고 <u>맛있더라구요</u>.
"The coffee was cheap and tasty, you know."
어머니께서 많이 <u>걱정하시더라구요</u>.
"My mother was really concerned, you know."
한국에 가니까 정말 <u>산이 많더라구요</u>.
"When I went to Korea, I noticed that there were really many mountains, you know."

68.3.3 The use of the retrospective noun-modifying ending ~던 (see 21.4)

A: 와, 맛있네요!
   "Wow, it is delicious!"
B: 미국에 있었을 때 자주 만들어 <u>먹던</u> 음식이에요.
   "This is food that I used to make and enjoy frequently when I was in the states."

친구들과 자주 <u>가던</u> 식당은 시내에 있어요.
"The cafeteria that I used to go to with my friends is located downtown."
제가 고등학교 때 자주 <u>듣던</u> 노래예요.
"It is a song that I used to listen to when I was a high school student."
저희가 주말이면 자주 <u>찾던</u> 커피숍이에요.
"This is the coffee shop that we used to visit every weekend."
옛 여자 친구하고 자주 <u>가던</u> 공원이에요.
"This is the park that I used to go to with my ex-girlfriend."

68.3.4 ~었/았던

This form is made of the past tense marker ~었/았 (see 11.1) and the retrospective noun-modifying ending ~던 (see 21.4).

A: 와, 이거 내가 고등학교 때 엄청 <u>좋아했던</u> 노래인데요.
   "Wow, this is the song that I liked when I was a high school student."
B: 아 그래요? 저도 자주 <u>듣던</u> 노래예요.
   "Oh, really? It's a song that I also used to listen to frequently."

작년에 한국을 방문했을 때 친구하고 <u>갔던</u> 식당이에요.
"It is the restaurant that I went to with my friend when I visited Korea last year."
언니가 결혼할 때 <u>입었던</u> 웨딩드레스를 입기로 했어요.
"I decided to wear the wedding dress that my older sister wore for her wedding."

The use of retrospective suffix ~더 (see 11.3) **68.3**

대학교 때 <u>좋아했던</u> 친구를 길거리에서 마주쳤다.
"I ran into the friend that I liked in college on the street."
여기가 우리가 신혼여행 때 <u>묵었던</u> 호텔이에요.
"This place is the hotel that we stayed in during our honeymoon."
눈이 유난히 <u>컸던</u> 친구였어요.
"He was my friend with unusually huge eyes."

68.3.5 ~던데요 "I perceived that . . ."

This form adds the retrospective noun-modifying ending ~던 (see 21.4) to ~데요. The meaning of ~던데요 is similar to ~데요 in that they both signal a perceived past event or state.

   A: 학교 앞에 새로 생긴 일식당에 가 보셨어요?
       "Have you been to the new Japanese restaurant in front of the school?
   B: 네, 지난 토요일에 갔는데 깨끗하고 음식이 아주 <u>맛있던데요</u>.
       "Yes, I went there last Saturday, and I perceived that the restaurant was really clean, and the food was really delicious."

노래를 굉장히 <u>잘 하던데요</u>.
"I perceived that she really sang well."
영화가 아주 재미있고 <u>감동적이던데요</u>.
"I perceived that the movie was really interesting and moving."
시험이 생각보다 아주 <u>쉽던데요</u>.
"I perceived that the exam was much easier than my expectations."
아주 <u>괜찮아 보이던데요</u>.
"I perceived that it looked nice."
학교 헬스클럽 시설이 아주 <u>좋던데요</u>.
"I perceived the facility of the fitness center was really good."

69

Regret and futility

This chapter discusses expressions that can be used to indicate regret or futility.

69.1 후회스럽다/유감스럽다 "regretful"

Korean nouns, adjectives, and verbs that explicitly denote a sense of regret include 후회 "regret/repentance," 후회하다 "to regret," 후회스럽다 "regretful," 유감 "regret/pity," 유감스럽다 "regretful/sorry," and so forth.

지난 날들이 정말 후회스러워요.
"My past days are really regretful."
지금 안 사시면 결국 후회하실 거예요.
"You will regret it eventually if you don't buy it now."
왜 그 생각을 못했을까 후회가 돼요.
"Why couldn't I think about it? I feel so regretful."
지금 와서 후회한들 무슨 소용있겠어요?
"What's the use even if you regret it not?"
그때 왜 병원에 안 갔을까 후회가 됩니다.
"I regret that I did not go to the hospital at that time."
그때 열심히 공부하지 않았던 것이 후회스럽습니다.
"I am regretful that I did not study hard at that time."
정말 유감입니다.
"It's really a great pity."
그 일에 대해서는 저희도 매우 유감스럽습니다.
"As for that matter, we are also very regretful."
유감스럽게도 참석 못 할 것 같습니다.
"To my regret, I will not be able to participate"

69.2 ~고 말다 "end up ~ing" (see 15.1)

어제 늦게 퇴근하는 바람에 오늘 아침 늦게까지 자고 말았어요.
"Because I left my work late yesterday, I ended up oversleeping this morning."
지난 며칠 동안 무리를 좀 했더니 감기에 걸리고 말았어요.
"I overworked myself the last few days, and I ended up catching a cold."
제 옛날 여자 친구 때문에 지금 여자 친구랑 헤어지고 말았어요.
"Because of my ex-girlfriend, I ended up breaking up with my current girlfriend."
경쟁이 너무 심해서 인터뷰에서 아깝게 떨어지고 말았어요.
"Because the competition was too severe, I didn't pass the interview."

69.3 왜 . . . 는지 모르겠다 "not sure why . . ."

This form is made up of the question word 왜 "why," the indirect question form ~는지 (see 31.1), and the verb 모르다 "do not know."

도대체 왜 그랬는지 모르겠어요.
"I don't know why I did that."
왜 거절했는지 모르겠어요.
"I am not sure why I refused it."
왜 가겠다고 했는지 모르겠어요.
"I don't know why I volunteered to go there."
왜 하겠다고 했는지 모르겠어요.
"I don't know why I said that I would do it."

69.4 ~(으)ㄹ걸 그랬다 "should have" (see 26.1)

A: 음식이 많이 남았네요. 더 드시지 그래요?
"So much food is left. Why don't you help yourself to more?"
B: 아니요. 배부른데요. 음식을 조금 시킬걸 그랬어요.
"No, I am full. I should have ordered fewer dishes."

그렇게 하지 말걸 그랬어요.
"I should not have done that."
그때 샀으면 좋았을걸 그랬어요.
"It would be nicer if I had bought it at that time."
가지 말고 좀 더 기다릴걸 그랬어요.
"I should have waited longer, and not gone back."
디저트까지 먹지 말걸 그랬어요.
"I should not have eaten dessert."

69.5 ~었/았더라면 ~(으)ㄹ 텐데 "if/when . . . I guess that . . ."

This construction is made of ~었/았더라면 (see 18.2.3) and ~(으)ㄹ 텐데 (see 17.1.2).

A: 시험 잘 보셨어요?
"Did you do well on the exam?"
B: 아니요. 좀 더 열심히 공부했더라면 좋았을 텐데 후회돼요.
"No. If I would have studied harder, I guess that I could have done better, so I feel regretful."

좀 더 일찍 출발했더라면 기차를 놓치지 않았을 텐데 뭐 어떻게 할 수 없지요.
"If I would have left earlier, I would not have missed the train, but I couldn't help it."
미리 예약하고 갔더라면 기다리지 않아도 됐을 텐데 말이에요.
"If I went there after making a reservation in advance, we wouldn't have to wait, you see."
그때 포기하지 않았더라면 의사가 될 수도 있었을 텐데 아쉬워요.
"If I did not give up at that time, I could have become a doctor, so it's a great pity."
그때 검사를 받았더라면 그 큰 병에 걸리지 않을 수도 있었을 텐데 후회돼요.
"If I could have received the check up, I would not have fallen ill, so I feel sorry about that."
물어보고 샀더라면 더 싸게 살 수 있었을 텐데 아쉽네요.
"If I bought that after finding out its price, I could have bought it cheaper, so it's a pity."
꽃이라도 사서 갔더라면 좋았을 텐데 할 수 없네요.
"If I at least bought some flowers and went there, it would have been nice, but it's too late."
10분 일찍 일어났더라면 버스를 놓치지 않았을 텐데 말이에요.
"If I could have gotten up ten minutes early, I would not have missed the bus, you see."

REGRET AND FUTILITY

병원에 더 빨리 도착했었더라면 돌아가지 않으셨을 텐데 정말 죄송합니다.
"If he had arrived at the hospital more quickly, he probably would have not passed away; I am really sorry."
담배를 피우지 않으셨더라면 더 오래 사셨을 텐데 지금 와서 어떻게 뭐 할 수 없지요.
"If he did not smoke, he probably would have lived longer, but it is too late to do anything now."
과식을 안 했었더라면 배탈이 안 났을 텐데 후회가 막심해요.
"If I did not overeat, I probably would not have an upset stomach, so I regret it very much."

69.6 ~었/았아야 했는데 "should have" (see 11.1, 15.9, 17.1.1)

지난 주에 찾아봤어야 했는데 늦었네요.
"I should have come last week, but it is too late."
진작 병원에 모시고 갔어야 했는데 죄송합니다.
"I should have taken her to the hospital beforehand; I am sorry."
그런 이야기를 꺼내지 말았어야 했는데....
"I should not have brought it up...."
좀 더 신중하게 생각했어야 했는데 뭐 할 수 없지요.
"I should have thought about it more, but well, it's too late."
계약서를 꼼꼼하게 읽어 봤어야 했는데 너무 서두르는 바람에 그랬네요.
"I should have read the contract more carefully. I guess I was in a rush."

69.7 ~(으)나 마나 "whether . . . or not" (see 17.2.3)

지금 전화하나 마나 집에 없을 거예요.
"Whether you give her a call or not, she will not be home."
약을 먹으나 마나 별로 효과가 없어요.
"Whether you take the medicine or not, it will have no effect."
이 시간에 가나 마나 안 열었을 거예요.
"Whether you go there or not at this hour, the store is not open."

69.8 ~어/아 봤자 "though you try . . . no use"

This form is made of the auxiliary verb ~어/아 보다 (see 13.6), the past tense ~었/았 (see 11.1), and the ending ~자.

지금 가 봤자 아무도 없을 거예요.
"Even if you go there now, there will be no one there anyway."
이야기를 해 봤자 믿지 않을 거예요.
"Even if you tell her, she will not believe it."
부탁해 봤자 소용없을 거예요.
"Even if you ask for it, it will be of no use."

69.9 ~(으)ㄴ들 "no matter how" (see 17.2.9)

머리가 아무리 좋은들 노력하지 않으면 실패하기 마련이에요.
"No matter how smart you are, if you don't make an effort, you are bound to fail."
아무리 돈이 많은들 건강을 잃으면 다 잃는 겁니다.
"No matter how rich you are, if you lose your health, you lose everything."
지금 와서 후회한들 아무런 소용없어요.
"No matter how sorry you feel about it, it's no use."

외국어 점수가 아무리 높은들 발음이 좋지 않으면 안 돼요.
"No matter how high your foreign language test score is, if your pronunciation is not good, it is of no use."
아무리 얼굴이 예쁜들 성격이 나쁘면 누가 좋아하겠어요?
"No matter how pretty she is, if her personality is bad, who will like her?"

69.10 ~(으)ㄴ 나머지 "as a result of, driven by"

This form consists of the noun-modifying ending ~(으)ㄴ (see 21.2) and the noun 나머지 "a leftover, remaining."

너무 놀란 나머지 무슨 말을 해야 할지 몰랐어요.
"I was so surprised that I didn't know what to say."
인터뷰할 때 너무 긴장한 나머지 실수를 많이 한 것 같아요.
"I was so nervous during the interview that I think I made many mistakes."
너무 바쁜 나머지 오늘이 제 생일인 것도 모르고 있었네요.
"I was so busy that I forgot today was my birthday."
아침 출근시간에 너무 서두른 나머지 지갑을 집에 두고 나왔어요.
"I was so rushed during the morning rush hour that I left my wallet at home and came out."

70

Requests

Korean has different linguistic structures and an intricate linguistic politeness system for indicating different degrees of social meanings, such as distance and power. A request in Korean can be direct/informal or can be extremely lengthy/indirect/formal. The degree of directness/formality/politeness of your request depends on who you are talking to. You need to consider the relationship between yourself and the listener. A single Korean request (e.g., requesting someone to turn on the air conditioner) can be performed at least in 35 ways:

Direct request (command)

(1) 에어콘 틀어.
(2) 에어콘 틀어요 (트세요).
(3) 에어콘 좀 부탁한다 (드립니다).

Indirect request (command)

(4) 에어콘 좀 틀어야지(요).
(5) 에어콘 좀 틀라고(요).
(6) 에어콘 좀 틀도록 해라 (하세요).
(7) 에어콘 좀 틀 거예요 (트실 거예요)?
(8) 에어콘 좀 틀래요 (트실래요)?
(9) 에어콘 좀 틀어 줘요 (주세요).
(10) 에어콘 좀 틀어 줄래요 (주실래요)?
(11) 에어콘 좀 틀어 주겠어요 (주시겠어요)?
(12) 에어콘 좀 틀어 줄 거지요 (틀어 주실 거지요)?

Indirect request (ability/possibility)

(13) 에어콘 틀 수 있어요 (트실 수 있으세요)?
(14) 에어콘 틀 줄 알아요 (틀 줄 아세요)?
(15) 에어콘 좀 틀어 줄 수 있어요 (주실 수 있으세요)?
(16) 에어콘 좀 틀어 줄 수 있겠어요 (주실 수 있으시겠어요)?
(17) 에어콘 좀 틀어 줄 수 있을까요 (주실 수 있으실까요)?
(18) 에어콘 어떻게 트는지 알아요 (트는지 아세요)?

Indirect request (permission)

(19) 에어콘 좀 틀어도 될까(요)?
(20) 에어콘 좀 틀어 주면 안 될까요 (틀어 주시면 안 될까요)?
(21) 에어콘 좀 틀어 주면 안 될까 해서요 (틀어 주시면 안 될까 해서요).

Indirect request (suggestion)

(22) 에어컨 틀자 (틉시다).
(23) 에어컨 좀 틀지 그래요?
(24) 에어컨을 켜는 것이 좋지 않을까요?
(25) 에어컨을 켜는 것이 어때요 (어떨까 싶네요.)?

Indirect request (wish/condition)

(26) 에어컨 좀 틀고 싶다.
(27) 에어컨 좀 틀었으면 좋겠다.
(28) 에어컨 좀 틀어 줬으면 하는데 (틀어 주셨으면 하는데요).
(29) 에어컨 좀 틀어 주면 고맙겠다 (주시면 감사하겠습니다).

Indirect request (need)

(30) 이 방에는 에어컨이 꼭 필요하겠다.
(31) 에어컨이 있어야 하겠다.
(32) 에어컨이 없으면 안 되겠네.

Indirect request (hint)

(33) 덥다. 창문이라도 열든지 뭐라도 좀 해봐.
(34) 에어컨은 그냥 폼으로 달아 놓으셨나?
(35) 방이 좀 덥지 않으세요?

All of the previous examples can be interpreted/used as requests. In addition, except for the first three, all of the examples may be called indirect requests, though with different degrees of indirection. In general, the longer a sentence is, the more indirect – and thus more polite – it is, since more hedges are included. Let's look at more examples.

70.1 Direct request/command (see 27.2)

제발 열심히 공부 좀 <u>해요</u>.
"Study hard, please."
오늘 집에 일찍 들어오도록 <u>해라</u>.
"Come home early today."
커피 두 잔 좀 <u>부탁할게</u>.
"Two cups of coffee, please."

70.2 ~어/아 주세요 "(Please) . . . for me." (see 14.3)

네 자전거 좀 <u>빌려 주라</u>.
"Please let me borrow your bike."
내일 아침 7시에 좀 <u>깨워 주세요</u>.
"Please wake me up at seven tomorrow morning."
여기, 양념치킨 하나하고 맥주 두 병 <u>주세요</u>.
"One order of fried chicken and two bottles of beer here, please."

70.3 ~(으)ㄹ 거지(요)? "You will . . ., right?" (see 12.1.1, 26.6)

내일까지 꼭 가지고 올 <u>거지</u>?
"You will bring it to me by tomorrow, right?"

REQUESTS

약속대로 이제부터 담배 안 피울 거지?
"As promised, you will not smoke from now on, right?"
이따가 시장실 때 같이 갈 거지요?
"Later when going to the market, we will go together, right?"

70.4 ~어/아 줄래(요)/주시겠어요? "Will/Would you . . . ?" (see 14.3, 12.1.2)

나 20달라만 좀 빌려 줄래?
"Will you lend me 20 dollars?"
가게 앞에서 내려 주시겠어요?
"Would you drop me off in front of the store?"
여자 향수 좀 보여 주실래요?
"Would you please show me some women's perfumes?"

70.5 ~(으)ㄹ 수 있으세요? "Can/Could you . . . ?" (see 23.11)

내일 오후 6시까지 데리러 올 수 있으세요?
"Can you please come and pick me up by 6 p.m. tomorrow?"
죄송하지만 TV 소리 좀 줄여 주실 수 있으세요?
"Sorry, but can you please turn down the TV volume for me?"
2층 방들도 보여 주실 수 있으세요?
"Can you please show us the rooms on the second floor as well?"

70.6 ~는지 아세요? "Do you know how to . . . ?" (see 31.1)

메리의 휴대 전화 번호 아세요?
"Do you know Mary's cell phone number?"
이 프린터 어떻게 사용하는지 아세요?
"Do you know how to use this printer?"
이 프로그램을 어떻게 다운로드 받는지 아니?
"Do you know how to download this program?"

70.7 ~어/아 주실 수 있을까(요)? "Would it be possible . . . ?" (see 14.3, 23.11, 26.2)

옆 머리가 아직 긴데 좀 더 잘라 주실 수 있을까요?
"The hair on the side of my head is still a bit long, so would you please cut it a little more?"
선생님, 허락을 해 주시면 안 될까요?
"Sir, wouldn't it be possible for you to give me permission?"
추천서 좀 써 주실 수 있으실까 해서요.
"I wonder if it would be possible for you to write a letter of recommendation for me."

70.8 ~어/아도 될까(요)/괜찮을까(요)? "Would it be fine even if . . . ?" (see 17.2.4, 26.2)

니 거 좀 써도 될까?
"Would it be okay even if I use yours?"

Indirect request (hint)

커피 좀 <u>부탁드려도 될까요</u>?
"Would it be okay even if I ask for a cup of coffee?"
저희가 먼저 <u>먹어도 괜찮을까요</u>?
"Would it be fine even if we eat first?"

70.9 ~읍시다/어떨까 싶네요 "How about . . . Let's . . . I wonder . . ." (see 27.2.1, 15.4)

2차로 노래방 <u>갑시다</u>.
"As for the second event, let's go to a noraebang."
레드와인으로 <u>하는 게 어때</u>?
"How about red wine?"
오늘 점심은 중식이 <u>어떨까 싶네요</u>?
"As for lunch today, how about Chinese food?"

70.10 ~(으)면 한다/고맙겠다/감사하겠습니다 "I would appreciate it if . . ." (see 57.3)

엄마, 제 겨울 코트 좀 <u>부쳐 주셨으면 하는데요</u>.
"Mom, I would appreciate it if you would send me my winter coat."
다음부터는 모자하고 장갑도 <u>준비해 오셨으면 감사하겠습니다</u>.
"I would appreciate it if you would come with a hat and gloves from the next time on."
이따가 올 때 내 거도 같이 <u>갖다 주면 좋겠다</u>.
"It would be nice if you bring mine as well when you come later."
삼일 정도 휴가를 <u>냈으면 하는데요</u>.
"I would appreciate it if I could take three days off."

70.11 Indirect request (want/need) (see 4.1.11, 15.3, 57.3)

찬물이 좀 <u>마시고 싶은데</u>.
"I want to drink cold water."
선생님의 수업을 꼭 <u>듣고 싶은데요</u>.
"I really wish to take your class, please."
내일 모두 아침 8시까지 강당으로 <u>모이시기 바랍니다</u>.
"I hope that everyone gathers in the assembly hall by eight tomorrow morning."
휴가를 좀 <u>냈으면 합니다</u>.
"I would like to take some days off."

70.12 Indirect request (hint)

어, 전화를 집에 나두고 왔네.
"Oh, I left my phone at home." (intending to borrow a friend's phone)
와, 진짜 맛있어 보인다. 그거 뭐니?
"Wow, it looks so delicious. What is it?" (wishing to get a piece of your friend's food)
집 안이 왜 이렇게 춥지요?
"Why is the house so chilly?" (wishing your friend turns on the heater)

Meanwhile, Koreans' requesting remarks tend to be more indirect than Americans. For instance, let's think of a situation in which you need to borrow your friend's virus protection software (since your notebook is infected with viruses). In American English, one tends to make an

REQUESTS

explicit request and then provide a reason/justification (e.g., *Hey, could I borrow your program? Because . . . my computer is infected with viruses*). However, in Korean, people tend to provide a reason first and then make a specific request (e.g., 미안, 내 컴퓨터가 고장이니 그런데, 괜찮다면 네 거 좀 빌려주면 안 될까?). Moreover, one commonly used strategy Koreans use when making requests is an apologetic remark (e.g., 미안한데, 죄송합니다, 실례합니다만, etc.). Note however, that these apologetic remarks are used as sort of protocols rather than genuine apologetic remarks.

과장님, 정말 죄송한데요. 지난 번에도 말씀드렸지만, 오늘 오후 2시에 저희 아버지 수술이 있어서요. 그래서 먼저 퇴근해도 될까 해서요.
"Manager, I am really sorry, but as I said last time, my father's surgery is scheduled at 2 p.m. today. So, I wonder if I can get off first."

선생님, 아시다시피 이번 학기로 제가 이제 4학년이고 이제 이 수업만 들으면 졸업이잖아요. 수업이 이미 꽉 차 있는 거 잘 알지만, 그래도 어떻게 좀 안 될까요? 선생님, 허락 해 주실 거지요, 네?
"Professor, as you know, I am a senior this semester, and all I need to graduate is to take this course. I know that the class is completely full, but I wonder if it is possible somehow. . . . Please, professor, you will give me permission to take the course, right?"

정수씨, 정말 미안해요. 이거 오늘 오후 5시 전까지 부장님한테 제출해야 되거든요. 정수씨도 바쁜 거 알지만, 저 먼저 좀 도와주시면 안 될까요?
"Jungsoo, I am really sorry. I need to submit this to the manager by 5 p.m. today. I know that you are also busy, but would you please help me first?"

71

Similarity

This chapter discusses a number of expressions that can be used to indicate similarity, likeness, or resemblance.

71.1 Indicating resemblance

71.1.1 N처럼 "like" (see 7.3.2)

A: 존이 일본어를 좀 하나요?
   "Does John speak Japanese?"
B: 그럼요. 일본 사람처럼 잘해요.
   "Sure. He speaks it well like a Japanese person."

언니가 요리사처럼 음식을 잘해요.
"My older sister cooks well just like a chef."
정말 소처럼 매일 일만 했어요.
"I really did nothing but work every day like a cow."
나이도 어린 놈이 도대체 왜 무슨 노인처럼 행동하지?
"Though he is a young man, why does he act like an old man?"

71.1.2 N같이 "like" (see 7.3.2)

A: 한국 사람같이 생겼어요?
   "Does he look like Korean?"
B: 아니요, 전혀요.
   "No, not at all."

말같이 얼굴이 길어요.
"His face is long like a horse's."
영훈이는 영화배우같이 잘생겼어요.
"Younghoon is handsome like a movie star."
천국같이 아름다운 하와이가 바로 제 고향이에요.
"My home town is Hawaii, which is beautiful like heaven."

71.1.3 닮다 "resemble, look alike, take after"

A: 동생이 형을 많이 닮았네요.
   "The younger brother looks like his older brother."
B: 그렇다는 소리 많이 들어요.
   "I hear people saying that so often."

그녀는 크면서 어머니를 닮아 갔다.
"She grew up to resemble her mother."

SIMILARITY

부부는 서로 닮는다고 하지요?
"People say that couples resemble each other, right?"
언니는 아빠를 닮고 나는 엄마를 닮았어요.
"My older sister took after my dad, and I took after my mom."

71.1.4 비슷하다 "similar"

A: 다른 멤버들도 그렇게 생각할까요?
   "I wonder if the other members think so too?"
B: 모두 비슷한 생각을 하고 있을 테니 너무 신경 쓰지 마세요.
   "I am certain that everyone has similar thoughts, so don't worry too much."

그들은 나이가 비슷해요.
"Their ages are about the same."
모든 회원들의 의견은 아주 비슷했다.
"The opinions of all members were similar."
제 성격하고 많이 비슷했어요.
"Her personality was really similar to mine."

71.1.5 흡사하다 "alike"

A: 보시는 바와 같이 이 두 그림은 아주 흡사합니다.
   "As you see here, these two paintings are very alike."
B: 와, 정말 뭐가 진짜인지 모르겠네요.
   "Wow, I really can't tell which is the real one."

이 두 제품은 색상과 모양이 매우 흡사합니다.
"These two products look very similar in color and appearance."
이 셔츠하고 그 넥타이하고 색상이 흡사하네요.
"The color of this shirt and that necktie are similar."
그 두 사람은 외모가 아주 흡사했습니다.
"Their appearances were very similar to one another."

71.2 Expressing sameness

71.2.1 같다 "the same"

A: 1 마일은 몇 킬로미터 정도 되나요?
   "How far is one mile in kilometers?"
B: 약 1.6킬로미터와 같습니다.
   "It is equivalent to about 1.6 kilometers."

집 크기가 웬만한 모텔과 같습니다.
"The size of the house is about the same as that of a regular motel."
제 여자 친구는 제 어머니와 키가 같아요.
"My girlfriend and my mother are the same height."
우리는 같은 점이 하나도 없어요.
"We have nothing in common."

71.2.2 마찬가지이다 "the same"

A: 상규 씨하고 많이 친하신가 봐요.
   "You seem to be close to Sangkyu."
B: 그럼요. 제 친동생이나 마찬가지예요.
   "Sure. He is like my real younger brother."

Expressing in the same manner or form

이것을 먹나 저것을 먹나 <u>마찬가지예요</u>.
"Whether you eat this or that, it's the same."
어쨌든 결과는 <u>마찬가지였어요</u>.
"Anyway, the result was the same."
너와 <u>마찬가지로</u> 나도 많이 힘들어.
"I also have a hard time just like you."
그 곳은 제 작업실이었지만 창고나 <u>마찬가지였어요</u>.
"That space was my workroom, but it was the same as storage."
불경기라 박사 학위 소유자들도 취업난을 겪기는 <u>마찬가지예요</u>.
"Due to the recession, experiencing difficulties in getting a job even for PhD holders is the same."

71.2.3 N(이)나 다름없다 "no different from"

This form is constructed from the particle (이)나 "about, or" (see 8.2.2) and the adjective 다름없다 "be not different."

A: 차가 아주 좋네요. 새 차 같아요.
   "Your car is nice. It looks like a new car."
B: 작년에 산 것이라서 <u>새 차나 다름없어요</u>.
   "I bought this last year, so it is the same as a new one."

저희들한테는 <u>아버지나 다름없는</u> 분이셨어요.
"For us, he was just like our father."
한 번 입어서 <u>새 옷이나 다름없어요</u>.
"I wore it only once, so it is not different from a new one."
거진 매일 술을 마시는 <u>거나 다름없어요</u>.
"He drinks almost every day."
빨래하고 설거지는 <u>제 일이나 다름없어요</u>.
"Doing laundry and dishes is like my work."

71.3 Expressing in the same manner or form

71.3.1 ~다시피 하다/되다 "as, in the same way, almost"

This form is made of the conjunctive ~다시피 "as if" (see 19.3.2) and the verb 하다 "do."

A: 연습 많이 하셨어요?
   "Did you practice a lot?"
B: 네, 골프장에서 매일 <u>살다시피 하면서</u> 연습했어요.
   "Yes, I practically lived at the golf range and focused on practicing every day."

아파서 하루종일 <u>물만 마시다시피 했어요</u>.
"I was sick, so I practically drank only water the whole day."
물에 빠져 <u>죽다시피 됐어요</u>.
"He nearly drowned."
할머니께서 저희를 <u>키우다시피 하셨어요</u>.
"My grandmother actually raised us."
<u>알고 계시다시피</u> 현재 상태가 굉장히 나쁩니다.
"As you know, the present condition is really bad."

71.3.2 ~듯이 "as, as if" (see 19.3.1)

A: 선생님, 그럼 어떻게 하면 좋을까요?
   "Doctor, then what should we do?"
B: 제가 전에도 <u>말씀드렸듯이</u> 곧 입원하셔야 할 것 같습니다.
   "As I said before, I think that he should be hospitalized soon."

SIMILARITY

비가 오듯이 땀이 나요.
"I am sweating like it is raining."
너도 알듯이 내가 좀 바쁘잖아.
"As you know, I am busy."
언제나 따지듯이 이야기하면 누가 좋아하겠어요?
"If you always talk like you are arguing, who will like you?"

71.3.3 ~는/(으)ㄴ 양 "as if"

This expression is the varied form of ~는/(은)ㄴ 모양이다 (see 23.3).

A: 준영이 아직도 안 일어났어요?
   "Junyoung did not get up yet?"
B: 네, 무슨 큰 병에 걸린 양 계속 누워 있네요.
   "Yes, he is on the bed as if he is terribly sick."

자기가 무슨 주인인 양 행동해요.
"She acts as if she is the owner."
한국에서 오래 산 양 경험담을 늘어 놓았어요.
"He bragged about his experiences as if he lived in Korea for a long period of time."
자기가 무슨 매니저라도 되는 양 자꾸 잔소리를 해 대요.
"He continues to nag them, as if he were a manager."

71.3.4 ~는/(으)ㄴ 척/체하다 "pretend" (see 24.7)

A: 정말 관심 없는 것 같아요?
   "Do you think that he is not really interested in her?"
B: 아니요, 엄청 좋아하면서 싫어하는 척하는 것 같아요.
   "No, though he really likes her, he pretends that he does not like her."

잘난 척 좀 하지 마세요.
"Don't act too arrogant."
일하기 싫으니까 자는 척했어요.
"Since he did not want to work, he pretended to be asleep."
학교에 가기 싫을 때면 아픈 척하면서 집에 있었어요.
"I pretended to be sick and stayed home whenever I didn't want to go to school."

72

Simultaneous actions and states

In Korean, the following expressions can be used to talk about actions or states that take place at the same time.

72.1 Indicating simultaneous actions by clausal conjunctives

72.1.1 ~다가 "while doing" (see 19.1.7)

책을 <u>읽다가</u> 잠이 들었어요.
"While reading a book, I fell asleep."
조깅을 <u>하다가</u> 발목을 삐었어요.
"While jogging, I hurt my ankle."
영화를 <u>보다가</u> 팝콘을 사러 나갔어요.
"While watching a movie, he went out to buy popcorn."
자전거를 <u>타다가</u> 넘어졌어요.
"While riding a bike, I fell."
<u>자다가</u> 알람 소리에 깨서 벌떡 일어났어요.
"While sleeping, I woke up due to my alarm and got up suddenly."

72.1.2 ~(으)면서 "while" (see 19.1.4)

A: 어제 많이 바쁘셨나 봐요.
"You seemed to be very busy yesterday."
B: 네. 점심 먹으러 나갈 시간도 없어서 김밥 <u>먹으면서</u> 일했습니다.
"Yes. Since I had no time to go out to eat lunch, I worked while eating gimbap."

<u>전화하면서</u> 운전하지 마세요.
"Don't drive while talking on the phone."
뭘 자꾸 <u>먹으면서</u> 전화하고 있어요.
"He is talking on the phone while eating something."
악보를 <u>보면서</u> 노래를 부르세요.
"Please sing while reading the notes."
노래방은 친구들하고 같이 <u>노래하면서</u> 노는 곳이에요.
"A noraebang is a place where you have fun while singing with friends."
피아노를 <u>치면서</u> 노래하던데요.
"He was singing while playing piano."

SIMULTANEOUS ACTIONS AND STATES

72.2 Indicating simultaneous actions or states by modifier clauses

72.2.1 ~는/(으)ㄴ 가운데 "while doing"

This form is made of the noun-modifying ending ~는/(으)ㄴ (see 21.1) and the word 가운데 "the middle."

바쁘신 가운데 와 주셔서 감사합니다.
"Thanks for coming in the midst of your busy schedule."
변 교수님을 기다리고 있는 가운데 전화가 왔습니다.
"While we were waiting for Professor Byon, the phone rang."
학생들하고 이야기하고 있는 가운데 새로운 사실을 알게 되었다.
"While talking to students, I found out a new fact."
국가가 울려 퍼지는 가운데 국기가 게양되었습니다.
"While the national anthem played, the national flag was raised up."
전국적으로 가뭄이 지속되고 있는 가운데 정부는 대책 마련에 고심하고 있습니다.
"While the drought continues nationwide, the government is struggling to come up with countermeasures."

72.2.2 ~는/(으)ㄴ 김에 "while you are at it" (see 22.5)

이렇게 만난 김에 어디 가서 차나 한 잔 합시다.
"Seeing as we met like this, let's go somewhere and have a cup of tea or something."
라면 끓이는 김에 한 개 더 끓이면 되지요.
"Seeing as you are cooking Ramen, just add one more to it."
스타벅스에 가는 김에 내 커피도 한 잔 부탁할게요.
"Seeing as you are going to Starbucks, let me ask you to get a cup of coffee for me too."
우체국에 가는 김에 제 편지도 부쳐 주실래요?
"Seeing as you are going to the post office, would you please send my letter as well?"

72.2.3 ~는 길에 "on the way to/from" (see 22.6)

은행에서 오는 길에 차 사고가 났어요.
"On my way from the bank, I had a car accident."
퇴근하는 길에 만나자.
"Let's get together on our way back from work."
병원에 가는 길에 저도 같이 좀 데려다 주실래요?
"On your way to the hospital, can you take me too?"
집으로 돌아오는 길에 커피 숍에 들렀어요.
"I stopped by a coffee shop on my way home."

72.2.4 ~는 동안(사이)에 "while" (see 22.10)

A: 비행기를 기다리는 동안에 뭐 하실 거예요?
   "What will you do while you wait for your flight?"
B: 점심도 먹고 면세점도 구경하려구요.
   "I intend to have a lunch and also visit duty free shops."

잠시 말씀 나누시는 동안 제가 서류를 준비하겠습니다.
"While you are having conversations, I will prepare some documents."
집사람이 설거지를 하는 사이에 제가 빨래를 했습니다.
"While my wife did dishes, I did laundry."
여기 구경하시는 동안 저는 호텔에 가서 기다리고 있을게요.
"While you are sightseeing here, I will wait for you at the hotel."

Indicating simultaneous actions or states by modifier clauses   **72.2**

화장실에 <u>가 있는</u> 사이에 전화가 왔어요.
"While you went to the restroom, there was a phone call for you."
친구를 <u>기다리는</u> 동안 커피를 마셨어요.
"While waiting for my friends, I had a cup of coffee."
저희가 밥 <u>먹는</u> 사이에 어디서 뭐 하실 건데요?
"What are you going to do while we have a meal?"

72.2.5 ~는 (도)중에 "in the middle of" (see 24.3)

A: 왜 전화 안 받았어요?
  "Why did you answer the phone?"
B: <u>샤워하는 중에</u> 전화가 와서요.
  "The telephone rang when I was in the middle of taking a shower."

<u>식사하는 중에</u> 전화를 받았어요.
"During my meal, I received a phone call."
지금 <u>샤워하는 중이니까</u> 10분 후에 전화 주시겠어요?
"I am in the middle of taking a shower, so can you call me back after ten minutes?"
<u>수업 중에는</u> 전화기를 꺼 주세요.
"During the middle of class, please turn off your cell phone."
지금 <u>공사하는 중이라</u> 길이 많이 막혀요.
"Because it is in the middle of construction, roads are blocked."

72.2.6 ~(으)ㄴ 채로 "just as it is, while" (see 24.6)

안경을 <u>쓴 채로</u> 잠이 들었어요.
"He fell asleep while wearing his glasses."
차에 열쇠를 <u>둔 채로</u> 나와 버렸어요.
"I came out, leaving my keys in the car."
신발을 <u>신은 채로</u> 그냥 들어오시면 안 되지요.
"You should not just enter with your shoes on."

72.2.7 ~(으)ㄹ 때 "when" (see 22.12)

A: 이 옷들은 비싼 옷이니까 <u>세탁할 때</u> 조심하셔야 돼요.
  "These clothes are expensive clothes, so you need to be careful when you do the laundry."
B: 네, 알겠습니다.
  "Okay, I got it."

다른 사람하고 <u>식사할 때</u> 코를 풀거나 방귀를 뀌면 안 됩니다.
"When you have a meal with others, you should not blow your nose or fart."
두통이 <u>심하실 때</u> 어떤 약을 주로 드세요?
"When you have a serious headache, what kind of medicine do you usually take?"
<u>운전하실 때</u> 절대로 전화기를 쓰지 마세요.
"When you drive, never use your phone."
여권을 <u>잃어 버렸을 때</u> 엄청 당황했었어요.
"I was in a panic when I lost my passport."
남자 친구하고 <u>헤어졌을 때</u> 무척 슬프고 괴로웠어요.
"When I broke up with my boyfriend, I was really sad and distressed."
제가 <u>젊었을 때</u> 운동을 아주 잘했었어요.
"When I was young, I used to be good at sports."

72.2.8 ~(으)ㄹ 때마다 "every time"

The form is made of ~(으)ㄹ 때 (see 22.12) and the particle 마다 "every" (see 7.4.1).

외로울 때마다 여자 친구한테 전화를 걸곤 했어요.
"Whenever I felt lonely, I used to call my girlfriend."
엄마의 얼굴이 그리울 때마다 어렸을 때 사진을 보곤 했어요.
"Whenever I miss my mother's face, I used to look at my childhood photos."
운동할 때마다 전화기로 최신 가요를 들어요.
"Whenever I exercise, I listen to the most recent pop songs using my phone."
스트레스가 쌓일 때마다 헬스클럽에 가서 운동을 했었어요.
"Whenever I felt stressed, I used to go to the fitness center and exercise."
기분이 좋을 때마다 콧노래를 흥얼거려요.
"Whenever I feel good, I hum."

73

Softening strategies

In general, Korean tends to be more indirect and vague than English, especially in so-called face-threatening situations, such as making requests, refusing, complaining, and advising. On this account, Korean has many means (e.g., words, verbs, sentence endings, formulaic expressions, etc.) of making these utterances more indirect or less assertive, and this chapter discusses these means.

73.1 좀 "please"

The noun 좀 is the contracted form of 조금, which means "a little bit." However, it is often used as a politeness strategy, meaning "please" when used colloquially.

> 저, 좀 도와 주시면 안 될까요? (vs. 저, 도와 주시면 안 될까요?)
> "Uh, would you please help me?"
> 좀 오세요. (vs. 오세요.)
> "Please come."
> 공부 좀 해라. (vs. 공부해라.)
> "Study."
> 이제 좀 괜찮아지셨어요? (vs. 이제 괜찮아지셨어요?)
> "Are you feeling better now?"

73.2 어떻게 "how"

One can use 어떻게 "how" instead of other question words, such as 왜 "why," 뭐 "what," and 몇 살 "how old." For instance, compare the following two questions:

> 이름이 뭐예요?
> "What is your name?"
> 이름이 어떻게 돼요?
> "What is your name?" (lit. "How does your name become?")

Notice that the former sounds more direct and blunt than the latter. By using 어떻게, you can render the message more indirect and less blunt. Here are more examples:

> 어떻게 오셨어요? (vs. 왜 오셨어요?)
> "What brought you here?"
> 휴대 전화 번호가 어떻게 되지요? (vs. 휴대 전화 번호가 뭐예요?)
> "What is your cell phone number?"
> 생일이 어떻게 돼요? (vs. 생일이 언제예요?)
> "When is your birthday?"

SOFTENING STRATEGIES

73.3 ~(으)ㄴ가(요)?/~나(요)?

One can use gentle question forms like ~(으)ㄴ가(요)?/~나(요)? instead of other questions forms, such as ~니?, ~어/아요?, and ~습니까?

~나(요)? (for verb stems)

보다 "see"	보나요?
믿다 "believe"	믿나요?
말하다 "study"	말하나요?
배우다 "learn"	배우나요?
만들다 "make"	만드나요?

언제 돌아오시나요? (vs. 돌아오세요?)
"When does he return?"
주말마다 운동하시나요? (vs. 운동하세요?)
"Do you exercise every weekend?"
보통 몇 시에 주무시나요? (vs. 주무세요?)
"What time do you usually go to bed?"
한국에서 영어를 가르치셨나요? (vs. 가르치셨어요?)
"Did he teach English in Korea?"
무슨 일이 생겼나요? (생겼어요?)
"Something happened?"

~(으)ㄴ가(요)? (for adjective and copula stems)

크다 "big"	큰가요?
쉽다 "easy"	쉬운가요?
따뜻하다 "warm"	따뜻한가요?
춥다 "cold"	추운가요?
작다 "small"	작은가요?
이다 "be"	인가요?

요즘 많이 바쁜가요? (vs. 바빠요?)
"Are you busy lately?"
물을 많이 마시네. 좀 매운가요? (vs. 매워요?)
"You are drinking water a lot. Is it a bit spicy?"
사무실이 조용한가요? (vs. 조용해요?)
"Is his office quiet?"
학생인가요? (vs. 학생이에요?)
"Is he a student?"
오늘이 며칠인가요? (vs. 며칠이에요?)
"What is the date today?"

73.4 ~지(요) (see 26.6)

As for requests/commands, you can use ~지(요) in place of other command/request endings, such as ~어/아(요) and ~ㅂ/읍시다.

이제 가시지요. (vs. 이제 갑시다)
"Let's go now."
고기는 그만 먹고 대신 샐러드 시키지. (vs. 샐러드 시켜)
"Stop eating meat and order a salad instead."
모두 얼마 나왔지요? (vs. 모두 얼마 나왔어요?)
"How much is it in total?"

73.5 ~게 되다 "to become" and 그렇다 "to be so"

~게 되다 is used to indicate an unplanned change in a situation that arises without your capability or control.

> 또 걱정을 끼쳐 드리게 돼서 죄송합니다. (vs. 끼쳐 드려서 죄송합니다.)
> "I am sorry for causing you to worry again."
> 제가 좋은 회사에 취직을 하게 돼서 기뻐하세요. (vs. 취직을 해서 기뻐하세요.)
> "She rejoices because I got employed at a good company."

In addition, by using 그렇다, you can avoid stating your message directly, allowing your listener to figure out your message.

> 기분이 좀 그래요. (vs. 기분이 좀 나빠요.)
> "I feel kind of bad."
> 야, 여기 음식이 좀 그렇다. (vs. 맛이 좀 없다.)
> "Hey, the food here is not that good."

73.6 ~는/(으)ㄴ 것 같다 "seems/appears to" and ~은/는 편이다 "tends to/kind of"

You can avoid saying something directly or bluntly, by using ~는/(으)ㄴ 것 같다 (see 22.1) or ~는/(으)ㄴ 편이다 (see 24.9).

> 이번 주말은 제 아들 놈 생일 파티 때문에 바쁠 것 같습니다. (vs. 바쁩니다.)
> "As for this weekend, because of my son's birthday party, I will be kind of busy."
> 난 이게 더 좋은 것 같다. (vs. 좋다.)
> "I kind of like this better."
> 고기는 거의 매일 먹는 편이에요. (vs. 먹어요.)
> "I tend to eat meat almost every day."
> 얼굴은 예쁜데 성격이 좀 까다로운 편이야. (vs. 까다로워.)
> "She is pretty but kind of hard to please."

73.7 ~어/아 주다 "do something" and ~어/아 보다 "to try something"

You can soften your message by using auxiliary verbs such as ~어/아 주다 (see 14.3) and ~어/아 보다 (see 13.6) as shown in the following examples:

> 이것 좀 마셔 보세요. (vs. 이것 좀 마시세요.)
> "Please try drinking this."
> 내일 오후 2시에 제 연구실로 와 주세요. (vs. 연구실로 오세요.)
> "Please come to my office at 2 p.m. tomorrow."
> 그럼 로비에서 잠시만 기다려 줘요. (vs. 기다려요.)
> "Then, please wait in the lobby for a moment."

73.8 ~는/(으)ㄴ 감이 있다 "feel like"

This form is equivalent to "feel like . . ." in English. It is constructed from the noun-modifying ending ~는/(은), the noun 감 "sense," the subject particle 이, and the verb 있다 "have/exist."

> 작년 학회 때보다 참석자가 줄어든 감이 있어요. (vs. 줄었어요.)
> "I feel like the number of participants decreased compared to the conference last year."

SOFTENING STRATEGIES   73.11

100불이면 조금 <u>비싼 감이 있네요</u>. (vs. 비싸네요.)
"I feel like 100 dollars was a bit too expensive."
하루 전에 예약하는 것은 <u>늦은 감이 있습니다</u>. (vs. 늦었어요.)
"I feel like it is late to make a reservation merely a day before."

73.9 The use of questions

You can also mitigate the message by changing your utterance into a question form.

저 여기 반찬 좀 더 <u>주시겠어요</u>? (vs. 반찬 좀 더 주세요.)
"Well, could you please give us some more side dishes here?"
내일 같이 점심 <u>먹지 않을래</u>? (vs. 내일 같이 점심 먹자.)
"Won't you have lunch together with me tomorrow?"
조금 더 싸게 주시면 <u>안 돼요</u>? (vs. 싸게 주세요.)
"Wouldn't it be possible for you to sell it at a cheaper price?"

73.10 The use of clausal conjunctives as sentence endings

The Korean language is a context-oriented language in that any contextually understood elements may be omitted unless they are indispensable. Consequently, a clausal conjunctive, such as ~는데 (see 17.1.1), ~어/아서 (see 16.2.1), and ~고 (see 19.1.1), can be used as a sentence ending, as its contextually understood main clause is omitted.

A: 요즘 많이 바쁘신가 봐요. 전혀 연락도 안 주시구요.
"You must be really busy lately. You have not contacted me at all for a while."
B: 죄송합니다. 요즘 회사에 일이 좀 <u>많아서요</u>. (연락을 못 드렸습니다.)
"My apologies. I have a lot of job-related matters recently, so (I was not able to get in touch with you)."
A: 왜 더 안 드세요? 더 드시지요.
"Why don't you eat more? Please help yourself to more."
B: 아니요, 이제 <u>배부른데요</u>. (어떻게 더 먹겠어요?)
"No, since I am full now (how can I eat more?)."

73.11 The use of fillers

A filler refers to a sound (or word/short phrase) that signals a pause (rather a conclusion) to other people involved. It is used to get the listener's attention, signaling that he/she has not finished speaking but simply paused to think what to say next, and so forth. Fillers are basically meaningless but serve as important conversational cues, contributing to smooth communication and making the speech more authentic. Examples of English fillers include "um," "you know," "I mean," "well," "uh," "so," and so on. Korean also makes use of fillers extensively, and here are some examples.

그러니까 "so, you mean ..."

<u>그러니까</u> 너무 비싸서 못 샀다는 거지요?
"So, you mean that you couldn't buy it because it was too expensive, right?"

그럼 "then, well"

<u>그럼</u> 먼저 가 볼게요. 천천히 놀다 오시고, 이따 뵈어요.
"Well, then, I will get going first. Take your time, and I'll see you later."

The use of fillers

그 왜 . . . 지요/잖아요 "you know"

그 왜 여기 유명한 박물관 있지요? 루브르인가 하는 박물관.
"Well, you know, there is a famous museum, right? It's called the 'Louvre' or something."

그래 "so"

그래, 공항에 도착하면 먼저 누구한테 연락할 거니?
"So, when you arrive at the airport, who will you call first?"

글쎄요 "well, let's see"

A: 미국에 가시면 차 먼저 사실 거지요?
   "When you go to America, you will buy a car first, right?"
B: 글쎄요, 일단 아파트 먼저 알아보고요. 그 다음 생각해 보려구요.
   "Well, let's see, I need to look for an apartment. Then, I will think about it."

뭐 "well, you know"

A: 이제 가셔도 될 것 같은데요.
   "It seems like you can leave now."
B: 아니에요. 아직 2시인데요. 뭐.
   "No. It's only 2 o'clock, you know."

~었지 뭐예요/뭐야 "you know"

요즘 바빠서 어제가 제 누나 생일인 것도 모르고 있었지 뭐예요.
"I am so busy nowadays, so I did not even realize that yesterday was my older sister's birthday, you know."

뭐랄까 "how should I put it?"

너무나도 충격적인 소식이라, 뭐랄까 다 남의 이야기같이 들렸어요.
"It was such shocking news. So how shall I put it; it sounded as if it were a stranger's story."

어 . . . 에 . . . 음 "uhm, uh"

어, 선생님 부탁드릴 말씀이 있어서 전화 드렸는데요.
"Um, professor, I called because I have a favor to ask."

어디 "well, now, let's see"

어디 누가 술이 더 센지 한 번 마셔 볼까?
"Well, to see who is stronger in alcohol, shall we drink it?"

자 "well"

자 이제 닫을까요?
"Well, shall I close it?"

SOFTENING STRATEGIES

저 "well"

저 혹시 선아 씨 아버님이 저희 학교 추장님 아니세요?
"Well, is Suna's father the president of our college by any chance?"

(저기) 있잖아요 "well, excuse me"

저기 있잖아요. 나가면서 문 좀 닫아 주실래요?
"Well, excuse me. Could you close the door on your way out?"

저기 말이에요 "well, you know"

저기 말이에요. 이번 주는 제가 아주 바쁜데요.
"Well, you know. I am really busy this week."

74

Telling the time, date, etc.

This chapter covers various expressions associated with telling times, dates, months, and so forth in Korean.

74.1 Telling the time

Koreans use native Korean numbers for 시 "o'clock" but Sino-Korean numbers for 분 "minutes." In addition, for a.m. and p.m., Koreans use the following five words: 아침 "morning" or 오전 "before noon" for a.m., and 오후 "afternoon," 저녁 "evening," and 밤 "night" for p.m., at the beginning of the expression.

7:36 a.m.	아침 (or 오전) 일곱 시 삼십육 분
8:10 a.m.	아침 (or 오전) 여덟 시 십 분
10:45 a.m.	오전 열 시 사십오 분
2:50 p.m.	오후 두 시 오십 분
6:17 p.m.	저녁 (or 오후) 여섯 시 십칠 분
9:24 p.m.	밤 (or 오후) 아홉 시 이십사 분
11:38 p.m.	밤 (or 오후) 열한 시 삼십팔 분

To say half past, you can either say "삽십 분" or the expression 반, meaning "a half." Consequently, the Korean expression for telling 11:30 p.m. can be 오후 (or 밤) 열 한시 삼십 분 (or 반).

As for seconds, you use Sino-Korean numbers for 초 "seconds."

One minute thirty seconds	일 분 삼십 초
Two minutes ten seconds	이 분 십 초

74.2 Counting days

Counting days with Sino-Korean numbers is regular. You need to add 일 "a counter for day" after the number, such as 일 일, 이 일, 삼 일, and so on. However, counting days with native Korean numbers is irregular in that there are special words for days up to 20 as shown in the following examples.

1 day	일 일	하루
2 days	이 일	이틀
3 days	삼 일	사흘
4 days	사 일	나흘
5 days	오 일	닷새
6 days	육 일	엿새
7 days	칠 일	이레
8 days	팔 일	여드레

TELLING THE TIME, DATE, ETC.

9 days	구 일	아흐레
10 days	십 일	열흘
11 days	십일 일	열하루
12 days	십이 일	열이틀
13 days	십삼 일	열사흘
...		
20 days	이십 일	스무날

After 20, only Sino-Korean expressions are used.

74.3 Counting months and years

Koreans use Sino-Korean numbers for counting calendar months. Hence, you need to add 월 "months" after a Sino-Korean number, as in 일월, 이월, 삼월, and so on. However, be careful that Koreans do not say June as 육월 but 유월 and October not as 십월 but 시월.

January	일월
February	이월
March	삼월
April	사월
May	오월
June	유월
July	칠월
August	팔월
September	구월
October	시월
November	십일월
December	십이월

For months (duration), however, you can use either native Korean numbers or Sino-Korean numbers. When counting with Sino-Korean numbers, you add 개월 after the number as in 일 개월, 이 개월, 삼 개월, and so on. When counting with native Korean numbers, you add 달 after the number, as in 한 달, 두 달, and so on.

1 month (duration)	일 개월	한 달
2 months	이 개월	두 달
3 months	삼 개월	세 달 (or 석 달)
4 months	사 개월	네 달 (or 녁 달)
5 months	오 개월	다섯 달
6 months	육 개월	여섯 달
7 months	칠 개월	일곱 달
8 months	팔 개월	여덟 달
9 months	구 개월	아홉 달

For years, Koreans normally use Sino-Korean numbers with 년 "year," such as 일 년, 이 년, 삼 년, and so on. They use native Korean numbers for years only with small numbers, such as 한 해 and 두 해. However, Koreans rarely use native Korean numbers beyond 두 해.

1 year	일 년	한 해
2 years	이 년	두 해
3 years	삼 년	–
4 years	사 년	–
5 years	오 년	–
60 years	육십 년	–
100 years	백 년	–

Asking and telling dates 74.5

Let's put all these expressions together. Koreans give dates starting from the largest unit to the smallest, which is the opposite in English. For instance, the date information such as "2:19 p.m., May 18th, 1970" is said as "(일)천구백 칠십년 오월 십팔일, 오후 두 시 십구 분." Here are more examples:

7:12 a.m., January 5th, 1982
(일)천구백팔십이 년, 일 월 오 일, 오전 일곱 시 십이 분
8:50 a.m., December 17th, 2006
이천육 년, 십이 월 십칠 일, 오전 여덟 시 오십 분
2:38 p.m., October 27th, 1979
(일)천구백칠십구 년, 시 월 이십칠 일, 오후 두 시 삼십팔 분

74.4 Asking and telling the time

The question word for asking time is 몇 시 "what time."

A: 지금 몇 시예요?
"What time is it now?"
B: 지금 7시 반이에요.
"It's 7:30 now."

A: 지금 몇 시쯤 됐어요?
"Approximately, what time is it now?"
B: 10시 10분 전인데요.
"It's ten before ten."

A: 지금 몇 시인지 아세요?
"Do you know what time it is now?"
B: 9시 조금 넘었습니다.
"It's a bit after nine."

A: 몇 시에 가게를 연대요?
"What time did they say they would open the store?"
B: 오전 10시래요.
"They say it's at ten."

아침 식사 시간은 9시까지입니다.
"Breakfast is served until nine."
점심 식사 시간은 12시부터 1시 사이입니다.
"Lunch break is between twelve and one."

74.5 Asking and telling dates

The following words are used to refer to days before/after today:

그저께   the day before yesterday
어제   yesterday
오늘   today
내일   tomorrow
모레   the day after tomorrow
글피   three days after today

A: 오늘이 며칠이지요?
"What's today's date?"
B: 3월 16일이네요.
"It's March 16th."

TELLING THE TIME, DATE, ETC.

A: 영훈이 생일이 언제예요?
"When is Younghoon's birthday?"
B: 6월 9일이에요. 다음 주 토요일이에요.
"It's June ninth. It's next week Saturday."

A: 오늘이 무슨 요일이지요?
"What day of the week is today?"
B: 목요일이에요.
"It's Thursday."

A: 장학금 지원 마감일이 언제지요?
"When is the deadline for scholarship application?"
B: 이번 주 금요일이래요.
"They said that it is Friday this week."

A: 요가 수업이 무슨 요일에 있어요?
"On what day do you have yoga class?"
B: 월요일이요.
"It's on Monday."

74.6 Asking and telling when something will happen or happened

A: 하경이 생일 파티가 몇시지요?
"What time is Hakyung's birthday party?"
B: 6시까지 오시면 돼요. 잊지 마세요.
"Please come by at 6 o'clock. Don't forget."

A: 그런데 요가 수업은 몇 시에 있어요?
"By the way, what time is yoga class?"
B: 매주 토요일 아침 10시요. 같이 가실래요?
"It is at 10 a.m. every Saturday. Would you like to go together?"

A: 한국 전쟁은 언제 일어났어요?
"When did the Korean War break out?"
B: 1950년에요.
"In 1950."

A: 서울 올림픽은 몇 년도에 있었지요?
"In what year was the Seoul Olympics held?"
B: 1988년에 열렸었어요.
"It was held in 1988."

74.7 Asking and telling how long something takes

To ask how long something takes, the following expressions can be used:

A: 뉴욕에서 서울까지 비행기로 몇 시간 걸리지요?
"How many hours does it take by airplane from New York to Seoul?"
B: 14시간 넘게 걸릴 거예요.
"I guess it takes more than 14 hours."

A: 집에서 학교까지 멀어요?
"Is it far from your home to school?"
B: 아니오. 버스로 10분쯤 걸려요.
"No. It takes about ten minutes by bus."

Asking and telling the time that has passed for a certain period

A: 오늘 강의가 얼마나 길지요?
"How long is the lecture today?"
B: 40분이나 아직 남았어요.
"There are still 40 minutes left."

A: 영화가 얼마나 길어요?
"How long is the movie?"
B: 두 시간인 것 같아요.
"It seems to be two hours."

요리하는데 두 시간이나 걸려요.
"It takes as long as two hours to cook."
대학을 졸업하는데 4년 걸렸어요.
"It took four years to graduate from college."
컴퓨터를 고치는데 이틀 걸렸어요.
"It took two days to repair the computer."

74.8 Asking and telling the time that has passed for a certain period

74.8.1 N동안 (see 22.10)

A: 태권도는 얼마 동안 배우셨어요?
"How long have you learned Taekwondo?"
B: 지난 6개월 동안이요.
"For the last six months."

A: 몇 시간 동안 연습했어요?
"How many hours have you practiced?"
B: 연습 시작한 지 아직 한 시간밖에 안 됐습니다.
"It has been only an hour since we started practicing."

74.8.2 ~(으)ㄴ 지 지나다/되다 (see 24.5)

A: 한국에 오신 지 얼마나 되셨어요?
"How long has it been since you came to Korea?"
B: 작년 봄에 왔거든요. 벌써 온 지 1년 넘었어요.
"I came last spring. It's already been one year."

A: 아직 신혼이시지요?
"You guys are still newly wed, right?"
B: 그럼요, 결혼한 지 6개월밖에 안 됐습니다.
"Sure, it's been only six months."

A: 런던으로 떠나신 지 얼마나 되셨어요?
"How long has it has been since he left for London?"
B: 아직 1주밖에 안 됐어요.
"It's been only one week."

A: 한국어를 배우기 시작한 지 얼마나 됐나요?
"How long has it been since you started learning Korean?"
B: 이제 일년 됐습니다.
"It's been a year now."

중국어를 공부한 지 5년 됐어요.
"It has been five years since I started studying Chinese."

TELLING THE TIME, DATE, ETC.   74.8

태권도를 배우기 <u>시작한 지</u> 이제 <u>4개월</u> 됐습니다.
"It has been four months since I started learning Taekwondo."
런던으로 이사온 지 한 달이 지났다.
"It has been a month since I moved to London."
담배를 <u>끊은 지</u> 오늘로 <u>2주</u> 되었어요.
"By today, it has been two weeks since I quit smoking."
하와이를 떠나 시카고로 <u>이사한 지</u> <u>10년</u>이 훨씬 넘었네요.
"It has been more than ten years since I left Hawaii and settled down in Chicago."
어머니께서 <u>돌아가신 지</u> <u>7년</u> 지났어요.
"It has been seven years since my mother passed away."
대학을 <u>졸업한 지</u> <u>3년</u>이나 <u>지났는데</u> 아직 직장을 찾지 못했어요.
"It has been three years since he graduated from college, but he was unable to find a job yet."
피아노를 <u>배우기 시작한 지</u> <u>1년</u>이 <u>지났어요</u>.
"It has been one year since I started learning piano."

75

Temporal relations

Temporal relations in English can be indicated by expressions such as "before," "after," "then," "as soon as," and so on. What follow are some expressions of temporal relations in Korean.

75.1 Expressing "before"

75.1.1 N전(에) "before N"

This form is made of the noun 전 "before" and the particle 에.

    A: 약은 언제 먹어야 되나요?
         "When should I take the medicine?"
    B: 식사 <u>30분 전에</u> 드세요.
         "Make sure you take this medicine 30 minutes before your meal."

한국에는 <u>3개월 전에</u> 갔다 왔어요.
"I visited Korea three months ago."
<u>시험 기간 전에</u> 많이 아팠었어요.
"I was very sick before the examination period."

75.1.2 ~기 전(에) "before ~ing" (see 4.1.20)

    A: 뉴욕으로 <u>이사를 오시기 전에</u> 어디에서 사셨어요?
         "Where did you live before moving to New York?"
    B: 시애틀에서 3년 정도 살았었어요.
         "I used to live in Seattle for about three years."

<u>조깅하기 전에</u> 준비 운동을 꼭 하세요.
"Before jogging, make sure you do some warm-up exercises."
<u>식사하기 전에</u> 감사의 기도로 시작하십시다.
"Let's start by saying grace before having a meal."
강의를 <u>시작하기 전에</u> 먼저 제 소개를 하겠습니다.
"Before starting my lecture, I would like to introduce myself first."

75.2 Expressing "after"

75.2.1 N다음/ 후(에) "after N"

This form consists of the noun 후 "after" (or 다음 "next") and the particle 에.

    A: 언제 한국으로 돌아가실 생각이세요?
         "When do you plan to return to Korea?"
    B: 인턴쉽 마치고 <u>3개월 후에</u> 갈 생각입니다.
         "I am thinking of going back after three months when I complete my internship."

TEMPORAL RELATIONS 75.2

사업 실패 후 그는 우울증 때문에 병원에 입원했었다.
"After his business went bankrupt, he was hospitalized for depression."
6개월 후에 비서 한 번 들르세요.
"Stop by here again after six months."

75.2.2 ~(으)ㄴ 후/다음(에) "after" (see 22.7)

A: 지금 먹을래요?
   "Do you want to eat now?"
B: 아니오. 샤워한 다음에 먹을게요.
   "No. I will eat after taking a shower."

월요일에는 수업이 끝난 다음에 학교 식당에서 아르바이트를 해요.
"On Monday, after class ends, I have a part-time job at the school cafeteria."
대학을 졸업한 후에 곧바로 미국으로 유학을 떠났어요.
"After graduating from college, I soon left for America to study abroad."

75.2.3 ~(으)ㄴ 끝에 "after"

This form is built on the noun-modifying ending ~(으)ㄴ, the noun 끝 "end," and the particle 에.

A: 6시간을 넘게 운전한 끝에 어젯밤 늦게 사무실에 도착했습니다.
   "After driving more than six hours, I arrived at the office late last night."
B: 정말 고생 많으셨어요.
   "Thank you for your hard work."

고된 훈련을 견딘 끝에 올림픽에서 결국 금메달을 따냈습니다.
"After enduring all those hard trainings, I finally got the gold medal at the Olympics."
4년간 열심히 공부한 끝에 서울대학교를 우수한 성적으로 졸업했어요.
"After studying hard for four years, I graduated from Seoul National University with honors."

75.2.4 N만(에) "after"

A: 잘 주무셨어요?
   "Did you sleep well?"
B: 아니요, 시차 때문에 잠든 지 1시간만에 또 깼어요.
   "No, I woke up again after sleeping one hour because of the time difference."

A: 잘 지내셨어요? 정말 오래간만이에요.
   "How have you been? It's been such a long time."
B: 그렇네요. 1년만에 뵙네요. 별일 없으시지요?
   "That's right. It has been a year. Everything okay for you too?"

대학을 3년만에 졸업했습니다.
"I graduated from college after three years."
운전해서 2시간만에 도착할 수 있었습니다.
"I was able to arrive there after two hours."
도서관에 들어갔다가 딱 10분만에 나왔어요.
"I went into the library and came out after just ten minutes."

75.2.5 ~고 나서 "after having (done something)"

This form is made of the auxiliary verb ~고 나다 "after finishing (something)" and the conjunctive ~어서/아서 "so, and then."

A: 언제쯤 출발하실 생각이세요?
   "When do you think you will leave?"

332

Expressing sequence "and then" 75.3

B: 일단 이 일을 <u>끝내고 나서</u> 출발할게요.
"I will finish this work first and then leave."

전화를 <u>받고 나서</u> 나갔습니다.
"He went out after receiving a phone call."
수영할 때는 꼭 먼저 준비 운동을 <u>하고 나서</u> 해야 됩니다.
"When you swim, you need to do some warm-up exercises first and then swim."
서류를 <u>받고 나서</u> 나가겠습니다.
"I will leave after receiving the document."
먼저 <u>빨래를 하고 나서</u> 요리를 시작하려고요.
"I will do the laundry first and then start cooking."
저녁 <u>식사를 하고 나서</u> 모두 함께 2차로 노래방에 갔습니다.
"After having dinner, we all went to a noraebang together for a second round."
대학을 <u>졸업하고 나서</u> 유학을 떠날 계획입니다.
"After I graduate from college, I plan to study abroad."

75.3 Expressing sequence "and then"

75.3.1 ~고 "and then" (see 19.1.1)

A: 박 과장님, 언제 서류를 드릴까요?
"Manager Park, when shall I give you the documents?"
B: 세미나 <u>끝나고</u> 주세요.
"Please give them to me after the seminar."

일단 창문을 <u>닫고</u> 에어컨을 켜세요.
"First shut the window and then turn on the air conditioner."
저녁 <u>먹고</u> 전화할게요.
"I will call you after eating dinner."
먼저 숙제<u>하고</u> 놀아라.
"Do your homework first and then play."

75.3.2 ~어/아서 "and then" (see 16.2.1)

A: 왜 학기 중에도 아르바이트를 하세요?
"Why are you doing that part-time job even during the semester?"
B: 돈 좀 <u>모아서</u> 여름 방학 때 여행가려고요.
"I intend to save some money to travel during summer vacation."

사과를 <u>씻어서</u> 먹었어요.
"I washed the apple and then ate it."
여자 친구에게 꽃을 <u>사서</u> 줬어요.
"I bought flowers and gave them to my girlfriend."
일단 <u>앉아서</u> 이야기합시다.
"Let's sit first and then talk."
일단 한국에 <u>돌아가서</u> 취직 준비하려구요.
"I will return to Korea first and then look for a job."
공항에서 같이 <u>만나서</u> 갔어요.
"We met at the airport and went there together."
과일을 <u>씻어서</u> 냉장고에 넣어 주세요.
"Please wash the fruits and then put them in the refrigerator."
사과는 <u>깎아서</u> 드세요.
"Please peel the apple and then eat it."

TEMPORAL RELATIONS

75.3.3 ~고서 "after, and then" (see 19.1.2)

A: 취직 준비 안 하세요?
"Don't you prepare for employment?"
B: 취직은 일단 대학을 <u>졸업하고서</u> 생각하려구요.
"I intend to think about employment after graduating from college."

친구들이 나를 <u>업고서</u> 병원에 데려다 줬어요.
"My friends took me to the hospital by carrying me on their backs."
남자 친구와 한 번 <u>싸우고서</u> 사이가 더 좋아졌어요.
"I became closer to my boyfriend after fighting once."

75.3.4 ~었/았다가 "did and then" (see 19.1.7)

A: 더운데 왜 에어컨 안 켰어요?
"It's hot, so why didn't you turn on the air conditioner?"
B: 에어컨을 <u>켰다가</u> 너무 시끄러워서 다시 껐어요.
"I turned on the air conditioner, but then I turned it off because it was too noisy."

창문을 <u>열었다가</u> 바람이 너무 세게 불어서 다시 닫았어요.
"I opened the window but then shut it because the wind was too strong."
커피를 사러 <u>갔다가</u> 줄이 너무 길어서 안 사고 그냥 돌아왔어요.
"I went out to buy coffee but then just returned without buying it because the line was too long."

75.4 Expressing "as soon as"

75.4.1 ~기가 무섭게 "just after" (see 4.1.2)

A: 케빈 어디 있어요?
"Where is Kevin?"
B: 날이 <u>밝기가 무섭게</u> 조깅하러 나갔어요.
"As soon as it was light out, he went out to jog."

가게 문이 <u>열리기가 무섭게</u> 손님들이 가게 안으로 들어왔어요.
"As soon as the store was open, customers rushed into the store."
회의가 <u>끝나기가 무섭게</u> 식당으로 달려가던데요.
"As soon as the meeting ended, he ran to the cafeteria."
말을 <u>꺼내기가 무섭게</u> 안 된다고 거절했어요.
"Just after I mentioned it, he said no."

75.4.2 ~는/(으)ㄴ 대로 "as soon as" (see 22.9)

A: 서류를 <u>찾는 대로</u> 보내 주십시오.
"Please send the document to me as soon as you find it."
B: 네, 알겠습니다.
"Sure, we will do so."

공항에 <u>도착하는 대로</u> 부모님께 전화 드려라.
"Give your parents a phone call as soon as you arrive at the airport."
비자를 <u>받는 대로</u> 떠나려구요.
"I plan to leave as soon as I get the visa."
<u>결정하시는 대로</u> 말씀해 주세요.
"Please let us know as soon as you decide."
호텔를 <u>예약하는 대로</u> 알려 드릴게요.
"I will let you know you as soon as I make a hotel reservation."

Expressing "about to"

집에 도착하는 대로 전화 주세요.
"Please give me a call as soon as she arrives home."
다음 기차가 도착하는 대로 떠납시다.
"Let's leave as soon as the next train arrives."

75.4.3 ~자마자 "as soon as" (see 19.1.6)

A: 침대에 눕자마자 잠 들었어요?
   "Did he fall asleep as soon as he lay on the bed?"
B: 네, 많이 피곤했나 봐요.
   "Yes, I assume that he was very tired."

신호등이 바뀌자마자 길을 건넜습니다.
"We crossed the street as soon as the traffic light changed."
저는 학위를 마치자마자 취직을 할 수 있었습니다.
"I was able to get a job as soon as I finished my degree."
에어컨을 켜자마자 금방 방이 시원해졌어요.
"As soon as I turned on the air conditioner, the room became cooler immediately."
3월이 지나자마자 날씨가 많이 따뜻해졌어요.
"As soon as March passed, it became much warmer."
경기 결과가 발표되자마자 모두 환호성을 지르며 기뻐했습니다.
"As the game result was announced, everyone rejoiced and shouted."
용돈을 받자마자 다 써 버렸어요.
"As soon as I received spending money, I ended up spending it all."
수업이 끝나자마자 모두들 나갔어요.
"As soon as the class ended, everyone went out."
집에 돌아오자마자 샤워하고 잤습니다.
"As soon as I returned home, I took a shower and went to bed."
배우가 무대에 등장하자마자 사람들이 모두 일어나서 박수를 치기 시작했다.
"As soon as the actor appeared on the stage, everyone stood up and started applauding."
우리 팀이 경기에서 결국 패하자마자 파티 분위기가 가라앉았다.
"As soon as our team eventually lost the game, the atmosphere of the party sunk."

75.5 Expressing "about to"

75.5.1 ~(으)려는 참이다 "is about to"

This form is made of the form ~(으)려고 하다 "intending to do" (the conjunctive ~으려고 + the verb 하다), the noun-modifying ending ~는 (see 21.1), the dependent noun 참 "the moment," and the copula 이다.

A: 커피 마시러 가는 길인데 같이 가실래요?
   "We are on my way to get some coffee; would you like to join us?"
B: 아, 네, 저도 마침 커피를 사러 가려는 참이에요. 같이 가요.
   "Oh, yes, I am also about to go get some coffee. Let's go."

아침을 아직 못 먹어서 지금 식당에 가려는 참이에요.
"I have not had breakfast, so I am about to go to a restaurant now."
호텔 프론트에 전화하려는 참이에요.
"I am about to call the hotel front desk."

75.5.2 ~(으)려던 참이었다 "was about to"

This form is made of the form ~(으)려고 하다 "intending to do," the noun-modifying ending ~던 (see 21.4), the dependent noun 참 "the moment," and the copula in the past tense 이었다.

같이 가자고 말하려던 참이었어요.
"I was about to say that we go together."
상의 드릴 일이 있어서 마침 뵈러 가려던 참이었습니다.
"I have something to get your feedback on, so I was about to visit you."

English Index

address terms 171–2; family members 172–4; non-family members 174–5
adjectives 46, 68
adnouns 159
adverbs 162; adverbials 164–5; conjunctional adverbs 162–3; degree adverbs 163; manner adverbs 163; mimetic/onomatopoeic words 165–6; proper adverbs 164; sentential adverbs 162; time adverbs 163
affixes 3–4
auxiliary verbs 62

bound/dependent nouns 6–8, 160

case particles 26; comitative 34–5; instrumental 33–4; location and movement 30–3; object 28–9; possessive 29; subject 27–8; vocative 172
causatives 150–2
clausal conjunctives 76; background 82–3; comparison 98–9; conditions 90–3; contrast 83–7; intention 88–90; option 97–8; reasons/cause 78–81; restrictions 76–7; sequence 94–7
collocation 9
copula 48–9
counters (classifiers) 15–16

demonstratives 160
derivation: derivational prefixes 5; derivation suffixes 5
descriptive verbs 46
determiners 159
direct quotations 155–6

endings 46–7; non-sentence-final endings 47–8; pre-final endings 47; sentence-final endings 48, 126
exclamatory remarks 233–4

fillers 322
formulaic expressions: condolences 201–2; congratulations 200; good wishes 200–1, 262; gratitude 202–3; greetings 242–3; leave taking 243–5
future tense 57

honorifics 135; addressee honorifics 135; honorific nouns 9, 144; honorific particles 32, 143; honorific verbs/adjectives 142–3; humble verbs 143; object honorifics 143–4; referent honorifics 136, 142; speech level endings 48, 136; subject honorific suffix 142

indirect questions 153–4
indirect quotations 156–8
inflection 3
irregular predicates 50–3

kinship terms 173–4

modifiers 105; past/retrospective modifier 106–7; present modifier 105–6; prospective/future modifier 106

negation 100; commands and proposals 103; long form negation 101–2; short from negation 100–1; Sino-Korean negative prefixes 104
nominalization 19; The nominalizing endings 19, 24–5
noun formation 4; compounding process 5–6; derivational process 5
nouns 3; collocations 9; gender 8; loan words 4; native Korean nouns 3–4; plurality 8; positions 8; Sino-Korean nouns 3–4
numbers 14; counters 15–16; native-Korean numbers 14–15, 17–18; ordinals 18; Sino-Korean numbers 14–15, 17–18

particles/postpositions 26–7
passives 146–9
past tense 54–5
prenouns 159
pronouns 10; first person pronouns 10; humble forms 10; indefinite pronouns 12–13; plain

ENGLISH INDEX

forms 10; second person pronouns 11; third person pronouns 12

reference terms 171

sentence types 48
special particles 26, 36; approximation and optionality 44–5; comparison/contrast 38–9; extent 41–3; frequency 40; topic/focus 37–8
speech levels: The blunt speech level 48, 140–1; The familiar speech level 48, 140; The formal speech level 48, 136–7; The intimate speech level 48, 138; The plain speech level 48, 138–40; The polite speech level 48, 137–8
stems 46–7

tense and aspect: continuous tense/aspect 60–1; double past tense 55–6; future tense 57; past tense 54–5; retrospective suffix 56

verbs 46

words: native Korean compound words 5; Sino-Korean compound words 6; word order 26–7

Korean Index

<ㄱ>

가/이 27
같이 39, 311
거/것 6
~거나 97, 184
~거니와 95, 265
~거든(요) 92, 126, 196, 229
~건 185
~건만 211
~게 (familiar speech level) 140
~게 90, 164, 291
~게 되다 74, 181, 321
~게 하다 152
~겠 59
~겠어요 204, 255
겸 6
~고 94, 263, 333
~고 나서 332
~고 말다 71, 302
~고 보다 71
~고 보니(까) 227
~고 싶다 72, 260
~고 싶어하다 72
~고 있다 60
~고 해서 294
~고도 86, 211
~고말고(요) 127
~고서 95, 334
~고자 90, 290
~곤 하다 299
곳 6
과/와 34
~군(요) 127, 226
~기 19
~기 나름이다 20, 199
~기 때문에 21
~기 마련이다 22, 288
~기 망정이지 249
~기 시작하다 22
~기 십상이다 22, 288
~기 위해서 23

~기 일쑤이다 23, 193
~기 전(에) 24, 331
~기 짝이 없다 24, 220
~기가 귀찮다 20
~기가 그지없다 230
~기가 무섭게 20, 334
~기가 쉽다 19
~기가 싫다 20
~기가 어렵다 19
~기가 이를 데 없다 230
~기가 재미있다 20
~기가 좋다 20
~기가 편하다 20
~기가 힘들다 19
~기나 하다 21
~기는(요) 20
~기는 하다 21
~기는 커녕 21, 230
~기도 하다 21
~기로 하다 22, 218
~기를 바라다 22, 261
~기로서니 87, 192
~기에 23, 294
~기에 따라서 23
~기에 앞서서 23
~길래 81, 294
까지 41, 269
~껏 165
께 32, 143
께서 143

<ㄴ>

나 10
~나/(으)ㄴ가 보다 73, 204
~나/(으)ㄴ가 했다 205
~나(요)? 320
너 11
~네 (familiar speech level) 140
~네(요) (mild exclamations) 128, 226
~느냐고 하다 157
~느니 87, 185

KOREAN INDEX

~느라고 80, 295
~는 (noun-modifying form) 105
는/은 37, 214, 261
~는 도중에 122, 317
~는 동안/사이에 112, 316
~는 법이다 288
~는 중이다 122
~는가/나? (familiar speech level) 140
~는가/(으)ㄴ가? (plain speech level) 139
~는가 하면 263
~는/ㄴ다고 하다 156, 246
~는/ㄴ다면 246
~는/ㄴ대요 158
~는/던 길에 111, 316
~는/(으)ㄴ 가운데 316
~는/(으)ㄴ 감이 있다 321
~는/(으)ㄴ 것 25
~는/(으)ㄴ 김에 111, 316
~는/(으)ㄴ 대로 112, 334
~는/(으)ㄴ 대신에 186
~는/(으)ㄴ 데다가 233, 265
~는/(으)ㄴ 마당에 289
~는/(으)ㄴ 바람에 116, 295
~는/(으)ㄴ 반면에 117, 215
~는/(으)ㄴ 법이다 117, 288-9
~는/(으)ㄴ 셈치다 249
~는/(으)ㄴ 양 314
~는/(으)ㄴ 이상 119, 295
~는/(으)ㄴ 척/체하다 124, 314
~는/(으)ㄴ 탓/통에 124, 296
~는/(으)ㄴ 편이다 124, 321
~는/(으)ㄴ 한 125
~는/(으)ㄴ데 82
~는/(으)ㄴ데도 85, 213
~는/(으)ㄴ/(으)ㄹ 것이다/거다 110
~는/(은)ㄴ/(으)ㄹ 듯하다/싶다 113, 206
~는/(으)ㄴ/(으)ㄹ 만큼 221
~는/(으)ㄴ/(으)ㄹ 모양이다 116, 206
~는/(으)ㄴ/(으)ㄹ 줄 알다/모르다 121, 207
~는/(으)ㄴ/(으)ㄹ/던 것 같다 109, 205
~는/(으)ㄴ/(으)ㄹ지 153, 308
는/은커녕 43
~는/ㄴ다/다 (plain speech level) 139
~니/(으)냐? (plain speech level) 139
~님 171

<ㄷ>

다 46
~다 못해(서) 170
~다가 97, 315
~다가 보니(까) 227
~다가 보면 228
~다고 하다 157
~다시피 99

~다시피 하다/되다 313
당신 11
대로 39
대신(에) 185
~더 56, 299
~더니 81
~더라(구요.) 300
~더라도 85, 212, 247
~던 (noun-modifying form) 107, 300
~던데(요) 301
데 6
~데요 299
도 42
~도록 90, 220, 291
~도록 하다 152, 177
동안 6, 329
~든지 98, 186
들 6
~듯이 98, 313
따라 39
따름 6
때 7
때문에 7, 179

<ㄹ>

~라고 하다 155, 157
랑/이랑 35
~래요 158
를/을 28

<ㅁ>

~ㅁ/음 24
마다 40
마저 42
만 7, 42, 219
만에 332
만큼 7, 39, 189
못 100
무렵 7

<ㅂ>

바 7
밖에 43, 220
보다 38, 188
부터 41
분 7
뿐 7, 43, 220

<ㅅ>

~세 (familiar speech level) 140
~소/(으)오 (blunt speech level) 140

KOREAN INDEX

~습니다/ㅂ니다 (formal speech level) 136
~습니까/ㅂ니까 (formal speech level) 136
씩 40

<ㅇ>

~아/야 (vocative particle) 172
안 100
안 ~(으)면 안 되다 273
안 ~(으)ㄹ 수 없다 289
~어/아 (intimate speech level) 138
~어/아 가다 62
~어/아 내다 63
~어/아 놓다/두다 63
~어/아 대다 64, 193
~어/아 버리다 65
~어/아 보다 65, 240
~어/아 보이다 67, 207
~어/아 본 적/일이 있다/없다 240
~어/아 봤자 304
~어/아 빠지다 67, 192
~어/아 오다 62
~어/아 있다 60
~어/아 주다 67, 307, 321
~어/아 치우다 68
~어/아도 84, 212
~어/아도 되다 277, 308
~어/아라 (plain speech level) 140
~어/아서 78, 296, 333
~어/아서라도 85
~어/아야 92, 197
~어/아야 되다/하다 74, 273
~어/아야겠다 255
~어/아야지(요) 193, 257, 274
~어/아요 (polite speech level) 137–8
~어/아지다 69, 148, 182
~어/아하다 68
~었/았 54, 298
~었/았겠다 129
~었/았니/(으)냐? 139
~었/았다(가) 334
~었/았더니 56, 228
~었/았더라면 91, 250, 303
~었/았던 300
~었었/았 55
에 30, 264, 267–8
에 관해서 252
에 대해서 252
에게 32
에게서 32
에다(가) 31, 265
에서 31, 269
와/과 34

우리 10
~(으)ㄴ (noun-modifying form) 105
~(으)ㄴ 끝에 332
~(으)ㄴ 나머지 305
~(으)ㄴ 다음/후에 111, 332
~(으)ㄴ 덕분에 112
~(으)ㄴ 반면에 117
~(으)ㄴ 일/적/경험이 있다/없다 119, 240
~(으)ㄴ 지 되다/지나다 123, 329
~(으)ㄴ 채로 123, 317
~(으)ㄴ가(요)? 320
~(으)ㄴ들 86, 304
~(으)나 84, 213, 250
~(으)나 마나 84, 304
~(으)니까 79, 226, 297
~(으)ㄹ (noun-modifying form) 106
~(으)ㄹ 거예요 57, 207, 256, 287
~(으)ㄹ 거지(요)? 307
~(으)ㄹ 것 57
~(으)ㄹ 게 뻔하다 288
~(으)ㄹ 겸 110, 257
~(으)ㄹ 계획/생각 110
~(으)ㄹ 때 113, 317
~(으)ㄹ 리가 없다 115, 286
~(으)ㄹ 만하다 115, 178
~(으)ㄹ 바에 116, 186
~(으)ㄹ 법하다 117, 287
~(으)ㄹ 뻔했다 118, 248
~(으)ㄹ 뿐 118, 232,
~(으)ㄹ 뿐더러 266
~(으)ㄹ 뿐만 아니라 266
~(으)ㄹ 수 있다/없다 118, 170, 285, 308
~(으)ㄹ 수밖에 없다 232, 289
~(으)ㄹ 정도로 121, 220
~(으)ㄹ 줄 알다/모르다 169
~(으)ㄹ 테니까 80, 209
~(으)ㄹ 텐데(요) 83, 131, 209, 303
~(으)ㄹ 필요 있다/없다 275–6
~(으)ㄹ걸(요) 130, 208, 303
~(으)ㄹ게(요) 58, 256
~(으)ㄹ까(요)? 130, 176, 208
~(으)ㄹ까 보다 73
~(으)ㄹ까 싶다 72
~(으)ㄹ까 하다/생각하다 73, 256
~(으)ㄹ래(요) 58, 256
~(으)ㄹ망정 87, 249
~(으)ㄹ수록 93, 181
~(으)ㄹ지도 모르다 208, 286
~(으)ㄹ지라도 86, 248
~(으)ㄹ지언정 87, 248
~(으)라 (plain speech level) 140
~(으)라고 하다 157
~(으)랴...~(으)랴 264
~(으)러 88, 290
~(으)려고 88, 291

KOREAN INDEX

~(으)려는 참이다 335
~(으)려던 참이었다 336
~(으)려다가 90, 267
~(으)려면 91, 197
~(으)렴 132
(으)로 33, 165, 268, 270
(으)로부터 32
~(으)로(서/써) 33-4, 271
~(으)리라 258
~(으)리만치 221
~(으)ㅁ 24
~(으)ㅁ에도 불구하고 215
~(으)며 95, 264
~(으)면 90, 196
~(으)면 되다
~(으)면 안 되다 278
~(으)면 좋겠다/하다 260, 309
~(으)면서 95, 192, 315
~(으)므로 80, 297
~(으)시 142
~(으)십시오 (formal speech level) 136
~(으)십시다 (formal speech level) 136, 309
~(으)오/구려 (blunt speech level) 140
은/는 37, 214, 251
은/는커녕 43
을/를 28
~음에도 (불구하고)
~읍시다/ㅂ시다 (blunt speech level) 140
의 29
이/가 27
~이 (nominal form) 25
~이 (familiar vocative) 172
(이)나 44, 187
(이)나 다름없다 313
(이)라도/(이)어도 187
(이)랑 35
~(이)며...~(이)며 264
(이)야 38
(이)야말로 38, 232
~이/히 (adverb) 165

~이/히/기/리 (passive) 146
~이/히/기/리/우/구/추 (causative) 150

<ㅈ>

~자 140
~자고 하다 157
자기 11
자네 11
~자마자 96, 335
~잖아(요.) 132, 229
~재요 158
저 10
저희 10
적 6
조차 42
좀 319
중/도중 7
~지 그래요? 176
~지 말다 103, 279
~지 못하다 101
~지 않다 101
~지 않아도 되다 275
~지 않으면 안 되다 273
~지만 83, 211
~지요 132, 320

<ㅉ>

쪽 7
쯤 44

<ㅊ>

채 8
처럼 39, 311

<ㅎ>

하고 35
한테 32
한테서 32

For Product Safety Concerns and Information please contact our EU representative GPSR@taylorandfrancis.com
Taylor & Francis Verlag GmbH, Kaufingerstraße 24, 80331 München, Germany

www.ingramcontent.com/pod-product-compliance
Ingram Content Group UK Ltd.
Pitfield, Milton Keynes, MK11 3LW, UK
UKHW051329100226
10621UKWH00031B/472